Lecture Notes in Computer Science   11005

Commenced Publication in 1973
Founding and Former Series Editors:
Gerhard Goos, Juris Hartmanis, and Jan van Leeuwen

More information about this series at http://www.springer.com/series/7411

Éric Renault · Selma Boumerdassi
Samia Bouzefrane (Eds.)

Mobile, Secure, and Programmable Networking

4th International Conference, MSPN 2018
Paris, France, June 18–20, 2018
Revised Selected Papers

Springer

Editors
Éric Renault
Télécom SudParis
Évry, France

Samia Bouzefrane
Conservatoire National des Arts et Métiers
Paris, France

Selma Boumerdassi
Conservatoire National des Arts et Métiers
Paris, France

ISSN 0302-9743   ISSN 1611-3349   (electronic)
Lecture Notes in Computer Science
ISBN 978-3-030-03100-8   ISBN 978-3-030-03101-5   (eBook)
https://doi.org/10.1007/978-3-030-03101-5

Library of Congress Control Number: 2018958773

LNCS Sublibrary: SL5 – Computer Communication Networks and Telecommunications

This Springer imprint is published by the registered company Springer Nature Switzerland AG
The registered company address is: Gewerbestrasse 11, 6330 Cham, Switzerland

Preface

The rapid deployment of new infrastructures based on network virtualization and cloud computing has triggered new applications and services that in turn have generated new constraints such as security and/or mobility. The International Conference on Mobile, Secure and Programmable Networking (MSPN) aimed at providing a top forum for researchers and practitioners to present and discuss new trends in networking infrastructures, security, services and applications while focusing on virtualization and cloud computing for networks, network programming, software-defined networks (SDN) and their security. In 2018, MSPN was hosted by CNAM Paris, one of the oldest teaching centers in Paris.

The call for papers resulted in a total of 52 submissions from all around the world. Every submission was assigned to at least three members of the Program Committee for review. The Program Committee decided to accept 27 papers. The accepted papers are from: Algeria, Argentina, Benin, China, Colombia, France, Germany, India, Morocco, Norway, The Netherlands, Tunisia, the UK, and Vietnam. Two intriguing keynotes from Prof. Ruben Milocco of the University of Comahue, Argentina, and Prof. Jean-Claude Belfiore, Head of the Communications Science Department at Huawei Technologies, France, completed the technical program.

We would like to thank all who contributed to the success of this conference, in particular the members of the Program Committee and the reviewers for carefully reviewing the contributions and selecting a high-quality program. Our special thanks go to the members of the Organizing Committee for their great help.

We hope that all participants enjoyed this successful conference, made a lot of new contacts, engaged in fruitful discussions, and had a pleasant stay in Paris, France.

June 2018

Selma Boumerdassi
Éric Renault

Organization

MSPN 2018 was organized by the CEDRIC Laboratory of CNAM Paris and the Wireless Networks and Multimedia Services Department of Télécom SudParis, a member of Institut Mines-Télécom and University of Paris-Saclay.

General Chairs

Selma Boumerdassi   CNAM, France
Éric Renault   Institut Mines-Télécom – Télécom SudParis, France

Publicity Chairs

Indayara Bertoldi Martins   PUC Campinas, Brazil
Gloria Elena Jaramillo   CNAM, France
Abdallah Sobehy   IMT-TSP, France

Organizing Committee

Fred Aklamanu   NOKIA Bell Labs, France
Lamia Essalhi   ADDA, France
Van Khang Nguyen   IMT-TSP, France
Van Long Tran   IMT-TSP, France

Technical Program Committee

Abdallah Adib   FST of Mohammedia, Morocco
Claudio A. Ardagna   Università degli Studi di Milano, Italy
Abdella Battou   NIST, USA
Bo Ai   Beijing Jiaotong University, China
Martin Barrère   Imperial College, UK
Indayara Bertoldi Martins   PUC Campinas, Brazil
Nardjes Bouchemal   University Center of Mila, Algeria
Selma Boumerdassi   CNAM, France
Ahcene Bounceur   University of Brest, France
Yuh-Shyan Chen   National Taipei University, Taiwan
Mathys Cornelius du Plessis   Nelson Mandela University, South Africa
Dabin Ding   University of Central Missouri, USA
Moez Esseghir   UTT, France
Eugène Ezin   University of Abomey-Calavi, Benin
Paul Farrow   BT, UK
Hacène Fouchal   Université de Reims Champagne-Ardenne, France

Mounir Ghogho	University of Rabat, Morocco
Aravinthan Gopalasingham	NOKIA Bell Labs, France
Alberto Huertas Celdran	University of Murcia, Spain
Al-Sakib Khan Pathan	Southeast University, Bangladesh
Ahmed Khattab	Cairo University, Egypt
Lobna Kriaa	ENSI-University of Manouba, Tunisia
Nadira Lammari	CNAM, France
Anis Laouiti	IMT-TSP, France
Adel Larabi	Ericsson, Canada
Cherkaoui Leghris	Hassan II University, Morocco
Véronique Legrand	CNAM, France
Ludovic Mé	Inria, France
Saurabh Mehta	Vidyalankar Institute of Technology, Mumbai, India
Natarajan Meghanathan	Jackson State University, USA
Ruben Milocco	Universidad Nacional del Comahue, Argentina
Pascale Minet	Inria, France
Michele Nogueira	Universidade Federal do Paraná, Brazil
Sabine Randriamasy	NOKIA Bell Labs, France
Éric Renault	IMT-TSP, France
Leonardo Rey Vega	Universidad de Buenos Aires, Argentina
Jihene Rezgui	LRIMA Lab, Maisonneuve, Canada
Sevil Sen	Hacettepe University, Turkey
Hamida Seba	University of Lyon, France
Mounir Tahar Abbes	University of Chlef, Algeria

Additional Reviewer

Inès Khoufi	Inria, France

Sponsoring Institutions

Conservatoire National des Arts et Métiers, Paris, France
Institut Mines-Télécom – Télécom SudParis, Évry, France

Contents

Surveying and Analyzing Urban Environment Approaches of Air Quality Monitoring

Rahim Haiahem[1]([✉]), Cherif Ghazel[1], Leila Azouz Saidane[1], and Selma Boumerdassi[2]

[1] RAMSIS Team, CRISTAL Laboratory, 2010 Compus University, Manouba, Tunisia
{rahim.haiahem,leila.saidane}@ensi-uma.tn,
Cherif.Ghazel@Email.ati.tn
[2] CEDRIC Laboratory, CNAM, Paris, France
Selma.Boumerdassi@cnam.fr

Abstract. Human beings need a regular supply of healthy food, clean water and especially intoxicated air. However, the increase in industrialization leads to high gas emissions, which effects badly the urban environment and people health. To measure, in real time, pollutants concentrations influencing the human health and natural environment, traditional equipment of air quality monitoring was substituted by new advanced wireless technologies. Using wireless technologies, air pollution data can be monitored and transmitted to remote servers in real time. In this paper, we present a survey related to the application of urban environmental monitoring. We also proposed a new methodology for air quality monitoring based on vehicular networks.

Keywords: Air quality · Air Quality Guidelines · WSN · VANET

1 Introduction

Every year, huge amount of chemicals are emitted from multiple natural and man-made sources, such as plants, forest and other geothermal sources, into the air. These pollutants have great harmful effect on human being and nature. To ensure a healthy physical atmosphere, it is necessary to provide clean environment where the levels of contaminates must not exceed the international agreed standards. Hence, Air Quality Guidelines (AQG) and technical measures were introduced to control and monitor indoor and outdoor air pollution [1].

In the last decades, pollution measurement methods have benefited from the laboratory analyses and monitoring stations. In fact, laboratory analyzes require high cost and complex equipment technology [2]. Thus, monitoring stations are expensive in terms of implementation and maintenance [3,4]. They are

© Springer Nature Switzerland AG 2019
É. Renault et al. (Eds.): MSPN 2018, LNCS 11005, pp. 1–12, 2019.
https://doi.org/10.1007/978-3-030-03101-5_1

also implemented in a limited number of cities limited within a country boundaries. Another weakness of these techniques is that they provide little information about how healthy the ambient air is.

Nowadays, the advances in wireless technologies, such Wireless Sensor Networks (WSN), Low Power Wide Area (LPWA) networks and cellular networks, allows a fine-grained monitoring of air quality. Using these technologies, small sensors are deployed everywhere in the urban environment to detect the concentrations of hundreds of pollutants in real time. Data gathered by the sensor are widely transmitted to governmental authorities and emergency numbers in order to take decisions and save human health.

The reminder of this paper is organized as follows: In the second section, we define some air pollution concepts and guidelines. The third section presents related work. The proposed architecture is presented in section four. Concluding remarks are given in the last section.

2   Air Pollution

The term "Atmospheric pollution" refers to the presence of airborne pollutants, such as fuels, carbon, bacteria and other microscopic particles, in the atmosphere [5]. The major factor behind air pollution is human-related activities like energy transformation, residential sector and transport [2–5]. These uncontrolled activities threaten man's well being and the human life, in general, by causing many diseases such as cancer, respiratory illnesses, cardio-vascular diseases, coma and death [1,6].

As stated by US EPA, six pollutants (ozone (O3), nitrogen dioxide (NO2), sulfur dioxide (SO2), carbon monoxide (CO) and two fine particulate matters (PM10, PM2.5)) are detrimental to both environment and public health [6]. Although no specific guideline value can be considered to protect human health, World Health Organization (WHO) working group introduced particular guideline values for these pollutants to show the health risk caused by these pollutants [1,7]. In fact, these standards and guidelines should be updated and reviewed periodically to protect sensitive and non sensitive populations and to save animals, buildings and cities. In Table 1, we present these pollutants and their corresponding guidelines.

Different models were developed to imitate the diffusion of gases in the air. For instance, Gaussian plum model permits computing pollutants concentration at a three-dimensional position, as shown in Eq. 1 [4,8]:

$$C(x, y, z) = \frac{M}{\sqrt[3]{2\Pi}\sigma_x\sigma_y\sigma_z}$$

$$\exp\left(-\frac{(x - x_0 - \mu(t - t_i))^2}{2\sigma_x^2} - \frac{(y - y_0)^2}{2\sigma_y^2}\right)$$

$$\left[\exp\left(\frac{(z - z_0)^2}{2\sigma_z^2}\right) + \alpha\exp(\frac{(z + z_0)^2}{2\sigma_z^2})\right] \tag{1}$$

Table 1. Major air quality pollutants and WHO Air Quality Guideline values

Pollutants	Sources	Health Implications	Averaging time	AQG value
NO2	Smoke Oxidation of nitric oxide (No)	Serious lung damage with a delayed effect	1 year	40 ($\mu g/m^3$)
			1 h	200 ($\mu g/m^3$)
CO	Fuels burning at very high temperature Road transport	Respiratory or heart diseases	8 h	9 ppm
			1 h	35 ppm
PM2.5	Industrial combustion, Wood burning, air pollution caused by different means of transport	Respiratory or heart diseases	1 year	10 ($\mu g/m^3$)
			24 h	25 ($\mu g/m^3$)
PM10			1 year	20 ($\mu g/m^3$)
			24 h	50 ($\mu g/m^3$)
SO2	Fossil fuels (Charbon, Gaz, Diesel)	Asthma	24 h	20 ($\mu g/m^3$)
			10 min	500 ($\mu g/m^3$)
O3	Reaction between primary pollutants (NOx, Co, COV)		8 h, daily maximum	100 ($\mu g/m^3$)

where C is the concentration of gas emissions in g/m^3, M represents the mass of the released product, μ denotes the average wind speed in m/s, t corresponds to the time since the emission of gas. α is the ground reflection coefficient. x, y, z are the coordinates of the points where the concentration is calculated, and x_0, y_0, z_0 present the initial source positions. σ_x, σ_y, σ_z, are the standard deviations of the Gaussian distribution of the gas quantity M. Equation 1 imitates an instantaneous diffusion of a gas quantity M. The continuous rejection consists in a succession of instantaneous rejections that evolve in a Gaussian way. The concentration C of the gas, in the atmosphere, at a point $A(x, y, z)$ is presented by Eq. 2 [8]:

$$C(x, y, z) = \sum_{i=1}^{n} \frac{M_i}{\sqrt[3]{2\Pi}\sigma_{x_i}\sigma_{y_i}\sigma_{z_i}}$$

$$\exp\left(-\frac{(x - x_0 - \mu(t - t_i))^2}{2\sigma_{x_i}^2} - \frac{(y - y_0)^2}{2\sigma_{y_i}^2}\right) \qquad (2)$$

$$\left[\exp\left(\frac{(z - z_0)^2}{2\sigma_{z_i}^2}\right) + \alpha\exp(\frac{(z + z_0)^2}{2\sigma_{z_i}^2})\right]$$

where M_i is the mass of the released product, n denotes the considered number of instantaneous releases and σ_i^{2x}, σ_i^{2y}, σ_i^{2z} are the standard deviations of the Gaussian distribution of the instantaneous releases of the emitted mass. The other parameters are presented above.

3   Air Quality Monitoring Methods

Due to the high importance of controlling and predicting the air quality in a given city, several approaches were introduced. They can be classified into three categories: approaches with fixed devices (static sensors), those with mobile devices (Cellphones, VSN) and Hybrid approaches (based on combining fixed and mobile devices).

3.1   Approaches with Static Coverage

Laboratory analyzes and monitoring stations are traditional solutions applied to measure air quality. They include high cost and complex equipment technology. Because air pollution level is not the same all over the world and it varies, from one country to another and from one city to another, according to human activities, these solutions cannot be applied to predict and monitor the overall pollution situation [2–4]. To resolve this problem, Abdulsalam et al. [9], proposed an algorithm called AQM-LEACH for monitoring pollutants. Their system is based on sending less data, when the air quality is good, and more data if the air quality is bad [9]. It allows the used equipment to switch to idle period then to sleeping periods for more time. Authors compared their algorithm with LEACH and they proved that the network lifetime can be better extended by applying it. Authors, in [10], developed a methodology for monitoring the environment by using sensor networks and Internet of Things (IoT). Their introduced system is based on four-layer architecture including traditional sensor network layer, processing layer, storage layer and application layer. The sensor network layer collects data and communicates directly via micro-controllers such as Arduino and Raspberry Pi. Then, the processing layer treats the collected data by employing these devices. Then, these data will be sent to the storage layer. Finally, the application layer displays and shows the measured data. In [11], a WSN to monitor, in real time, the environment pollutants, like CO2, CO and NO2, was proposed by Pavani et al. [11]. It is based on a multi-hop mesh network topology to increase the coverage of the monitoring area. Sensors, in this system, were deployed on Libelium Wasp motes equipped with a ZigBee module that sends data to the base station. This system permits a real access to the harvested data. Despite its advantages, such network topology is expensive and results in a high redundancy of network connections. In [2], researchers presented a prototype for a low indoor air quality monitoring device to measure the concentration of CO and HCHO gases. Their efficient and scalable platform is composed of a PC, marvell board, sensors and mobile phone. In their approach, sensor-readings are transmitted periodically to the AWS cloud via WiFi. Using a python scripts, data are either transmitted to user by e-mails and text messages or monitored by the users themselves through cellphones and laptops. To assure a fine-granularity and spatial coverage of pollutants, authors suggested exploiting low cost sensors pervasiveness where data are transmitted via GSM cellular networks. However, such networks are still expensive and unable to support optimally the requirements of nowadays smart city applications [12]. It is obvious that the a fore-mentioned works did not consider the weather and geographical conditions which affect highly the air pollution concentration and polluting source diffusion [3]. In [3] researchers proposed a method combining IoT technology with environment monitoring. The system perception layer was realized by employing environmental and meteorological sensors in selected monitoring sites (e.g. production area). The readings obtained from meteorological and environmental sensors were submitted in real time to a server then to a data center by using XML as transmission exchange language. Using neuronal network technique, a 24-h prediction network was established based on the current and the past 24-h air pollution concentrations. Although such forecasting and estimation techniques are efficiently applied to predict future air pollutants levels, their application may decrease the accuracy of real world pollutants. In [13], researchers developed an outdoor air quality monitoring system relying on a ZigBee multi-hop transmission. The introduced system is composed of coordinators, routers and terminals. The latter transmit the collected CO, NO2, SO2, O3 and NO concentrations to routers in order to be forwarded to the coordinator then to the server. Considering the ZigBee transmission range (270 m) [14], the system cost increases by widening the coverage area. In order to spread data over long distance and avoid the energy consumption occurring in multi-hop networks, Zheng et al. [15], introduced a monitoring system based on LPWA networks. The sensing devices are placed in a fixed position within the range of 3 Km from the Access Point (AP), forming a star topology. In the proposed system, the collected information are communicated directly to the access points. Then, it is transmitted every 10 min to the cloud where they would be pre-processed, analyzed, stored and finally displayed or sent to users. In order to extend network lifetime over several years, each monitoring node is powered by using battery and solar panel. In [14], authors presented an IoT-based air quality monitoring using LoRa. The system controls several pollutants and ensures a communication over long distance with high coverage and a long devices battery power. In [14,15] authors addressed the pervasiveness of sensors devices without taking into account collisions that may happen in such LPWA networks, especially in the case of a large network size. From the above-mentioned ideas, we may conclude that the monitoring of a large area requires using a large number of sensors. In fact, such static WSN solution lacks flexibility to collect and monitor all air pollution situations. Thus, as vehicles and mobile devices move anywhere in the urban environment, several approaches adopted these alternatives to ensure a high coverage of urban environment.

3.2 Approaches with Dynamic Coverage

In [16], authors developed a platform based on the implication of mobile phones in recording PM 2.5 and CO2 in the ambient air. The everyday sampled data taken from mobile phones are transmitted to the server using GSM messages. Thereafter, the server displays the analyses via a web interface. To reduce the cost of monitoring the air quality, [17] adopted Internet-connected PM2.5 monitors and a cloud-based Air Quality Analytics Engine. In their system, the sensing data are transmitted to the cloud via Ethernet or mobile phones. Then, the cloud engine uses multiple machine learning techniques to calibrate and infer PM2.5 measurements. In order to monitor the CO concentration caused by vehicle emissions in Taipei city, Liu et al. [18], introduced a system with high-resolution of air pollution data in real time. Sensor nodes use Octopus II containing a low-power CC2420 wireless transceiver adapted to a ZigBee specification for wireless communication [18]. Before switching to sleeping period, the nodes find their appropriate parents to which they send the collected data. Then, parent nodes transmit the collected data to the gateway which forwards them to the server. Users will be informed about the collected data by SMS sent by LabVIEW program. In [19], authors presented a system composed of a set of gas sensors installed on vehicles for measuring O3, Co and No2 pollutants. The system uses its Bluetooth enabled interface to send samples to the user's laptops or smartphones. When the car is in motion, the device samples data, for each minute, and stores them with the location and time (using GPS receiver). The collected data are uploaded to the server when cars enter a WiFi covered area. In the server, data are shown on Google maps. In [20], authors suggested a hardware mobile unit (MU) composed of many pluggable sensors dedicated to sense multiple parameters such as CO, combustible gas, temperature and air contamination. Devices are also equipped by a GPS module. The MUs are embedded on cars and are powered only by vehicles power. They switch up only when the car engine is running. Periodically, devices reading are stored in flash memory and displayed in mobile LCD interface. Every hour, the data are transmitted to the server using 2G communication. Using Google map API, the received data are visualized on a map of cities and are accessible through an online web server. Some latency were generated, in [19], because data transmission is dependent on the cars accessibility to WiFi zones. Thus, in [20], a high data isolation may be caused when cars engines is off. Hu et al. [21], developed a monitoring system based on using vehicular sensor networks (VSNs). These cars are equipped by different external and central units to detect CO2 data and send reports to the server via GSM short messages, respectively. Authors divided the region of interest into fixed grids. They also adopted variation-based (VAR) and gradient-based (GRA) schemes to adjust the sampling rates in order to reduce the communication overhead on the cellular networks. Authors, in [4], proposed an efficient data gathering and estimation (EDGE) mechanism. To adjust sampling rates, EDGE uses region quadtree technique to maintain the dynamic grid partition based on the variation of pollutants concentration. Moreover, authors adopted SUMO (open source package to model real roads and car traffic) and ISC3 (steady-state Gaussian plume model) to model the real urban traffic and air pollution dispersion, respectively. Vehicles, in this study, were equipped by a set of gas sensors, GPS receiver and wireless interfaces (WiFi or LTE-A). In contrast to the previous study, authors applied Delaunay Triangulation Technique to infer missing air quality data. At another scale, due to the incapability of mobile units (vehicles, bikes and phones) to collect data from all position in the urban environment in consequence of obstacles, such as building and secured regions, other studies proposed the combination of the previously-mentioned static and dynamic deployment approaches.

3.3   Approaches with Hybrid Coverage

To monitor carbon dioxide (CO2) in the urban environment, Fu et al. [22], developed a distributed system that uses sensors and robots networks. In their system, the region of interest is divided into sub-regions; each of which is equipped by a fixed sensors (e.g. placed over the buildings, etc.) and dynamic sensors (e.g. fixed to bicycle, cars, scooter, etc.). In their approach, a node gets its GPS coordinates using the GPS receiver, detects the degree of CO2 then forwards the data to the server through a 3G network. The air quality data, for each sensing region and best healthful routes, were dynamically shown on Google maps. Although this system assures a high coverage of the urban environment, the employed cellular networks are expensive and high energy-consuming. Mendez et al. [23], presented a participatory sensing system composed of sensing devices and mobile phones. The sensing device contains a set of external sensors integrated in an Arduino BT development board to provide a multi-sensing parameters [23]. A static wireless sensor networks were also integrated into the system and all data coming from either dynamic or static networks were stored in the same storage server. Users employ their own devices to view data and take decision. Sensing devices, in this system, do not have a long lifetime due to the constantly-opened Bluetooth communication with the first integrator level. Authors, in [24], proposed a collaboration between static and dynamic nodes to monitor the air quality. Static devices were implemented and deployed in bus stations and form a cluster topology based on ZigBee. Each device, in this system, collects and transmits information about different gas pollutants to the cluster head. Devices mount on public transport: buses and vehicles modulate mobile nodes. When buses arrive at the bus stations, devices collect and store data from all ZigBee static cluster head in the pathway. Finally, data will be analyzed when cars return to their destinations. Authors also discussed a new architecture relying on LTE-M technology. Devices with an LTE-M module installed on public transportation means collect data from ZigBee static coordinators and send them directly to the cloud computing.

4   Proposed Architecture

Smart environment was introduced as evolutionary development concept to construct home, environmental, industrial and transportation systems automation [25, 26]. Indeed, smart environment is based essentially on sensory data taken from the real world. Regarding the necessity of having a real world physical parameters, a promising solution consists in introducing multiple sensors, in distributed locations, to sample, process and deliver information to external systems such Internet [25, 27]. However, the networking of large numbers of tiny sensor nodes requires a careful selection of both wireless technology and efficient, reliable and scalable networking protocols [28], as shown in Fig. 1.

The implication of cellular networks (mobile phones), in the air pollution perception, allows fast access with low latency for data transmission. However, apart from the high energy consumption, these technologies (2G, 3G, and 4G) exploit licensed frequency bands and each message transmitted should be paid. Since the environment monitoring domain is required to send continuously messages, the cost of the system implementation is expensive [29]. Thus, WSNs are frequently considered as a solution for large-scale tracking and monitoring applications [27] thanks to their low data rate, low implementation complexity and low energy consumption. However, their short sensing and communication range create the need for multi-hop networks in order to satisfy the requirement of large coverage of air pollution monitoring. This fact increases latency, energy consumption (in receiving, transmitting and forwarding) and, consequently, the network cost. For more flexibility, efficient solutions belonging to LPWA class become popular by providing promising advantages such as increasing battery lifetime and communication range and decreasing latency and cost [30]. In fact, The LPWA technologies exploit both licensed (NB-IoT, LTE-M) and unlicensed frequency bands (LoRa). For instance, LoRa permits a communication range over 3 Km in urban environment and 14 Km in line of sight by exploiting the frequency free ISM band [31]. Using this technology, devices have a high autonomy and can communicate over long distances with a remote server in direct M2M access [14], which makes this technology efficient and appropriately used in the monitoring cities. In addition, because of the high vehicles motion, many studies included the context of dynamicity in the air pollution monitoring. Devices are mounted onto cars and wireless technologies are exploited to ferry the collected atmospheric pollutants to remote servers. However, some technologies, such as IEEE 802.15.1 (Bluetooth), IEEE 802.15.4 (Zigbee) and IEEE 802.11 (WiFi), cannot optimally operate in such mobility context. Nowadays, another area of study, namely vehicular ad-hoc networks (VANETs), is dedicated to support wireless access in vehicular environments (WAVE) and expected to improve excellent network performances for smart city applications [26]. VANETs improve broad

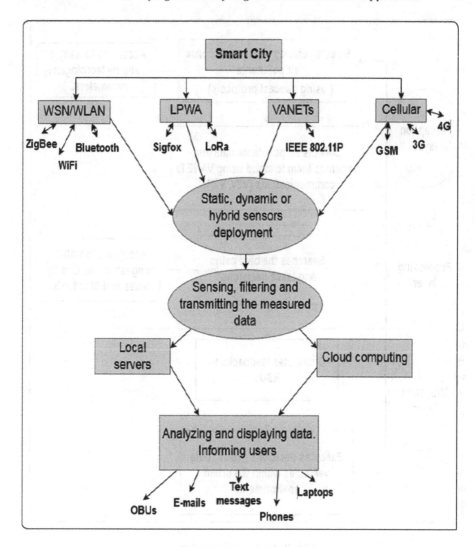

Fig. 1. Wireless technologies and air quality monitoring process

range of safety and non-safety applications including vehicular traffic, congestion avoidance, location-based services as well as travel time, fuel consumption
and energy reduction [26,32]. VANETs communications, including Vehicle-to-
Vehicle (V2V), Vehicle-to-Roadside (V2R) or Vehicle-to-Infrastructure (V2I),
spread on Dedicated Short Range Communication (DSRC) band. The latter,
using 75 MHz of spectrum at 5.9 MHz, provides high data transmission rate
(UP to 27 Mbits/s) and low communication latency in a maximum coverage of
1000 meters [32]. Using VANETs and cloud computing, we suggest a new air
pollution monitoring and mitigation system. The architecture of our system is
shown in Fig. 2:

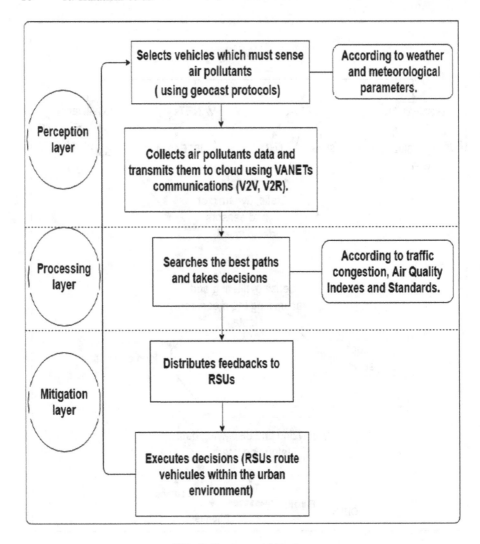

Fig. 2. System architecture

Our architecture is composed of three layers: the perception layer, the processing layer and the mitigation layer. In the perception layer, our system selects the vehicles that will participate in the monitoring round according to the meteorological parameters. Then, data will be sent to high processing and computing stations hosted in a cloud computing using vehicular communications. In the processing layer, the system looks for less polluted routes according to the traffic congestion as well as air pollution levels and guidelines. The mitigation layer transmits decisions and results to Roadside Units (RSUs). Based on the received results, RSUs will route cars in the urban environment.

5   Conclusion

In this survey, we presented the existing air quality monitoring solutions and the corresponding functionalities. We also detailed the air pollution concepts including: criteria pollutants, health effects and guideline values. Besides, we show how we can simulate their dispersion in the environment. A classification between the developed approaches in the field of the urban environment protection was also presented. The proposed architecture presented a new methodology based on vehicular networks for air quality monitoring while covering a wide range of environment elements.

References

1. World Health Organization (WHO and others). Air quality guidelines for Europe (2000)
2. Tapashetti, A., Vegiraju, D., Ogunfunmi, T.: Iot-enabled air quality monitoring device: a low cost smart health solution. In: Global Humanitarian Technology Conference (GHTC) 2016, pp. 682–685 (2016)
3. Chen, X., Liu, X., Xu, P.: Iot-based air pollution monitoring and forecasting system. In: International Conference on Computer and Computational Sciences (ICCCS), pp. 257–260 (2015)
4. Wang, Y.-C., Chen, G.-W.: Efficient data gathering and estimation for metropolitan air quality monitoring by using vehicular sensor networks. EEE Trans. Veh. Technol. **66**(8), 7234–7248 (2017)
5. Mendez, D., Diaz, S., Kraemer, R.: Wireless technologies for pollution monitoring in large cities and rural areas. In: 24th Telecommunications Forum (TELFOR), pp. 1–6 (2016)
6. Mintz, D.: Technical assistance document for the reporting of daily air quality-the air quality index (AGI): Us environmental protection agency. Office of Air Quality Planning and Standards (2012)
7. Krzyzanowski, M., Cohen, A.: Update of who air quality guidelines. Air Qual. Atmos. Health **1**(1), 7–13 (2008)
8. Jakeman, A.J., Simpson, R.W., Taylor, J.A.: A simulation approach to assess air pollution from road transport. IEEE Trans. Syst. Man Cybern. **SMC–14**(5), 726–736 (1984)
9. Abdulsalam, H.M., Ali, B.A., AlYatama, A., AlRoumi, E.S.: Deploying a leach data aggregation technique for air quality monitoring in wireless sensor network. Procedia Comput. Sci. **34**, 499–504 (2014)
10. Li, W., Kara, S.: Methodology for monitoring manufacturing environment by using wireless sensor networks (WSN) and the internet of things (IoT). Procedia CIRP **61**, 323–328 (2017)
11. Pavani, M., Rao, P.T.: Real time pollution monitoring using wireless sensor networks. In: IEEE 7th Annual Information Technology, Electronics and Mobile Communication Conference (IEMCON), pp. 1–6 (2016)
12. Oppitz, M., Tomsu, P.: Internet of things. Inventing the Cloud Century, pp. 435–469 (2018)
13. He, Y.-L., Geng, S.-Q., Peng, X.-H., Hou, L.-G., Gao, X.-K., Wang, J.-H.: Design of outdoor air quality monitoring system based on zigbee wireless sensor network. In: 13th IEEE International Conference on Solid-State and Integrated Circuit Technology (ICSICT), pp. 368–370 (2016)

14. Liu, S., Xia, C., Zhao, Z.: A low-power real-time air quality monitoring system using lpwan based on lora. In: 13th IEEE International Conference on Solid-State and Integrated Circuit Technology (ICSICT), pp. 379–381 (2016)
15. Zheng, K., Zhao, S., Yang, Z., Xiong, X., Xiang, W.: Design and implementation of lpwa-based air quality monitoring system. IEEE Access **4**, 3238–3245 (2016)
16. Mun, M., et al.: Peir, the personal environmental impact report, as a platform for participatory sensing systems research. In: Proceedings of the 7th International Conference on Mobile Systems, Applications, and Services, pp. 55–68 (2009)
17. Cheng, Y., et al.: Aircloud: a cloud-based air-quality monitoring system for everyone. In: Proceedings of the 12th ACM Conference on Embedded Network Sensor Systems, pp. 251–265 (2014)
18. Liu, J.-H., et al.: Developed urban air quality monitoring system based on wireless sensor networks. In: Fifth International Conference on Sensing Technology (icst), pp. 549–554 (2011)
19. Völgyesi, P., Nádas, A., Koutsoukos, X., Lédeczi, Á.: Air quality monitoring with sensormap. In: Proceedings of the 7th International Conference on Information Processing in Sensor Networks, pp. 529–530 (2008)
20. Tudose, D.Ş., Pătraşcu, T.A., Voinescu, A., Tătăroiu, R., Ţăpuş, N.: Mobile sensors in air pollution measurement. In: 8th Workshop on Positioning Navigation and Communication (WPNC), pp. 166–170 (2011)
21. Hu, S.-C., Wang, Y.-C., Huang, C.-Y., Tseng, Y.-C.: Measuring air quality in city areas by vehicular wireless sensor networks. J. Syst. Softw. **84**(11), 2005–2012 (2011)
22. Fu, H.-L., Chen, H.-C., Lin, P.: Aps: distributed air pollution sensing system on wireless sensor and robot networks. Comput. Commun. **35**(9), 1141–1150 (2012)
23. Mendez, D., Perez, A.J., Labrador, M.A., Marron, J.J.: P-sense: a participatory sensing system for air pollution monitoring and control. In: IEEE International Conference on Pervasive Computing and Communications Workshops (PERCOM Workshops), pp. 344–347 (2011)
24. Jamil, M.S., Jamil, M.A., Mazhar, A., Ikram, A., Ahmed, A., Munawar, U.: Smart environment monitoring system by employing wireless sensor networks on vehicles for pollution free smart cities. Procedia Eng. **107**, 480–484 (2015)
25. Lewis, F.L., et al.: Wireless sensor networks. Smart Environ. Technol. Protoc. Appl. **11**, 46 (2004)
26. Alsabaan, M., Alasmary, W., Albasir, A., Naik, K.: Vehicular networks for a greener environment: a survey. IEEE Commun. Surv. Tutor. **15**(3), 1372–1388 (2013)
27. Yang, K.: Wireless sensor networks. Principles, Design and Applications (2014)
28. Perillo, M.A., Heinzelman, W.B.: Wireless sensor network protocols (2005)
29. Wang, L., Manner, J.: Energy consumption analysis of wlan, 2g and 3g interfaces. In: IEEE/ACM International Conference on Cyber Physical and Social Computing (CPSCom), Green Computing and Communications (GreenCom), pp. 300–307 (2010)
30. Sinha, R.S., Wei, Y., Hwang, S.-H.: A survey on lpwa technology: Lora and nb-iot. ICT Express **3**(1), 14–21 (2017)
31. SEMTECH. Lora sx1276/77/78/79 datasheet, August 2016. https://www.semtech.com/uploads/documents/sx1276.pdf
32. Zeadally, S., Hunt, R., Chen, Y.-S., Irwin, A., Hassan, A.: Vehicular ad hoc networks (vanets): status, results, and challenges. Telecommun. Syst. **50**(4), 217–241 (2012)

A Novel Color Image Encryption Scheme Using Logistic Map and Quadratic Map Systems

Djamel Herbadji[1(✉)], Aissa Belmeguenai[1], Nadir Derouiche[1], Youcef Zennir[2], and Salim Ouchtati[1]

[1] Laboratoire de Recherche en Electronique de Skikda,
Université 20 Août 1955- Skikda, BP 26 Route d'El-hadaeik, 21000 Skikda, Algeria
herbadjidjamel@gmail.com, {a.belmeguenai,n.derouiche}@univ-skikda.dz,
ouchtatisalim@yahoo.fr
[2] Laboratoire d'Automatique de Skikda,
Université 20 Août 1955- Skikda, BP 26 Route d'El-hadaeik, Skikda, Algeria
y.zennir@univ-skikda.dz

Abstract. In this work, we propose a color image encryption scheme based on logistic map and quadratic map systems. First, the color image is divided into three components (red (R), green (G), and blue (B)). The three components are mixed as single grayscale image, to permute the pixels positions; we have used two permutation index vectors for changing rows and columns position. Finally, the permuted grayscale image is encrypted. In order to evaluate the security of the proposed scheme, the entropy, key space analysis, key sensitivity analysis, the correlation of two adjacent pixels and differential attack were performed. The Experimental results and analyses show that the proposed scheme enable to reduce computing effort, to allow efficient and outperform many schemes given in the literature.

Keywords: Color image encryption · Logistic map · Quadratic map

1 Introduction

In recent years, encryption has become a fundamental tool to provides a security for data that is transferred on the computer and communications networks, therefore, this is considered as an important method to protect digital images, image encryption has become a very attractive research field.

Due to the image features that are different to the text such as big data space and the high correlations within adjacent pixels, therefore, some traditional encryption schemes are effective for text encryption but not effective for digital image encryption such as RivestShamir-Adleman (RSA), advanced encryption standard (AES) and data encryption standard (DES) [1]. Recently, image encryption schemes based on chaotic maps have attracted the attention of

© Springer Nature Switzerland AG 2019
E. Renault et al. (Eds.): MSPN 2018, LNCS 11005, pp. 13–23, 2019.
https://doi.org/10.1007/978-3-030-03101-5_2

many researches because of their important characterizes such as highly sensitive dependence on initial conditions and control parameters, ergodicity, unpredictability, pseudo randomness [2], which can satisfy the requirements such as diffusion and mixing in the sense of image encryption, these good features make chaos-based encryption algorithms very efficient in terms of speed and security.

The image encryption schemes that have been proposed in literature are adopted on many chaotic maps and using different methods in the encryption process. A new color image encryption using combination of the 1D chaotic map in [3] where they have used deference of the output a sequences of some existing one-dimensional chaotic maps, as given by the authors in [4]. Digital RGB Image Encryption Based On 2D cat mapand shadow numbers are proposed where this is based on the concept of scrambling the pixels's positions, and changing the pixels values, Huang et al. [5] proposed a color image encryption based on logistic mapping and double random-phase encoding by using logistic map to diffuse the color image, the results are scrambled by replacement matrices generated by logistic map. On the other hand, the security of chaos-based image encryption algorithm usually depends on two part, changing the pixel positions of the image (permutation) and changing the values of pixels(diffusion) [6].

In this paper, the color image encryption based on logistic map and quadratic map systems is introduced. This paper is organized as follows. In the next section, Logistic Map, Quadratic Map systems are shown. In Sect. 3, we describe the proposed color image encryption algorithm. In Sect. 4, the experimental setting is presented. Finally, in Sect. 5, it is outlined some concluding remarks.

2   Logistic Map and Quadratic Map Systems

2.1   Logistic Map

The logistic map is considered as simply model of chaotic system, with a non linear equation as follows [1] and [5]:

$$x_{k+1} = \mu x_k(1 - x_k). \tag{1}$$

Where $\mu \in [0, 4]$ is a control parameter and $x \in [0, 1]$ is a real number, where the chaotic behavior is shown when $\mu \in [3.57, 4]$ as shown in Fig. 1.

2.2   Quadratic Map

The quadratic map is considered one of the chaotic maps, because it offers chaotic behavior and also it is non lineare equation is defined as follows [1]:

$$n_{k+1} = r - n_k^2. \tag{2}$$

where $r \in [0, 2]$ is a control parameter and $n \in [0, 1]$ is a real number, where the chaotic behavior is shown when $r \in [1.5, 2]$ [1].

3   Proposed Color Image Encryption Algorithm

In this section, a novel color image encryption schemea is presented. First, the color image is divided into three components (red, green, and blue), this three components are mixed as single grayscale image, to permute the pixels positions, we have used two permutatation index vectors for changing rows and columns position. Finally, the permuted grayscale image is encrypted. The encryption algorithm details are shown in following steps.

Step 1: Load the color image $I_{n\times m\times 3}$ of $n \times m \times 3$ pixels and divided it into three separate components (red, green, and blue), then are mixed as single gray scale image $P_{n\times 3m}$ of $n \times 3m$ pixels.

Step 2: We choose the secret keys that are the control parameters and initial values of chaotic systems that are used in our algorithm $(\mu_1 = 4, x_1 = 0.2), (\mu_2 = 3, x_1 = 0.4)$, $(r_1 = 1.6, n_1 = 0.5)$ and $(r_2 = 1.7, n_2 = 0.4)$ by using the Eqs. 1 and 2 respectively.

Step 3: We generate four different chaotic sequences $key1 = x_1, x_2, ..., x_{n\times 3m}$ of size $n\times 3m$, $key2 = y_1, y_2, ..., y_{n\times 3m}$ of size $n\times 3m$, $key3 = z_1, z_2, ..., z_{3m}$ of size $3m$, and $key4 = w_1, w_2, ..., w_n$ of size n, by using the Eqs. 1 and 2 respectively.

Step 4: We reshaped the two sequences key1 and key2 to two matrices and each matrices is converted its values into integers by using the following formula:

$$Key1(i,j) = mod(floor(key1(i,j) \times 10^{15}), 256). \tag{3}$$

$$Key2(i,j) = mod(floor(key2(i,j) \times 10^{15}), 256). \tag{4}$$

Step 5: We obtain the shuffled index vectors by sorting the chaotic sequences key3 and key4 in ascending, the Fig. 2 is shown the process.

Step 6: We confuse and diffuse the color image at the same time by using the following algorithms as shown in Fig. 3:

Algorithm 1.rows substitution and diffusion
Input: $(P_{n\times 3m}, key1_{n\times 3m}, index - key3_n)$.
Output: encrypted grayscale image $C_{n\times 3m}$.
For i=1 to n
    For j=1 to 3m
    $C(i,j) = bitxor(P(index - key3_n(i), j), key1(i,j))$;

    End
End
Algorithm 2.columns substitution and diffusion
Input: $(C_{n\times 3m}, key2_{n\times 3m}, index - key4_n)$.
Output: encrypted grayscale image $encrypted - image_{n\times 3m}$.
For j=1 to 3m
    For j=1 to n
    $encrypted - image(i,j) = bitxor(C(i, index - key4_n(j)), key2(i,j))$;

End
End

Step 7: We convert *encrypted – image* into three components R, G, and B, then we compos the final color encrypted image by using these three components.

4   Experimental Results and Analyses

The simulation results of the proposed algorithm are illustrated in Fig. 4, where is observed that all encrypted images are noise-like ones. The performance tests of the proposed algorithm are shown in follows analyses.

4.1   Key Space Analysis

A good encryption algorithm should have is characterized by its sufficiently large key space in order to enhance its resistance to brute force attack, and have key space more than 2^{128} [5] and [7]. Our algorithm has 8 key: the initial values and control parameters of the chaotic systems that are used in encryption process, we suppose that the values precision is 10^{-15}, so the key space is $10^{15 \times 8} = 10^{120}$, therefore the total key space able overcome the brute force attack.

4.2   Histogram Analysis

The histogram is used to compare between the distribution of pixel of the encrypted image and the original image, the histogram of the encrypted image should have uniform and different from the original image histogram. it is observed in the Figs. 5 and 6, the distribution of the encrypted red image, green image and blue image is very close to the uniform distribution, which can well protect the information of the image to withstand the statistical attack.

4.3   Key sensitivity Analysis

The most important features of a good cryptographic system are its high sensitivity to changes in the keys used in the encryption and decryption process. For example, a tiny change in the secret key leads to a faulty decryption of the data. In order to confirm the degree of sensitivity of the secret key, a small modification of one of the control parameters or one of the initial values, fails completely the decryption, see Fig. 8.

4.4   Information Entropy Analysis

The information entropy refers to the degree of information source randomness, the mathematical formula defined as [8]:

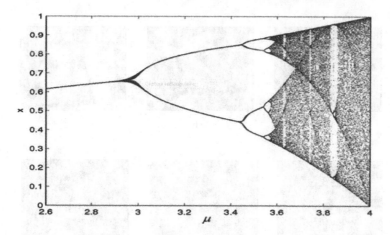

Fig. 1. Bifurcation graph of Logistic Map.

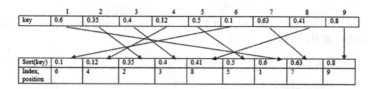

Fig. 2. Example of the generation of permutation position vector.

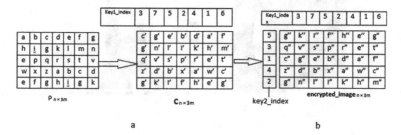

Fig. 3. Example of confusion and diffusion: (a)columns substitution and diffusion, (b) rows substitution and diffusion.

$$H(m) = -\sum_{i=0}^{255} pr(m_i)logpr(m_i). \tag{5}$$

Where, $Pr(m_i)$ is the probability of the symbol m_i, the ideal entropy for a 256- level greyscale image is 8. The Table 1 gives the values of entropy of the original image and their encryption image.

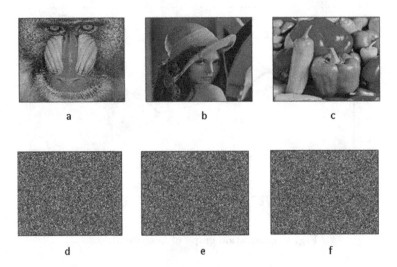

Fig. 4. Plain images: (a) Baboon, (b) Lena, (c) Pepper and encrypted images: (d) Baboon, (e) Lena, (f) Pepper.

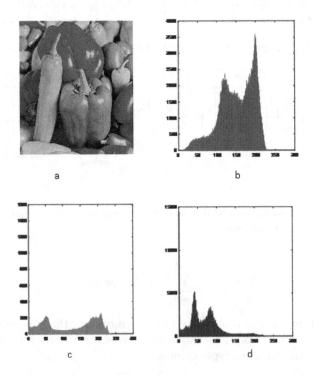

Fig. 5. (a) Original image, (b, c, d) Histograms of the R, G, B components of the original image. (Color figure online)

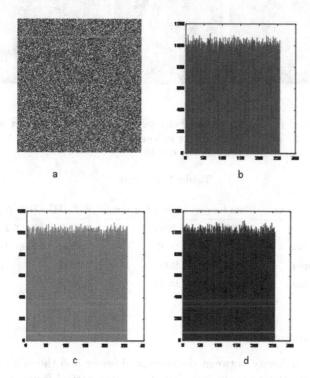

Fig. 6. (a) Encrypted image, (b, c, d) Histograms of the R, G, B components of the encrypted image. (Color figure online)

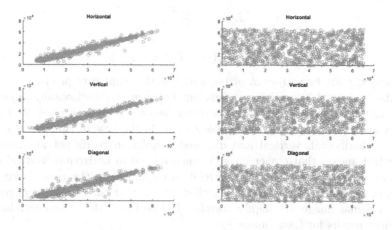

Fig. 7. The correlation of Lena image:(left frame) image original and (right frame) encrypted image.

Fig. 8. Decrypted images with a small change of the keys: (a) Incorrect independent parameter $\mu_1 = 4 + 10^{-15}$, (b) Incorrect independent parameter $x_2 = 0.4 + 10^{-15}$, (c) Incorrect independent parameter $r_1 = 1.6 + 10^{-15}$.

Table 1. Entropy.

Image name	Plain image	Encrypted image	Ref. [11],	Ref. [9]
Leana	7.4767	7.9998	7.9997	7.9972
Baboon	7.6885	7.9997	7.9989	7.9989
Pepper	7.6698	7.9998	7.9984	-
Barbara	7.72068	7.9999	7.9985	-

4.5   Correlation Analysis

The degree of similarity between the encrypted image and the original image is measured by correlation coefficients [10], the mathematical formula defined as:

$$r_{xy} = \frac{N^2.Cov(x,y)}{\sum_{i=1}^{N}(xi - E_x)^2.\sum_{i=1}^{N}(y_i - E_y)^2}. \tag{6}$$

$$E_x = \frac{\sum_{i=1}^{N}x_i}{N}. \tag{7}$$

$$Cov(x,y) = E((x - E_x)(y - E_y)). \tag{8}$$

where x; y are two adjacent pixels, and N is the number of pixels.

Table 2 gives the correlation coefficient between two horizontally adjacent pixels, two vertically adjacent pixels and two diagonally adjacent pixels for Lena, Pepper and Banana images. The Table 2 show, in the case of cipher image the values of horizontal, vertical and diagonal correlation coefficient are near to zero, which means that cipher image is uncorrelated in horizontal, vertical and diagonal direction. The values of correlation coefficient in the case of original image, in all directions are close to 1, which means that the two adjacent pixels in the original image are highly correlated. The Fig. 7 shows the correlation coefficient results for Lena image.

Table 2. Correlations coefficients of original image and encrypted image.

Correlation	Vertical	Horizontal	Diagonal
Original Leana	0.9798	0.9739	0.9631
Original Pepper	0.9820	0.9786	0.9694
Original Baboon	0.9259	0.9447	0.9046
Encrypted Leana	−0.000929	−0.000717	−0.000680
Encrypted Pepper	−0.000887	−0.000570	−0.000803
Encrypted Baboon	0.000129	0.000821	0.000606
Pepper in [11]	0.0160	−0.0074	−0.0235
Lena in [11]	0.0107	−0.0064	0.0051
Pepper in [3]	0.000169	0.002175	0.001039
Baboon in [3]	0.000397	−0.004717	0.000057

4.6 Differential Attack Analysis

The most important criteria to resist differential attack are NPCR (number of pixels change rate) and UACI (unified average changing intensity), where the theoretical values of NPCR and UACI are 0.99 and 0.33 respectively, the mathematical formulas defined as:

$$NPCR(p,q) = \frac{1}{H \times W} \sum_{ij} D(i,j) \times 100\%. \tag{9}$$

Where $D(i,j) = 0$, if $q_1(i,j) = q_2(i,j)$ and $D(i,j) = 1$, if $q_1(i,j) \neq q_2(i,j)$, where $q_1(i,j)$ and $q_2(i,j)$ are two different encrypted-images whose corresponding plain-images are differ by only one bit, where W and H are the width and height of encrypted-images q_1 and q_2

$$UACI(p,q) = \frac{1}{H \times W} \sum_{ij} \frac{D(i,j)}{255} \times 100\%. \tag{10}$$

A sufficiently high NPCR/UACI score is usually considered to be a strong resistance against attacks.

The NPCR and UACI test results are shown in Tables 3 and 4. The results demonstrate that the proposed scheme can resist to differential attack.

4.7 Speed analysis

The speed evaluation of a cryptosystem is an important factor that influences the cost of the proposed image encryption algorithm, our proposed encryption algorithm is carried out using a Matlab, on a PC with 2 GHz processor Intel Core i3-5005 CPU, 4 GB RAM, and Windows 7, 64-bit operation system to show encryption/decryption time takenof the proposed algorithm, the speed analysis

Table 3. NPCR (%) results.

Image	R	G	B
Leana	99.592	99.61	99.61
Baboon	99.59	99.63	99.59
Pepper	99.60	99.61	99.60
Leana [11]	99.65	99.62	99.58
Baboon [11]	99.62	99.62	99.62
Pepper [11]	99.61	99.61	99.61

Table 4. UACI (%) results.

Image	R	G	B
Leana	29.99	30.92	32.32
Baboon	33.34	29.30	33.17
Pepper	28.95	33.91	33.90
Leana [11]	33.48	33.41	33.34
Baboon [11]	33.46	32.22	34.23
Pepper [11]	31.03	34.00	34.78

test results for Lena image with 512 * 512 are shown in Table 5. The time costs for encryption faster than the two existing ones. Therefore, the proposed algorithm is suitable for real applications.

Table 5. Encryption time(s).

Image	Proposed scheme	[7]	[3]
Leana	0.134684	0.8193	0.1748522

5   Conclusion

We have proposed a novel color image encryption scheme by using logistic map and quadratic map systems. In order to evaluate the security of the proposed method a series of tests such as entropy, key space analysis, key sensitivity analysis, correlation of two adjacent pixels and differential attack was performed and compared with other methods. The Experimental results and analyses show that the proposed algorithm is characterized by reducing the computing effort, high efficiency and outperform many schemes given in the literature. We suggest that this encryption scheme is suitable for applications like secure transmission of confidential data in the Internet.

References

1. Mokhtar, M.A., Sadek, N.M., Mohamed, A.G.: Design of image encryption algorithm based on different chaotic mapping. In: 2017 34th National Conference on Radio Science Conference (NRSC), pp. 197–204 (2017)
2. Wu, J., Liao, X., Yang, B.: Color image encryption based on chaotic systems and elliptic curve ElGamal scheme. Sig. Process. **141**, 109–124 (2017)
3. Pak, C., Huang, L.: A new color image encryption using combination of the 1D chaotic map. Sig. Process. **138**, 129–137 (2017)
4. El Abbadi, N.K., Yahya, E., Aladilee, A.: Digital RGB image encryption based on 2D cat map and shadow numbers. In: 2017 Annual Conference on New Trends in Information and Communications Technology Applications (NTICT), pp. 162–167 (2017)
5. Huang, H., Yang, S.: Colour image encryption based on logistic mapping and double random-phase encoding. IET Image Process. **11**(4), 211–216 (2016)
6. Jeng, F.-G., Huang, W.-L., Chen, T.-H.: Cryptanalysis and improvement of two hyper-chaos-based image encryption schemes. Sig. Process. Image Commun. **34**, 45–51 (2015)
7. Liu, H., Kadir, A., Sun, X.: Chaos-based fast colour image encryption scheme with true random number keys from environmental noise. IET Image Process. **11**(5), 324–332 (2017)
8. Murugan, B., Nanjappa Gounder, A.G.: Image encryption scheme based on block-based confusion and multiple levels of diffusion. IET Comput. Vis. **10**(6), 593–602 (2016)
9. Wu, X., Zhu, B., Hu, Y., Ran, Y.: A novel color image encryption scheme using rectangular transform-enhanced chaotic tent maps. IEEE Access **5**, 6429–6436 (2017)
10. Belmeguenai, A., Ahmida, Z., Ouchtati, S., Djemii, R.: A novel approach based on stream cipher for selective speech encryption. Int. J. Speech Technol. **20**(3), 685–698 (2017)
11. Yang, B., Liao, X.: A new color image encryption scheme based on logistic map over the finite field Z_N. Multimed. Tools Appl. **77**, 21803–21821 (2018). https://doi.org/10.1007/s11042-017-5590-0

Evolutionary Multi Optimization Business Process Designs Using MR-Sort NSGAII

Nadir Mahammed[1(✉)], Sidi Mohamed Benslimane[1],
Ali Ouldkradda[2], and Mahmoud Fahsi[3]

[1] LabRI-SBA, Ecole Supérieure en Informatique, Sidi Bel Abbes, Algeria
{n.mahammed,s.benslimane}@esi-sba.dz
[2] LRIIR Laboratory, Ahmed Ben Bella University of Oran 1, Oran, Algeria
ould.kradda.ali@edu.univ-oranl.dz
[3] EEIDIS Laboratory, Djillali Liabes University Sidi Bel Abbes,
Sidi Bel Abbes, Algeria
mfahci@univ-sba.dz

Abstract. In this paper, a research was carried out on the problem of evolutionary multi objective business process optimization. It does involve (i) to construct feasible business process designs with optimum attributes, and (ii) to classify the obtained solutions using a simple and scientific approach understandable by the decision maker. The business process evolutionary multi objective optimization (BPMOO) approach involves the generation of a series of diverse optimized business process designs for the same process requirements using an evolutionary algorithm (EA). The work presented in this paper is aimed to investigate the benefits that come from the utilization of multiple-criteria decision analysis methods (MCDA) with an evolutionary multi objective optimization algorithms (EMOA) execution process. The experimental results clearly bring that the proposed optimization Framework is capable of producing an acceptable number of optimized design alternatives to simplify the decision maker's choice of solutions in a reasonable runtime.

Keywords: Multi objective optimization · Evolutionary algorithm
Business process · Multiple-criteria decision analysis

1 Introduction

According to [1], optimization refers to finding the best possible solution to a problem given a set of constraints. Firstly, when a single objective has to be optimized, the aim is to find the best possible solution available called "global optimum". Secondly, the case where there is not one but several objectives to optimize simultaneously. Actually, these objectives are most often in conflict with each other. These problems are called "multi-objective optimization" (MOO) that leads to a set of solutions. Therefore, a solution in a MOO is Pareto optimal [2] if it exists no other feasible solution which would decrease some criterion without causing a simultaneous increase in at least one other criterion. Such problems can be mostly solved using metaheuristics [3]. Evolutionary algorithms are particularly recommended because of their ability to handle a set

© Springer Nature Switzerland AG 2019
É. Renault et al. (Eds.): MSPN 2018, LNCS 11005, pp. 24–31, 2019.
https://doi.org/10.1007/978-3-030-03101-5_3

of solutions simultaneously, and their capability to deal with problems of various kinds [4]. Having said that, evolutionary multi objective optimization (EMOO) was introduced in the 1980s [5], and used in a lot of disciplines, nowadays, and business process optimization (BPO) is, by no means, an exception. BPO is considered the problem of building feasible business processes (BPs) while optimizing conflicting criteria [6].

This article proposes a Framework that deals with a business process multi objective optimization dealing with 02 conflicting optimization criteria. MRS-NSGAII, for Majority Rule Sorting NSGAII is used by the Framework as enhanced EA. It tests and experiments the influence of using an MCDA in BPMOO. Section 2 presents a state of the art on BPMOO. Section 3 presents the main contribution of the paper, the optimization Framework with its proposed Fitness function and introduces MRS-NSGAII. Experiments are performed and the results are presented in Sect. 4. Finally, Sect. 5 summarizes the proposed research and provides perspectives.

2 Related Work

NSGAII is one of the most widely used evolutionary algorithms to overcome the question of multi objective (up to 03 criteria) of business processes [7]. The first work to mention is [8]. It focuses on how to appropriately allocate resources to activities in BP designs to ensure its high performance. A series of work on BPMOO with evolutionary algorithms are introduced by [9]. The proposed approach uses a formal definition of a BP. It proposed and tested a Framework using NSGAII to generate new BP designs. Thereafter, [10–12] present the most important work in this field. The authors have improved [9] work by adding (i) the ability to review or reconfigure any unfeasible BP design and (ii) using other EAs. They finally propose a Framework where each task can be regarded as a Web service. [13] proposed an optimization Framework using Petri networks for modeling. [14] resumed the work of [10] by modifying the mutation and crossover operators used within NSGAII. [15] are interested in a BPMOO (up to three criteria) by implementing a Framework using NSGAII with a modified crossover's operator and different selection techniques. [16] worked on a novel selection operator within NSGAII tested with a real BP scenario.

The present work is an enhancement of the optimization Framework proposed in [16]. We propose to add a step on the EA progress while generating and evaluating processes with diverse designs constructed based on a predefined business process.

3 Proposed Approach

3.1 Overall Architecture of the Proposed Framework

A BP is defined as a collective set of tasks when properly connected perform a business operation, e.g. a product or a service providing value to the organization [17]. The main elements involved are tasks, resources and attributes of the BP. The attributes provide the capability of evaluating a BP design. The problem of BPMOO can be defined as follows:

$P = (BPS, F, C)$ with BPS is the BP designs search space $(sol \in BPS)$. F is the Fitness function that assigns a numerical score $F(sol)$ for each BP design. C is a set of constraints to optimize. The optimization problem aim is to find either the instance of:

- Global optimal BP sol_{opt}, such as $\forall sol \in BPS$, $F(sol_{opt}) < F(sol)$ or
- A near-optimal BP sol_{nopt}, such that $F(sol_{opt}) - F(sol_{nopt}) < \delta$.

Throughout the Framework course (Fig. 1); each BP design must fulfill a certain amount of constraints. MRS-NSGAII is used to generate BP designs. Each solution set has (i) a feasible graphical representation and (ii) optimized' attributes values.

Create an Initial Population. A random population of BP designs is generated. It takes place only once in the Framework's progress. The steps 2–5 are repeated for a predefined number of iterations.

Create Designs Representation. For each BP design, a matrix tasks/task is generated to represent the relationship between tasks and resources composing a potential design (compared to [16] with 02 matrix).

Verify and Apply the Restraints. The Framework verifies a set of constraints because a design might be modified thereafter. As restraints, we quote that (i) a task must appear once in each design and (ii) verify inputs and outputs of each BP design.

Assess Designs. BP design's Fitness value is calculated based on its attributes values. The proposed Framework uses a Fitness function using with 02 optimization criteria.

Perform EA. MRS-NSGAII is applied (simulated binary tournament selection, simulated binary crossover and mutation operators). The process does not check whether a solution is feasible (step 3). Subsection III-B introduces MRS-NSGAII.

3.2   MRS-NSGAII

MRS-NSGAII is an enhanced version of NSGAII proposed by [17] (see Fig. 2). The authors propose to add the majority rule sorting method (MR-sort) to the non-dominated sorting stage into NSGAII execution. MR-sort is a simplified version of the ELECTRE TRI sorting model [19, 20]. The general principle of MR-sort is to assign alternatives by comparing their performances to those of profiles delimiting proposed categories. To the authors' knowledge this technique has never been used with NSGAII and particularly in a BPMOO, by the past. MRS-NSGAII is summed up as follows:

1. A parent population called P_t is randomly generated and an offspring population Q_t is created from it.
2. Both populations P_t and Q_t are combined into population R_t with $2N$ size.
3. The population R_t is categorized by going through the MR-sort model where all members are classified and put into categories.

4. The non-dominated sorting is applied on all categories except the last category (i.e. the worse according to the sorting by MR-sort).
5. The best remaining N individuals from R_t are selected using the crowding distance and so form the next generation's parent population P_{t+1}.
6. The steps 1–5 are repeated until the stopping criteria have been satisfied.

MR-sort method works as follows [21]: Let X be a set of objects evaluated on n ordered criteria, $F = \{1, \ldots, n\}$. We assume that X is the Cartesian product of the criteria scales, $X = \prod_{j=1}^{n} X_j$. An object $a \in X$ is a vector $(a_1, a_2, \ldots, a_n)$, where $a_j \in X_j$ for all j. The ordered categories which the objects are assigned to by the MR-sort method are denoted by C_h, with $h = 1, \ldots, p$. We denote by $P = \{1, \ldots, p\}$, the list of category indices. An object is assigned to a category if its criterion values are at least as good as the category lower profile values on a weighted majority of criteria while this condition is not fulfilled when the object's criterion values are compared to the category upper profile values.

4   Experimentation and Results

In order to generate satisfactory results, the proposed Framework needs to achieve two goals (i) obtain optimal business process designs by converging to the Pareto-optimal front and (ii) obtain a variety of different sizes of BP designs while maintaining the population diversity. This suggests that the features of the problem that require more attentions are:

- The number of feasible non-dominated solutions.
- The different acceptable BP designs sizes.
- The execution time.

Each of these problem features is related with the performance goals of the Framework. The optimization Framework is expected to increase the quality of generated solutions in shorter time periods. The work presented is aimed to investigate the benefits that come from the utilization of MRS-NSGAII. This feature puts to test both the convergence and diversity capabilities of MRS-NSGAII execution. It must not content itself by discovering feasible solutions but also to converge towards the optimal, in reasonable time frames.

Table 1 shows the parameters used by the proposed Framework. The problem is set up to deal with 02 criteria. MRS-NSGAII performs 500 iterations, it might seem excessively low but initial experiments showed that it produced better quality results in comparison with higher numbers and in a timely fashion. Initial population is limited to 500. Table 2 shows the parameters of the test scenarios. To apply correctly MR-sort, we propose 03 categories: "*Good*", "*medium*" and "*bad*" ranked from most important (to the decision maker) to least important, respectively. The limit profiles are resulting from [16] experiments. NetBeans 8.1 IDE and Java 8 on a machine with Intel Core i7-4810MQ (Quad-Core 2.8 GHz) and a 16 Go RAM have been used in the experimentation phase. This article proposes to add MR-sort to the canonical non-dominated sorting used within NSGAII, and compare the results using traditional NSGAII.

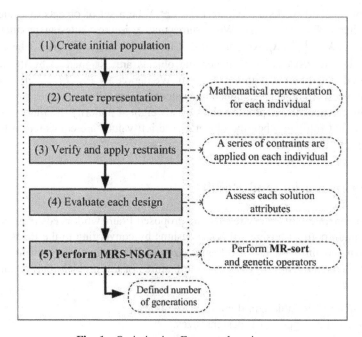

Fig. 1. Optimization Framework main steps

MR-sort has proved to enhance the performance of MRS-NSGAII used by the proposed Framework in the optimization of the business processes scenarios by reducing its execution time while finding more non dominated solutions. As shown on Table 3, MR-sort has a very good impact on the runtime of the Framework for all scenarios. Resulted in execution time decrease rate to 44.44% with scenario B. MR-sort method assists NSGAII in generating more non-dominated solutions. The increase rate of the solutions comes up to 56.41% for scenario C. The Framework has better solutions using MRS-NSGAII both from the point of you of the convergence towards optimal solutions and maintaining the population diversity.

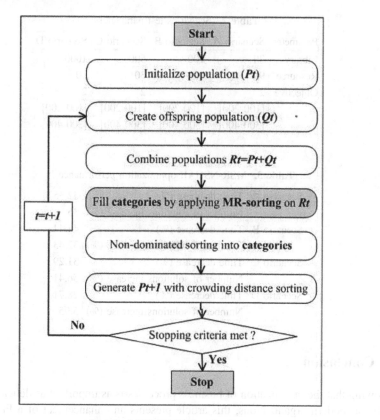

Fig. 2. MRS-NSGAII main steps

Table 1. Framework parameters

Parameter	Value
Crossover probability	0.8
Mutation probability	0.2
Optimization criteria	2
Categories	$\{C_3$: good, C_2: medium, C_1: bad$\}$
Limit profiles Scenario A	$\{b_{1,1} = 1003, b_{1,2} = 1801, b_{2,1} = 4084, b_{2,2} = 4935\}$
Limit profiles Scenario B	$\{b_{1,1} = 1663, b_{1,2} = 1870, b_{2,1} = 4205, b_{2,2} = 5191\}$
Limit profiles Scenario C	$\{b_{1,1} = 1788, b_{1,2} = 2001, b_{2,1} = 4387, b_{2,2} = 5267\}$
Limit profiles Scenario D	$\{b_{1,1} = 1850, b_{1,2} = 2113, b_{2,1} = 4712, b_{2,2} = 5374\}$
λ	0.86

Table 2. Scenarios test parameters

Parameter	Scenario A	Scenario B	Scenario C	Scenario D
Library	30	100	500	1000
Resource	9	30	30	30
Objective	2	2	2	2
a_1	[100 200]	[100 200]	[100 200]	[100 200]
a_2	[300 400]	[300 400]	[300 400]	[300 400]

Table 3. MSR-NSGAII optimization performance

Scenario A	Time decrease (%)	32.35
	Number of solutions increase (%)	36
Scenario B	Time decrease (%)	44.44
	Number of solutions increase (%)	32.43
Scenario C	Time decrease (%)	31.29
	Number of solutions increase (%)	56.41
Scenario D	Time decrease (%)	28.71
	Number of solutions increase (%)	5.95

5 Conclusion

Knowing that the optimization of business processes is as important as delicate to deal with for modern organizations, this article presents an enhancement of a Framework capable of generating optimal feasible BP designs. It involves a quantitative representation for each solution, a modified optimization EA that generates diverse optimized designs using a MCDA method for the categorization of the solutions. The results have demonstrated that the Framework with the aid of the MR-sort method has increased its capability of generating diverse solutions and selecting the optimal ones in less time. Which pave the way to further experimentations as using another type of MCDA (e.g. for ranking), adding more optimization criteria and rewrite the Fitness function as well. Using MR-sort method needs to set several parameters and it is not easy for a decision maker to assess such parameters. In the present article, we choose to assess these parameters regarding to previous work and automate the proceeding is the next step to achieve.

References

1. Coello, C.A.C.: Evolutionary multi-objective optimization: a historical view of the field. IEEE Comput. Intell. Mag. 1(1), 28–36 (2006)
2. Pareto, V.: Cours d'Economie Politique, vol. I and II. F. Rouge, Lausanne (1896)
3. Coello, C.A.C., Lamont, G.B., Van Veldhuizen, D.A.: Evolutionary Algorithms for Solving Multi-Objective Problems, vol. 5. Springer, New York (2007). https://doi.org/10.1007/978-0-387-36797-2

4. Deb, K., Goel, T.: Controlled elitist non-dominated sorting genetic algorithms for better convergence. In: Zitzler, E., Thiele, L., Deb, K., Coello Coello, C.A., Corne, D. (eds.) EMO 2001. LNCS, vol. 1993, pp. 67–81. Springer, Heidelberg (2001). https://doi.org/10.1007/3-540-44719-9_5

5. Schaffer, J.D.: Multiple objective optimization with vector evaluated genetic algorithm. In: 1st International Conference of GA and their Application, pp. 93–100 (1985)

6. Mahammed, N., Benslimane, S.M.: Toward multi criteria optimization of business processes design. In: Bellatreche, L., Pastor, Ó., Almendros Jiménez, J.M., Aït-Ameur, Y. (eds.) MEDI 2016. LNCS, vol. 9893, pp. 98–107. Springer, Cham (2016). https://doi.org/10.1007/978-3-319-45547-1_8

7. Goel, T., Vaidyanathan, R., Haftka, R.T., Shyy, W., Queipo, N.V., Tucker, K.: Response surface approximation of pareto optimal front in multi-objective optimization. Comput. Methods Appl. Mech. Eng. **196**(4), 879–893 (2007)

8. Hofacker, I., Vetschera, R.: Algorithmical approaches to business process design. Comput. Oper. Res. **28**(13), 1253–1275 (2001)

9. Vergidis, K., Tiwari, A., Majeed, B.: Business process improvement using multi-objective optimisation. BT Technol. J. **24**(2), 229–235 (2006)

10. Vergidis, K., Saxena, D., Tiwari, A.: An evolutionary multi-objective framework for business process optimisation. Appl. Soft Comput. **12**(8), 2638–2653 (2012)

11. Vergidis, K., Turner, C., Alechnovic, A., Tiwari, A.: An automated optimisation framework for the development of re-configurable business processes: a web services approach. Int. J. Comput. Integr. Manuf. **28**(1), 41–58 (2015)

12. Georgoulakos, K., Vergidis, K., Tsakalidis, G., Samaras, N.: Evolutionary multi-objective optimization of business process designs with pre-processing. In: IEEE Congress on CEC 2017, pp. 897–904. IEEE (2017)

13. Wibig, M.: Dynamic programming and genetic algorithm for business processes optimisation. Int. J. Intell. Syst. Appl. **5**(1), 44 (2012)

14. Farsani, S.T., Aboutalebi, M., Motameni, H.: Customizing NSGAII to optimize business processes designs. Res. J. Recent Sci. **2**, 74–79 (2013)

15. Mahammed, N., Benslimane, S.M.: An evolutionary algorithm based approach for business process multi-criteria optimization. IJOCI **7**(2), 34–53 (2017)

16. Mahammed, N., Benslimane, S., Hamdani, N.: Evolutionary multi-objective optimization of business process designs with MA-NSGAII. In: Amine, A., Mouhoub, M., Ait Mohamed, O., Djebbar, B. (eds.) CIIA 2018. IAICT, vol. 522, pp. 341–351. Springer, Cham (2018). https://doi.org/10.1007/978-3-319-89743-1_30

17. Deb, K., Pratap, A., Agarwal, S., Meyarivan, T.A.M.T.: A fast and elitist multi objective genetic algorithm: NSGA-II. IEEE Trans. Evol. Comput. **6**(2), 182–197 (2002)

18. Bouyssou, D., Marchant, T.: An axiomatic approach to noncompensatory sorting methods in MCDM, I. Eur. J. Oper. Res. **178**(1), 217–245 (2007)

19. Yu, W.: Aide multicritère à la décision dans le cadre de la problématique du tri: concepts, méthodes et applications, Doctoral dissertation, Paris 9 (1992)

20. Roy, B., Bouyssou, D.: Aide multicritère à la décision: méthodes et cas. Economica, Paris (1993)

21. Sobrie, O., Mousseau, V., Pirlot, M.: Learning the parameters of a non compensatory sorting model. In: Walsh, T. (ed.) ADT 2015. LNCS (LNAI), vol. 9346, pp. 153–170. Springer, Cham (2015). https://doi.org/10.1007/978-3-319-23114-3_10

Design and Implementation of an Intrusion Prevention System for Wi-Fi Networks 802.11 AC

Julián Francisco Mojica Sánchez[1], Octavio José Salcedo Parra[1,2(✉)], and Javier Medina[3]

[1] Department of Systems and Industrial Engineering, Faculty of Engineering, Universidad Nacional de Colombia, Bogotá D.C., Colombia
{jfmojicas, ojsalcedop}@unal.edu.co
[2] Faculty of Engineering, Intelligent Internet Research Group, Universidad Distrital "Francisco José de Caldas", Bogotá D.C., Colombia
osalcedo@udistrital.edu.co
[3] Faculty of Engineering, GEFEM Research Group, Universidad Distrital "Francisco José de Caldas", Bogotá D.C., Colombia
rmedina@udistrital.edu.co

Abstract. In this document, related works are evaluated with theory of games applied to IPS (Intrusion Prevention System) in terms of wireless networks and a model of game theory that allows the detection of intrusions in WI-FI networks 802.11 ac.

Keywords: IPS · Intrusions · Wi-Fi 802.11 n · Theory of games

1 Introduction

The Internet is now part of everyday life of people and each time is more linked due to the introduction of the Internet of Things concept, where all things have a digital identity and can communicate or share information through a network of the who are part [1].

With this massive connection of devices that handle sensitive information and the intrinsic vulnerabilities of wireless communications, the infrastructure of the networks of the Internet of things becomes a point of interest for criminals, for which it is necessary to ensure privacy of this information through security mechanisms that adapt to different types of attacks [2].

A possible solution that guarantees the security of the information is the encryption of the information, but this is not viable in a large number of Internet devices of things because they have small batteries, for which your operation requires low energy consumption and the implementation of an encryption module would increase said consumption [3].

The simple of Internet devices of things allows them to be a gateway for attackers because they do not have measures that guarantee the communication security, between attacks to which Wi-Fi networks are exposed by communicating with these devices are low password exploitation, remote code execution, hidden monitoring functions,

© Springer Nature Switzerland AG 2019
É. Renault et al. (Eds.): MSPN 2018, LNCS 11005, pp. 32–41, 2019.
https://doi.org/10.1007/978-3-030-03101-5_4

reverse engineering hardware and man in the middle. One of the main uses of control of Internet devices of things by hand of criminals is the denial of services, through which they can charge money for preventing access to a website [4].

Due to the importance of information and vulnerabilities of wireless networks are being carried out efforts in research and development both in new Internet devices of things as in problems of existing security. It should be noted that the information that share through these devices is done in real time it is necessary to identify the events, process them and react to these in real time so that the information traveling to through the network is not compromised [5].

In the present document, a model based on in game theory to establish the detection criteria of intrusions of an IPS (Intrusion Prevention System) for Wi-Fi 802.11 n networks, from the review of works related previously developed.

2 Related Works

In 2016, Sharma, Moon, Moon and Park designed a DFA-AD (distributed framework architecture for the detection of advanced persistent threats), in which one of the 4 traffic classification modules was Dynamic Bayesian game model Based, in this case the game model is dynamic as each player selects his behavior depending on the current state of the system and the information that has. Attackers identify users and objectives system specials exhaustively, therefore, the attackers have more data on the module than the protectors, which creates a system in incompleteness and asymmetry. They define the model through 7 components of the following way [4]:

$$DBG - Model = (S, E, V, B, X, W, R)$$

Where:

- $S = (s_1, s_2, .., s_n)$ refers to the state space of the target system and contains all possible system states. The change of state of the system gives with each behavior of the players. Rule of change is limited by the use of vulnerabilities of the system, the nodes of the connection system and the capabilities of the players.
- $E = \{E_A, E_D\}$ are the entities that can choose their behavior autonomously during the game. It can be a group, an association or an individual. The protectors are denoted with D and attackers with A.
- $V = (V_A; V_D)$ are the rewards granted to players. This is the key variable of the model since the players choose their behaviors to amplify your own results.
- $B = \{B_A, B_D\}$ is the space of behavior of the players, while $B_A = (b_A^1, b_A^2, \ldots, b_A^k)$, $B_D = (b_D^1, b_D^2, \ldots, b_D^k)$ refers respectively to all the behavior of attackers and defenders.
- $X = \{X_A, X_B\}$ denotes the previous probability of each played and used to evaluate the type of other players on the basis of the known information.
- $W = \{W_A; W_B\}$ is the space for type of players, where $W_A = (w_1, w_2, \ldots, w_m)$; $W_B = (w_1, w_2, \ldots, w_m)$ represents, respectively, all types of attackers and defenders The players that come in different types they refer to different levels of behavior.

R is the result of the game model, which can be used to predict the behavior of players.

In this work after making the classification by 4 different methods then perform event correlation to from each of the classifications and then a vote to establish what behaviors correspond to an attack.

In 2016 Wang, Du, Yang, Zhu, Shen and Zhang propose an attack-defense game model for detecting malicious nodes in Embedded Sensor Networks (ESNs) using a repeated game approach, where they define the function of rewards that attackers will receive and defenders for their actions [6]. To solve the errors detection and detection absences use a model of game tree. They show that the game model it does not have a Nash equilibrium of pure but mixed strategy, where the nodes are changing due to the strategies of attackers and defenders so that they are in dynamic equilibrium, where resources are used limited and security protection is provided at the same weather. Finally, they perform simulations where they show that with the proposed model can reduce consumption of energy 50% compared to the existing model All Monitor (AM) and improve the detection percentage of 10% to 15% compared to the existing Cluster Head (CH) model.

In 2013 Manshaei, Zhu, Alpcan, Bacşar and Hubaux conducts a review of the investigations in privacy and security in communication networks and computation with a game theory approach [7]. In their content they have an Intrusion Detection section Systems where they present the different works found in the review of the literature; the way they are configured the IDS; Networked IDS, where different networks operate in the network IDS independent way and the security of each subsystem which they protect individually depends on the performance of the other IDS; Collaborative Intrusion Detection System Networks, in this case in the network operate different IDS collaborative way, that is, they share the knowledge of the new attacks that they detect, but the system can be see compromised if the control of an IDS is taken by an attacker and finally the response to intrusions, where expose an intrusion response system based on Stackelberg stochastic game called Response and Recovery Engine (RRE).

In 2012 Rafsanjani, Aliahmadipour and Javidi propose a method to prevent and detect intrusions internal networks in ad hoc mobile networks using game theory [8]. To reduce the consumption of resources generated by the detection external intruders choose a cluster head in each cluster to provide the service to detect intrusions to other nodes in the cluster, in this way they call it normal mode and only you can be in this when the attack probability is low. When the attack probability is high, the victim nodes they must activate their own IDS to detect and counteract intrusions, in this way they call it perfect mode. In this work the cluster head should not be malicious and should detect external intrusions in your cluster with enough resources and honest behavior. This is a hybrid system of three phases: the first phase is the relationship construction of trust between nodes and the estimation of the trust value of each node to prevent internal intrusions. In the second phase, they propose an optimal method for the choice of cluster head by using the trust value, and in the third phase the determination of the confidence value to notify to the victim node that must activate its IDS once the attack probability exceeds that value. In the first and third phase apply Bayesian game.

In conclusion they propose a hybrid method that uses game theory to improve the security and performance of the network and reduces the consumption of means.

In 2013 Kantzavelou, Tzikopoulos and Katsikas they model a non-cooperative three-player game for study the interactions between an insider and the systems of detection of intrusions used in a WSN (Wireless Sensor Network) [9]. To solve the game, they place the balance of Nash to determine how the players should play it. By examining this balance, it is possible to perform suggestions and recommendations of strategies to identify and isolate a compromised node.

· In the proposed architecture, each cluster of devices has a local IDS that communicates to the global IDS when detects suspicious activity and makes suggestions trust, this is the first player, the second player is the global IDS, this is separated from the others devices in a base station and admits or excludes action of users if it is normal or intrusive respectively and the third player is the Potential Attacker, which is any node of the sensor network, is a user completely authorized and can perform a normal action or attack.

3 Models of Game Theories

The prevention of intrusions can be understood as an attack scenario - defense, in which the person in charge of the security of the network decides whether it is necessary or not to put in operation the system of prevention of intrusions, because this operation has a cost that would not be necessary if the network is not being attacked.

The game consists of a defender (the one in charge of putting in March or not the IPS) and an attacker (which seek to enter the network and take advantage of such intrusion), this was taken of the model proposed by Wang in 2016 [6] but limited to a single attacker and defender, as he took multiple attackers and defenders in multiple nodes and periods of weather.

As for the defender, he has two strategies (UD): defend or not defend and in the case of the attacker (UA): attack or not attack. The realization of these strategies has some rewards and costs that will determine the way act of the two actors. These are defined below costs and rewards:

- Cost of starting the IPS Cm
- Average loss when the system is attacked Ci
- Cost to attack by the attacker Ca
- Cost of not attacking by the attacker Cw
- Payment to the defender for taking an action strategy defensive Ui
- Payment to the attacker for taking an action strategy offensive Ua.

Now you can understand that the reward of the attackers Pa is equal to average losses when the system is attacked, that is:

$$Pa = Ci \tag{1}$$

Now it is necessary to define when it is profitable for the attacker perform the attack:

$$Cw < Pa - Ca \tag{2}$$

The above equation means that the attacker will perform an attack when its reward minus the cost of attacking greater than the cost of not attacking.

On the other hand, the attacker will not make an attack when the cost of starting the IPS is much lower than the loss average when the system is attacked, because in this case surely the defender would have started the IPS, therefore this will be in operation and the attack will be detected and the attacker isolated from the network.

From this it is possible to define the reward matrix as:

$$\begin{bmatrix} P_a - C_a, U_i - C_i & -U_a, U_i - C_m \\ C_w, U_i & C_w, U_i - C_m \end{bmatrix}$$

Where the columns correspond to the strategies of the defender, that is, not defend and defend; and the rows do reference to the attacker's strategies, that is, attack and not attack.

Now it is necessary to analyze the Nash equilibrium by analyzing the payments of each actor depending on the strategy he takes the other actor.

When the defender does not defend the attacker has two strategies possible, but by Eq. (1) we know that

$$Cw < Pa - Ca \tag{3}$$

Therefore, the attacker will always choose to attack.

In second place when the defender defends the same mind the attacker can choose between attacking and not attacking, but as

$$-Ua < Cw \tag{4}$$

The attacker would always choose not to attack.

Now you must fix the behavior of the attacker and analyze what strategy the defender will carry out.

First, when the attacker decides to attack

$$Ui - Ca = Ui - Cm \tag{5}$$

The defender will always choose to defend.

Second, when the attacker decides not to attack

$$Ui > Ui - Cm \tag{6}$$

Therefore, the defender will always choose not to defend.

To analyze the previous strategies that the actors will take depending on the behavior of the other one can say that there is no pure Nash equilibrium, since there is no place in the matrix in which both actors are satisfied with their reward.

Because there is no pure Nash equilibrium, it is necessary analyze if the game model is in mixed equilibrium of Nash, for this the probability is defined that the attacker attack δ and the probability that the defender defends σ.

The attacker's mixed strategy is:

$$U_A = (P_a - C_a)(1 - \delta)\sigma + (-U_a)\delta\sigma + C_w(1 - \sigma) \tag{7}$$

The mixed strategy of the defender is:

$$U_I = (U_i - C_i)(1 - \delta)\sigma + (U_i - C_m)\delta + U_i(1 - \delta)(1 - \sigma) \tag{8}$$

$$U_I = U_i + C_i\delta\sigma - C_i\sigma - C_m\delta \tag{9}$$

Now using the extreme value method to solve the strategy of the Nash mixed model, the equations are derived (7) and (9) regarding σ and δ respectively.

$$\frac{\partial U_A}{\partial \sigma} = (P_a - C_a)(1 - \delta) + (-U_a)\delta - C_w = 0 \tag{10}$$

$$\frac{\partial U_I}{\partial \delta} = C_i\sigma - C_m = 0 \tag{11}$$

Clearing from Eq. (10) is it possible to find δ

$$\delta = \frac{P_a - C_a - C_w}{P_a - C_a + U_a} \tag{12}$$

Clearing from Eq. (11) is it possible to find σ

$$\sigma = \frac{C_m}{C_i} \tag{13}$$

With these rewards depending on the probability of take the strategy of attacking and defending, we can find the rewards of not attacking and not defending like $(1 - \delta)$ and $(1 - \sigma)$ respectively. Therefore, the strategies of the Attackers under a mixed Nash equilibrium model are:

$$(\delta, 1 - \delta) = \left(\frac{P_a - C_a - C_w}{P_a - C_a + U_a}, \frac{U_a + C_w}{P_a - C_a + U_a} \right) \tag{14}$$

$$(\sigma, 1 - \sigma) = \left(\frac{C_m}{C_i}, \frac{C_i - C_m}{C_i} \right) \tag{15}$$

To analyze the Nash equilibrium by mixed strategy, you can start assuming that the probability of attacking δ be high, for this to be $Cm \gg Ci$, that is, the attack occurs when it is not profitable to start the IPS, which makes the probability of defense is low.

In case the defense probability is high, he wants say that IPS has probably been put in place due to that the losses from being attacked are greater than the cost to have the IPS in motion, that is, $Cm \ll Ci$ which indicates that the probability of attack must be low.

In conclusion, the chances of attack and defense are inversely proportional and the system will be found in Mixed Nash equilibrium when:

$$\delta = \sigma \tag{16}$$

Now Manshaei [7] explains a Bayesian game of two players, a defense node and a malicious or regular one. He malicious node can choose between attacking and not attacking, while that the defense node can choose between monitoring and not monitor The defender's security is quantifiable from according to the property that protects w, therefore, when there is a safety failure the damage is represented by -w. Below is the matrix of rewards:

$$\begin{bmatrix} (1-\alpha)w - C_a, (2\alpha-1)w - C_m & w - C_a, -w \\ 0, \beta w - C_m & 0, 0 \end{bmatrix}$$

In this matrix the columns represent the behaviors of the defender (monitor and not monitor) and the rows attacker behaviors (attack and not attack), Ca and Cm do they refer to the costs of attacking and monitoring, α and β are the detection rate and the false alarm rate of the IDS respectively and μ_0 the probability that a player is malicious.

Finally they show that when $\mu_0 < \frac{(1+\beta)w + Cm}{(2\alpha+\beta-1)w}$ the game supports a strategy of pure balance (attack if it is malicious, do not attack if it is regular), do not monitor, μ_0 and when $\mu_0 > \frac{(1+\beta)w + Cm}{(2\alpha+\beta-1)w}$ the game does not have a pure strategy.

4 Proposed Model

From the model described by Manshaei and establishing that the two players are intruder and defender, since the intruder is ready to carry out the attack because has done a vulnerability study and has planned the different strategies to follow in order to enter authorized to the network, the time when no attack represents a Cw cost (waiting cost) because the network can change and the investment mentioned above both of time and of resources can be lost. Therefore, the payment matrix is:

$$\begin{bmatrix} (1-\alpha)w - C_a, (2\alpha-1)w - C_m & w - C_a, -w \\ -C_w, -\beta w - C_m & -C_w, 0 \end{bmatrix}$$

Next, each of the scenarios is explained possible and the respective payments for the intruder and the defender:

- When the intruder attacks and the defender monitors: Reward of the attacker, the times the system fails of detection for the good that protects less the cost to attack; the defender's reward, the times the system works less the times it fails for the good that protects, all this except the cost of monitoring.
- When the intruder attacks and the defender does not monitor: the reward of the attacker, the good that one wants to obtain minus the cost of attacking; the defender's reward, in this case is the loss of good.
- When the intruder does not attack and the defender monitors: reward of the attacker, in this case it is the loss for waiting to perform the attack; the reward of defender, false alarm rate degrades the good and its It also has the cost of monitoring.
- When the intruder does not attack and the defender does not monitor: reward of the attacker, in this case it is the loss wait to perform the attack; the reward of the defender, in this case it is null since it does not spend on monitoring and it is not attacked.

5 Evaluation of the Model

Since there is no point in the rewards matrix in which both defender and attacker feel comfortable with the situation, it is necessary to determine if the model is in mixed Nash equilibrium, for this the probability of that the attacker attack δ and the probability that the defender defend σ.

The mixed strategy of the attackers is

$$U_A = [(1 - \alpha)w - C_a]\delta\sigma + [w - C_a](1 - \delta)\sigma + (-C_w)\delta(1 - \sigma) + (-C_w)(1 - \delta)(1 - \sigma) \tag{17}$$

The mixed strategy of the defender is

$$U_I = [(2\alpha - 1)w - C_m]\delta\sigma + (-w)(1 - \delta)\sigma + [-\beta w - C_m]\delta(1 - \sigma) \tag{18}$$

Using the extreme value method to solve the strategy of the Nash mixed model, the equations are derived (17) and (18) regarding δ and σ respectively and are equal to zero.

$$\frac{\partial U_A}{\partial \sigma} = -\delta\alpha w + w - C_a + C_w = 0 \tag{19}$$

$$\frac{\partial U_I}{\partial \sigma} = 2\sigma\alpha w - \beta w - C_m + \sigma\beta_w = 0 \tag{20}$$

Clearing from Eq. (19) is it possible to find

$$\delta = \frac{w - C_a + C_w}{w\alpha} \tag{21}$$

Clearing from Eq. (20) is it possible to find δ

$$\sigma = \frac{\beta w + C_m}{2\alpha w + \beta_w} \tag{22}$$

To analyze the Nash equilibrium by mixed strategy, you can start assuming that the probability of attacking δ be high, for this to be $Cm \gg 2\alpha w$, this means that the attacker could attack comfortably when the goods that protects the defender are not so valuable to him, which is why I will not have activated the IPS. In the case where you come from protect are valuable the defense probability will increase and the probability of attack will decrease.

Therefore, it is found again that the probabilities of attack and defense are inversely proportional and the system will be in mixed Nash equilibrium when:

$$\delta = \sigma \tag{23}$$

Additionally, in case the probability of defense be high, this situation occurs when the cost of waiting for attacker is greater than the cost of attacking, that is, when it is more profitable for the attacker to effect his attack than to follow waiting for the right moment.

6 Discussion

The presented model is based on the model described by Manshaei [7] but this does not have a pure Nash equilibrium because in this new model it is defined that there are two players: a defender and an attacker, while in the presented by Manshei it is possible that the attacker is not malicious in which if there is a pure balance and it is the one of not attacking and not monitoring.

Regarding the model presented by Wang [6], the same conclusion that the system will be in equilibrium when the probability of attacking

$$\sigma = \frac{\beta w + C_m}{2\alpha w + \beta_w}$$

Be equal to the probability of defending

$$\delta = \frac{w - C_a + C_w}{w\alpha}$$

And in case these are not equal the model is regulated to over time until you reach this balance even though you in this case the detection rate and false are taken into account IPS alarms, which is raised in the model described by Manshaei [7] and makes the model closer to reality.

7 Conclusions

This model of game theory adds a characteristic new for intrusion prevention systems, where you can evaluate how complex it is to make an analysis of vulnerabilities to the network that defends itself. Because if it is much less expensive to perform the analysis that the attack would be more profitable for the attackers launch your attack plan and therefore the IPS has to be in operation to prevent such attacks and avoid loss of information, money and reputation.

The proposed model is regulated over time until reach the equilibrium point at which the probability of attack δ is it equal to the probability of defending σ.

$$\sigma = \frac{\beta w + C_m}{2\alpha w + \beta_w} = \frac{w - C_a + C_w}{w\alpha} = \delta$$

References

1. Adat, V., Gupta, B.B.: Security in internet of things: issues, challenges, taxonomy, and architecture. Telecommun. Syst. **67**, 1–19 (2017). https://doi.org/10.1007/s11235-017-0345-9
2. Sforzin, A., Marmol, F.G., Conti, M., Bohli, J.M.: RPiDS: raspberry Pi IDS - a fruitful intrusion detection system for IoT. In: Proceedings - 13th IEEE International Conference on Ubiquitous Intelligence and Computing, 13th IEEE International Conference on Advanced and Trusted Computing, 16th IEEE International Conference on Scalable Computing and Communications, IEEE International, pp. 440–448 (2017). https://doi.org/10.1109/UIC-ATC-ScalCom-CBDCom-IoPSmartWorld.2016.0080
3. Saeed, A., Ahmadinia, A., Javed, A., Larijani, H.: Intelligent intrusion detection in low-power IoTs. ACM Trans. Internet Technol. **16**(4), 1–25 (2016). https://doi.org/10.1145/2990499
4. Sharma, P.K., Moon, S.Y., Moon, D., Park, J.H.: DFA-AD: a distributed framework architecture for the detection of advanced persistent threats. Cluster Comput. **20**(1), 597–609 (2017). https://doi.org/10.1007/s10586-016-0716-0
5. Chen, J., Chen, C.: Design of complex event-processing IDS in internet of things. In: Proceedings - 2014 6th International Conference on Measuring Technology and Mechatronics Automation, ICMTMA 2014, pp. 226–229 (2014). https://doi.org/10.1109/ICMTMA.2014.57
6. Wang, K., Du, M., Yang, D., Zhu, C., Shen, J., Zhang, Y.: Game-theory-based active defense for intrusion detection in cyber-physical embedded systems. ACM Trans. Embed. Comput. Syst. **16**(1), 1–21 (2016). https://doi.org/10.1145/2886100
7. Manshaei, M.H., Zhu, Q., Alpcan, T., Bacşar, T., Hubaux, J.-P.: Game theory meets network security and privacy. ACM Comput. **45**, 25 (2013). https://doi.org/10.1145/2480741.2480742
8. Rafsanjani, M.K., Aliahmadipour, L., Javidi, M.M.: A hybrid intrusion detection by game theory approaches in MANET. Indian J. Sci. Technol. **5**(2), 2123–2131 (2012)
9. Kantzavelou, I., Tzikopoulos, P.F., Katsikas, S.K.: Detecting intrusive activities from insiders in a wireless sensor network using game theory. In: ACM International Conference Proceeding Series (2013)

DoTRo: A New Dominating Tree Routing Algorithm for Efficient and Fault-Tolerant Leader Election in WSNs and IoT Networks

Ahcène Bounceur[1,2,5(✉)], Madani Bezoui[1,3], Loic Lagadec[1,4],
Reinhardt Euler[1,2], Laouid Abdelkader[5,6], and Mohammad Hammoudeh[7]

[1] Lab-STICC CNRS UMR 6285, Brest, France
Ahcene.Bounceur@univ-brest.fr
[2] Université de Bretagne Occidentale, Brest, France
[3] Department of Mathematics, Université de Boumerdes, Boumerdes, Algeria
[4] ENSTA Bretagne, Brest, France
[5] LIMED Laboratory, Bejaia, Algeria
[6] University of El-oued, El Oued, Algeria
[7] Manchester Metropolitan University, Manchester, UK

Abstract. A leader node in Ad hoc networks and especially in WSNs and IoT networks is needed in many cases, for example to generate keys for encryption/decryption, to find a node with minimum energy or situated in an extreme part of the network. In our work, we need as a leader the node situated on the extreme left of the network to start the process of finding its boundary nodes. These nodes will be used to monitor any sensitive, dangerous or non-accessible site. For this kind of applications, algorithms must be robust and fault-tolerant since it is difficult and even impossible to intervene if a node fails. Such a situation can be catastrophic in case that this node is the leader. In this paper, we present a new algorithm called DoTRo, which is based on a tree routing protocol. It starts from local leaders which will start the process of flooding to determine a spanning tree. During this process their value will be routed. If two spanning trees meet each other then the tree routing the best value will continue its process while the other tree will stop it. The remaining tree is the dominating one and its root will be the leader. This algorithm turns out to be low energy consuming with reduction rates that can exceed 85%. It is efficient and fault-tolerant since it works in the case where any node can fail and in the case where the network is disconnected.

Keywords: Wireless Sensor Network · IoT · Leader election
Distributed algorithms · Dominating Tree Routing

This project is supported by the French National Research Agency ANR PERSEP-TEUR - REF: ANR-14-CE24-0017.

© Springer Nature Switzerland AG 2019
É. Renault et al. (Eds.): MSPN 2018, LNCS 11005, pp. 42–53, 2019.
https://doi.org/10.1007/978-3-030-03101-5_5

1 Introduction and Related Work

This paper comes within the context of secured sites where one needs to find the boundary nodes of wireless sensor and IoT networks. Many algorithms exist in the literature. A recent algorithm, called D-LPCN [1], can be used for this purpose. This algorithm starts from the node which is on the extreme left of the network, that we suppose to be embedded in the plane with nodes being identified by their coordinates. To find this particular node, one can use any Leader Election algorithm, which is a process of electing one particular node in a network. Usually, the leader process is required to play a particular role for coordination or control purposes. There is no solution for this problem in the case of anonymous systems [2], i.e., systems with nodes having no identifiers. In other words, there is no way to differentiate a process p_i from another process p_j. Due to this problem, we assume in this paper that each process p_i has a unique identifier id_i. Moreover, it is assumed that the identifiers can be compared with each other.

In the literature, one can define two main families of leader election methods. The leader election for ring topologies and the leader election for arbitrary topologies (e.g., ad hoc networks).

Regarding the first case of ring topologies, authors of [3] have presented an algorithm for bidirectional rings, where each process has a left and a right neighbor, and where it can send and receive messages from any neighbor. Authors of [4] have presented an algorithm for unidirectional rings, in which the channels are receiving messages in FIFO mode. As in [3], initially, all processes compete to be elected as a leader, and execute consecutive rounds to that end. During each round, at most half of the processes that are competitors remain competitors in the next round.

Regarding the second case of arbitrary topologies, in [5,6], two leader election protocols have been presented for static networks. In these algorithms, several minimum-weight spanning trees are established, which will be reduced to only one spanning tree. Then the root will be the leader. In [7], two leader election algorithms have been proposed for mobile ad hoc networks. The algorithms assume that each connected component of the graph has exactly one leader. They are based on a routing algorithm TORA presented in [8]. Another algorithm is presented in [9,10] for asynchronous mobile ad hoc networks AEFA (Asynchronous Extrema Finding Algorithm), which is a weakly self-stabilizing algorithm in which each node possesses some weight representing the criteria to elect the best-node. It constructs and maintains a spanning tree using the diffusion computation to elect a leader. The paper [11] introduces a leader election algorithm for mobile ad hoc networks, which is based on an extrema-finding concept that elects a unique node and, on the basis of specific characteristics, outperforms all the other nodes in the network. Another algorithm is proposed in [12] for the election of a leader in an asynchronous network with dynamically changing communication topology. In the last decade, several clustering and leader election algorithms has been developed and tested to address the challenges of communication efficiency and fault tolerance in Wireless Sensor Networks (WSN) [13,14].

In this paper, we propose a new algorithm for arbitrary networks. This algorithm starts with a given set of local minima, each of which will start as a root the process of flooding in order to determine a spanning tree on which to route its value. If two spanning trees meet, the one routing the better value will continue the flooding process and the other one will stop it. After a given time, only one spanning tree will remain and its root will be the leader.

The remainder of the paper is organized as follows: Sect. 2 presents the classical Minimum Finding algorithm. Section 3 introduces the Local Minima Finding algorithm. Section 4 is dedicated to the proposed DoTRo algorithm. The used simulator is briefly presented in Sect. 5 and the simulation results are presented in Sect. 6. Finally, Sect. 7 concludes the paper.

2   The Minimum Finding Algorithm

In this section, we will present a distributed algorithm that allows to determine a leader node representing the node with minimum or maximum value v. This value can represent the local energy of the battery, the residual energy, the x-coordinate in a network, etc. Let us first define in Table 1 the functions used in the algorithms that will be presented in this paper.

Table 1. Functions of the proposed algorithms.

Function	Definition
getId()	Returns the node identifier
delay(t)	Waits t milliseconds before going to the next instruction
stop()	Stops the execution of the program
send(a,b)	Sends the message a to the sensor node having the identifier b or in a broadcast (if $b = *$)
read()	Waiting for receipt of messages. This function is blocking, which means that if there is no received message any more, it remains blocked in this instruction
read(t)	Waiting for receipt of messages. If there is no received message after t milliseconds then the execution will continue and go to the next instruction

The Minimum Finding Algorithm presented in [15,16] relies on the tree-based broadcast algorithm. Indeed, it can also be used to find the maximum value. The principle of this algorithm can be described as follows. First, each node of the network assigns its local value to the variable x_{min} assumed to represent the minimum value of the network (the leader). Then it will broadcast this value and wait for other x_{min} values coming from its neighbors. If a received value x_{min} is less than its local x_{min} value then this one will be updated and broadcasted again. This process is repeated by each node as long as a received value is less than its local x_{min} value. After a certain time t_{max}, there will be only one sensor node that has not received a value that is smaller than its local x_{min} value. This node is the leader. The pseudo-code of this process is given by Algorithm 1, where t_0 is the time of the first execution of the algorithm, which can correspond to the first powering-on of a sensor node, t_c the current local time of a sensor node, and t_{max} the maximally tolerated running time of the algorithm from the first execution to the current time of a sensor node.

Algorithm 1. *MinFind*: The pseudo-code of the classical Leader Election Algorithm

---

Input: wt, x
Output: *leader*
1: *leader* = true
2: $x_{min} = x$
3: send(x_{min}, *)
4: **while** (true) **do**
5:     x_r = read(wt)
6:     **if** (x_r == null) **then**
7:         stop()
8:     **end if**
9:     **if** ($x_r < x_{min}$) **then**
10:         *leader* = false
11:         $x_{min} = x_r$
12:         send(x_{min}, *);
13:     **end if**
14: **end while**

---

3   The Local Minima Finding Algorithm

A local minimum node, also called *Local Leader*, is the node which has no neighbor with a value smaller than its own value. But, this value is not necessarily a global minimum.

The Local Minima Finding (LMF) Algorithm uses the same principle as the previously presented *MinFind* algorithm to determine if a node is a local minimum or not, with the exception that each node will send its coordinates only once, and after reception of messages from all its neighbors, it decides if it is a local minimum or not in case it has received a smaller value than its own. The algorithm of finding local minima is given as follows:

Algorithm 2. *LMF*: The pseudo-code of the Local Minima Finding Algorithm

Input: wt, v
Output: *local_min*
1: *local_min* = true;
2: $x_{min} = v$;
3: send(x_{min}, *);
4: **while** $(((x = \text{read}(wt)) \neq \text{null})$ and *local_min*) **do**
5:    **if** $(x < x_{min})$ **then**
6:       *local_min* = false;
7:    **end if**
8: **end while**

4   The Proposed DoTRo Algorithm

4.1   The DoTRo Algorithm

The DoTRo algorithm is is based on a tree routing protocol. It starts from local leaders which will run, as a root, the process of flooding [19] to determine a spanning tree. During this process the value of the leader (root) will be routed. If two spanning trees meet each other then the tree routing the best value will continue its process while the other one will stop it. Based on the example of Fig. 1, we present in the following the main steps of the DoTRo algorithm, where we assume that the leader is the node having the maximum value:

1. *Step 1:* For the network of Fig. 1(a) we run the LMF algorithm (cf. Algorithm 2) to determine the local minima. The obtained result is shown by Fig. 1(b) where we have two local minima: 1 and 4 because they are the only nodes that don't have any neighbor with a value smaller than their own value.
2. *Step 2:* Each local minimum will start the flooding process to route the leader value (local minimum) over the tree (cf. Fig. 1(c)).
3. *Step 3:* If two trees meet, as is the case of the center node in Fig. 1(c), the red tree chooses the center node with value 1 and the blue tree will choose the same center node with value 4. Since 1 is less than 4, the center branch of the blue tree will stop the flooding process, whereas the other branch will continue, and the center branch of the red tree will continue the flooding process. The obtained result is shown by Fig. 1(d). Figures 1(e) and (g) show another meeting and Figs. 1(f) and (h) show the result of the DoTRo algorithm after this meeting.
4. *Step 4:* Each local minimum will wait for a given time, assumed to be sufficient to finish the process of flooding. If after this time there is no received message anymore, the corresponding local minimum will become the leader.

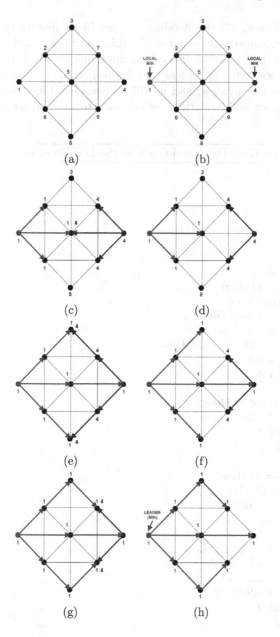

Fig. 1. DoTRo algorithm illustration. (Color figure online)

4.2 The DoTRo Pseudo-code

The pseudo-code of the DoTRo algorithm is given by Algorithm 3. It is composed of three main parts that are: (1) the initialization part (lines 1 to 4) where each node is considered as a leader (line 4), (2) the LMF algorithm (line 5 and from line 8 to line 18) and (3) the flooding process (from line 21 to line 30). The second part is explained above and in the third part, each node will wait for a message representing the value of the local minimum routed during the flooding process. If the received value is less than its own value then it will route it to continue the flooding process, and it will be considered as a non-leader node. Otherwise, the node will do nothing, which will stop the process of flooding.

Algorithm 3. *DoTRo*: The pseudo-code of the DoTRo algorithm

Input: x, wt_1, wt_2
Output: *leader*
  1: $id = \text{getId}()$
  2: $x_{min} = x$
  3: $step = 1$
  4: $leader = \text{true}$
  5: $\text{send}(x, *)$
  6: **while** (true) **do**
  7:     **if** ($step == 1$) **then**
  8:         $rx = \text{read}(wt_1)$
  9:         **if** ($rx ==$ null) **then**
 10:             $step = 2$
 11:             **if** ($leader ==$ true) **then**
 12:                 $\text{send}(x, *)$
 13:             **end if**
 14:         **else**
 15:             **if** ($rx < x$) **then**
 16:                 $leader = \text{false}$
 17:             **end if**
 18:         **end if**
 19:     **end if**
 20:     **if** ($step == 2$) **then**
 21:         $rx = \text{read}(wt_2)$
 22:         **if** ($rx ==$ null) **then**
 23:             $\text{stop}()$
 24:         **else**
 25:             **if** ($rx < x_{min}$) **then**
 26:                 $leader = \text{false}$
 27:                 $x_{min} = rx$
 28:                 $\text{send}(rx, *)$
 29:             **end if**
 30:         **end if**
 31:     **end if**
 32: **end while**

---

5   CupCarbon Simulator and SenScript

The simulation of networks is an essential tool for testing protocols and their prior-performance deployment. Indeed, such an establishment may be costly and challenging, especially when a large number of nodes are to be distributed at a large scale. This is why the simulation of networks is essential. CupCarbon is a Smart City and Internet of Things Wireless Sensor Network (SCI-WSN) simulator. Its objective is to design, visualize, debug and validate distributed algorithms for monitoring, tracking, collecting environmental data, etc., and to create environmental scenarios such as fires, gas, mobiles, and generally within educational and scientific projects. It can help to visually explain the basic concepts of sensor networks and how they work; it may also support scientists to test their wireless topologies, protocols, etc. (cf. Fig. 2).

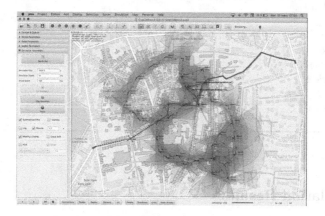

Fig. 2. CupCarbon user interface.

Networks can be designed and prototyped by an ergonomic and easy to use interface using the OpenStreetMap (OSM) framework to deploy sensors directly on the map. It includes a script called SenScript, which allows to program and configure each sensor node individually. The energy consumption can be calculated and displayed as a function of the simulated time. This allows to clarify the structure, feasibility and realistic implementation of a network before its real deployment. CupCarbon offers the possibility to simulate algorithms and scenarios in several steps. For example, there could be a step for determining the nodes of interest, followed by a step related to the nature of the communication between these nodes to perform a given task such as the detection of an event, and finally, a step describing the nature of the routing to the base station in case that an event is detected [17, 18]. SenScript is the script used to program sensor nodes of the CupCarbon simulator. It is a script where variables are not declared, but can be initialized. For string variables, it is not necessary to use the quotes. A variable is used by its name (e.g., x), and its value is determined by

$ (e.g., x). Algorithm 4 shows an example of a SenScript code. The command **atget id cid** of line 1 allows to assign to variable *cid* the identifier of the current node. The command **loop** allows to start the loop section, where all the code situated after will be executed infinitely. The command textbfwait will allow to wait for a received message. This command is blocking and the next code will not be executed until a message is received. The command **read** of line 4 will assign the received message in the buffer to x. In the line 5, we test if the received message (an identifier) is less than the value of the current identifier cid. If is the case, the line 6 will be executed, and the node will be marked (**mark 1**), otherwise (line 7), the line 8 will be execute, where the current sensor will be unmarked (**mark 0**).

Algorithm 4. *SenScript example*

```
1: atget id cid
2: loop
3:    wait
4:    read x
5:    if($x < $cid)
6:        mark 1
7:    else
8:        mark 0
9:    end
```

---

6   Simulation Results

To compare our algorithm with the classical *MinFind* algorithm, we have generated 9 networks in a rectangular area of $(z \times z)\,\mathrm{m}^2$, where z is varied from 200 to 1000 with n randomly generated nodes. The value of n is fixed so that the density of the nodes in each network remains the same. We have fixed it to 10 *nodes*/hm^2 (*hm*: hectometer), i.e., 10 nodes in an area of $100\,\mathrm{m} \times 100\,\mathrm{m}$. Note, that we consider symmetric communications between nodes.

We have considered two cases. In the first case (case 1), each node generates a value representing its x-coordinate. In the second case (case 2), the considered value represents a random value. For each network, we have calculated the number of transmitted and received messages (exchanged messages) in order to compare their energy consumption which is directly related to this metric. We have obtained the graph of Fig. 3. In both cases, we have executed the algorithm MinFind [15]. The obtained results are shown by the black curves of Fig. 3 labeled as MinFind1 (case 1) and MinFind2 (case 2) and the red curve for DoTRo1 (case 1) and the blue curve for DoTRo2 (case 2). As we can see, the DoTRo algorithm is less energy consuming than the MinFind algorithm. This is confirmed by Fig. 4 which shows the reduction rate between the MinFind algorithms for both cases defined above. In the case where the leader represents the smallest x-coordinate value, we can see that the reduction rate reaches 83% for a network with 1000 nodes and it is growing for larger networks. This kind of leader is needed in the case of the D-LPCN algorithm [1] which starts from the node situated on the extreme left. In the case of other kinds of leaders (random, id, etc.) the proposed algorithm can reach a reduction rate of 30%. Altogether, we can conclude that the proposed algorithm is less energy consuming than the classical algorithm MinFind.

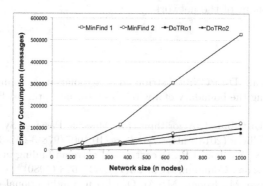

Fig. 3. Simulation results. (Color figure online)

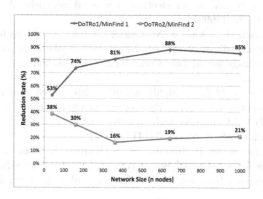

Fig. 4. Reduction rate.

7   Conclusion

We have presented a new algorithm called DoTRo (Dominating Tree Routing) which starts from the local minima found using the LMF algorithm. Then each local minimum starts as a root the process of flooding in order to determine the spanning tree while routing its value over it. If two spanning trees meet, the one routing the better value will continue the flooding process and the other one will stop it. After a given time, only one spanning tree will remain and its root will be the leader. The obtained results show that the proposed algorithm is less energy consuming with rates that can exceed 85% when searching the minimum x-coordinate and 30% when searching the minimum random value. Another advantage of the proposed algorithm is that it is fault tolerant since it starts even when there are failing nodes and it also finds the leader of each connected component of the network.

References

1. Saoudi, M., et al.: D-LPCN: a distributed least polar-angle connected node algorithm for finding the boundary of a wireless sensor network. Ad Hoc Netw. **56**(1), 56–71 (2017)
2. Raynal, M.: Distributed Algorithms for Message-Passing Systems, vol. 500. Springer, Heidelberg (2013). https://doi.org/10.1007/978-3-642-38123-2
3. Hirschberg, D.S., Sinclair, J.B.: Decentralized extrema finding in circular configuration of processors. Commun. ACM **23**(11), 627–628 (1980)
4. Dolev, D., Klawe, M., Rodeh, M.: An O(n log n) unidirectional distributed algorithm for extrema finding in a circle. J. Algorithms **3**(3), 245–260 (1982)
5. Gallager, R.G., Humblet, P.A., Spira, P.M.: A distributed algorithm for minimum-weight spanning trees. ACM Trans. Program. Lang. Syst. (TOPLAS) **5**(1), 66–77 (1983)
6. Peleg, D.: Time-optimal leader election in general networks. J. Parallel Distrib. Comput. **8**(1), 96–99 (1990)
7. Malpani, N., Welch, J.L., Vaidya, N.: Leader election algorithms for mobile ad hoc networks. In: Proceedings of the 4th International Workshop on Discrete Algorithms and Methods for Mobile Computing and Communications, pp. 96–103. ACM (2000)
8. Park, V.D., Corson, M.S.: A highly adaptive distributed routing algorithm for mobile wireless networks. In: The Proceedings of the Sixteenth Annual Joint Conference of the IEEE Computer and Communications Societies. Driving the Information Revolution, vol. 3, pp. 1405–1413 (1997)
9. Vasudevan, S., DeCleene, B., Immerman, N., Kurose, J., Towsley, D.: Leader election algorithms for wireless ad hoc networks. In: The Proceedings of the IEEE DARPA Information Survivability Conference and Exposition 2003, vol. 1, pp. 261–272 (2003)
10. Vasudevan, S., Kurose, J., Towsley, D.: Design and analysis of a leader election algorithm for mobile ad hoc networks. In: The Proceedings of the 12th IEEE International Conference on Network Protocols. ICNP 2004, pp. 350–360 (2004)
11. Boukerche, A., Abrougui, K.: An efficient leader election protocol for mobile networks. In: Proceedings of the ACM International Conference on Wireless Communications and Mobile Computing, pp. 1129–1134 (2006)
12. Ingram, R., Shields, P., Walter, J.E., Welch, J.L.: An asynchronous leader election algorithm for dynamic networks. In: IEEE International Symposium on Parallel and Distributed Processing, IPDPS 2009, pp. 1–12 (2009)

13. Hammoudeh, M.: Modelling clustering of sensor networks with synchronised hyper-edge replacement. In: Ehrig, H., Heckel, R., Rozenberg, G., Taentzer, G. (eds.) ICGT 2008. LNCS, vol. 5214, pp. 490–492. Springer, Heidelberg (2008). https://doi.org/10.1007/978-3-540-87405-8_42

14. Hammoudeh, M., Alsbou'i, T.A.A.: Building programming abstractions for wireless sensor networks using watershed segmentation. In: Balandin, S., Koucheryavy, Y., Hu, H. (eds.) NEW2AN/ruSMART -2011. LNCS, vol. 6869, pp. 587–597. Springer, Heidelberg (2011). https://doi.org/10.1007/978-3-642-22875-9_53

15. Santoro, N.: Design and Analysis of Distributed Algorithms, vol. 56. Wiley, Hoboken (2007)

16. Lynch, N.A.: Distributed Algorithms. Morgan Kaufmann, Burlington (1996)

17. CupCarbon simulator. http://www.cupcarbon.com

18. Mehdi, K., Lounis, M., Bounceur, A., Kechadi, T.: CupCarbon: a multi-agent and discrete event wireless sensor network design and simulation tool. In: IEEE 7th International Conference on Simulation Tools and Techniques (SIMUTools 2014), Lisbon, Portugal (2014)

19. Tanenbaum, A.S., Wetherall, D.J.: Computer Networks, 5th edn, pp. 368–370. Pearson Education, London (2010)

An Enhancement Approach for Securing Neighbor Discovery in IPv6 Networks

Ali El Ksimi[✉] and Cherkaoui Leghris

L@M, RTM Team, Faculty of Sciences and Technologies,
University Hassan 2 of Casablanca, Mohammedia, Morocco
ali.elksimi@yahoo.fr, cleghris@yahoo.fr

Abstract. IPv6 is willing to be the most used protocol in the future Internet even its deployment takes more time due to some constraints. Indeed, IPv6 allows addressing all objects on the Internet with public addresses. One of the new associated IPv6 protocols is Neighbor Discovery Protocol (NDP). Duplicate address detection (DAD) is one of the functions of NDP to make sure a generated IPv6 address is unique. However, since the NDP is not secure by default, the DAD is vulnerable to attacks. The attacker can prevent a new node from using a new address by failing the DAD procedure. The purpose of our technique is to secure the DAD process in an IPv6 network using a new field in NS message called Hash_Target_64. Our algorithm called DAD-Hide-Target is going to secure the DAD process by using a hash function SHA-256 and hiding the target address. Overall, the experimental results show a significant effect in term of Address Configuration Success Probability.

Keywords: IPv6 · DAD · Security · SHA-256 · ACSP

1 Introduction

The routing protocol mainly used today for Internet communications is the Internet Protocol (IP). The current IPv4 protocol suffers from many weaknesses and the main problem is the address space. Indeed, the IPv4 addresses are 32 bits long, which represents about 4,3 milliard possible addresses. Following the explosion of network growth Internet and wastage of addresses due to the class structure, the number of IPv4 addresses has become insufficient. Another problem is the saturation of the routing tables in the main routers of the Internet. Even if since 1993, emergency measures have been taken, this only allows delaying the deadline. Also, the Internet Engineering Task Force (IETF) launched work in 1994 to specify the new Internet protocol version IPv6 [1] who will be in replacing IPv4. IPv6 is nowadays ready to support the new Internet trends with more address space and other more important functionalities like neighbor discovery capacity of an IPv6 host.

The Neighbor Discovery (NDP) [2] is the most important part in IPv6; it allows a node to easily integrate into the local network environment, that is, the link on which IPv6 packets are physically transmitted. This protocol makes possible for a host to

É. Renault et al. (Eds.): MSPN 2018, LNCS 11005, pp. 54–69, 2019.
https://doi.org/10.1007/978-3-030-03101-5_6

interact with the equipment connected to the same support (stations and routers). It is important to note that for a given piece of the node, the discovery of the neighbors does not consist in establishing an exhaustive list of the other entire node connected to the link. Indeed, it is only to manage those with whom it dialogues. This protocol performs the following functions: Address Resolution, Neighbor Unreachability Detection, Autoconfiguration, and Redirect Indication using five messages including Router Solicitation, Router Advertisement, Neighbor Solicitation, Neighbor Announcement, and Indication redirection. The IPv6 stateless address Autoconfiguration (SLAAC) [3] is primarily based on the NDP process. This mechanism uses Duplicate address detection (DAD) [4] to verify the uniqueness of the addresses on the same link. However, it is vulnerable to attack, and some solutions have been standardized to minimize this vulnerability, particularly Secure Neighbor Discovery (SEND) [5]. But, they are subject to certain limitations.

To study this vulnerability, we chose omnet++ simulator to simulate an IPv6 networks. This paper defines the SLAAC phases and explains the problems associated with them.

In order to optimize IPv6 security in IPv6 network, we develop a new algorithm DAD-Hide-Target based on SHA-256 [6].

This paper is organized as follows. Section 2 presents a related work to our field. Section 3 describes some IPv6 functionalities, in particular, the DAD process. Section 4 presents the parameters and methodology following in this work. In Sect. 4.3, we will detail our proposed algorithm model. Section 5 includes the implementation and evaluation. Section 6 concludes this paper and addresses some prospects.

2 Related Work

Security attacks in the operation of IPv6, especially DAD process in the NDP, have become one of the interesting research fields. Several proposals have been made by researchers to address security issues in IPv6 DAD.

In [7], the authors have presented a new algorithm for address generation, this mechanism has a minimal computation cost as compared to CGA. Nevertheless, this mechanism uses SHA-1 hash encryption which is vulnerable to collisions attacks.

In [8], the authors have proposed a scheme to secure IPv6 address, this method includes the modifications to the standard RFC 3972 by reducing the granularity factor of the sec from 16 to 8, and replacing RSA with ECC and ECSDSA, using SHA-256 [6] hash function. This method improves the address configuration performance, but it does not eliminate the address conflict.

In [9], the authors have utilized a novel approach for securing IPv6 link-local communication. They have used an alternative approach for the CGA and SEND protocols which still represent a limitation to the security level.

Another approach such as; a secure IPv6 address configuration protocol for vehicular networks [10] was proposed to ensure security in IPv6 without DAD process. However, this method is used only when the distance between a vehicle and its serving AP is one-hop.

In [11], the authors have proposed a new method to secure Neighbor Discovery Protocol in IPv6 which is based on SDN controller to verify the source of NDP packets. However, this method is not efficient because it does not handle the detection of NDP attacks.

Another method was used in [12] to secure the DAD; it is called trust-ND. It is used to detect fake NA messages. However, the experiments show some limits of this method.

In [13], the authors have presented a technique for detecting neighbor solicitation spoofing and advertisement spoofing attacks in IPv6 NDP. However, this method can only detect NS spoofing, NA spoofing, DoS attacks. The disadvantage of this method is that it does not detect other attacks like Duplicate Address Detection attacks.

In [14], the authors have proposed a new method to secure NDP attacks; this method is based on the digital signature. It detects the messages NS and NA spoofing and DOS attacks, router redirection and Duplicate Address Detection, but this mechanism is seen as not complete.

In [15], the authors describe and review some of the fundamental attacks on NDP, prevention mechanisms, and current detection mechanisms for NDP-based attacks.

In this paper, we propose to study and evaluate the security in the NDP within the network based on IPv6 protocol. Indeed, we suggest a new algorithm which could secure the attacks in the DAD process. The experimental results showed that DAD process could be secured by introducing a new field in the NS and NA messages and hide the target address; the hash of the new node's target address. Overall, this method showed a significant effect in term of address configuration success probability.

3   Duplicate Address Detection (DAD)

The Neighbor Discovery Protocol (NDP) mechanism provides IPv6 with some number of essential features for the proper functioning of the IPv6 protocol. The best known is the address resolution feature that matches what is an ARP in IPv4. This protocol also offers other features. The one that will interest in our paper, Duplicate Address Detection (DAD), allows detection when two nodes want to use the same address and avoids the future collision by refusing the assignment of the address. This is equivalent to "gratuitous ARP" in IPv4. This feature is even more important, that in IPv6, new nodes can use the "stateless auto configuration" and assign themselves an address (self-generated).

3.1   DAD Process

The Neighbor Discovery Protocol mechanism uses ICMPv6 type messages [2]. Under the DAD mechanism, only we are interested in two types of messages, the message Neighbor Solicitation (NS) and the message Neighbor Advertisement (NA). When resolving an address, the message Neighbor Solicitation is used to request the physical address of a node (e.g. MAC address) with it want to communicate by contacting it via his IPv6 address. This message contains a target field that is populated with the node's (IPv6) address that we want to contact. If this target exists, it responds with a message intended for the node that issued the request and contains in one of its fields an option carrying the physical address of this node for the network interface concerned. This association, between the logical and physical addresses, will then be kept in the neighbor cache table.

The DAD mechanism is not infallible, especially if it occurs during the time when several nodes of the same network are temporarily "separated" (loss of connecting or dropping a link between the nodes) and that one or more of the nodes perform a DAD procedure. They can assign the same address without the procedure detects the collision.

For the node, the procedure starts by listening to the multicast group "all-nodes multicast" and the multicast group of the solicited-node ("solicited-node multicast"). The first allows it to receive address resolution requests ("Address Resolution") for this address and the second will allow it to receive the messages sent by other nodes also making a DAD on this address. In order to listen to these, the node must issue a Multicast Listener Discovery (MLD) [16] request; when a node triggers the DAD procedure, it sends a Neighbor Solicitation message, an ICMPv6 type message.

- Algorithm DAD description
  - The first step is to generate an IPv6 address with either autoconfiguration or other methods;
  - In the second step, the node will subscribe to multicast groups: all-nodes multicast and solicited-node multicast;
  - There are three cases:
    - A NA message is received: the tentative address is used as a valid address by another node. The tentative address is not unique and cannot be retained;
    - A NS message from a neighbor is received as part of a DAD procedure; the tentative address is also a tentative address for another node. The tentative address cannot be used by any of the nodes;
    - Nothing is received after one second (default value): the tentative address is unique, it passes from the state of provisional to that of valid and it is assigned to the interface.

Figure 1 shows the DAD algorithm:

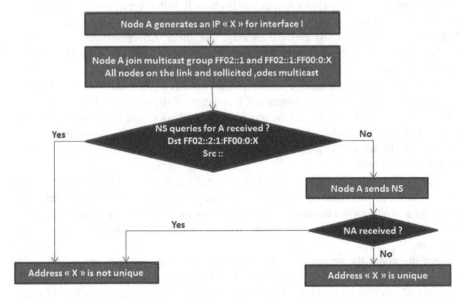

Fig. 1. The flowchart of the DAD process

3.2 The Attack on DAD Process

An attack on the DAD mechanism was identified in [10], the attack is composed as follows: the attacker will deceive the DAD mechanism and make it succeed in one of the two cases where it fails so that the victim cannot claim an address. Since there is a finite number of tries to get an address, the DAD always ends up failing, it's a DoS attack [11]. For the attack to be feasible the attacker must be able to listen on the network any query necessary to perform the DAD procedure (e.g. the NS messages with the unspecified address as the source address are characteristics of the DAD procedure); this implies being able to join the multicast group "Solicited-Node". He then has two choices; he can send an NS message with, as source address, the unspecified address and, as the target address, the address of the victim or an NA message with, as the target address, the "tentative" address of the victim. He can thus prevent the arrival of new nodes having no address yet. The effectiveness of the attack depends strongly on the type of links because it is necessary that the attacker can receive the first NS sent by the victim and that he can answer them. Indeed the attacker must be able to join the multicast group "Solicited-Node", which is not easy in the case of a level 2 point-to-point technology, for example, ADSL.

3.3   Vulnerabilities of Multicast Communications

In IPv6 multicast DAD process, groups are identified by a group address and any node in the network can join or leave the group when it wishes. This simplicity, which is the power of multipoint routing, presents however vulnerabilities:

- IPv6 multicast does not support the notion of the closed group. Indeed, multicast addresses are public: joining a group or leaving a group is an operation that does not require special permissions. This allows any node to join a group and receive messages for it;
- Access to the group is not controlled: an intruder can send data to the group without being part of it, disrupt the multipoint session, and possibly cause congestion in the network;
- The data intended for the group can cross several unsecured channels before reaching all members of the group. This increases listening opportunities to potential intruders;
- Group communications offer more opportunities for intercepting communications, proportional to the number of participants;
- A vulnerable point in the group implicates the safety of all members of the group;
- The large-scale publication of the group's identity and address helps intruders focus their attacks;
- Attackers can impersonate the legitimate members of the group.

To counteract these attacks, group communication requires security services such as authentication, data privacy, confidentiality of the traffic flow…

3.4   Security Needs in Multicast

Multicast requires the set of security mechanisms in a unicast communication in addition to some needs inherent to its nature which is the group communication. These needs can be divided into three main parts:

A. Authentication

All participants in a multicast session must self-authenticate before joining the group. Authentication [17] may be restricted to group members: sources and receivers, or possibly extended to the routing infrastructure: designated routers.

Among other authentication mechanisms, the certification scheme with a third authority can be used.

B. Integrity

This ability ensures that the multicast stream reaches the recipients without falsification. This option is usually provided by cryptographic, hash and digital signature mechanisms [18].

C. Confidentiality

This confidentiality [19] must be provided at several levels:

- Past privacy (backward confidentiality): We can imagine that a hacker can store the multicast stream for a time interval $[t_0, t]$, join the group at time t to acquire the keys needed to decrypt this stream "past". Past privacy alters such a hacking scheme by, for example modifying decryption keys for the stream, once a new member joins the group;
- Forward Confidentiality: A system with this ability prevents any member excluded from the multicast group at time t from having the keys necessary for decrypting the multicast stream at times $t + \mu$. This usually results in a modification of these keys and then their redistribution to the remaining members;
- Group Privacy: Only authenticated members must have the keys to decrypt multicast messages.

4 Proposed Technique

In this section, we present the description of our algorithm which makes it possible to secure the target address used in NS message in the DAD process.

4.1 Hash Function

A hash function [20] is a method for characterizing information, a data. By having a sequence of reproducible treatments at an input, it generates a fingerprint to identify the initial data.

A hash function, therefore, takes as input a message of any size, applies a series of transformations and reduces this data. We get at the output a string of hexadecimal characters, the condensed, which summarizes somehow the file.

We define a hash function as an application:

$$h:\{0,1\}^* \rightarrow \{0,1\}^n, n \in N.$$

A hash function is considered safe if the following three properties are satisfied:

1. Resistance to a pre-image attack (one-way). For any given output y, finding an x, which makes $h(x) = y$, is computationally infeasible;
2. Resistance to a second pre-image attack. For any given input x, finding an input x' that is unequal to x, which makes $h(x) = h(x')$, is computationally infeasible;
3. Resistance to a collision attack: Finding two unequal inputs x and x0, such that $h(x) = h(x')$, is computationally infeasible.

The SHA - secure hash algorithm – [21] is a hash algorithm used by certificate authorities to sign certificates and CRL (certificate revocation list). Introduced in 1993 by the NSA with the SHA0, it is used to generate unique condensates (thus for "chopping") of files.

4.2   Hash-TargetAdd-DAD

Hash-TargetAdd-DAD (Hash target address) is a new definition of the ICMPv6 packet (for NS and NA).

Since the standard DAD is not secure, in order to fulfill such security requirement, a "Hash Secure Target" can be applied on NS and NA messages to ensure that only nodes which possess this hash are able to communicate in the IPv6 local network.

In our algorithm, when the node sends an NS message, it assigns the unspecified address to the target address (::), so the target address is hidden. Only nodes that have a specific address can know the target address.

Figure 2 shows the formatted message of Hash-TargetAdd-DAD.

Ethernet header	Dest MAC Src MAC Type
IPv6 header	Src IP address Dest IP address Next header
ICMPv6 header	Type Target address Options ICMPv6 Hash_target_64

Fig. 2. The message format of Hash-TargetAdd-DAD.

The message format of Hash-TargetAdd-DAD is illustrated in Fig. 3. Hash-TargetAdd-DAD uses two new message types, namely, $NS_{hash\text{-}targetAdd\text{-}DAD}$ and $NA_{hash\text{-}targetAdd\text{-}DAD}$, and its "Type" fields are 138 and 139, respectively. Compared with the NDP packet, Hash-TargetAdd-DAD adds a new field "Hash_target_64", which stores the last 64 bits of the SHA-512 result.

The hash_target_64 calculation method is illustrated in Fig. 3.

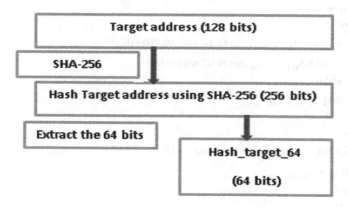

Fig. 3. The message format of Hash-Target-DAD

Figure 4 shows the $NS_{DAD\text{-}Hide\text{-}Target}$ message.

Target address	:: (hidden address)
Hash_Target_64	H64 (IPv6x)
options	Mac address

Fig. 4. The $NS_{DAD\text{-}Hide\text{-}Target}$

Figure 5 shows the $NA_{DAD\text{-}Hide\text{-}Target}$ message.

Target address	IPv6y
Hash_Target_64	H64 (IPv6y)
options	Mac address

Fig. 5. The $NA_{DAD\text{-}Hide\text{-}Target}$

4.3   Algorithm DAD-Hide-Target

We present now the two algorithms; the first one represents the sending phase of NS and the receipt of NA, and the second one represents the receipt of NA and its verification.

Algorithm 1: send $NS_{DAD\_Hide\_Target}$ and receive $NA_{DAD\_Hide\_target}$

1: **Input:** address $IPv6_X$

2: **Output:** true: DAD_Hide_Target success; false: DAD_Hide_Target fail

3: broadcast $NS_{DAD\text{-}Hide\text{-}Target}$

4: **while** DAD_Hide_Target timeout ≠ true **do**

5:   receive $NA_{DAD\_Hide\_target}$

6:   **if** $NA_{DAD\_Hide\_target}.Hash\_64 == H64\ (IPv6_X)$ **then**

7:     **if** $NA_{DAD\_Hide\_target}.Target\ address == IPv6_X$ **then**

8:       **return** false

9:     **else**

10:       **if** $H64\ (NA_{DAD\_Hide\_target}\ Target\ address) \neq H64\ (IP_X)$**then**

11:         add $NA_{DAD\text{-}Hide\text{-}Target}.Src\ MAC$ into blacklist

12:       **end if**

13:       drop $NA_{DAD\_Hide\_target}$

14:     **end if**

15:   **else**

16:     add $NA_{DAD\_Hide\_target}.Src\ MAC$ into blacklist

17:     drop $NA_{DAD\text{-}Hide\text{-}Target}$

18:   **end if**

19: **end while**

20: **return** true

When another node MN2 receives the $NS_{DAD\_Hide\_Target}$, it will search in its address pool to find an IP address (IP_Y) that satisfies the equation:

$$H64\,(IPv6_Y) \;=\; NS_{DAD\_Hide\_Target}.Hash\_64$$

The existence of IP_Y indicates a conflicting address and node MN2 needs to send a $NA_{DAD\_Hide\_Target}$ as a reply to node MN1. The algorithm used in this process is shown in Algorithm 2.

Algorithm 2: receive and verify $NS_{DAD\_Hide\_Target}$

1: **Input:** $NS_{DAD\_Hide\_Target}$
2: **Output:** true: with with $NA_{DAD\_Hide\_target}$; false: drop $NS_{DAD\_Hide\_Target}$
3: receive $NS_{DAD\_Hide\_Target}$
4: **while** address pool is not empty **do**
5:    remove out an IP address as $IPv6_Y$
6:    **if** H64 $(IPv6_Y)$ == $NS_{DAD\_Hide\_Target}.Hash\_64$ **then**
7:       send out $NA_{DAD\_Hide\_target}$
8:       **return** true
9:    **endif**
10: **end while**
11: drop $NS_{DAD\_Hide\_Target}$
12: **return** false

In the Algorithm 1, we have 2 principles:

- *Principle 1*: The "Hash_Target_64" field value in $NS_{DAD\text{-}Hide\text{-}Target}$ is known; hence, if the "Hash_64" in $NA_{DAD\text{-}Hide\text{-}Target}$ does not match that in $NS_{DAD\text{-}Hide\text{-}Target}$, then the node should be considered malicious, and its MAC address should be added into the blacklist;
- *Principle 2*: If the "Hash_Target_64" field in $NA_{DAD\text{-}Hide\text{-}Target}$ is consistent with that in $NS_{DAD\text{-}Hide\text{-}Target}$ but the "Target address" field is not identical to IPv6X and H64 (TargetAddress) $\neq$ Hash_Target_64, then $NA_{DAD\text{-}Hide\text{-}Target}$ is considered a spoofing attack. Hence, the MAC address of the node should be added to the blacklist.

We present an example to demonstrate the DAD_Hide_Target process. The assumptions are that three nodes, namely, MN1, MN2, and MN3, are present in the network, and their address configuration information is as shown in Table 1.

Assume that node MN1 generates a new address B::1:1. To determine whether the address is occupied, node MN1 has to send $NS_{DAD\text{-}Hide\text{-}Target}$ to perform DAD. Node

Table 1. Example of DAD_Hide_Target algorithm:

Node	IPv6	MAC address	SHA256 of IPv6
MN1	A::1:1	08:00:27:0C:00:01	8fd9edea25e6d3adcc5444d2d70b8cdd2242881127 876503a010abe2b56e8ab9
MN2	B::1:1	08:00:27:0C:00:02	1868dc0b983ecb96392c6c879007a2b857c00e1ce 7ad94eef88f7a7ef5095660
MN3	C::1:1	08:00:27:0C:00:03	b0fc16b8bd08391200bec60e554cc6bbd53bc00bbb b6578acba2bf0eef78e856

MN1 fills in the "Hash_64" field with the last 64 bits of the hash value and fills in the "Target address" field with "::", which is an empty address. Both nodes MN2 and MN3 will receive this $NS_{DAD\_Hide\_Target}$.

Node MN3 removes an IPv6 address C::1:1 from the address pool and the calculated hash value is being different from the "Hash_64" field of $NS_{DAD\_Hide\_Target}$, and no more address is found in the address pool. Thus, node MN3 drops $NS_{DAD\_Hide\_Target}$. If node MN3 wants to attack node A, then it should forge $NA_{DAD\_Hide\_Target}$ and fill in the "Target address" of the forged $NA_{DAD\_Hide\_Target}$ with a correct address (B::1:1). However, node MN3 only knows the hash value of the correct address and cannot obtain the original address according to the hash value; thus, MN3 cannot launch DoS attacks.

4.4   Security Analysis

- Security of "Hash_target_64" field

It supposed that n nodes are present in LAN network, wherein each node has m IPv6 addresses. The length of "Hash_target_64" field is L.

We put l = m × n

The hash collision probability in DAD-Hide-Target process is:

$$P(Collision) = 1 - \prod_{i=1}^{l}\left(1 - \frac{i}{2^L}\right)$$

Proof

First, we assume that the hash function is perfect, so the hash value is random and non-repetitive.

Given that n nodes are present in LAN network, each node has m addresses. Thus, the total number of addresses in LAN is l = m × n, which means that l hash random values exist. Suppose the probability that these hash values do not collide with the "Hash_target_64" is P. Then,

$$P = \left(\frac{2^L - 1}{2^L}\right) \times \left(\frac{2^L - 2}{2^L}\right) \times \left(\frac{2^L - 3}{2^L}\right) \times \ldots \times \left(\frac{2^L - l + 1}{2^L}\right)$$

So,

$$P = \left(1 - \frac{1}{2^L}\right) \times \left(1 - \frac{2}{2^L}\right) \times \left(1 - \frac{3}{2^L}\right) \times \cdots \left(1 - \frac{l-1}{2^L}\right)$$

$$P(non\ Collision) = \prod_{i=1}^{l} \left(1 - \frac{1}{2^L}\right)$$

Thus, the probability of collision is:

$$P(Collision) = 1 - \prod_{i=1}^{l} \left(1 - \frac{i}{2^L}\right)$$

Thus, a longer L increases the possibility of node's attack; against a smaller L make the node more secure.

In this work, we set L to 64. In our algorithm DAD-Hide-Target, if 2^8 nodes are present, with each node having 2^{10} IPv6 addresses, then the number of reply messages is:

$$1 - \prod_{i=1}^{2^8 \times 2^{10}} \left(1 - \frac{i}{2^{64}}\right) = 1 - e^{-1/29}$$

This value tends to 0, so it is negligible.

5 Performance Evaluation

5.1 Network Topology

The network environment includes a gateway router, an Ethernet switch, a new node (MN1), two existing nodes (MN2 and MN3) and an attacker. Figure 6 shows the network topology. The simulated network is a LAN network using omnet++ simulator.

The network node is less in order to simplify the experimental design and reduce the experimental error. We chose a LAN to simulate our algorithm, since a LAN can have attacks.

After node MN2 receives $NS_{DAD\_Hide\_Target}$, it removes B::1:1 from its address pool and determines that the hash value of B::1:1 is equal to the "Hash_64" field in $NS_{DAD\_Hide\_Target}$. Thus, node MN2 replies with a $NA_{DAD\_Hide\_Target}$. If Node MN2 has

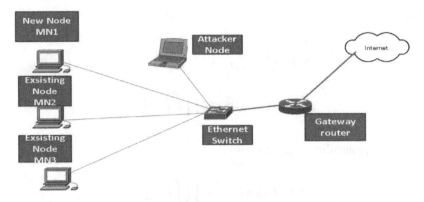

Fig. 6. The network topology

another address IP_Z with a hash value of "edce7a8659a73312" (i.e. the last 64 bits also match the "Hash_64" field), then node MN2 must reply again with $NA_{DAD\_Hide\_Target}$.

Each node can have several addresses and centralized random address space to increase the probability of address conflict.

5.2 Simulation Results and Evaluation

The simulation results show the following performances:

- Address Configuration Failure Probability (ACFP): When a mobile node uses DAD process to configure its address in the presence of an attack. If a DAD process (DAD-P) is performed n times, and m times have failed, then the ACFP of DAD-P is:

$$ACFP = \left(\frac{m}{n}\right) \tag{1}$$

- So, since Address Configuration Success Probability (ACSP) is the complement of ACFP then it is defined as follow:

$$ACSP = 1 - (m/n) \tag{2}$$

From the definition of ACSP, we can conclude that if ACSP is equal to 0, it means that the DAD-Hide-Target is failed n times; then the attack is fully functional in DAD-Hide-Target. Thus, we can use the ACSP to measure a DAD-Hide-Target.

The results of the simulation in Fig. 7 show when there is an attacker in the network, with the standard DAD, the configuration of the address generated to the new node fails, which shows that ACSP tends to 0. However, with our algorithm, the

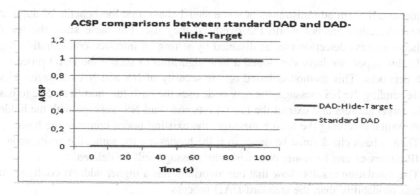

Fig. 7. ACSP comparisons between standard DAD and DAD-Hide-Target

attacker cannot decrypt the sent message because he does not have the private key, which shows that ACSP tends to 1.

We can see in Fig. 7 that ACSP with our algorithm is higher to that found with standard DAD.

5.3 Effectiveness of Our Algorithm

By combining the Algorithm 1 and 2 and the example, we can observe that the main differences between DAD-Hide-Target and DAD are as follows:

- DAD-Hide-Target uses a new message format that adds a new field "Hash_target_64." This format stores the hash value of the "Target address" field to ensure that the real target address of detection does not leak;
- DAD-Hide-Target adds a verification process. After host A receives the NADAD–Hide-Target, according to the "Hash_target_64" field and "Target address" field, the verification process can effectively filter out false replies;
- Hash collision probability is negligible.

6 Conclusion and Perspectives

In order to ensure that all configured addresses are likely to be unique on a given link, IPv6 nodes execute a duplicate address detection algorithm on the requested IPv6 addresses. Nodes must execute the algorithm before assigning addresses to an interface.

For security reasons, the uniqueness of all addresses must be verified prior to their assignment to an interface. The situation is different for IPv6 addresses created by stateless automatic configuration. The uniqueness of an address is determined primarily by the portion of the address formed from an interface ID. Therefore, if a node has already verified the uniqueness of a link-local address, you do not need to test the additional addresses individually. The addresses must be created from the same interface ID. All manually obtained addresses must be individually tested for their uniqueness. System administrators at some sites believe that the benefits of duplicate address detection are not worth the overhead they use. For these sites, the use of duplicate address detection can be disabled by setting an interface configuration flag.

In this paper, we have developed a new algorithm to secure the DAD process in IPv6 networks. This method is based on the security of NS and NA messages. First, before sending the NS message, the new node uses the hash function SHA-512 to hash to the target address and extract the last 64 bits and send NS message with the hidden target. When receiving the secure message, the existing nodes compare the hash.

Then, a hash check must be done; so if the hashes are the same, the verification of the IP addresses can be done; otherwise, the message will be deleted.

The simulation results show that our algorithm has a higher address configuration success probability than the standard DAD process.

Although IPv6 node communications are limited to NDP and DAD protocols when IPv6 is not officially deployed, there are still attacks that can affect network performance by exploiting only these two protocols as we have been able to see it. Our future work will be focalized on others Neighbor Discovery messages security.

References

1. Deering, S., Hinden, R.: Internet Protocol, Version 6 (IPv6) Specification. IETF, RFC 8200, July 2017
2. Ahmed, A.S.A.M.S., Hassan, R., Othman, N.E.: IPv6 neighbor discovery protocol specifications, threats and countermeasures: a survey. IEEE. Access. 5, 18187–18210 (2017). Electronic ISSN: 2169-3536
3. Gont, F., Cooper, A., Thaler, D., Liu, W.: Recommendation on stable IPv6 interface identifiers. IETF, RFC 8064, February 2017
4. Alisherov, F., Kim, T.: Duplicate address detection table in IPv6 mobile networks. In: Chang, C.-C., Vasilakos, T., Das, P., Kim, T., Kang, B.-H., Khurram Khan, M. (eds.) ACN 2010. CCIS, vol. 77, pp. 109–115. Springer, Heidelberg (2010). https://doi.org/10.1007/978-3-642-13405-0_11
5. Moslehpour, M., Khorsandi, S.: A distributed cryptographically generated address computing algorithm for secure neighbor discovery protocol in IPv6. Int. J. Comput. Inf. Eng. 10(6) (2016)
6. Dobraunig, C., Eichlseder, M., Mendel, F.: Analysis of SHA-512/224 and SHA-512/256. In: Iwata, T., Cheon, J.H. (eds.) ASIACRYPT 2015. LNCS, vol. 9453, pp. 612–630. Springer, Heidelberg (2015). https://doi.org/10.1007/978-3-662-48800-3_25
7. Shah, J.L., Parvez, J.: Optimizing security and address configuration in IPv6 SLAAC. Procedia Comput. Sci. 54, 177–185 (2015)
8. Shah, J.L., Parvez, J.: IPv6 cryptographically generated address: analysis and optimization. In: AICTC 2016 Proceedings of the International Conference on Advances in Information Communication Technology & Computing, 12–13 Aug 2016 (2016)
9. Shah, J.L.: A novel approach for securing IPv6 link local communication. Inf. Secur. J.: Glob. Perspect. 25, 136–150 (2016). ISSN: 1939–3555
10. Wang, X., Mu, Y., Han, G., Le, D.: A secure IPv6 address configuration protocol for vehicular networks. Wireless Pers. Commun. 79(1), 721–744 (2014)
11. Lu, Y., Wang, M., Huang, P.: An SDN-based authentication mechanism for securing neighbor discovery protocol in IPv6. J. Secur. Commun. Netw. 2017, 9 (2017)

12. Praptodiyono, S., et al.: Improving security of duplicate address detection on IPv6 local network in public area, 31 Oct 2016 (2016). ISSN: 2376-1172
13. Barbhuiya, F.A., Bansal, G., Kumar, N., et al.: Detection of neighbor discovery protocol based attacks in IPv6 network. Netw. Sci. 2(3–4), 91–113 (2013)
14. Hassan, R., Ahmed, A.S., Othman, N.E.: Enhancing security for IPv6 neighbor discovery protocol using cryptography. Am. J. Appl. Sci. 11(9), 1472–1479 (2014)
15. Anbar, M., Abdullah, R., Saad, R.M.A., Alomari, E., Alsaleem, S.: Review of security vulnerabilities in the IPv6 neighbor discovery protocol. Information Science and Applications (ICISA) 2016. LNEE, vol. 376, pp. 603–612. Springer, Singapore (2016). https://doi.org/10.1007/978-981-10-0557-2_59
16. Sridevi, : Implementation of multicast routing on IPv4 and IPv6 networks. Int. J. Recent. Innov. Trends Comput. Commun. 5, 1455–1467 (2017). ISSN: 2321-8169
17. Cunjiang, Y., Dawei, X., Li, J.: Authentication analysis in an IPV6-based environment. IEEE, 01 Dec 2014 (2014)
18. Nia, M.A., Sajedi, A., Jamshidpey, A.: An introduction to digital signature schemes. IEEE (2014)
19. Chittimaneni, K., Kaeo, M., Kaeo, M.: Operational security considerations for IPv6 networks. Internet-Draft, 27 Oct 2014 (2014)
20. Abdoun, N., et al.: Secure hash algorithm based on efficient chaotic neural network. IEEE, 04 Aug 2016 (2016)
21. Aggarwal, S., Aggarwal, K.: A review of comparative study of MD5 and SHA security algorithm. Int. J. Comput. Appl. 104(14), 0975–8887 (2014)

Dynamic Team Access Control
for Collaborative Internet of Things

Hadjer Benhadj Djilali[1]($\boxtimes$) and Djamel Tandjaoui[2]

[1] LSI, USTHB: University of Sciences and Technology Houari Boumediene,
Algiers, Algeria
h.benhadjdjilali@usthb.dz
[2] Computer Security Division, CERIST: Research Center on Scientific
and Technical Information,
Algiers, Algeria
dtandjaoui@cerist.dz
http://www.usthb.dz/fr
http://www.cerist.dz

Abstract. The article presents a new access control model for IoT (Internet of Things), which is based on a dynamic approach. Our aim is to change the access control design concept from a static to a dynamic model in order to fit to characteristics and features of IoT. We do so by adapting TMAC (Team Access Control) model to IoT dynamic environment. DTMAC (Dynamic Team Access Control) allows the creation of dynamic teams that are deleted when the collaborative activities are over. In addition, it offers an easy management of the teams in a decentralized manner. We implement DTMAC as a web application using a relational database management to assess its security. The assessment of DTMAC shows that it adapts well to IoT dynamic network. Moreover, the model is user-driven, flexible and scalable. It also provides fine-grained access control, supports the well-known least privileges principle and separation of duties for the team members.

Keywords: Internet of Things · Access control · Team Access Control
Collaborative activities · Dynamic environment · Security

1 Introduction

After the revolutionary technology of the internet that changed the world, today IoT is another game changer that marks and changes the history of the humankind. IoT introduces a new concept which is connecting objects to the internet offering relevant services and applications in order to facilitate the human life. Many sectors benefit from IoT intelligence. Indeed, we find IoT applications everywhere, such as in e-government, e-health, smart-cities, e-learning, Smart-Grid...

Although the promising future of IoT, the security issues in IoT delays its big scale deployment because connected devices are difficult to secure due to their

© Springer Nature Switzerland AG 2019
É. Renault et al. (Eds.): MSPN 2018, LNCS 11005, pp. 70–85, 2019.
https://doi.org/10.1007/978-3-030-03101-5_7

constrained and limited resources. Among security challenges in IoT, the access control is an important one to keep the confidentiality and the integrity of data and to prevent from unauthorized access.

In collaborative IoT, users and sensors are dynamic. They join the network while others leave. They also collaborate to achieve a common goal. In order to make the management of collaborative activities easier, we should consider creating teams of users and sensors to minimize the load of addressing permissions to each user for each instant of IoT objects.

The existing traditional solutions for access control in IoT context are limited in dynamicity. In fact, the proposed models are static and do not fit well to the umbrella of IoT and dynamic environment especially in collaborative IoT. These limitations motivate us to change the access control design concept from a static to a dynamic model. For this, we are creating dynamic access control on demand of the users by creating teams dynamically. The teams have a short lifetime that can go from days to months and they will be removed when the collaborative activities are over. Moreover, the teams are dynamic because: (a) from one day to another there are newly deployed sensors added to the team, (b) new users join the team while others leave, (c) exhaustion of sensors implicit deleting sensors from the team...

In this paper, we propose a DTMAC (Dynamic Team Access Control) model for the collaborative IoT where users collaborate to do a collaborative activity. DTMAC adapt TMAC (Team access control) to make it dynamic. It relies on the top of RBAC (Role Based Access Control). As a result, it adopts features of trusted and largely used of RBAC and preserves the advantages of scalable security administration that RBAC model offers. In addition, the access control permissions are suitable for the dynamic environment of IoT because DTMAC creates dynamic teams that provide a fine-grained access control based on the session role permission and team based permission which leads to the separation of duties for team members. DTMAC has also the capability to model a rich set of security policies and to tune permissions activation and deactivation in a flexible way. Furthermore, DTMAC decentralizes the access control management and it is user-driven unlike traditional system that requires contacting security administrator to get the required access permission and needs.

The remainder of the paper is organized as follows. In Sect. 2, IoT characteristics and features are presented briefly. In Sect. 3, related work of access control of IoT is presented. Section 4 presents and details DTMAC model. In Sect. 5, we implement and run security analysis of our model. Finally, Sect. 6 concludes this paper.

2   Internet of Things Features

Beside the characteristics of distributed systems, IoT has it is own characteristics and features that make it different and difficult to tackle. We mention a few of them [1],[2]:

- Dynamic environment: IoT is a dynamic network where object joins the network while others leave.
- Short life cycle: IoT has a short life cycle due to its limited low battery.
- Scalability: IoT is characterized by a huge number of connected systems and devices so it should consider scalability in different levels.
- Heterogeneity: IoT devices have different computational and communication capabilities. That should be supported in both architectural and protocol levels to ensure the interoperability.

The designed access control model should consider IoT features and characteristics to propose a suitable and flexible model that provides fine-grained access control permissions.

3   Related Work

In literature, there are many access control models: RBAC, ABAC (Attribute Based Access Control), TMAC, CapBAC (Capability Based Access Control), TrustBAC (Trust Based Access Control), OrgBAC (Organizational Based Access Control), UCON (Usage Based Access Control). Almost all of them have been adapted to the IoT context. However, each one of them has a different level of security and usability. The big challenge here is: how to define a smooth model that provides fine grained access control and adapts to the context and features of the IoT applications and environment.

RBAC [3] is a model that controls the access of users to objects based on their roles. Reference [4] reinforced RBAC using contextual information like time, location and state of the environment. Authors of [5] integrated social media network services in role based access control to enable users to share their IoT devices. RBAC from collaborative IoT perspective is limited in dynamicity and not user driven with critical scalability and difficult permission management in dynamic network of users and IoT objects.

ABAC [6] is an access control model that grants access to objects according to attributes presented by a subject. Authors of [7] adopted ABAC based authorization method as an access control policy and authentication based on Elliptic Curve Cryptography. ABAC From IoT perspective is very complex to implement, especially in a dynamic environment like IoT where object join and leave the network autonomously. Moreover, ABAC is not user-driven.

OrgBAC [8] model is conceived to extend the RBAC model by introducing the organizational notion and separating between the concrete level and the abstract level. SmartOrBAC [9] and extended OrBAC [10] models for IoT environment include the context of application like smart cities to fit the IoT features. However, OrgBAC model is very complex and cannot be supported by constrained devices and difficult to handle.

TrustBAC [11] is an access control model based on trust score and trust relationships. The models FTBAC (Framework for Trust Based Access Control) [12] and TACITO (trust-aware access control system for IoT) [13] propose a trust based access control that calculates the trust value based on different factors like experience, knowledge and recommendation, reputation. Then the trust score is mapped to different access control levels. TrustBAC from collaborative IoT perspective is an interesting point of research but is still subject to malicious nodes/users that can ruin the system.

CapBAC is a token-based access control model firstly presented in [14] which is very much used in the actual control systems. Authors of [15] proposed Cap-Bac system for IoT that provides delegation and capability support and information granularity in a centralized approach. Reference [16] presented a distributed capability access control where the access control decision is made by the objects, the token includes a digital signature using ECDSA (Elliptic Curve Digital Signature Algorithm)[17] using a public key cryptography and other fields. The CapBAC is a very popular repeated model in IoT access control thanks to it is simplicity. But the token key management is still a challenging factor in the context of collaborative IoT devices/users, CapBAC also does not take context into consideration.

The UCON model [18] is a generalization of access control to cover obligation, condition, continuity (ongoing control) and mutability. From the study in [19] UCON for IoT presents a high dynamicity, mutability of attributes, a fine-grained access and a flexible scalable model. But the model is too complex to implement and beyond the capacity of IoT devices. It is also not user-driven, does not support delegation and there is no functionality for administration. A full state of art of access control for IoT can be found in the following references [20], [21].

The TMAC was introduced par Thomas in 1997 in [22], in purpose to apply the concept of RBAC in collaborative environments. To the best of our knowledge, there are no preliminary work that integrates TMAC in IoT, so we integrate and adapt it to the context of IoT by proposing DTMAC.

4   Dynamic Team Access Control Model

In this section, we present our proposed access control model DTMAC. Besides the existing access control models in the company, the purpose of our proposed DTMAC is to control the access of a team of users that are collaborating to monitor physical phenomenal data collected by sensors. Like: sugar level and heartbeats in e-health, humidity and acidity in e-farming, environmental metrics about extraction sites in oil, gas and mining. So only authorized users from the company staff that are working in a collaborative activity can create dynamic teams and access to sensors data easily in decentralized manner that does not require security administrator intervention for the team creation, management and access permission. As a consequence, different users with relevant roles can create, delete and manage teams dynamically according to local policies.

Georgiadis et al. [23] presented a Flexible Team-Based Access Control using contexts. The teams are static, fixed pre-created by an administrator. The authors enforced security of the teams using contextual information. Unfortunately, their work cannot be applied directly to the IoT ecosystem because IoT is a dynamic environment where users and sensors join the network while others leave. To overcome dynamicity issue, we extend their work and make the model dynamic by considering IoT features and integrating IoT devices part of the team. We make DTMAC dynamic by creating teams dynamically. Here the teams are not created in advance but dynamically according to the requests of users. The team can be deleted when the collaborative activity is over. We approach to create a team in demand by users with specific roles that is explained in Sect. 4.1. DTMAC model relies on the top of RBAC model. As a result, it adopts features of trusted and largely used of RBAC.

We make the following assumptions:

- All workers of the company have a unique id which is registered in the database and related to their roles.
- All sensors have a unique id which is registered in the company database.
- Each team has a unique id in the system.
- Only users with specific superior roles can create a team.
- Users can be members of different teams but one sensor belongs to one team for security reasons.

The team architecture is presented in "Table 1" which is composed of:

- Team id which is unique and generated by the ACP(Access Control Provider).
- Team admin is the user who created the team.
- Team members are users with specific roles from the company (Master and Slave role) as defined in the company policies.
- Team sensors are IoT sensors that belong to the company registered sensors.
- Team permissions are enabled by default when the team is created and can be disabled by the local policy of the company or by the team admin for security or functional measurement.

Table 1. Dynamic team access control architecture

Team	Team Id
Team admin	$ID(User_1)$
Team members	$ID(User_1)$, $ID(User_2)$, $ID(User_3)$
Sensors	$ID(Sensor_1)$, $ID(Sensor_2)$, $ID(Sensor_3)$
Team permission	Enabled or disabled

We choose to implement DTMAC in a centralized architecture in order to minimize the load on sensors. Doing so, sensors only collect data to preserve their energy and their life cycle. The ACP represents the company server that hosts its data in an organized manner (security policies, databases of employees, teams and sensors...). The ACP handles the access control decision of users' requests either by granting or denying access according to DTMAC model.

4.1   Roles Definitions

Our proposed model DTMAC relies on the top of RBAC model, focusing on the team flow. We consider and define the following two levels of roles:

- **Master Role:** The definition of this role represents the user with the important and high permissions in the team. It's different from one field to another. For instance, in the e-health field the master role is the physician who creates a team to monitor the sensors of the patient. In oil, gas and mining filed the head engineer is the master role that can create a team that contains other engineers and technicians to control and monitor connected sensors used to provide environmental metrics about extraction sites and many other use cases.
- **Slave Role:** The definition of this role represents the users with low permissions in the team. These users can only be a member of a team and do not have permissions to create teams. For instance, a nurse or technician cannot create a team, but they can be a member of existing teams.

We emphasize that the master role is superior than the slave role in the hierarchy of the company. The role definition leads to a different access role permissions. Users with the master role can create, delete and manage a team. They also have read and write permissions to sensors data. Users with slave role have only reading permission to read sensors data.

The master and slave roles differ from a policy to another. As a consequence, we have different teams with different access control permissions where each team is associated with one policy. For instance T_1 is associated with P_1 and T_2 is associated with P_2 where P_1 and P_2 have a different master and slave role definition. As a result T_1 will have different access control permissions than T_2.

4.2   Team Creation

Whenever there is a dynamic activity that needs a collaboration of different users to monitor a special task with sensors (monitor patients, forest, new work zone, new construction site...), a team needs to be created. A user with a master role creates a team by adding other users and sensors to the team by sending a team creation request that includes users and sensors IDs to the company ACP server.

The ACP server evaluates a team creation request by checking the session role permissions of the user (if the user has the appropriate role (Master Role) to create a team according to the local company policy). It also checks the team members and the team sensors. If all is true the team is successfully created and validated in the database through a trigger, otherwise the team will be created with notification errors sent to the team admin. For instance, the selected user with $id = 600$ is not allowed to be a team member because his role is neither master nor slave, the selected sensor $id = 506$ is wrong does not exist in sensor database, the selected sensor $id = 1006$ is used in another team...

4.3   Action that Can Be Performed

DTMAC considers the following actions that can be requested by users in collaborative and dynamic activity:

- **Add-user(user, team):** Add a user to an existing team.
- **Delete-user(user, team):** Delete a user from an existing team.
- **Add-Sensor(Sensor, team):** Add a sensor to an existing team.
- **Delete-Sensor(Sensor, team):** Delete a sensor from an existing team.
- **Team-activate(team):** Enable the team permissions so the team members can access the sensor data.
- **Team-deactivate(team):** Disable the team permissions for the entire team.
- **Delete-Team(team):** Delete the team when the collaborative work is over.
- **Read-Data(sensor, team):** Read data of sensor.
- **Write-Data(Sensor, team):** Write data in the sensor (if there is a need of sensor configuration).

4.4   Formal Description of Dynamic Team Access Control

The formalization of DTMAC definition is based on RBAC0. The model is presented in "Fig. 1".

Definition: DTMAC has the following components:

- U, R, IoT, P, S, T, TA stand for users, roles, Internet of things devices, permissions, sessions, teams and team administrator respectively.
- PRS $\subseteq$ P $\times$ R, is a many to many permission to role assignment relation.
- URS $\subseteq$ U $\times$ R, is a many to many user to role assignment relation.
- UTS $\subseteq$ U $\times$ T, is a many to many user to team assignment relation.
- TATS $\subseteq$ TA $\times$ T, is a one to many Team Administrator to team assignment relation|TA $\subseteq$ U.
- TIoTS $\subseteq$ T $\times$ IoT, is a many to one team to IoT assignment relation.
- session-user: S $\longrightarrow$ U, is a function that map each session s_i to a single user: user(s_i) which is constant for the session is lifetime.
- session-roles: S $\longrightarrow$ 2^R is a function that map each session s_i to a set of roles: roles(s_i) $\subseteq$ {r | user(s_i), r) $\in$ URS}, which can change in time when the user log with different roles. the session s_i has the permission $\cup$ r $\in$ roles(s_i) {$p|(p,r) \in PRS$ referred to as a Session role permissions.
- session-teams: S $\longrightarrow$ 2^T is a function that map each session s_i to a set of teams: teams(s_i) $\subseteq$ {t | user(s_i), t) $\in$ UTS}, which can change with time.
- team-users: T $\longrightarrow$ 2^u, is a function that map each team t_i to a set of users: user(t_i) $\subseteq$ {u | (u, t_i) $\in$ UTS } $\wedge \exists s_j$: user(s_j) = u}.
- team-roles: T$\longrightarrow$ 2^R is a function that map each team t_i to a set of roles. roles(t_i) $\subseteq$ {r | (u, t_i) $\in$ URS}, which can change in time. The team t_i has the permission $\oplus$ r $\in$ roles(t_i) {$p|(p,r) \in PRS$. Referred to as team roles permission.

- team-team administrator: $T \longrightarrow 2^{AT}$, is a function that map each team t_i to a one team administrator: Team Administrator $TA(t_i) \subseteq \{ta|(ta, t_i) \in TATS\} \wedge \exists s_j$: $user(s_j) = TA\}$.
- $ACD(s_i, T_i, A \longrightarrow P)$ is a function that handles the access control decision to respond with the appropriate permission to the request. As parameters, it takes the current session s_i to retrieve the permissions that are related to the user role for the active session, the team t_i to retrieve the team-based permissions and the action A that the user wants to do.

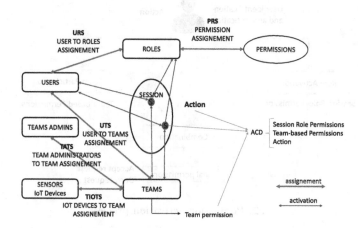

Fig. 1. Dynamic team access control approach

4.5 User Permission Access Activation Process

The process of enabling access permissions for users who request to perform an action in the system of our proposed model uses: role-based permissions and team-based permissions. "Fig. 2" depicts the permission access activation process. The process starts with a log-in phase where the user will have to authenticate himself by presenting suitable credentials (such as user-id and password information for local networks, or present digital certificates for internet/intranet environments) to be identified in the system. Then the user has to select a role from a set of roles assigned to him. According to this selection, a particular set of role-based permissions are granted and these are called session-roles permissions.

After the role selection where the role must exist in the team roles, the user has to select the team and/or sensors that he wants to process an action to it through a mobile application with a friendly user interface to lead a better user experience. Following the team selection procedure, the team-based permissions are set to the user request. The components of team-based permissions differ according to the action requested by the user. Basically, it is composed of team permissions (enabled or disabled), team membership and team admin.

The final permission of the user is a combination of role-based permissions and team-based permissions.

The final permission = Session Role Permissions ⊕ Team-based Permissions (Action).

The ACP server evaluates the request using the final permission. If the final permission is verified and valid, the APC grants access to the user to perform the request otherwise it rejects it.

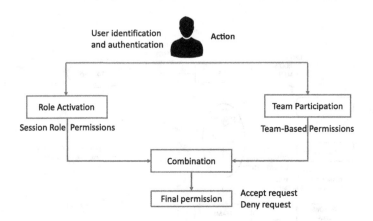

Fig. 2. Permission activation process

5   Security Analysis of the Proposed Scheme

In order to show the security efficiency of the proposed access control model, we conduct a security analysis on it. Our proposed model offers a resistance to several possible authorized and unauthorized requests like: team creation request, access request and team management request.

We implement DTMAC in relational database management system MySQLI using Apache WampServer and we simulate users' requests through a web application. The company database server basically stores two tables: company employees and senors. The first one, stores the company's employees information: first/last name, id of the employee, user name, password, department... The second one, stores the Ids of sensors and a column available to check if the sensor is used or not in a team. In addition, "teams" is a database that stores all the dynamic teams of the company created through DTMAC model.

A team is technically represented by the following three tables:

- team(idteam)info: is a table that stores team id, team permissions and the team related information.
- team(idteam)members: is a table that stores information of team members that consists of idemployee, employee role and a column admin to distinguish the team admin from the team members.
- team(idteam)sensors: is a table that stores the ids of sensors of the team.

We analyze security of DTMAC model by considering the team with the id = 2001 that is presented in "Table 2". The team members are composed: of the head engineers, engineers and technicians that collaborate to monitor sensors that collect environmental metrics about extraction sites in oil, gas and mining IoT applications. The team is associated with policy P_1 where the role of the head engineers is defined as a master role and the roles engineer and technician are defined as slave role.

Table 2. Team 2001

Team ID	2001
Team admin	ID(Head engineer$_{Sam}$ = 100)
Team Members	ID(engineer$_{Dave}$) = 201, ID(engineer$_{Mate}$) = 202
	ID(Technician$_{John}$) = 501, ID(Technician$_{Adam}$) = 502
Sensors IDs	1000, 1001, 1002, 1003, 1004, 1005
Team permission	Enabled

5.1   Team Creation

The ACP server evaluates the team creation requests as explained in Sect. 4.1.

"Figure 3" illustrates, the head engineers Sam with the id = 100 sends a request to create a team. The ACP evaluates the request and creates the team without any notification errors.

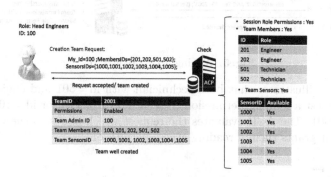

Fig. 3. Team creation request 1

"Figure 4" illustrates that both technician with id = 502 and engineer with id = 201 request to create a team. The ACP evaluates the request and rejects it because both users do not have enough session role permissions to create a team (Slave role).

Fig. 4. Team creation request 2

5.2   Access Request

We specify that reading permission is represented by a select request and writing permission is represented by an update request on the teams database. The ACP server evaluates access requests by checking the following conditions: if the user is a member of the team, the team permissions are enabled and the session role permissions of the user.

"Figure 5" illustrates that the head engineers with id = 100 request a writing permission to write data into sensor id = 1002 of the team id = 2001, this can be used to reset or change the configuration of the sensor. The ACP server evaluates the request which obeys to the conditions. As a consequence, it grants a writing access permission to the head engineers.

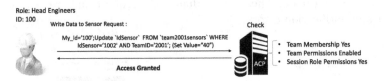

Fig. 5. Writing access request 1

"Figure 6" illustrates that both technician with id = 501 and engineer with id = 201 request a reading permission to read data from sensor id = 1001 of the team id = 2001. The ACP evaluates the request which obeys to the conditions as a result, it grants them a reading access permission.

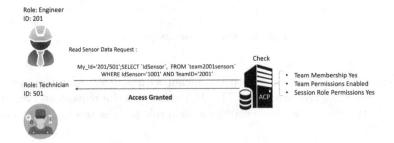

Fig. 6. Reading access request 1

"Figure 7" illustrates that both technician with id = 501 and engineer with id = 201 request a reading permission to read data from sensor id = 1001 of the team id = 2001. The ACP evaluates the request and denies access because the team permissions are not enabled.

Fig. 7. Reading access request 2

"Figure 8" illustrates that both technician with id = 505 and engineer with the id = 203 request a reading permission to read data from sensor id = 1001 of the team id = 2001. The ACP evaluates the request and denies access because both users are not team members of the team id = 2001.

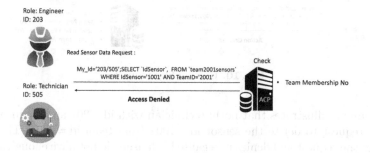

Fig. 8. Reading access request 3

"Figure 9" illustrates that both technician with id = 202 and engineer with id = 502 request a writing permission to write data into sensor id = 1002 of the team id = 2001. The ACP evaluates the request and denies access because both users do not have enough session role permissions to perform a writing action (slave role).

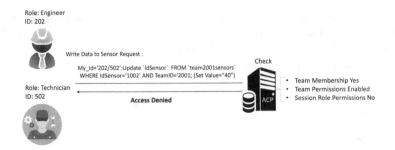

Fig. 9. Writting access request 2

5.3   Team Management

The ACP server evaluates a team management request by checking the following conditions: if the user is a member of the team, the session role permissions of the user, if the team permissions are enabled and if the user is the team admin.

"Figure 10" illustrates that the head engineers with id = 100 request to add a new user to the team id = 2001. The ACP evaluates the request which obeys to the conditions. As a result, it adds the new user with id = 203 as a team member of the team 2001.

Fig. 10. User adding request

"Figure 11" illustrates that both: technician with id = 201 and engineer with id = 501 request to delete the sensor id = 1002 from team id = 2001. The ACP evaluates the request and denies it because both users do not have enough session role permissions to manage the team (slave role).

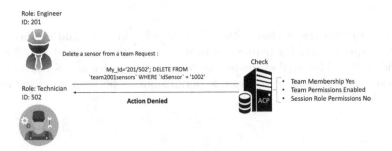

Fig. 11. Deleting sensor request

As the two previous figures illustrate, only the team admin can: add and delete a sensor/user, activate or deactivate team permissions and delete the team.

We justify the last assumption "one sensor belong to one team" presented in Sect. 4 Of DTMAC for the following reason: if we have a sensor that is shared between two team T_1 and T_2 that have different policies P_1 and P_2 respectively where the role R_1 is defined as a slave role in P_1 and as a master role in P_2. A user with the role R_1 that is a team member of both teams T_1 and T_2 can only read data from the shared sensor with T_1 permissions. He can also write data to the sensor with T_2 permissions which lead to a security breach of data and access control permission non-integrity.

Unlike the centralized one security administrator and manager of the teams, DTMAC uses a decentralized approach of creating collaborative teams to minimize the cost of time and management of the teams especially in dynamic environment of IoT. The access control decision is made by the ACP server of the company to minimize the load and energy consumption of IoT due to its limited constrained devices characteristics. Besides, IoT devices are not trusted to make access control decision because they easy to circumvent them.

From the above security assessment, we conclude that DTMAC provides a secure fine-grained access control and separation of duties for team members thanks to session role permission and role hierarchy definition of master and slave role. It also preserves the privacy of data by rejecting unauthorized access request from non-team members. Additionally, DTMAC preserves the advantages of scalable security administration that RBAC model offers and yet offers the flexibility to activate permissions for individual users and to a specific object instance. Furthermore, DTMAC regarding to IoT features is user-driven, scalable and dynamic (by creating, deleting and management of team in a dynamic manner) which adapts well to IoT dynamic environment.

6   Conclusion

To sum up, we presented a new access control model that integrates the classic TMAC model and we adapted it to the IoT dynamic environment for collaborative activities. Our DTMAC relies on the top RBAC model which preserves the advantages of scalable security administration that RBAC model offers with a flexibility to activate permissions for individual users and to a specific object instance. Furthermore, DTMAC has the capability to model a rich set of security policies and to tune permission activation and deactivation in a flexible way and it adapts well to IoT dynamic environment and features. We believe that DTMAC and its variations will prove to be an interesting starting point for further investigation of security models for next-generation of collaborative and dynamic environment for IoT applications.

References

1. De Pellegrini, F., Miorandi, I., Daniele, C., Sicari, S.: Internet of things: vision, applications and research challenges. Ad Hoc Netw. **10**, 1497–1516 (2012)
2. Lopez, J., Roman, R., Zhou, J.: On the features and challenges of security and privacy in distributed internet of things. Comput. Netw. **57**, 2266–2279 (2013)
3. Sandhu, R.S.: Role Based Access Control (1998)
4. Zhang, G., Tian, J.: An extended role based access control model for the Internet of Things. In: ICINA (2010)
5. Jindou, J., Xiaofeng, Q., Cheng, C.: Access control method for web of things based on role and SNS. IEEE (2012)
6. Yuan, E., Tong, J.: Attributed based access control (ABAC) for web services. In: IEEE International Conference. IEEE (2005)
7. Ye, N., Zhu, Y., Wang, R.-C., Malekian, R., Qiao-min, L.: An efficient authentication and access control scheme for perception layer of Internet of Things. Appl. Math. Inf. Sci. Int. J. **4)(2014**, 1617–1624 (1624)
8. Kalam, A., et al.: Organization based access control. IEEE (2003)
9. Ouaddah, A., Bouij-Pasquier, I., Abou Elkalam, A., Ait Ouahman, A.: Security analysis and proposal of new access control model in the Internet of Thing. IEEE (2015)
10. Bouij-Pasquier, I., El Kalam, A.A., Ouahman, A.A., De Montfort, M.: A security framework for Internet of Things. In: Reiter, M., Naccache, D. (eds.) CANS 2015. LNCS, vol. 9476, pp. 19–31. Springer, Cham (2015). https://doi.org/10.1007/978-3-319-26823-1_2
11. Kagal, L., Finin, T., Joshi, A.: A Trust-Based Access Control Model for Pervasive Computing Applications. IEEE (2001)
12. Malhalle, P.N., Thakre, P.A., Prasad, N.R., Prasad, R.: A fuzzy approach to trust based access control in Internet of Things. IEEE (2013)
13. Bernabe, J.B., Ramos, J.L.H., Gomez, A.F.S.: TACIoT: multidimensional trust aware access control system for the Internet of Things. Soft Comput. **20**, 1763–1779 (2016)
14. Dennis, J.B., Van Horn, E.C.: Programming semantics for multiprogrammed computations. Commun. ACM **9**, 143–154 (1966)
15. Gusmeroli, S., Piccione, S., Rotondi, D.: A capability based security approach to manage access control in the Internet of Things. Math. Comput. Modell. **58**, 1189–1205 (2013)
16. Hernandez-Ramos, J.L., Jara, A.J., Marin, L., Skarmeta, A.F.: Distributed capability-based access control for the Internet of Things. JISIS **3**, 1–16 (2013)
17. Johnson, D., Menezes, A., Vanstone, S.: The elliptic curve digital signature algorithm (ECDSA). Int. J. Inf. Secur. **1**, 36–63 (2001)
18. Sandhu, R., Park, J.: Usage control: a vision for next generation access control. In: Gorodetsky, V., Popyack, L., Skormin, V. (eds.) MMM-ACNS 2003. LNCS, vol. 2776, pp. 17–31. Springer, Heidelberg (2003). https://doi.org/10.1007/978-3-540-45215-7_2
19. Zhang, G., Gong, W.: The research of access control based on UCON in the Internet of Things. J. Softw. **6**, 724–731 (2011)
20. Zhang, Y., Wu, X.: Access Control in Internet of Things: A Survey (2016)

21. Ait Ouahman, A., Ouaddah, A., Mousannif, H., Abou Elkalam, A.: Acess control in the Internet of Things: big challlenges and new opportunities. Comput. Netw. **112**, 237–262 (2017)
22. Team-based access control (TMAC): a primitive for applying role-based access controls in collaborative environments. ACM (1997)
23. Georgiadis, C.K., Thomas, K., Mavridis, I., Pangalos, G.I.: Flexible team-based access control using contexts. In: SACMAT (2001)

Road Anomaly Detection Using Smartphone: A Brief Analysis

Van Khang Nguyen[1,2(✉)], Éric Renault[1], and Viet Hai Ha[2]

[1] Institut Mines-Télécom/Télécom SudParis, CNRS UMR 5157 SAMOVAR,
9 rue Charles Fourier, 91011 Evry Cedex, France
{van_khang.nguyen,eric.renault}@telecom-sudparis.eu
[2] College of Education, Hue University, Hue, Vietnam
haviethai@gmail.com

Abstract. Identification of road anomaly not only helps drivers to reduce the risk, but also support for road maintenance. Arguably, with the popularity of smartphones including multiple sensors, many road anomaly detection systems using mobile phones have been proposed. This paper aims at analyzing a number of typical road anomaly detection methods in terms of resource requirements, energy consumption, fitness conditions. From these measurements, we suggest some improvement directions to build road anomaly detection algorithms appropriate for smartphones.

Keywords: Road anomaly · Pothole · Road condition
Sensors network

1 Introduction

Today, road systems are dense all over the world. Unfortunately, under the influence of vehicles and weather, roads gradually deteriorate, to get poorer and poorer and lead to the appearance of anomalies. This causes huge economic losses and endangers people in traffic. Determining the quality of roads and finding potholes to repair is a very challenging and much needed effort. As a result, many systems for road monitoring and identification of potholes have been developed or proposed.

The pothole detection is based on a variety of information like audio, image, video, 3D laser or vibrations [11]. Sensors used to identify potholes can be either dedicated hardware mounted on vehicles or smartphone sensors [4]. Recently, smartphones have become very popular with low-cost Internet, and many researches on pothole detection based on smartphones' accelerometer and GPS sensors have been conducted.

Anomaly detection can be processed on phones or in a center or both. If the processing is done in a datacenter, a large amount of data might be exchanged the smartphone and the datacenter, while if the processing is done in the smartphone, the detection program should be designed so that it does not consume too

© Springer Nature Switzerland AG 2019
É. Renault et al. (Eds.): MSPN 2018, LNCS 11005, pp. 86–97, 2019.
https://doi.org/10.1007/978-3-030-03101-5_8

much resources like CPU, memory and energy. The purpose of this article is to analyse and compare current road anomaly detection methods that aim at being executed on the phone in real time. The main focus is set on vibration-based solutions.

The rest of the paper is organized as follows: Sects. 2 and 3 describe different pioneering researches on pothole detection based on acceleration and GPS data. These methods are divided into two classes: *threshold based* and *classification based*. In Sect. 4, each method described in Sects. 2 and 3 is analyzed in terms of (a) memory requirements and computing resources, (b) compatibility with qualitative conditions like road quality, vehicle speed and type of vehicle, and (c) applicability under unspecified telephone conditions. Improvements to some issues are also discussed in this section. Finally, Sect. 5 concludes the paper.

2   Threshold-Based Methods

The common feature of threshold-based methods is the use of simple algorithms to determine potholes according to the principle that if a component or a derivative of the components of a measured acceleration exceeds a specific threshold: a road abnormally is detected (see Fig. 1).

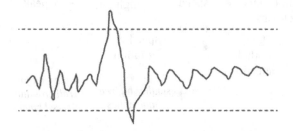

Fig. 1. Ideal of threshold-based methods.

The Pothole Patrol System [8]. Eriksson et al. proposed a system called Pothole Patrol (P^2). In order to detect road anomalies, they use accelerometers and GPS sensors installed in taxis. Gathered information from the sensors are:

```
< time, location, speed, heading, 3-axis acceleration >
```

The detection is made by a vehicle embedding a computer. The results (potholes) are sent to a control center through a WiFi network. The server compute clusters of potholes to prevent false positive analysis. The pothole detection algorithm proposed in P^2 consists of five filters. Information received from the sensors are first segmented into windows of 256 samples. Each window then is tested by the filters to reject non-pothole event types (see Fig. 2). These filters are:

- **Speed:** this filter rejects windows in which the speed is too small.
- **High-pass:** this stage rejects low-frequency components from acceleration measurement in x-axes and z-axes. This filter removes events like acceleration, turning, veering and braking.
- **z-peak:** this important filter rejects all windows with a z-axis of acceleration less than threshold t_z.
- **xz-ratio:** this step rejects events that affect both sides of a car such as railway crossings, speed bumps and expansion joints. A window is rejected if the x-acceleration peak in a sub-window from the read z-acceleration peak, is less than some factor t_2 times the z-acceleration peak. Let $\triangle w = 32$ samples be the size of the subwindow.
- **speed vs. z-ratio:** this step removes windows in which the z-acceleration peak is less than factor t_s times the speed.

In order to detect parameters t_z, t_x and t_s, authors use sample data to train the pothole detector.

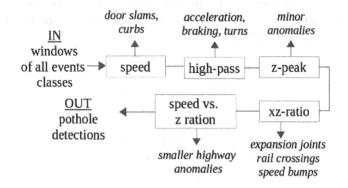

Fig. 2. P^2's pothole detector.

Nericell Road System Monitoring [13]. Mohan et al. present a system to monitor road conditions. Detection is performed on a smartphone. The system uses accelerometer, microphone, GSM radio and GPS sensors to detect potholes, bumps, brakings and honkings. Authors also propose to use Euler's angles to represent the orientation of the accelerometer and a method to estimate the angles based on gravity, and braking actions or accelerations.

Algorithms Used to Determine Anomalies:

- **Braking Detection:** Let a_x be the acceleration on the x-axis. The algorithm consists in computing $\overline{a_x}$ over a sliding window. When $\overline{a_x}$ is greater than threshold T, a braking event is detected. The windows size used by the authors is $4\,\text{s}$.

- **Bump and pothole detection:** Nericell does not distinguish between bump types such as potholes and speed bumps. At high speed, (i.e ≥ 25 km/h), authors use the z-peak method [8]: a bump is detected when a_z is greater than a given threshold. At low speed, authors propose a filter called z-sus. With z-sus, a bump is detected when there is a sustained dip, e.g a_z is less than threshold T for at least 20 ms.

Mednis et al. [12] proposed four algorithms for real-time road anomaly detection on smartphone sensing system. All of these algorithms are based on 3-axis acceleration data:

- **Z-THRESH:** is similar to the z-peak algorithm used in [8] and [13]. Events are detected when the amplitude of the z value of the acceleration exceeds a specified threshold.
- **Z-DIFF:** events are detected when the difference between two consecutive values is greater than a specific threshold.
- **Z-STDDEV:** the standard deviation on a small sliding window is computed. When the standard deviation is greater than a specific threshold, an event is detected.
- **G-ZERO:** an event is detected when the value of all three axes is less than a specific threshold.

Vittorio et al. [18] applied a anomaly detection method on mobile devices based on both acceleration signal and GPS signal but using only the vertical acceleration. Authors proposed to apply a partial ri-orientation to recompute the vertical value of acceleration (a_z). Since GPS data's frequency was 1 Hz and acceleration data's frequency was at least 5 Hz, authors grouped accelerometer data in groups of 1 s by computing a_{z_min}, a_{z_max} and a_{z_avg}. The detection is based on the vertical acceleration impulse (DVA) defined by DVA $= a_{z\_max} - a_{z\_min}$.

Authors have proposed a background noise removal:

$$DVA = \begin{cases} 0 & \text{if } DVA \leq DVA^{st} \\ DVA - DVA^{st} & \text{if } DVA > DVA^{st} \end{cases}$$

where DVA^{st} is the maximum DVA in a stationary condition. In order to filter anomalies, DVA is filtered as following:

$$DVA = \begin{cases} 0 & \text{if } DVA \leq DVA^{th} \\ DVA & \text{if } DVA > DVA^{th} \end{cases}$$

where DVA^{th} is a reference set of DVA values. Experiments allow to determine the optimal DVA^{th} value.

3   Classification-Based Methods

For classification-based methods, firstly features are extracted from the data collected by various methods. Then a classification will be applied to these features to classify them to detect road abnormally and types of abnormally (see Fig. 3).

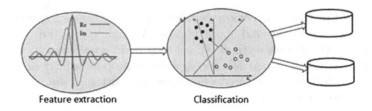

Fig. 3. Ideal of classification-based methods.

Perttunen et al. [15] proposed a road anomaly detection method which consists of many complex stages. Data (GPS and acceleration signals) first pass a preprocessing in which GPS outlier rejection and Kalman filters are applied to reduce noise. Then, the signals are framed using a sliding window to extract some features. Many of them are extracted from the acceleration signal: mean, variance, standard deviation, peak-to-peak, signal magnitude area, 3-axis autoregressive coefficients, tilt angles, root mean square for x-axis, y-axis and z-axis, correlation of signals between three dimensions. A Fast Fourier Transformation is also applied to incorporate information from specific frequencies. Authors also apply a removing linear dependence method [17] to remove dependence speed from the features. Finally, they apply support vector machines [6] to classify the windows. The result of this classification allows them to identify the road anomalies.

Cong et al. [5] proposed to apply Wavelet Packet Decomposition (WPD) and One-Class Support Vector Machine (SVM) on acceleration data to detect road anomaly. WPD is used for feature extraction. Acceleration signal is segmented into 114 sample windows. Then, a WPD using Daubecheis wavelet [7] is applied to extract features. The second stage is feature selection. Authors tested four selection methods: forward selection [2], backward selection [2], genetic algorithms [10] and Principal component analysis (PCA) [2]. At the end, a one-class SVM is used to classify the features to detect road anomalies.

Seraj et al. [16] proposed the Road pavement Anomaly Detection System (RoSDS), a smartphone-based system. Sensor data are first preprocessed to remove speed dependency by an empirical decomposition mode [9]. Like other classification-based methods, RoSDS extracts features form data. The window size is 256 samples with a 170-sample overlap for data sampled at 93 Hz or 128/85 samples with a data frequency of 43 Hz. The extracted features are:

- Time-domain: mean, variance, standard deviation, root mean square, peak to peak, zero crossing rate, mean of absolute value, correlation between the axis, tilt angles, etc.
- Frequency-domain by means of a Fast Fourier transform.
- Stationary Wavelet Transform [14].

Finally, support vector machines are applied to classify the features. The classification consists of two steps: the first step identifies the anomalous windows and the second step classifies the type of anomaly. The training is performed using labelled data consisting of 3066 windows including 2073 normal windows and 993 anomalous windows to detect the parameters.

Wolverine method [3] introduced by Bhoraskar et al. uses smartphone sensors to monitor road condition and detect bumps. Authors have proposed a reorientation using magnetometer beside accelerometer and GPS sensors. The reading of acceleration on axes of the vehicle could be recalculated by rotation matrices based on Gravity vector, Magnetic vector and vehicle motion direction. A bump detection method and a braking detection method based on an SVM classifier [1] has been proposed in Wolverine. Reoriented accelerometer data are devised into 1 s duration windows (i.e 50 samples). Several features are computed from these windows: means and standard deviations in three axes (μ_x, μ_y, μ_z, σ_x, σ_y and σ_z) which are used to detect bumps and three difference values (δ_x, δ_y and δ_z) which are used for the braking detection. Features δ_x, δ_y and δ_z are defined as follows:

$$\delta_x = \max a_x - \min a_x \qquad \forall a_x \in \text{window}$$
$$\delta_y = \max a_y - \min a_y \qquad \forall a_y \in \text{window}$$
$$\delta_z = \max a_z - \min a_z \qquad \forall a_z \in \text{window}$$

The features are then classified by SVM to predict the vehicle state. In order to create labelled data for SVM training, authors used the K-means clustering algorithm to classify the features into two classes and manually labelled smooth or bumpy (for bump detection) and "brake" or not (for braking detection).

4   Comparison of Road Anomaly Detection Methods

This section presents an analysis of some of the methods developed above for the purpose of examining the relevance of such methods when installed on a smartphone. The results are not compared as each research was examined on separate data. The comparison is made in terms of resource requirements, ability to adapt to different road conditions, vehicle type and speed. Table 1 qualitatively summarizes the results of the evaluation.

4.1   Memory and Computational Resources

The first part of this section is dedicated to the resource requirements as this determines the power consumption of the smartphone. However, note that most of the detection methods need a training. The training needs to be realised one time and it can be performed on computers. Thus, there is no need to mention the resources needed for the training or for the experiments. As a result, only the detection after the training, that can be executed on a smartphone, is considered.

Threshold-Based Methods. All these algorithms require the least memory and computational resources. As the algorithms use direct data gathered from sensors, the current window is the only one that needs to be stored in memory. In addition, the complexity of these threshold-based algorithms is quite small.

- The P^2 *system.* Assume n is the number of acceleration samples captured on the entire road that need to be monitored. The signal is segmented into windows of size k. Each window passes through five filters. For filters *speed*, *High-pass*, *z peak* and *speed vs. z ratio*, the detector has to loop through windows one time only. However, for filter *xz-ratio*, the program first searches for the peak on the z-axis of acceleration and then, for each peak of the z-acceleration, it searches for a peak on the x axis of the acceleration in $\triangle w$. Since the size of $\triangle w$ is composed of only 32 samples, the complexity of the z-acceleration peak filter is $O(k)$. As a result, the complexity of the algorithm becomes $O(n)$.
- The *Nericell system* uses a sliding window. The time complexity of the algorithm is $n \times k$ where n is the total number of acceleration samples and k is the window size. As a result, the complexity is $O(k \times n)$.
- For the *bump detector*, both z-peak and z-sus cases may loop through samples one time. Thus, the complexity of bump detector is $O(n)$. When two detectors are applied, the total complexity becomes $O(n \times k)$. Authors chose a window size of 4 s, i.e. $k = 4 \times f$, where f is the frequency of the accelerometer.
- Mednis et al. also proposed four different algorithms. One can easily domnstrate that the complexity for three first ones, namely *Z-THRESH*, *Z-DIFF* and *G-ZERO* is $O(n)$. For *STDEV(Z)*, the complexity is $O(n * k)$ where k is the window size, since the standard deviation must be computed on a sliding window. However, the complexity of *STDEV(Z)* may be reduced to $O(n)$ if the standard deviation can be progressively computed.
- The algorithm proposed by Vittorio et al. [18] is the same as *Z-THRESH* ans its complexity is $O(n)$.

Classification Methods. In contrast to the previous algorithms, these methods require much more resources. Moreover, all the following algorithms share a common aspect: before being proceed, the data from the sensors are first divided into windows. Then, a feature extraction method such as a *Fast Fourier Transformation* (FFT) or a *Wavelet Packet Decomposition* (WPD) is applied. After the feature selection, a classification using SVM (for Support Vector Machine) is done.

- Perttunen et al. [15] have used several tools like Kalman filters, FFTs, linear dependence methods and/or SVM with many extracted features.
- In Cong et al. [5], WPD is used to extract the features, then one selection feature method is applied, and finally a SVM is executed.
- FFT, Stationary Wavelet Transform and SVM are also used in RoSDS [16].
- Wolverine [3] is the least computationally intensive method in the set of classification-based methods. Nine features are computed from the windows and are classified using a SVM.

In short, these methods require more memory and computation. Therefore, if these methods would be deployed on a smartphone, they would consume a lot of energy. In addition, the detection program should run in the background. If the program takes up too much resources, they can be prioritized and/or cleaned by the operating system.

Processing time is also a factor to be considered. Typically, a condition for which an algorithm can execute in real time without losing data is that the processing time of a data block is smaller than the time between two block arrivals. Moreover, the anomaly detection program should not take up a large portion of the smartphone's processor.

4.2   Adaptation to Real Conditions

One of the main challenges for road-anomaly detection algorithms based on vibrations is that aptitude and vibration frequency both depend on road conditions, speed, vehicle type and suspension system quality, etc.

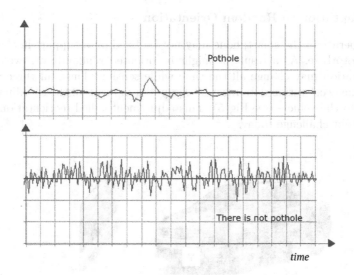

Fig. 4. Two different examples of road conditions

Current Threshold-Based Algorithms are Less Adaptable to Real Conditions. They use fixed thresholds and compare sensed data to peak values or the standard deviation of vertical values of acceleration data to find out road anomalies. Although these thresholds are determined from experiments or machine learning, they cannot be applied to all conditions where the magnitude and the standard deviation of the acceleration depend on the velocity, the road type and/or the vehicle type. As shown on Fig. 4, the amplitude of the acceleration (vertical component from the accelerometer) as the vehicle enters the pothole is smaller than in the other cases when the car does not pass through the pothole, but is driven on the worse roads. In both cases, cars run at about 7 m/s. As a result, a dynamic threshold, that would adapt to the quality of the road, would be far more appropriate for these algorithms. A dynamic threshold would be computed/adapted regularly to suit the current road conditions.

Classification-Based Methods Promise Better Adaptability. Window classifications based on many attributes allow a better identification of potholes under different conditions of speed, quality, etc.

However, to be able to classify accurately, training data should be a combination of different types of roads and vehicles at different speeds. In fact, building a complete labelled data set is practically difficult. It might be interesting to consider unsupervised learning approaches to improve the training. In addition, the training should be done in a data center and the parameters later uploaded on the smartphone to save energy.

4.3   Adaptation to Random Orientation

During operation, the smartphone may not be fixed on a support in the car or on the motorbike. As a result, it might be oriented randomly or, even worse, the orientation may change all the time while sensing. Thus, all three components of the acceleration data must be computed in terms of the coordinate axes attached to the vehicle (see Fig. 5). This adjustment called reorientation is also an important challenge today.

Fig. 5. The coordinate system of the car and of the phone do not coincide.

Tools have been used to determine the orientation of a smartphone, like Euler angles [13,18] or rotation matrices [3]. The general idea for determining the direction of a smartphone is based on two directions: the first one consists in considering the vertical direction that can be determined from gravity, and the second one is the motion direction. In [13], the motion direction is determined when there is a braking on the straight line as the deceleration is necessarily in the direction of the rotation. Another way to determine the motion direction consists in using the magnetic sensors: the combination of the magnetic vector and the vehicle motion direction (based for example on the GPS) allows to determine the angle of the smartphone deviation from the vehicle [3].

In fact, determining the orientation of the smartphone may face some difficulties. For example, the use of the vehicle braking to determine the vehicle direction from the smartphone may not be straightforward. If the smartphone is rotated but the vehicle does not change the speed at the same time or if it does not move in a straight line, one cannot determine the vehicle direction from the acceleration data. If the motion direction is determined using a magnetic sensor, the main difficulty is that many smartphones do not include such a magnetic sensor... Moreover, it is also important to bear in mind that a magnetic sensor may produce inaccurate results when located close to iron, which is often the case in a vehicle.

4.4 Removal of User Actions

At last, another very important element always omitted in the literature is the exclusion of the actions taken by the smartphone's user. Mohan et al. [13] are able to detect user interactions by looking for pressed keys, mouse events and/or phone calls. However, the user can move the smartphone without typing any key and/or touching the screen. In order to overcome this issue, it seems necessary to take into account the variations of the acceleration vector to identify the unusual motions of the device.

Table 1. Summary of methods based on features that are suitable for smartphones.

Method	Complexity	Memory[1]	Conditions[2]	Orientation[3]
Threshold-based methods				
Pothole Patrol [8]	Low	Low	Low	Low
Nericell [13]	Low	Low	Low	Good
Algorithm Z-THRESH Z-DIFF, STDEV(Z) [12]	Low	Low	Low	Good
Algorithm G-ZERO[12]	Low	Low	Low	Medium
Method of Vittorio et al. [18]	Low	Low	Low	Good
Classification-based methods				
Perttunen et al. [15]	High	High	Good	Medium
Method of Cong et al. [5]	High	Medium	Medium	Medium
RoSDS [16]	High	Medium	Medium	Medium
Wolverine [3]	Medium	Medium	Medium	Good

[1]Use of the memory—[2]Adaptation to real conditions—[3]Adaptation to random orientation

5 Conclusion and Future Work

Connecting smartphones to take advantage of their sensors to monitor road condition promises to be widely applied in the near future. This field of research has been active for few years and several researches have been conducted in this way. However, no method has proven enough accuracy to be used in widespread applications. This article explored the different pothole detection methods that have been released so far and presented both advantages and drawbacks. We showed that threshold-based methods require the least resources but are less adapted to effective road conditions. As a conclusion, we suggest using dynamic thresholds for these methods. For the classification-based methods, data required for the training are usually quite large. In the future, it shall be considered to train these algorithms at a data center constantly and then send the parameters back to the smartphones.

In the future, we will concentrate on determining the best way to divide the data processing between smartphones and datacenters to reduce communications and limit energy consumption.

References

1. Support vector machine. https://en.wikipedia.org/wiki/Support_vector_machine
2. Alpaydin, E.: Introduction to Machine Learning. Adaptive Computation and Machine Learning, 2nd edn. MIT Press, New York (2010)
3. Bhoraskar, R., Vankadhara, N., Raman, B., Kulkarni, P.: Wolverine: traffic and road condition estimation using smartphone sensors. In: 2012 Fourth International Conference on Communication Systems and Networks (COMSNETS), pp. 1–6. IEEE (2012)
4. Chugh, G., Bansal, D., Sofat, S.: Road condition detection using smartphone sensors: a survey. Int. J. Electron. Electr. Eng. 7(6), 595–602 (2014)
5. Cong, F., et al.: Applying wavelet packet decomposition and one-class support vector machine on vehicle acceleration traces for road anomaly detection. In: Guo, C., Hou, Z.-G., Zeng, Z. (eds.) ISNN 2013. LNCS, vol. 7951, pp. 291–299. Springer, Heidelberg (2013). https://doi.org/10.1007/978-3-642-39065-4_36
6. Cortes, C., Vapnik, V.: Support-vector networks. Mach. Learn. 20(3), 273–297 (1995)
7. Daubechies, I.: Ten Lectures on Wavelets. Society for Industrial and Applied Mathematics, Philadelphia (1992)
8. Eriksson, J., Girod, L., Hull, B., Newton, R., Madden, S., Balakrishnan, H.: The pothole patrol: using a mobile sensor network for road surface monitoring. In: Proceedings of the 6th International Conference on Mobile Systems, Applications, and Services, pp. 29–39. ACM (2008)
9. Feldman, M.: Signal Demodulation. Wiley, New York (2011)
10. Holland, J.H.: Adaptation in Natural and Artificial Systems: An Introductory Analysis with Application to Biology, Control, and Artificial Intelligence, pp. 439–444. University of Michigan Press, Ann Arbor (1975)
11. Kim, T., Ryu, S.K.: Review and analysis of pothole detection methods. J. Emerg. Trends Comput. Inf. Sci. 5(8), 603–608 (2014)
12. Mednis, A., Strazdins, G., Zviedris, R., Kanonirs, G., Selavo, L.: Real time pothole detection using android smartphones with accelerometers. In: 2011 International Conference on Distributed Computing in Sensor Systems and Workshops (DCOSS), pp. 1–6. IEEE (2011)
13. Mohan, P., Padmanabhan, V.N., Ramjee, R.: Nericell: rich monitoring of road and traffic conditions using mobile smartphones. In: Proceedings of the 6th ACM Conference on Embedded Network Sensor Systems, pp. 323–336. ACM (2008)

14. Nason, G.P., Silverman, B.W.: The stationary wavelet transform and some statistical applications. In: Antoniadis, A., Oppenheim, G. (eds.) Wavelets and Statistics. LNS, vol. 103, pp. 281–299. Springer, New York (1995). https://doi.org/10.1007/978-1-4612-2544-7_17

15. Perttunen, M., et al.: Distributed road surface condition monitoring using mobile phones. In: Hsu, C.-H., Yang, L.T., Ma, J., Zhu, C. (eds.) UIC 2011. LNCS, vol. 6905, pp. 64–78. Springer, Heidelberg (2011). https://doi.org/10.1007/978-3-642-23641-9_8

16. Seraj, F., van der Zwaag, B.J., Dilo, A., Luarasi, T., Havinga, P.: RoADS: a road pavement monitoring system for anomaly detection using smart phones. In: Atzmueller, M., Chin, A., Janssen, F., Schweizer, I., Trattner, C. (eds.) Big Data Analytics in the Social and Ubiquitous Context. LNCS (LNAI), vol. 9546, pp. 128–146. Springer, Cham (2016). https://doi.org/10.1007/978-3-319-29009-6_7

17. Tanaka, N., Okamoto, H., Naito, M.: Detecting and evaluating intrinsic nonlinearity present in the mutual dependence between two variables. Phys. D: Nonlinear Phenom. **147**(1–2), 1–11 (2000)

18. Vittorio, A., Rosolino, V., Teresa, I., Vittoria, C.M., Vincenzo, P.G., et al.: Automated sensing system for monitoring of road surface quality by mobile devices. Procedia - Soc. Behav. Sci. **111**, 242–251 (2014)

Quality of Service Applied to Li-Fi Networks in 5th Generation Environments

Jesús Manuel Paternina Durán[1], Octavio José Salcedo Parra[1,2]([⊠]), and Danilo Alfonso López Sarmiento[1]

[1] Faculty of Engineering, Internet Inteligente Research Group, Universidad Distrital "Francisco José de Caldas", Bogotá, D.C., Colombia
{jmpaterninad, osalcedo, dalopezs}@udistrital.edu.co
[2] Department of Systems and Industrial Engineering, Faculty of Engineering, Universidad Nacional de Colombia, Bogotá, D.C., Colombia
ojsalcedop@unal.edu.co

Abstract. This document corresponds the application of services that requires QoS in Li-Fi networks oriented towards 5th generation networks. This work served as the basis to establish the quality assurance of this type of networks in a methodology that will be described in detail in a future publication. It's taking into account the inherent characteristics of these technologies.

Keywords: Li-Fi · 5G · QoS · NS-2

1 Introduction

In today's world, wireless communications handle such high percentage of users and information that focusing efforts in research and innovation is crucial in this sector of technology. The major telecommunication operators aim their initiatives at meeting the high demand needs of all markets and industries. Technologies of 4th and 5th generation are present in most countries, however, some of their advantages have not been used in the best way. Consequently, it is of vital importance to start working on analyses and evaluations focused on obtaining the requirements of the networks and their integration, which is a fundamental feature that provides a greater bandwidth and processing possibilities of decentralization. Special emphasis was placed on the MAC layer and physical characteristics of the Li-fi networks to obtain similar conditions to the real ones. The results were compared with three research documents that allowed establishing the viability of the proposed algorithm.

2 Background

IntServ (Integrated Services) has been known since 1990, supporting this feature for end-to-end services. The resources were pre-reserved while traffic was transferred between the two nodes. The resources were reserved according to priorities for each new session. The packages had to be processed in each intermediate node to locate the corresponding resources [1].

© Springer Nature Switzerland AG 2019
É. Renault et al. (Eds.): MSPN 2018, LNCS 11005, pp. 98–106, 2019.
https://doi.org/10.1007/978-3-030-03101-5_9

Differentiated services (Diffserv) were introduced to provide greater efficiency and less complexity in the systems for extensive networks. Diffserv applies packet classification in the autonomous computers of the network. It provides QoS end-to end, which is based on aggregation of PHB traffic. Traffic is categorized into flows to which a codepoint is assigned according to the way in which the resources of the system will interconnect with the routing equipment.

In the Diffserve architecture, there is a Classification, Marking, metric and scheduling process. The first interaction with the incoming packets is presented in the classification. The classification rules are specified according to several parameters. The classifier marks the packets according to the specified rules. In the marking, the traffic is differentiated to which no profile was assigned. The marking is done with DS codepoints in the IP packet header.

In the process of the metric the decisions are made according to modification or discarding of packages. Here we store data like the current rat, the size of the buffer, etc.; and also, it is checked if the traffic obtained an appropriate profile.

Once the package has been classified and marked, it is sent to the corresponding queue. Here the transmission of the package to the medium is scheduled [1]. This antecedent in traffic treatment to provide QoS to networks is a fundamental part of the present work since it allowed to determine the way in which a algortimo can interject with the specific process, in this specific case, the process of QoS over communication networks.

3   Selection of Tools and Simulation Criteria

In this section, the simulation criteria established to implement QoS in Li-Fi networks over 5th generation environments are mentioned. Taking into account that the methodology was oriented solely towards the quality of service in terms of Li-Fi networks, it was necessary to delimit the observation framework in items to relate this optical network with 5th generation environments. This relationship is found in Table 1.

Table 1. Simulation criteria.

Criterion	Definition
Efficient use of the spectrum	This is evidenced by the efficient use of technologies, as in this case, optical frequencies in wireless environments. At this point it is important to highlight the importance of load balancing mechanisms that allow an efficient interaction between conventional radiofrequency networks and Li-Fi networks. Additionally, the simulation tools must be adapted to multiple optical connection environments without guided media (Li-Fi Networks)

(continued)

Table 1. (*continued*)

Criterion	Definition
Low latency	The delay in the networks is what is commonly known as latency. One of the fundamental parameters in 5th generation networks will be a very low latency. This is one of the fundamental criteria to guarantee quality of service in terms of a good perception of it, including in this latter part additional criteria such as network availability and coverage
Coverage and perception of the service	The most important limitation in Li-Fi networks is the need for line of sight to guarantee the communication process. With this in mind, one of the challenges in the simulation process lay in the correct arrangement of scenarios and their interpretation in terms of algorithm development, focusing this analysis on latency metrics, availability times and load balancing

For the development of the methodology, the chosen simulation tool allowed to guarantee the representation of the aforementioned metrics. Initially, in terms of network infrastructure, it was determined that this should include at least wireless radio frequency scenarios and visible optical connections. These scenarios would allow adjustments in frequency ranges. Additionally, the tool had to have the property of delimiting areas and interaction with optical signals to guarantee the reflection effects of light fronts on specific media, a parameter of special importance for the analysis of the behavior of the optical communications process. The losses due to refraction, diffraction or reflection of the light did not form part of the object of the present investigation, reason why this parameter was not taken into account for the selection of the tool.

Table 2. Simulation tools.

Tool	Observation
Opnet (riverbed)	It requires a license and does not allow modification of libraries and protocols. It has a high learning time but its robustness makes it very reliable
NS-2	Does not require licensing. He has an enthusiastic support community. It allows modification of protocols and changes in models from the coding point of view is very agile. It is reliable and highly used by the academic community
Omnet ++	Does not require licensing. It is reliable and highly used by the academic community. Modular configuration and programming based on C++. An important effort is required to create the simulation scenarios, but in specialized forums they agree that it is the most robust tool
Estinet	Requires license. It has a short learning time but does not allow modification of libraries

From the point of view of required protocols, the protocols for the transmission of video in streaming mode and real time are of certain relevance for the analysis, being their presence in the configuration parameters of the simulation tool to a certain extent necessary for get an approximation as close as possible to reality. Table 2 lists the verified tools.

For the reasons mentioned above, the NS-2 tool was chosen for the development of the project. The relevant point for this decision was the agility in the process for coding changes in the model.

4 Definition of QoS Metrics and Services

The metrics chosen for the analysis, according to the specific objectives, were the following: Latency, packet loss and bandwidth. The analysis of the set of these metrics allowed to identify the perception of the end user with respect to the services in real time mentioned above.

The QoS services that were validated in the development of the project should be those that require greater network characteristics for the end users. These are undoubtedly real-time traffic services, Voice over IP, video and streaming. For purposes of the work, the traffic of video streaming through UDP packets was specifically analyzed, because many of the entertainment applications use this service to broadcast content.

With respect to QoS, the following processes were taken into account for the treatment of real-time traffic in the Li-Fi network:

a. Marking and classification
b. Policing and Droping
c. Queuing and Scheduling
d. Shaping
e. Post-Queuing.

5 Algorithm Design

Starting from the flow diagram of the previous section, we proceeded to design a new algorithm that would allow to establish QoS on optical media, in this case Li-Fi networks, this with respect to the latency, packet loss and bandwidth metrics.

This new algorithm relied on the development of mathematical modeling based on the interaction of each of the components involved in the communication process.

It is important to bear in mind that one of the main differences between the simplified algortimo of the previous section and this algortimo proposal, lies in the processes carried out in the stages of policy identification, Dropping and queuing. This difference is based on the specific needs of the environment that are fundamental in these stages. The visible light spectrum for Li-Fi networks should also be taken into account, which is between 400 and 800 THz, in addition to the characteristics specified in the IEEE 802.15.7 standard.

For modeling, the following considerations were taken into account:

- Components: Transmitter, receiver and medium. All these elements are optical and open air, respectively.
- Descriptive variables: Latency, packet loss and bandwidth (QoS metrics)
- Identification of interaction rules: Packages must pass a marking and classification process to prioritize services. Privilege processing rules should be assigned according to the identified service. Subsequently, Policing, Dropping and Queuing processes must be executed to improve the perception of services in real time by end users.
- Descriptive parameters of the interactions: The interactions between the afore-mentioned processes and the marked packets are given by the characteristics of the Li-Fi network, from the point of view of bandwidth, latency and packet loss, in addition to the layer of liaison and physics, the latter described in detail in standard 802.15.7.

According to the limitations expressed in the previous sections, this algorithm allowed a better management of real-time service traffic for Li-Fi networks. A comparison of the proposed algorithm with the conventional results of Token Bucket with two token storage containers was carried out. The variation lies mainly in the treatment of the packets before assigning the corresponding token. One of the most important achievements in the development of Token bucket for QoS had been the implementation of a low priority traffic allocation in high priority queues based on the availability of space, this without affecting the performance of the routing elements, improving in this way the loss of packages [2].

Two physical buckets are proposed, taking into account that a greater number of containers would increase the level of processing, but the main innovation lies in the fact that apart from making an evaluation of space in the bucket and the tail according to the present traffic in a dynamic way, the optical characteristics of Li-Fi networks are included in the analysis, which demand agile procedures.

As there is currently no specific standard for Li-Fi, it is important to mention that the proposed algorithm (OLLQ) is based on the general needs to provide QoS in communications networks.

Initially, in the classification process, the kind of service that could be treated should be taken into account. Very probably, in the standard that will be socialized at the end of 2017 by the IEEE with respect to the modifications of IEEE 802.15.7, it will be necessary to specify the classes of service for the traffic of applications in real time, this for packages and arrivals of the same in variable and constant sizes and times. The treatment of the packages must also be included with respect to the best applicable effort. Additionally, due to the variation of the traffic pattern, parameters must be taken into account that define the minimum transfer rate that is required for the applications to remain functional, in addition to the maximum rate that should not be exceeded for the defined time intervals.

For purposes of the OLLA algorithm, the following classes of service shall be taken into account for the purposes of multimedia traffic in Li-Fi networks:

- Service for real-time applications with packet sizes and constant arrivals.
- Service for real-time applications with constant packet sizes and variable arrivals.
- Service for real-time applications with packet sizes and variable arrivals.
- Finally, best effort service for applications that are not in real time and do not require QoS guarantees.

Once the package is classified, the metrics that will apply for the optical Token Bucket process are calculated. These metrics are associated with the maximum and minimum average bandwidth, the size of the packets and the information associated with the service class defined in the previous step.

The decisions made in the optical Token Bucket process will make the packages marked for their queuing according to priorities. Finally, the package will be scheduled to exit to the corresponding interface.

Taking into account that 4 types of packet flows will be presented, the proposal is based on four queues for data processing. As the resources are limited, we worked 2 queues of physical type and 4 queues of virtual type, which will finally receive traffic dynamically. The packet flow will be assigned to certain queues according to conditions of availability of buffers and queues. This adaptive management with respect to changing data flow conditions will allow effective management of resources for Li-Fi networks.

6   Algorithm Simulation

Before starting the simulation process on the NS-2 tool, matlab tests and processing of the states raised in the previous section were made in Matlab with respect to the optical Bucket Token, the latter being the main object of code analysis and the starting point for further development, this also because Li-fi technology is so recent that the real data for comparison are extremely scarce.

6.1   Simulation in Ns-2

For the purposes of the simulation in the NS-2 tool, software version 2.35 of November 2011, downloaded directly from the NS 2 website, was used. The software was implemented on an operating system Ubuntu version 16.04 of 64 bits, which in turn was installed on a VMware virtual machine type Workstation Pro version 12.5.0.

For the purposes of the work done, it is important to highlight that the ns-2 tool has native protocols, which can be used in the development of a algortimo or, failing that, can be modified from its source code with some specific procedures. It started from the need to modify the conventional Token Bucket algortimo, identified as TBF (Token Bucket Filter) inside the tool in the "adc" folder located in the following route: / home/ns-allinone-2.35/ns-2.35/adc.

The following simulation corresponds to the implementation of the Token Bucket Optical algortimo according to the proposal of the work with a Li-Fi scenario, responding to needs of 5th Generation.

The scenario of the simulation and its respective justification are described below:

- Five nodes are located in the space (n0 to n4) without a wired connection. Four of these elements represent Li-Fi users, with the remaining being the access point (or LED lamp). In this simulation scenario, five elements are established by the effects of conventional disposition in a determined enclosure. The relevance in the connectivity lies in the line of sight of the devices and light power of the central node. The number of nodes and their arrangement in the space is due to the electrical characteristics of the devices, taking into account VLC type communications and possible smart applications in the remaining devices.
- The nodes are arranged in such a way that all the packets between them must necessarily pass through the central node, which is the Access Point of the Li-Fi network. This arrangement of the elements around the central device is based on the VLC facilities, the basis for this work of Li-Fi communications. The differences between the packet flows in this node will be crucial to determine the success of the proposal.
- Modify the characteristics of the netif variables with respect to the bandwidth and MAC characteristics of the network so that this wireless network has the characteristics of a Li-Fi network. This is done in this way to take advantage of the algorithms developed in the simulator by the community.
- Initially, a simulation is performed without preferential treatment of data. With this, a point of reference with respect to the performance of the proposed algorithm is sought.

In the following simulation, the data with optical bucket token is sent on nodes 1 and 3 to compare the differences with respect to the initial traffic treatment (Table 3).

Table 3. Results of Li-Fi network simulation with optical token bucket.

Node	Discarded packages	Failed packages	Packages received	Packages sent	Total packages
_0_	39	0	13546	13540	27125
_1_	0	0	7223	7238	14461
_2_	3	0	9717	9730	19450
_3_	0	0	6294	6309	12603
_4_	15	0	9722	9722	19459
Grand total	57	0	46502	46539	93098

Additionally, Fig. 1 shows the behavior of the packets in the network to determine the performance of the same from the point of view of the bandwidth for Li-Fi network.

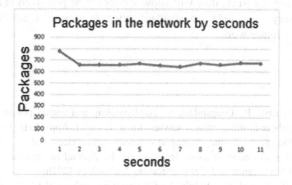

Fig. 1. Packages in the network by seconds.

7 Results Analysis

The performance of the Li-Fi work network is taken with respect to the number of packets that were taken on the network. It is possible to determine that the packet average per second is 671 packets. With this value a performance of 38.5% is obtained, but it is important to emphasize that the number of failed packages is null. With respect to the reference article, there is a decrease in the performance of the network but the quality of the link increases because the collision of packets disappears.

Finally, the delays object of comparison of [3], of the third article of reference; added, allow to obtain the latency of the system. The minimum delay is 105 ms and the maximum delay is 2 s. In the reference article tests are performed with different gluing configurations, so it is assumed that the delays vary according to the performance of the configurations, but it is clear that in the best of cases, the best response was obtained in the 105 ms. In the simulation object of this work, the minimum delay was 8.4 us and the maximum of 137.7 us. By a quite wide margin a very good response with respect to the delays of the packages is evidenced.

8 Conclusions

Through the use of the mechanisms proposed in this work, it was possible to obtain delays less than the 105 ms proposed as a reference. The delays obtained are in the order of the microseconds, evidencing an appropriate management of the criteria present in the proposed methodology. With the results obtained in the present work, it is possible to affirm that Li-Fi networks are a real option in the context of communication networks that will improve the use of spectrum, since their frequency of operation does not currently have services and has all the potential of integration with conventional networks through load balancing. From the point of view of the coverage and perception of the service, with the results of the simulation it is clear that a correct line of sight of the communication elements and the application of the mechanisms proposed in the present work, they will allow services to be perceived in a correct way, but it is necessary to include the standardization features that are close to being socialized within future work.

References

1. Kulhari, A., Avinash, P., Deepshikha, S.: Implementing and testing priority scheduler and token bucket policer in differentiated service. Int. J. Comput. Appl. **101**(13) (2014)
2. Kulhari, A., Pandey, A.: Traffic shaping at differentiated services enabled edge router using adaptive packet allocation to router input queue. In: Second International Conference on Computational Intelligence and Communication Technology (2016)
3. Bahaweres, R.B., Ahmad, F., Mudrik, A.: Comparative analysis of LLQ traffic scheduler to FIFO and CBWFQ on IP phone-based applications (VoIP) using Opnet (Riverbed). In: 2015 1st International Conference on Wireless and Telematics (ICWT). IEEE (2015)

Mobile Agent System Based Cloud Computing for Ubiquitous Telemonitoring Healthcare

Nardjes Bouchemal[1,2(✉)], Ramdane Maamri[2], and Naila Bouchemal[3]

[1] University Center of Mila, Mila, Algeria
n.bouchemal.dz@ieee.org
[2] LIRE Laboratory of Constantine2, Constantine, Algeria
ramdane.maamri@univ-constantine2.dz
[3] Altran Technology of Paris, Paris, France
naila.bouchemal@altran.com

Abstract. Distributed computing through a handheld/mobile device has to be considered with carefulness because of the limited capabilities on these devices. Especially in Ubiquitous Telemonitoring Healthcare, which refers to the disposition of any type of health services such that medical staff members, through mobile computing devices, can access them and expect data to be made available. In this paper, we present a new system based on mobile agent to assist monitor physician and cloud computing concept to allow him easy storage and remote access of healthcare data.

Keywords: Ubiquitous Telemonitoring Healthcare · Agent technology
Cloud computing

1 Introduction

Ubiquitous telemonitoring healthcare refers to the disposition of any type of health services such that individual consumers through mobile computing devices can access them.

Patients will be monitored at long distance, and medical control support devices may be embedded in devices collecting vital-sign information from sensors (blood pressure, temperature, etc.), [15–17].

It is clear that these systems must have special characteristics such as permanent connection, storage capability for patient's healthcare information and intelligence.

That requires the introduction of new technologies such as cloud computing for the storage and accessibility and intelligent agent for the assistance and decisions.

Indeed, cloud computing has become a vital tool in the healthcare field for better collaboration. It allows easy storage and remote access of healthcare data to professionals, [19].

The other key aspect is the use of context-aware technologies. It is not enough to gather information about the context, but that information must be processed by self-adaptable and dynamic mechanisms and methods that can react independently of each particular situation that arises.

É. Renault et al. (Eds.): MSPN 2018, LNCS 11005, pp. 107–116, 2019.
https://doi.org/10.1007/978-3-030-03101-5_10

In this sense, agents and Multi-Agent Systems comprise one of the areas that can contribute expanding the possibilities of ubiquitous healthcare systems and telemonitoring systems.

An agent can be defined as a computational system situated in an environment and is able to act autonomously in this environment to achieve its design goals [18].

But the use of the cloud concept and agents technology does not guaranty a permanent connection with the medical staff. Indeed, in the context of ubiquitous environments devices have reduced energy autonomy, storage capability and can be off-line at any time.

For that, we propose in this paper an approach based on Mobile Agent System and Cloud Computing, we called it MAC system (for Mobile Agent and Cloud).

Indeed, such as many other users, monitor physician is surrounded by many mobile and ubiquitous devices. We want to take advantages of this diversity to guaranty a permanent connection.

The goal of the mobile agent is to recognize medical employee devices and to migrate from one device to another in order to connect him with his patients.

On the other hand, the goal of the cloud is to hold a maximum of data. Cloud computing can improve medical services and benefit biomedical research providing Centralization, Collaboration and Virtualization, [19].

The rest of the paper is organized as follows: Sect. 2 summarizes some works based on the use of agents in telemonitoring systems. We present in Sect. 3 our contribution: MAC system, the implementation and experimentations on JADE-LEAP. Finally, some conclusions are drawn.

2   Related Work

Intelligent agents have the ability to make decisions defined by their inherent properties, such as: reactivity, pro-activity and sociability. These properties are intended to enable the agent to meet the objectives for which they were designed, following rules of behavior that enable them to communicate with their environment [18]. Recent research has discussed the benefits of using agent technology and applications in the health care and telemonitoring domain [5].

De Paz et al. presented a project: Autonomous aGent for monitoring ALZheimer's patients (AGALZ), which facilitates the monitoring and tracking of patients with Alzheimer's [4].

A telemonitoring system aimed at enhancing remote healthcare of dependent people at their homes has also been developed. The main contribution is the use of an experimental architecture that allows the interconnection of heterogeneous Wireless Sensor Networks [14].

De Meo et al. presented multi-agent system that supports personalized patient access to health care services. The proposed system combines submitted queries with the corresponding patient profiles to identify services likely to satisfy patient needs and desires [6].

Vaidehi et al. presented a design for a health care monitoring system based on multi-agent and wireless sensor networks which can collect, retrieve, store and analyze patient vital signs. The multi-agent system is applied to manage these sensors and to collect and store data in a database [9].

Camarinha-Matos and Vieira presented an MA-based architecture for health care centers to remotely observe and help elderly people living alone at home [3].

Wu et al. proposed a multi-agent web service framework based on a service-oriented architecture to support qualified and optimized medical data translation in an e-healthcare information system [8].

Su and Wu designed a highly distributed information infrastructure—MADIP—by using the multi-agent and MA paradigm, which can automatically notify the responsible care-provider of abnormalities, offer remote medical advice, and perform continuous health monitoring as needed [10].

Kim proposed a methodology for the design and implementation of u-healthcare, linking distributed mobile agents with medical entities into acollaborative environment [11].

Authors in [2] presents the design and development of a mobile multi-agent platform based open information systems (IMAIS)with an automated diagnosis engine to support intensive and distributed ubiquitous fetalmonitoring.

In most of presented systems, permanent connection is needed with healthcare staff. It is easy when using traditional wire-based communication systems, where users are connected to their desk PC.

But nowadays, users (including healthcare staff) need to have information anywhere and anytime to monitor patients and disabled persons.

For this, most of existing systems introduce ubiquitous devices and agents concept, but the problem is when these devices are offline (ex. problem of connection or insufficient battery), not available or does not have enough resources, Table 1.

Table 1. Agent based healthcare and tele-monitoring systems analysis

Systems	Domain	Type of agents	Ubiquitous devices	Devices limitation considered		
				Autonomy of energy	Connection quality	Storage quality
De Meo et al. [6]	Personalized e-Health service access	Stationary	Yes	No	Low	Low
Wu et al. [8]	Medical data transmission	Stationary	Yes	No	Low	Low
Vaidehi [9]	In-home monitoring	Stationary	Yes	No	Low	Low
De Paz et al. [4]	In-home monitoring	Mobile	Yes	No	Medium	Low
Su and Wu [10]	Health care monitoring	Mobile	Yes	No	Low	Low
Alonso et al. [14]	Health care monitoring	Stationary	Yes	No	Low	Low
Kim [11]	Ubiquitous health care systems	Mobile	Yes	No	Low	Low
Su and Chu [2]	Ubiquitous fetal monitoring	Mobile	Yes	No	Low	Low

3 MAC System: Mobile Agent System Based Cloud Computing

The monitor physician, such as most of today's users, has many handheld devices (smart phones, laptops, tablet, smart swatch, etc.) that provide him access to patient information.

The process may operate even if devices have limited energy capabilities or have no connectivity.

The idea is to connect monitor physician with his patients anywhere and anytime, through Mobile Agent and the cloud, [20]. Mobile agent can migrate from one device to another and takes advantages from all of them especially in case of energy insufficiency or failure connectivity. To resolve the problem of limited storage space, we introduce the cloud.

3.1 The System Components

The system is composed essentially of three parts: Monitor physician, Patients and the Cloud.

At the monitor physician level, we create Mobile Agent (*MA*) and Device Agent (*DevA*) embedded in each device.

In patients' side, we propose Patient Agent (*PatA*) for assistance, information collection and communication assurance with the monitor physician (*MA*).

We use cloud computing concept to assure healthcare data storage and mobile communications.

For that, we create cloud manager agent (*CMA*) to manage messages, information and to guarantee the communication between *MA* and *PatA*, Fig. 1. Below, we detail each component.

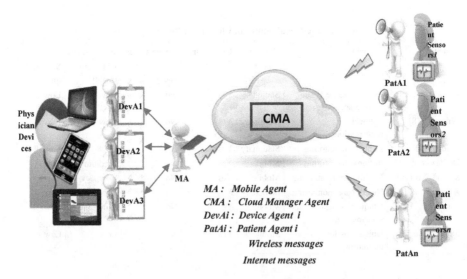

Fig. 1. Components of MAC system (case of n patients)

- *Mobile Agent (MA)*.
  - MA has the list of monitor physician devices: *ListDevice* = {*D1, D2,..,Dn*}. It is initially embedded on one of them (ex. smart phone).
  - MA establishes a wireless network including all *ListDevice* devices.
  - MA must have a permanent communication with the patient through Patient Agent (*PatA*) and with devices through Device Agent (*DevA*).
  - MA has a detailed status of each device *StatusDevice* including:
    - *EnergyCapacity* (time of battery),
    - *Connected* (yes or no),
    - *StorageCapacity*.
  - *StatusDevice* is collected from Device Agents. Table 2 summarizes example of status devices of laptop, smartphone and tablet.
- *Device Agent(DevA)*.
  It is a stationary agent embedded in each device. Its role is to collect and transmit *StatusDevice* to *MA*.
- *Patient Agent (PatA)*.
  At the patient level, we planned to install Patient Agent (*PatA*) to communicate with *MA*. It transmits health status information or alerts in emergency situations.
- *Cloud Manager Agent*.
  CMA is a stationary agent hosted in the cloud. Its role is to manage messages received from *PatA* and sent to *MA*.

Table 2. Example of **StatusDevice** of three devices

Device	Status device		
	Energy capacity	connected	Storage capacity
Lap Top	Low	Yes	Low
Smart phone	Low	No	High
Tablet	Medium	Yes	Medium

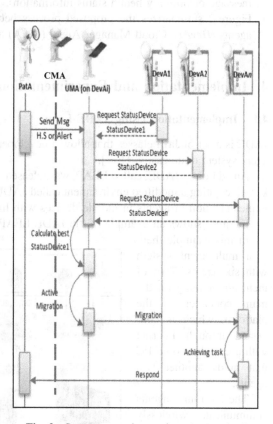

Fig. 2. System agent interactions (one patient)

3.2 Process Description

- Initially, we suppose that *MA* is embedded in *Di* from *ListDevice*.
- When **MA** receives information from *PatA* through *CMA* (Health Status or Alert Messages), it verifies capabilities of its actual device.
- If *StatusDevice* is weak (example: *EnergyCapacity = "low", Connected = "No"* or *StorageCapacity = "low"*), *MA* requests *StatusDevice* from all devices by contacting *DevA* of each one.
- *MA* evaluates the most powerful device, migrates and concludes its task (alert message or ordinary health status information).
- Figure 2 summarizes the proposed process between mobile agent (*MA*), device agents *(DevAi)*, Cloud Manager Agent (*CMA*) and patient agent*(PatA)*.

4 Implementation and Experimentation

4.1 Implementation Using JADE-Leap

JADE is a set of Java classes that allow a developer to build a FIPA-compliant multi-agent system quite easily, [1, 7].

An add-on to JADE, called LEAP, was released. It replaces some parts of the JADE kernel, creating a modified environment called JADE-LEAP [12, 13], which allows the implementation of agents in mobile devices with limited resources.

Figure 3 shows an example of the JADE-LEAP execution environment.

In this example there is a multi-agent system with six agents. Two of them are running on the main container of the platform, which is connected through Internet with a container on a PC that holds another two agents.

These four agents communicate wirelessly with two agents running in mobile devices (one on a tablet and one on a smart phone).

Note that in JADE-LEAP each agent is represented by a container.

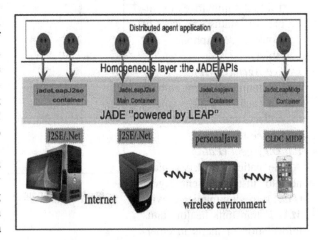

Fig. 3. JADE-leap agents' communication

The rest of programming (behaviors, messages, etc.) is identical to JADE.

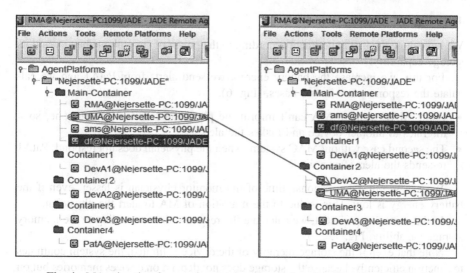

Fig. 4. MA migration from main container (smartphone) to Container2 (Tablet)

To implement the proposed system using JADE-Leap, we create agents for each device and containers as follows:

- We propose three devices to the monitor physician: Laptop, Smartphone and Tablet. So, we create three agents: **DevA1** *for* Laptop, **DevA2** for Tablet and **DevA3** for Smartphone.
- We create two patient agents: **PatA1** and **PatA2** to connect with **CMA**, (Fig. 4).
- **CMA** resides in the cloud and manages connections between **MA** and **PatAi**. The cloud is simulated by a container and **CMA** resides in it.
- **PatA1** sends information about the patient to **CMA**. It transmits this information to **MA** which was initially on the physician smartphone (Fig. 5).
- The smartphone has low battery and **MA** can't inform the physician. **MA** looks for available devices (tablet in this case), migrates and alerts the physician.
- Figure 4 presents proposed agents and containers. We can see **MA** migration from Main-container, simulating the smartphone, to Container2 simulating the tablet.

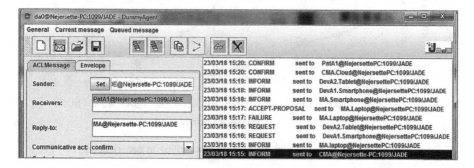

Fig. 5. Interactions of system agents using dummy agent of JADE.

4.2   Experimentation Results

We have done the first experiment according to the power of smartphone battery and its storage capability.

For this, we increase the battery energy, we send alerts from PatA1 and we calculate the response time in two cases, (Fig. 6).

- Using MAC system: MA can't inform the physician from the smartphone, so it migrates to another device and makes the alert.
- The second case without MAC system: when the physician does not respond, PatA1 re-sends the alert after a while.

We can see that the response time of the monitor physician is lesser, even if the battery energy is low. This is due to the migration of MA to alert the physician.

In the second experiment, we calculate the response time according to the memory storage capability, Fig. 7.

Note that even if the storage memory of the device is limited, the system continues to function efficiently, because the storage does not depend on devices memories but on the cloud.

We observe that even if the memory storage capability is low, the response time is less because of the use of cloud. This is not the case in the second graph showing that when the memory is not available the response time increases.

In the third experiment, we want to demonstrate that the number of messages processed is positively influenced by the number of devices. Indeed, when the number of devices increases, the AM is more likely to migrate and inform the physician. This explains the graph in Fig. 8.

This is not the case when we do not take into account the devices, because the processing of messages is done sequentially.

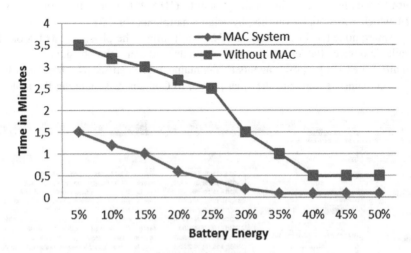

Fig. 6. Response time using MAC system according to battery energy.

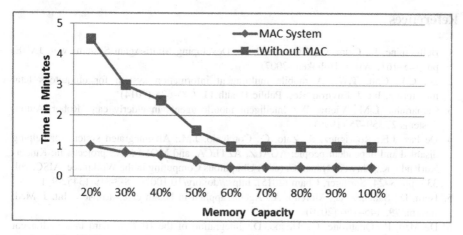

Fig. 7. Response time using MAC system according to memory capacity

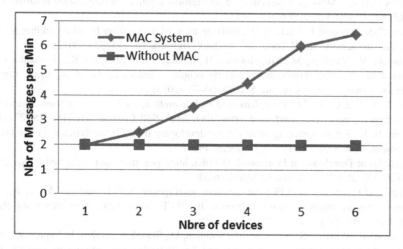

Fig. 8. Number of treated messages according to the number of devices

5 Conclusion

Mobile Agent based Cloud, or MAC system, is based on mobile agent and cloud computing in order to assist monitor physician to telemonitor his patients.

The monitor physician hands several mobile and restricted devices. The goal of MAC system is to take advantages of all devices surrounding him by allowing the mobile agent to migrate on, in order to complete its task (alerting the physician or just receiving health status information).

At patient level we designed patient agent. Its role is to have permanent communication with MA through the cloud. We have done the implementation and experimentation of our proposal using JADE-LEAP framework.

References

1. Bellifemine, F., Caire, G., Greenwood, D.: Developing Multi-Agent Systems with JADE, pp. 145–161. Wiley, Hoboken (2007)
2. Su, C.J., Chu, T.W.: A mobile multi-agent information system for ubiquitous fetal monitoring. Int. J. Environ. Res. Public Health **11**, 600–625 (2014)
3. Camarinha, L.M., Vieira, W.: Intelligent mobile agents in elderly care. Robot. Auton. Systems **27**, 59–75 (1999)
4. De Paz, J.F., Rodríguez, S., Zato, C., Corchado, J.M.: An integrated system for helping disabled and dependent people: AGALZ, AZTECA, and MOVI-MAS projects. In: Kinder-Kurlanda, K., Ehrwein Nihan, C. (eds.) Ubiquitous Computing in the Workplace. AISC, vol. 333, pp. 3–24. Springer, Cham (2015). https://doi.org/10.1007/978-3-319-13452-9_1
5. Isern, D., Sánchez, D., Moreno, A.: Agents applied in health care: a review. Int. J. Med. Inform. **79**, 145–166 (2010)
6. De Meo, P., Quattrone, G., Ursino, D.: Integration of the HL7 standard in a multiagent system to support personalized access to e-health services. IEEE Trans. Knowl. Data Eng. **23**, 1244–1260 (2011)
7. FIPA ACL Message Structure Specification. http://www.fipa.org/specs/fipa00061/SC00061G.pdf. Accessed 6 Nov 2013
8. Wu, C.-S., Khoury, I., Shah, H.: Optimizing medical data quality based on multiagent web service framework. IEEE Trans. Inf. Technol. Biomed. **16**, 745–757 (2012)
9. Vaidehi, V., Vardhini, M., Yogeshwaran, H., Inbasagar, G., Bhargavi, R., Hemalatha, C.S.: Agent based health monitoring of elderly people in indoor environments using wireless sensor networks. Proc. Comput. Sci. **19**, 64–71 (2013)
10. Su, C.-J., Wu, C.-Y.: JADE implemented mobile multi-agent based, distributed information platform for pervasive health care monitoring. Appl. Soft Comput. **11**, 315–325 (2011)
11. Kim, H.-K.: Convergence agent model for developing u-healthcare systems. Future Gener. Comput. Syst. (2013, in Press). Corrected Proof
12. Java Agent Development Framework (JADE). http://jade.tilab.com. Accessed 6 Nov 2013
13. JADE-LEAP. http://sharon.cslet.it/project/jade
14. Tapia, D.I., et al.: SYLPH: an ambient intelligence based platform for integrating heterogeneous wireless sensor networks. In: IEEE International Conference on Fuzzy Systems (FUZZ), pp. 1–8 (2010)
15. Koehler, F., Winkler, S., Schieber, M., Sechtem, U., Stangl, K., Bohm, I.: Impact of remote telemedical management on mortality and hospitalizations in ambulatory patients with chronic heart failure: the telemedical interventional monitoring in heart failure study. Circulation **123**(17), 1873–1880 (2011). On behalf of the telemedical interventional monitoring in heart failure
16. Miller, A.B., Pina, I.L.: Understanding heart failure with preserved ejection fraction: clinical importance and future outlook. Congest Heart Fail. **15**(4), 186–192 (2009). https://doi.org/10.1111/j.1751-7133.200900063.x
17. Qinghua, Z., et al.: Research on home health care telemedicine service system concerned with the improvement of medical resources utilization rate and medical conditions. In: The 12th International Conference on Advanced Communication Technology (ICACT), vol. 2, pp. 1555–1559 (2010)
18. Wooldridge, M.: An Introduction to Multi Agents Systems. Wiley, Sussez (2002)
19. Cloud Standards Customer Council: Impact of Cloud Computing on Healthcare Version 2.0. Annual report (2017)
20. Raza, K.: How the cloud is transforming healthcare. Forbes Technology Council (2017)

Alternative Connectivity Metric for Routing in VANETs

Frank Phillipson[1(✉)], Hacène Fouchal[2], and Kim van Gulik[1,3]

[1] TNO, The Hague, The Netherlands
frank.phillipson@tno.nl
[2] CReSTIC, Université de Champagne-Ardenne, Reims, France
[3] Erasmus University, Rotterdam, The Netherlands

Abstract. In vehicular ad-hoc networks a path has to be found to send a message from one vehicle to another vehicle. This path has to have a connectivity rate that is high enough to obtain a high probability of arrival of the message. In other approaches, the average distance between vehicles on a link of the network is used as metric for connectivity. In this paper, an other metric is proposed, based on the average and standard deviation of the distances between the vehicles to reach a metric that performs better.

Keywords: VANET · Location based routing · Metrics

1 Introduction

A Vehicular Ad Hoc Network (VANET) is a specific type of Mobile Ad Hoc Networks (MANET). In a MANET mobile nodes are connected wirelessly, without any central infrastructure, (possibly) moving around without any restrictions. In VANETS the mobility of the nodes is higher and the communication has higher demand regarding delay. The former one makes it more difficult to capture the topology of the nodes, where the latter one asks for a smarter and faster way of discovering the topology. However, in a VANET the mobile nodes are cars driving along a street pattern. These street patterns give the opportunity to recognize and use paths for communication.

The special characteristics of VANETs make it hard to use specific topology-based routing protocols for MANETs. However, the possibility to work with GPS systems within the nodes/cars makes it possible to use position based routing protocols like GSR [5], GPSR [4], A-STAR [8], GyTAR [3] and IDTAR [1].

Routing of packets is very important for the success of VANETs, it will make the difference whether network and application requirements will be met. In [6,7] a routing algorithm is proposed based on a simple location system represented by RSUs (Road Side Units). This routing algorithm is able to send a message from a source to the destination by using the most dense path based on a connectivity metric. They assume that at each road junction, a RSU is installed, and each

© Springer Nature Switzerland AG 2019
E. Renault et al. (Eds.): MSPN 2018, LNCS 11005, pp. 117–122, 2019.
https://doi.org/10.1007/978-3-030-03101-5_11

vehicle has a static digital map to get position of all RSUs. Next to this, each vehicle has knowledge of its geographic position by using its GPS, speed and direction of movement. This allows the vehicle to find the closest RSU in order to request it about the path to the destination, based on the connectivity metric. The information is then sent in the direction of the given path, using Improved Greedy Forwarding [2,3].

However, the used connectivity metric can be improved. It is now based on an average distance between vehicles, where big gaps between two consecutive vehicles are not noticed. In this paper we propose a different metric to improve the method of [6].

2   Connectivity Metric

2.1   Current Approach

In the current implementation of the Location Service of [6] the Link Connectivity (LC) is based on the average distance between consecutive vehicles on a road. For this a link between two vehicles is defined as:

$$Link(v_i, v_j) = \begin{cases} R_{tr} - dist(v_i, v_j) & \text{if } dist(v_i, v_j) \le R_{tr}, \\ 0 & \text{otherwise.} \end{cases}$$

Here R_{tr} denotes the transmission radius and $dist(v_i, v_j)$ the distance between vehicles i and j. Note that $Link$ represents the remaining communication distance between two vehicles. The Mean Link (ML) for all N vehicles on a specific road, which has two endpoints, junctions J_n and J_m, is expressed as:

$$ML_{road} = \frac{Link(J_n, v_1) + \sum_{i=1}^{N-1} Link(v_i, v_{i+1}) + Link(v_N, J_m)}{(N+1)}.$$

From this connectivity metric can be defined as

$$LC_{road} = \frac{ML_{road}}{R_{tr}},$$

which is a function on $[0, 1]$.

The drawback of the proposed metric is indicated using the following example. Assume we have a road and two possible distributions of vehicles on that road, as shown in Table 1. The road is 180 m and the transmission radius $R_{tr} = 50$ m. Here we see that, however Distribution 1 has a gap between two vehicles of 80 m, which is bigger than the transmission radius of 50 m, the Link Connectivity score is 0.45 which is better than the 0.3 of the other, more even, Distribution 2.

Table 1. Two distributions of vehicles on a road.

Variable	Distribution 1	Distribution 2
$dist(J_1, v_1)$	20	35
$dist(v_1, v_2)$	20	35
$dist(v2_1, v_3)$	80	35
$dist(v_3, J2_1)$	20	35
LC_{road}	0.45	0.3

2.2 Improved Metric

To improve the Connectivity Metric, several directions can be chosen. A simple metric would be the connectivity probability of the road CP_{road}, which is one if all distances are smaller than the transmission radius and zero otherwise, e.g., using

$$CP_{road} = \mathbb{1}_{\{Link(J_n, v_1)>0\}} \prod_{i=1}^{N-1} \mathbb{1}_{\{Link(v_i, v_{i+1})>0\}} \mathbb{1}_{\{Link(v_N, J_m)>0\}}.$$

This metric is clear and distinctive, but lacks a degree of nuance. This could be added by introducing speed, direction and a certain time frame (which are all known in the proposed approach of [6]) into the calculations, giving not only the probability of connection now, but also some prediction of the connection within the coming time frame.

We propose here however, to use the sum of the average and standard deviation of the distances between the cars and the junctions. Define $X_1 = dist(J_1, v_1)$, $X_{N+1} = dist(J_2, v_N)$ and $X_i = dist(v_i - 1, v_i)$ for $i = 2, ...N$. Using

$$\overline{X} = \frac{\sum_{i=1}^{N+1} X_i}{N+1},$$

now the new metric can be defined as

$$LC_{road}^{ASD} = \overline{X} + \sqrt{\frac{\sum_{i=1}^{N+1}(X_i - \overline{X})^2}{N+2}}.$$

We use the following 5 examples to indicate the strengths and weaknesses of this choice. Let us look at 5 different distributions of vehicles over a road. The used patterns are:

1. All distances are a result of a uniform distribution $[25, 35]$;
2. Using the sequence $\{1, 50, 1, 50, 1, 50, ...\}$;
3. Using the sequence $\{15, 15, 15, 80, 15, 15, 15, 80, ...\}$;
4. Using the sequence $15, 15, ..., 15, 200, 15, ... 15$;
5. Using the sequence $\{60, 60, ...\}$;

For all those patterns we can calculate the metric LC_{road} as proposed in [6], the connection probability CP_{road} as defined above and the proposed metric, the average plus standard deviation, noted as LC_{road}^{ASD}. First we could say something of our expectations of the desired outcome. Naturally, the first pattern is the best for connectivity; quite evenly distributed and the distances are within scope of the transmission radius. The second pattern is worse than the first, in terms of spread, but still acceptable; connectivity is still possible. The third and fourth have a big 'gap' in the path, ruining the connectivity. From these two the third is preferable, where movements in the coming time period could overcome this gap. The last one has the smallest number of vehicles on the (fixed) length of the road, making sure that the current situation has no connectivity but also in short term no improvement is expected.

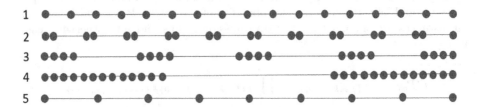

Fig. 1. Schematic overview of the used patterns.

The scores of the metrics on the five patterns can be found in Table 2 and, as impression, in Fig. 1.

Table 2. Scores of the metrics.

Pattern	LC_{road}	CP_{road}	LC_{road}^{ASD}
Pattern 1	0.40	1	35.04
Pattern 2	0.53	1	50.50
Pattern 3	0.56	0	57.93
Pattern 4	0.67	0	58.40
Pattern 5	0	0	60.00

Note that we would expect the patterns to be in decreasing order of score. Note also that for the current metric LC_{road} a higher score is better, and for the new metric LC_{road}^{ASD} a lower score is better. We see in Table 2 that LC_{road}^{ASD} and CP_{road} give results as expected and desired. The original metric however, scores in opposite direction, except for pattern 5, who scores the worst.

To make this a metric that scores between zero and one, giving the best value at one, we propose to use

$$LC_{road}^* = \frac{\max(0, 2R_{tr} - LC_{road}^{ASD})}{2R_{tr}}.$$

This metric is in the interval $[0, 1]$, because if $LC_{road}^{ASD} = 0$, the metric equals $2R_{tr}/2R_{tr} = 1$. If $LC_{road}^{ASD} \geq 2R_{tr}$, the term $2R_{tr} - LC_{road}^{ASD}$ becomes negative, so the denominator becomes zero, so does the total metric. The metric is also greater than zero if there is connectivity[1], meaning all distances are smaller than R_{tr}. For this we will have to prove that if all distances are smaller than R_{tr}, that then holds $2R_{tr} > LC_{road}^{ASD}$. Remember that $LC_{road}^{ASD} = \overline{X} + SD(X)$, where $SD(X)$ is the standard deviation of X. Then first, if $X_i < R_{tr}$ for all i, also $\overline{X} < R_{tr}$. Next, if $0 \leq X_i < R_{tr}$ for all i and $0 \leq \overline{X} < R_{tr}$, then $|X_i - \overline{X}| < R_{tr}$:

$$\sqrt{\frac{\sum_{i=1}^{N+1}(X_i - \overline{X})^2}{N+2}} < \sqrt{\frac{\sum_{i=1}^{N+1}(R_{tr})^2}{N+2}} = \sqrt{\frac{(N+1)(R_{tr})^2}{N+2}} < R_{tr}.$$

Concluding, if both $\overline{X} < R_{tr}$ and $SD(X) < R_{tr}$, then $\overline{X} + SD(X) < 2R_{tr}$ under the given conditions. The results of this adjusted defintion can be found in Table 3.

Table 3. Scores of the metrics.

Pattern	LC_{road}	CP_{road}	LC_{road}^*
Pattern 1	0.40	1	0.65
Pattern 2	0.53	1	0.50
Pattern 3	0.56	0	0.42
Pattern 4	0.67	0	0.42
Pattern 5	0	0	0.4

3   Conclusion and Further Research

In this paper the current implementation of the VANET Location Service of [6] is considered in which the Link Connectivity (LC) is based on the average distance between consecutive vehicles on a road. This metric has some drawbacks, for which a new metric was proposed, based on the average and standard deviation of the distances between the vehicles and the junctions. For a number of special examples the value of this new metric was calculated and was concluded that this value meets the expectation better than the previous metric.

In future research the results of this metric on the main performance indicators of VANETs should be determined, using road network simulations.

---

[1] Note that this is only one way: if there is no connectivity the metric is not necessarily zero.

References

1. Ahmed, A.I.A., Gani, A., Ab Hamid, S.H., Khan, S., Guizani, N., Ko, K.: Intersection-based distance and traffic-aware routing (IDTAR) protocol for smart vehicular communication. In: 2017 13th International Wireless Communications and Mobile Computing Conference (IWCMC), pp. 489–493. IEEE (2017)
2. Jerbi, M., Senouci, S.M., Meraihi, R., Ghamri-Doudane, Y.: An improved vehicular ad hoc routing protocol for city environments. In: IEEE International Conference on Communications, ICC 2007, pp. 3972–3979. IEEE (2007)
3. Jerbi, M., Senouci, S.M., Rasheed, T., Ghamri-Doudane, Y.: Towards efficient geographic routing in urban vehicular networks. IEEE Trans. Veh. Technol. **58**(9), 5048–5059 (2009)
4. Karp, B., Kung, H.T.: GPSR: Greedy perimeter stateless routing for wireless networks. In: Proceedings of the 6th Annual International Conference on Mobile Computing and Networking, pp. 243–254. ACM (2000)
5. Lochert, C., Hartenstein, H., Tian, J., Fussler, H., Hermann, D., Mauve, M.: A routing strategy for vehicular ad hoc networks in city environments. In: Intelligent Vehicles Symposium, 2003. Proceedings, pp. 156–161. IEEE (2003)
6. Nebbou, T., Fouchal, H., Lehsaini, M., Ayaida, M.: A cooperative location service for VANETs. In: 2017 IEEE Symposium on Computers and Communications (ISCC), pp. 54–58. IEEE (2017)
7. Nebbou, T., Fouchal, H., Lehsaini, M., Ayaida, M.: A realistic location service for VANETs. In: Eichler, G., Erfurth, C., Fahrnberger, G. (eds.) I4CS 2017. CCIS, vol. 717, pp. 191–196. Springer, Cham (2017). https://doi.org/10.1007/978-3-319-60447-3_14
8. Seet, B.-C., Liu, G., Lee, B.-S., Foh, C.-H., Wong, K.-J., Lee, K.-K.: A-STAR: a mobile ad hoc routing strategy for metropolis vehicular communications. In: Mitrou, N., Kontovasilis, K., Rouskas, G.N., Iliadis, I., Merakos, L. (eds.) NETWORKING 2004. LNCS, vol. 3042, pp. 989–999. Springer, Heidelberg (2004). https://doi.org/10.1007/978-3-540-24693-0_81

Num Ant Factor Based Comprehensive Investigations over Linguistic Trust and Reputations Model in Mobile Sensor Networks

Vinod Kumar Verma[✉]

Sant Longowal Institute of Engineering and Technology,
Deemed to be University, Longowal 148106, India
vinod5881@gmail.com

Abstract. Trust is the prime concern for the evaluations of mobile sensor network-based applications. Trust in terms of human intractable levels is being expected form nowadays mobile sensor networks. In this paper, a linguistic trust and reputation model has been investigated in an exhaustive manner. The performance parameters like accuracy, path length, and energy consumption have been evaluated. Moreover, satisfaction factor has been investigated with the inference power of the fuzzy sets. Num ant factor has been considered as the major factor for this investigational analysis. The effects of num ant factor on the operations of the mobile sensor networks system have been observed. Simulations have been performed to validate the results.

Keywords: Trust · Reputation · LFTM · Num ant · Accuracy
Path length · Energy · Satisfaction

1 Introduction

The real-time applications of the mobile sensor networks used in the daily sphere of the life need trustworthiness. If you trust on the application then the scope of use of that application will surely enhance to a wider context. Even more, if the mobile-based application works on the pattern is human intractable terms than the scenario becomes more interesting and efficient. Trust and reputation based models are the solution to incorporate trustworthiness in the mobile sensor-based applications. The performance of the designated system can not only be enhanced by the performance parameters like scalability, coverage, adaptability, mobility etc. but also through the human intractable terms like accuracy, path length, energy, and satisfaction. The focus of this paper is to incorporate the human intractable terms in the investigations over mobile sensor networks.

The structure of this paper is as follows. Section 2 depicts the related work corresponds to the trustworthy mobile sensor networks. Section 3 shows the description of linguistic fuzzy trust and reputation model in a brief manner. Section 4 presents the detailed setup for the proposed scenario. Section 5 highlights the results and discussions of the evaluations. Lastly, Sect. 6 concludes the summarization of the proposed work.

2 Related Work on Trustworthy Mobile Sensor Networks

Trustworthiness can serve as the paramount factor for all the distributed applications deployed through wireless sensor networks. This aspect is applicable to both static and mobile sensor networks. Different research areas and their applications are being affected by the trustworthiness of the backbone deployed the system. The major research efforts in this direction are as follows. Tang et al. [1] proposed a research on subjective trust management model using fuzzy set concepts. A trust model was proposed by Ramchurn et al. [2] for multi-agent interaction to evaluate confidence and reputation. Shuqin et al. [3] suggested a fuzzy set based trust and reputation model for peer to peer networks. A strategy for linguistic fuzzy enhancement for distributed networks was proposed by Gómez Mármol et al. [4]. A LFTM based mechanism to improve the performance of distributed network was suggested in reference [5]. A comparative analysis of trust and reputation models has been reported by Gómez Mármol et al. [6]. A more rigorous investigation of trust and reputation model was suggested by Verma et al. [7]. A thorough investigation over the collusion aspect was represented in reference [8]. Two major aspects of trustworthiness namely; pheromone and path length based estimation were suggested in reference [9]. Next section describes the LFTM model used in further sections.

3 Linguistic Fuzzy Trust and Reputation Model (LFTM)

This model has been considered for the comprehensive investigational purpose in the deployed scenario. In this trust and reputation model, the outcome has been evaluated on the basis of human understanding levels like very high, high, medium, low and very low. The resultants of this model show the trustworthiness of the deployed scenario. This model uses the inference power of the fuzzy logic. Moreover, satisfaction criteria have also been evaluated in this model. The motive of this model focuses on the human intractable outcome. Linguistic fuzzy sets have been considered to give the trustworthiness of the entire systems. The num ant factor of the LFTM model has been considered for the major investigational purpose in the deployed scenario.

4 Detailed Setup

In this section, the detailed setup for the evaluations has been described for the deployed scenario. The scenario has been deployed over an area of 100 m × 100 m. TRM-WSN simulator [10] has been used for the investigation purpose. The value of execution number remained 10, network number is taken as 100. Minimum value 10 and maximum value 100 for sensors has been used in the networks. The percentage of client sensors has been considered 15, relay sensors 5, malicious sensors 70, radio range as 12 m and no delay has been considered. LFTM model has been used in the proposed scenario. Table 1 summarizes the parameters considered for the investigations.

Table 1. Scenario parameters.

Parameters	Values
Num execution	10
Num network	100
Min. sensor	10
Max. sensor	100
Client (%)	15
Relay servers (%)	5
Malicious servers (%)	70
Radio range (%)	12
Delay	0
Phi	0.01
Rho	0.87
Num iteration	0.59
Alpha	1
Beta	1
Initial pheromone	0.85
Punishment threshold	0.48
Path length factor	0.71
Transition threshold	0.66

In the TRM-WSN simulator, the area is divided into four parts: (i) setting area (ii) network area (iii) outcome area (iv) messages area. Yellow dots show client nodes, green dots represent benevolent nodes, red dots depict malicious nodes, blue dots present relay nodes and black dots show idle nodes. The simulation setup scenario has been shown in Figs. 1 and 2 respectively.

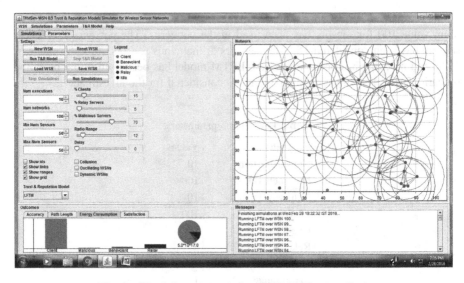

Fig. 1. Simulation setup window 1 (Color figure online)

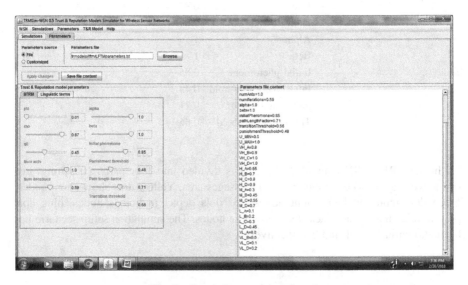

Fig. 2. Simulation setup window 2

5   Results and Discussion

This section presents the detailed investigation of the proposed scenario in mobile sensor networks domain. The focus of the investigation remained on four major factors namely: (i) Accuracy (ii) Path Length (iii) Energy consumption (iv) Satisfaction.

5.1   Accuracy Evaluation

In this evaluation, the behavior of accuracy versus Num Ant value has been observed as depicted in Fig. 3. Accuracy can be defined as the probability of the trustworthiness of the sensor nodes in the entire networks. The accuracy has been evaluated with two viewpoints: current and average. Current accuracy refers to the value obtained at the last monument of the evaluation in the network. Average accuracy denotes the summation of the accuracy obtained for the entire system. The observations reveal that the current accuracy depicts more non-linear behavior as compared to the average accuracy with respect to the num ant value in the network. The value of current accuracy remained highest at 0.8 num ant values and lowest at 0.1 num ant value. This seems a good agreement with the work reported in reference [6].

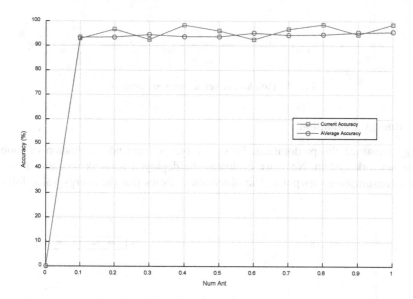

Fig. 3. Accuracy versus num ant analysis

5.2   Path Length Evaluation

This evaluation has been observed for the path length aspect for the deployed scenario as shown in Fig. 4. Path Length represents the value of resources being consumed for the operations in the mobile sensor networks. This evaluation has been performed on the consistent pattern of accuracy. The investigation shows that current path length follow non-linear behavior and average path length depicts linear behavior with respect to the num ant value. The value of the current path length remained highest for 0.2 num ant value and lowest for the 0.3, 0.4 and 0.6 in the deployed scenario. The work reported in reference [7] has been enhanced from a newer facet.

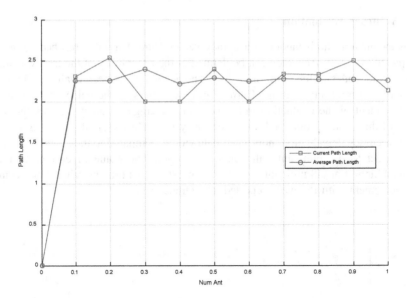

Fig. 4. Path length versus num ant analysis

5.3 Energy Evaluation

Energy remained the predominant factor for the performance evaluation of mobile sensor network system. Next, we evaluated the deployed network scenario from the energy consumption viewpoint. The observation shows that the energy value follows

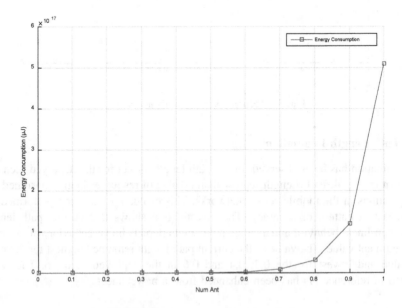

Fig. 5. Energy versus num ant analysis

linear incremental behavior with respect to the rise in the Num ant value as shown in Fig. 5. The energy consumption value remained highest for the num ant value 1.0 and lowest for the num ant value 0.1. The work proposed by reference [8] has been extended.

5.4 Satisfaction Evaluation

Lastly, the focus remained on the investigation of important aspect satisfaction which may be referred as the percentage of trustworthiness of the sensor nodes given by the neighbor nodes deployed in the whole network. This is the probability by which a node can request about the trustworthiness of a neighbor node from the network. This is based on the past behavior of the nodes. Two major levels have been focused here: Very High and Very Low. Satisfaction analysis shows linear behavior at both the levels as depicted in Fig. 6. This work on the consistent pattern with the work proposed in reference [9].

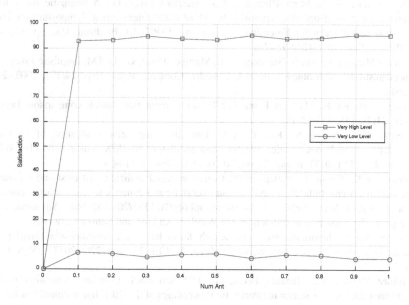

Fig. 6. Satisfaction versus num ant analysis

6 Conclusions

The focus remained on the investigational analysis of the mobile sensor networks from trustworthiness aspect. Initially, the scenario with sensor nodes has been deployed with linguistic fuzzy trust and reputation model for the mobile sensor networks. Num Ant value has been considered for the pervasive investigations of mobile sensor network system form performance viewpoints. Four major factors have been addressed from investigational views namely: accuracy, path length, energy, and satisfaction. Lastly, the observations reveal that there is a strong influence of the num ant value on the performance parameters of the mobile sensor network system. Additionally, it is also affecting the trustworthiness of the deployed system. More the value of num ant leads to more resource utilization and higher energy consumption in the deployed scenario.

References

1. Tang, W., Chen, Z.: Research of subjective trust management model based on the fuzzy set theory. Chin. J. Softw. **14**(8), 1401–1408 (2003)
2. Ramchurn, S.D., Sierra, C., Godo, L., Jennings, N.R.: A computational trust model for multi-agent interactions based on confidence and reputation. In: Proceedings of 6th International Workshop of Deception, Fraud and Trust in Agent Societies, pp. 69–75 (2003)
3. Shuqin, Z., Dongxin, L., Yongtian, Y.: A fuzzy set based trust and reputation model in P2P networks. In: Yang, Z.R., Yin, H., Everson, R.M. (eds.) IDEAL 2004. LNCS, vol. 3177, pp. 211–217. Springer, Heidelberg (2004). https://doi.org/10.1007/978-3-540-28651-6_31
4. Gómez Mármol, F., Marín-Blázquez, J.G., Martínez Pérez, G.: A linguistic fuzzy logic enhancement for distributed networks. In: Third IEEE International Symposium on Trust, Security and Privacy for Emerging Applications, TSP 2010, Bradford, UK, pp. 838–845 (2010). ISBN 978-1-4244-7547-6
5. Gómez Mármol, F., Marín-Blázquez, J.G., Martínez Pérez, G.: LFTM, linguistic fuzzy trust mechanism for distributed networks. Concurr. Comput.: Pract. Exp. **24**(17), 2007–2027 (2012)
6. Gómez Mármol, F., Martínez Pérez, G.: Trust and reputation models comparison. Internet Res. **21**(2), 138–153 (2011)
7. Verma, V.K., Singh, S., Pathak, N.P.: Towards comparative evaluation of trust and reputation models over static, dynamic and oscillating wireless sensor networks. Wirel. Netw. **23**, 335 (2017). https://doi.org/10.1007/s11276-015-1144-4
8. Verma, V.K., Singh, S., Pathak, N.P.: Collusion based realization of trust and reputation models in extreme fraudulent environment over static and dynamic wireless sensor networks. Int. J. Distrib. Sens. Netw. (2014). https://doi.org/10.1155/2014/672968. Advanced Convergence Technologies and Practices for Wireless Ad Hoc and Sensor Networks
9. Verma, V.K.: Pheromone and path length factor-based trustworthiness estimations in heterogeneous wireless sensor networks. Sens. J. IEEE **17**, 215–220 (2017). ISSN 1530-437X
10. Gomez Mármol, F., Martínez Perez, G.: TRMSim-WSN, trust and reputation models simulator for wireless sensor networks. In: Proceedings of the IEEE International Conference on Communications, IEEE ICC 2009, Communication and Information Systems Security Symposium, Dresden, Germany, June 2009

Position Certainty Propagation: A Location Service for MANETs

Abdallah Sobehy[1], Eric Renault[1(✉)], and Paul Muhlethaler[2]

[1] Samovar, CNRS, Télécom SudParis, University Paris-Saclay,
9 Rue Charles Fourier, 91000 Évry, France
{sobehy,eric.renault}@telecom-sudparis.eu
[2] INRIA Roquenourt, BP 105, 78153 Le Chesnay Cedex, France
Paul.Muhlethaler@inria.fr

Abstract. Localization in Mobile Ad-hoc Networks (MANETs) and Wireless Sensor Networks (WSNs) is an issue of great interest, especially in applications such as the IoT and VANETs. We propose a solution that overcomes two limiting characteristics of these types of networks. The first is the high cost of nodes with a location sensor (such as GPS) which we will refer to as anchor nodes. The second is the low computational capability of nodes in the network. The proposed algorithm addresses two issues; self-localization where each non-anchor node should discover its own position, and global localization where a node establishes knowledge of the position of all the nodes in the network. We address the problem as a graph where vertices are nodes in the network and edges indicate connectivity between nodes. The weights of edges represent the Euclidean distance between the nodes. Given a graph with at least three anchor nodes and knowing the maximum communication range for each node, we are able to localize nodes using fairly simple computations in a moderately dense graph.

Keywords: Location service · MANETs · WSNs

1 Introduction

Localization in MANETs has been the focus of attention in recent years as it is used in various applications such as routing, autonomous air-vehicles, network security, environment surveillance for military purposes, etc. For instance, in [1–3], the location information is used in various ways to improve routing decisions. A straightforward method to locate network nodes is to equip each of them with a location sensor such as a GPS and broadcast the location information. In SFLS location service [4], the location information is forwarded with higher frequency to close neighbors in terms of the number of hops and lower frequency to further nodes to decrease bandwidth consumption while maintaining adequate knowledge of neighbors' positions. Since IoT networks have limiting characteristics, it

© Springer Nature Switzerland AG 2019
E. Renault et al. (Eds.): MSPN 2018, LNCS 11005, pp. 131–142, 2019.
https://doi.org/10.1007/978-3-030-03101-5_13

is rather expensive to equip each node with a GPS sensor. Thus, different solutions attempt to locate nodes where only a subset of network nodes are equipped with a location sensor.

To estimate the position of non-anchor nodes, additional information is required to relate nodes to each other. According to the classification specified in [5], node relations can be as simple as being in connection with anchor nodes or not. This is used in [6] where a node's position is assumed to be the average of the known positions of the other nodes. Another approach is range-based where the distance between nodes is computed either through RSSI (Received Signal Strength Indicator), TOA (Time Of Arrival) or TDOA (Time Difference Of Arrival) [7]. TOA and TSOA require external hardware to synchronize a transmitter and a receiver, while RSSI does not since the distance is derived from a signal attenuation model that relates the signal strength to the distance [7]. Knowing the relative distances is obviously an added benefit that helps to improve the accuracy of the location. However, using RSSI is subject to errors due to environmental factors (indoors or outdoors), multi-path fading and noise [7]. In [8], RSSI was found to vary consistently with a distance up to 50 meters. In [5,9,10], the probability distribution is integrated in the location process instead of concluding a single position for each node. Such a method allows the uncertainty of measurements to be taken into account, be it is the GPS position or the relative distance between nodes [5].

2   Related Work

Consider the location problem as an undirected graph $G = (V, E)$ where V is the set of the nodes in the network and E is the set of edges connecting two nodes located within communication range of each other. In this context, the given information is the position of anchor nodes and edge weights which are relative distances between nodes within communication range. The aim is to compute the position of all non-anchor nodes. This can be seen as an optimization problem that can be solved using numerical techniques such as SDP [11] or linear programming [12]. To avoid inaccuracies of signal propagation models when using RSSI for distance measurements, some studies [13–15] have used interval-analysis. In interval-based analysis, instead of computing direct distances from RSSI, a set of inequalities is formulated to indicate that a node is on a ring between 2 radii based on its relative position to other nodes. Then, the defined areas for nodes can be further restrained using the Waltz algorithm [16].

Some approaches divide the problem into sub problems as in [8] where (1) base stations classify ordinary nodes into clusters based on their proximity to anchor nodes and (2) within each cluster, a node seen by three anchor nodes is located using a simple geometrical computation. In [7], the region where the network is deployed is divided into rectangular grids as a first step, then within each small grid the location is refined. However, in the previously mentioned approaches the number of GPS nodes needs to be high in order to satisfy the necessary constraints.

Generally speaking, if the distance of a non-anchor node to three anchor nodes is known, it can be located with simple geometric computations except in the rare cases where the nodes are collinear or when some nodes overlap. This might imply a conclusion that at least three GPS nodes in the network are needed for location. However, in [5], the proposed solution attempts to locate the network with a single anchor node. Each node starts with a uniform probability distribution over the deployment region and as the roaming anchor node passes by the ordinary nodes it tweaks the distribution to locate nodes. In this context, the authors experiment their solution where the anchor nodes use a random model to traverse the network and have a reasonable claim that traversing the network can be optimized to improve the location process. In [5,9] negative information about the absence of a node in the proximity of the anchor nodes is used in the location process. This kind of information is used as a basis for our algorithm.

An approach which is seemingly far from the mentioned methods, yea interesting to address the node location problem, is Graph Layout Algorithms such as FDP [17] and neato [18]. Even though the objective of these algorithms is generally to create an easy-on-the-eye graph, some variations make it possible to fix the positions of some nodes (the anchor nodes) and to set the suitable edge length (i.e., is the distance between nodes). We have tested these algorithms using graphviz [19] and the estimated node positions are satisfactory.

Other methods, which use a set of distance equations and optimization techniques usually require high computation power, which is impractical for these networks. In this case, the computation is done remotely in a centralized fashion. The graph structure might not yield a unique solution. Even if the graph has a unique solution, finding this solution is proved to be NP-hard [20].

We address the problem from the graph point of view aiming at pinpointing the location of as many anchor nodes as possible. We first introduce our algorithm. Then we move on to explain how it can be implemented distributively over the nodes.

In Sect. 3, the system model is presented and the centralized version of the algorithm is introduced. In Sect. 4, the distributed version of the algorithm is explained and how each node acquires awareness of its location and the location of other nodes. Next, the algorithm is compared with an existing method in Sect. 5. Section 6 contains the conclusion, and possible future work.

3   System Model

3.1   Overview

Let us consider the network as an undirected graph $G = (V, E)$ where $V = \{0, 1, ..., n\}$ are the nodes of the network and $E = \{(0, 1), (0, 2)...\}$ where each pair represents an edge connecting two nodes located within the communication range of each other. Each edge is assigned a weight indicating the distance between the two nodes. We assume a subset of the network nodes m are anchor nodes where m includes at least three nodes of the network and for our evaluation we use exactly three anchor nodes. We also assume there is at least one node within communication range of at least three anchor nodes.

3.2 Position Certainty Propagation Algorithm

To illustrate the algorithm, let's relate its steps to a 15-node network with three anchor nodes in a region of 20×20 square meters and a maximum communication range of 8 meters. Figure 1 presents an example of such a network.

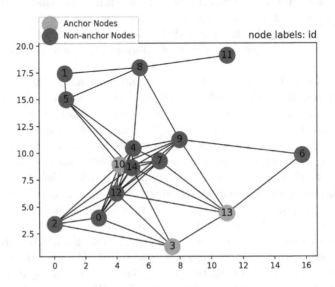

Fig. 1. 15-node network example

The algorithm starts by computing the position of the nodes with the most anchor nodes (or nodes with found positions) in their vicinity. Thurs, the first step is computing for each node the number of the neighbours with known position (whether anchor nodes or computed position nodes). Recall that for the algorithm to start, there must exist at least one node with at least three anchor nodes in its vicinity. Each anchor node forms a circle centered at the anchor node with a radius equal to the edge weight between the anchor node and the node in question. The node position is chosen to be the intersection of the three circles. Whenever a node position is found, it changes its state to a known position node. Whenever a node position is computed, all nodes recompute the number of neighbors with known positions in their vicinity. Then, the algorithm computes the position of the other nodes with the most known position nodes in their vicinity. Figure 2 illustrates the step of computing the number of nodes with known positions in vicinity (left) and the computation of the position of node 12 by computing the intersection of the three circles formed by the known position nodes: 3, 10 and 13 (right).

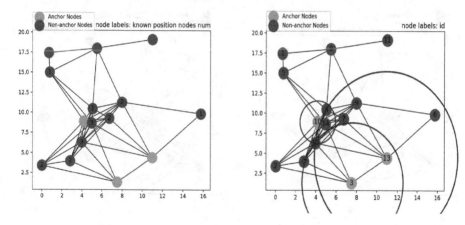

Fig. 2. Counting number of known position neighbours (left). Computing position from the intersection of three circles (right)

As the position of nodes are computed, the probability of finding nodes with known positions in the vicinity increases. Continuing to compute the position of nodes, one can reach the case where the maximum number of known position nodes in the vicinity is 2 for all nodes in the network. In this case, the intersection between the two circles formed by the two known position nodes in the vicinity would generally yield two possible positions. To choose one of these two positions, the node is assumed to be at both positions and the set of neighbors from the known position nodes that are within a radius of maximum communication range is computed at each of the two potential positions. The position where wrong nodes would have been neighbors, i.e. if one potential node position would be within the communication range of another node n while n is not actually sensed as a one-hop neighbor, is eliminated and the other position is chosen for this node. Figure 3 shows this case and the simulated two positions for node 6 are presented as blue octagons. The lower of the two possible positions can be eliminated because at this position node 6 would have had other neighbors which are not it actual neighbors in the network.

There might be cases where the elimination is not needed e.g. when the two generated circles are tangent at one point or when of the two positions are out of the deployment region. The algorithm continues to compute the position of nodes with the two previously mentioned cases until no more positions can be estimated. This is the case when a node sees two known position nodes within its vicinity but neither of the two possible positions introduces wrong neighbors and thus cannot be eliminated. Also, when a node is seen only by one known position neighbor, it may be located anywhere on the circle centered on the known position node and of radius the distance between the two nodes. Therefore, its position cannot be effectively established. This can be seen when attempting to compute the position of node 11, where its only known position

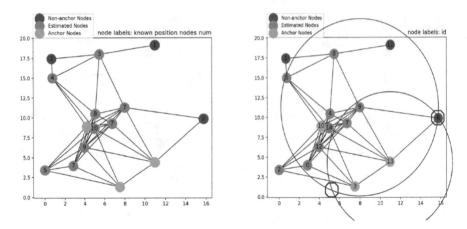

Fig. 3. Counting number of known position neighbours (left). Computing position from the intersection of two circles (right) (Color figure online)

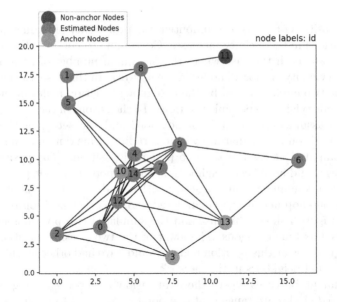

Fig. 4. The final result of the algorithm

neighbor is node 8. The final outcome of the algorithm in Fig. 4 shows that only node 11's position cannot be computed.

The main advantage of this algorithm is its lightness as it comes down to a series of triangulation steps. The next section discusses the implementation of the proposed solution in a distributed manner.

4 Distributed Implementation of the Algorithm

To cope with the distributive nature of MANETs, we introduce here a possible algorithm to run at each node either to establish its own position or the position of all the nodes in the network. First, we assume that a node with a known position broadcasts its own position through the network. To mitigate overloading the network bandwidth, position updates are spread over the network using a bandwidth conserving method like SFLS [4]. This method is based on sending the updates with the highest frequency to one-hop neighbors, and for each increment of hop-count the frequency of updates is halved. This method is compatible with our approach since the information needed to eliminate wrong positions relies on neighbors which are a few hops away. A node that needs to compute its own position receives position information from other nodes. It also computes the distance to one hop neighbors using any of the previously mentioned methods. When sufficient information has been received, it computes its own position as shown in Algorithm 1.

Algorithm 1. Position Certainty Propagation

1: N (list of received node positions) and N_1 (1-hop neighbours with known positions)
2: Id_1 list of IDs of all one-hop neighbors
3: **procedure** RECEIVE($sender, n, pos, timeStamp$)
4:     **if** $sender == n$ and (n not in N_1 or $timeStamp > N_1[n].timeStamp$) **then**
5:         update N_1 with n, pos and $timeStamp$
6:     **end if**
7:     **if** n not in N or $timeStamp > N[n].timeStamp$ **then**
8:         update N with n, pos and $timeStamp$
9:     **end if**
10: **end procedure**
11: **do**
12:     $receive(sender, n, pos, time())$
13:     **if** N_1 has 3 or more nodes **then**
14:         $selfPos = intersection(N_1)$
15:     **else if** N_1 has 2 nodes **then**
16:         [pos1, pos2] $= intersection(N_1)$
17:         $P1Neighbors = $ n **for** each $n \in N$ where $distance(n, pos1) <= CommRange$
18:         $P2Neighbors = $ n **for** each $n \in N$ where $distance(n, pos2) <= CommRange$
19:         $pos1IsCompatible \iff$ **for** each $n \in P1Neighbors, n \in Id_1$
20:         $pos2IsCompatible \iff$ **for** each $n \in P2Neighbors, n \in Id_1$
21:         **if** $pos1IsCompatible$ and not $pos2IsCompatible$ **then**
22:             $selfPos = pos1$
23:         **else if** $pos2IsCompatible$ and not $pos1IsCompatible$ **then**
24:             $selfPos = pos2$
25:         **end if**
26:     **end if**
27: **while** $selfPos$ not found

Let N_1 be the list of detected known position neighbors within communication range of the node. When N_1 includes two or three nodes, the position of the node can be made certain using the *intersection* method. If N_1 includes two nodes, the *intersection* method returns the two possible positions from which one is to be eliminated if possible. Let N be the list containing position information of all received positions of network nodes. The *receive* method is called when a message is received from a *sender* node within communication range that contains the node ID n and the corresponding position *pos*. Id_1 contains the list of IDs of all one-hop neighbors whether their position is known or not.

When positions are computed, the nodes start broadcasting their own position using SFLS [4]. Also, to take into account the continuous change of node positions, nodes should re-run the position computation algorithm whenever a change in the parameters used to compute its position is received. To make it clearer, if any of the three nodes used to compute a node's position send a message indicating a position change, the node should update its own position.

5   Performance Evaluation

5.1   Comparable Method: Gps-Free

In order to assess our algorithm we compare it with an existing solution [21], which we will refer to as Gps-free. We implemented the first part of the Gps-free algorithm where node positions are computed in a local coordinate system of one of the nodes in the network. The paper further explains how to choose a stable coordinate system for the network, which does not concern us since we evaluate the solution for a static instance of the network. The algorithm compromises the following steps:

1. Each node creates a local map composed of itself and the maximum possible number of 1-hop neighbours via triangulation making itself the origin.
2. Node k can transfer its coordinate system to node i if both nodes exist in the local map of one another in addition to a third node common in both local maps.
3. All nodes in the network attempt to transfer their coordinate system to node i so that all node positions are computed in one common coordinate system.

We refer the reader to the Gps-free article [21] for further details of how these steps are executed. Observing the behaviour of Gps-free in some graphs we figured an improvement that can increase the percentage of localized nodes. The improvement concerns the condition that only nodes who cannot build a local map are transferred to another coordinate system via triangulation. We quote from the Gps-free paper: "The nodes that are not able to build their local coordinate system but communicate with three nodes that already computed their positions in the referent coordinate system can obtain their position in the Network Coordinate System by triangulation" [21]. We extended this behaviour to nodes who built their local map but still cannot transfer their local coordinate system to the referent coordinate system; only the node compute its position in the referent coordinate system.

5.2   Experimental Setup

Our objective is to compute the positions in the global coordinate system using GPS information of three nodes. In the Gps-free method, even though the positions are computed in a local coordinate system, it is possible to transfer the node positions to the global coordinate system if the 3 GPS nodes have their positions computed. Each simulation run is a connected geometric graph (aka disc graph) where nodes are randomly positioned in a 100 m × 100 m grid. Three anchor nodes are randomly chosen so that at least one non-anchor node is within their communication range. Our algorithm is run to compute the positions of the non-anchor nodes as previously described. Gps-free is run where the node chosen to have all nodes transferred to its coordinate system is the one the maximizes the number of estimated nodes, this ensures extracting the best possible result from the Gps-free method without taking into account whether the GPS nodes are among the nodes with the computed positions. The success percentage is the percentage of nodes with their position computed. Two experiments are conducted, one varying the maximum communication range [14, 15, 16.., 23] while keeping the average number of nodes constant at 100 nodes. In the other experiment the communication range is kept constant at 14 m while the average number of nodes is varied [100, 115, 130, 145, 160]. The number of nodes in each experiment follows a poisson distribution with the given average. In each graph configuration the experiment is repeated 1000 times and the confidence interval is shown as a vertical bar around the point.

5.3   Experimental Results

Figure 5 shows the comparison between PCP, Gps-free and Gps-free extended version. We start with a maximum communication range of 14 m and increment by 1 m for each new configuration. We show on the graph the average node degree at each maximum communication range. Put differently, for the first configuration each node has a maximum communication range of 14 m and the average node degree over the 1000 simulations is approximately 5.5, the next configuration is with a range of 15 m which gives an average node degree of ∼6.3 etc. It can be clearly seen that the maximum communication range has a direct impact on the number of localized nodes. As the maximum communication range increases and consequently the average node degree, it is possible to estimate positions of more nodes. When the average degree is $\approx$ 10, our algorithm is able to compute the positions of $\approx$ 90% of nodes. Also, our algorithm shows a higher success percent at all configurations compared to Gps-free and the extended version. In another attempt to study the effect of varying the number of nodes keeping the maximum communication range constant at 14 meters, increasing the number of nodes has a similar effect to increasing the maximum communication range. Here, the node density (nodes/meter^2) is shown against the success rate.

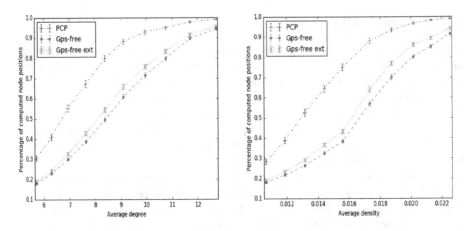

Fig. 5. Comparing PCP to Gps-free and Gps-free ext methods

6   Conclusion

This article presented a simple algorithm to compute the positions of nodes
when a network has a very limited number of anchor nodes (the minimum is set
to 3). The algorithm has an initial condition, which is the presence of a node
that is within the vicinity of at least three anchor nodes. It might appear that
the starting condition is hindering the utility of the approach, however it can
be partially mitigated by assuming three non-anchor nodes that are within each
other's vicinity and satisfy the initial condition as anchor nodes. These virtual
anchor nodes are given assumed positions so that they form a triangle from the
known distance between them. For instance, assume non-collinear nodes i, j, k
see each other and at least a forth node. Node i is positioned at the origin, node j
is on the horizontal axis with at a distance equal to $dist(i, j)$ and node k is added
to have a positive y-value using triangulation. The algorithm then treat them
as anchor nodes and compute the position of the rest of the nodes as previously
explained. When at least three real anchor node positions are computed, all
the nodes can then be transferred to the global coordinate system using there
computed positions and actual positions [21]. It has been shown statistically that
with a fairly dense network (average degree ≈ 10), the algorithm is able to quickly
and efficiently compute the position of $\approx 90\%$ the nodes whose positions are not
known. The next step is to test our algorithm with the inevitable uncertainty of
measurements using a tool such as NS3. Additionally, the impact of the node's
velocity, delay of receiving information on the accuracy of the estimation of the
node's position are also to be considered.

References

1. Jung, W.-S., Yim, J., Ko, Y.-B.: QGeo: Q-learning-based geographic Ad Hoc routing protocol for unmanned robotic networks. IEEE Commun. Lett. **21**(10), 2258–2261 (2017)
2. Terao, Y., Phoummavong, P., Utsu, K., Ishii, H.: A proposal on void zone aware greedy forwarding method over MANET. In: 2016 IEEE Region 10 Conference (TENCON), pp. 1329–1333. IEEE (2016)
3. Ko, Y.B., Vaidya, N.H.: Location aided routing (LAR) in mobile ad hoc networks. Wireless Netw. **6**(4), 307–321 (2000)
4. Renault, E., Amar, E., Costantini, H., Boumerdassi, S.: Semi-flooding location service. In: 2010 IEEE 72nd conference on Vehicular Technology Conference Fall, VTC 2010-Fall, pp. 1–5. IEEE (2010)
5. Huang, R., Záruba, G.V.: Monte Carlo localization of wireless sensor networks with a single mobile beacon. Wirel. Netw. **15**(8), 978 (2009)
6. Bulusu, N., Heidemann, J., Estrin, D.: GPS-less low-cost outdoor localization for very small devices. IEEE Pers. Commun. **7**(5), 28–34 (2000)
7. Chen, Z., Xia, F., Huang, T., Fanyu, B., Wang, H.: A localization method for the internet of things. J. Supercomput. **63**(3), 657–674 (2013)
8. Sallouha, H., Chiumento, A., Pollin, S.: Localization in long-range ultra narrow band IoT networks using RSSI. In: 2017 IEEE International Conference on Communications (ICC), pp. 1-6. IEEE (2017)
9. Peng, R., Sichitiu, M.L.: Robust, probabilistic, constraint-based localization for wireless sensor networks. In: 2005 Second Annual IEEE Communications Society Conference on Sensor and Ad Hoc Communications and Networks, 2005, IEEE SECON 2005, pp. 541–550. IEEE (2005)
10. Sichitiu, M.L., Ramadurai, V.: Localization of wireless sensor networks with a mobile beacon. In: 2004 IEEE International Conference on Mobile Ad-hoc and Sensor Systems, pp. 174–183. IEEE (2004)
11. Biswas, P., Ye, Y.: Semidefinite programming for ad hoc wireless sensor network localization. In: Proceedings of the 3rd International Symposium on Information Processing in Sensor Networks, pp. 46-54. ACM (2004)
12. Larsson, E.G.: Cramer-Rao bound analysis of distributed positioning in sensor networks. IEEE Sig. Process. Lett. **11**(3), 334–337 (2004)
13. Mourad, F., Snoussi, H., Abdallah, F., Richard, C.: Guaranteed boxed localization in MANETs by interval analysis and constraints propagation techniques. In: Global Telecommunications Conference 2008, IEEE GLOBECOM 2008, pp. 1–5. IEEE (2008)
14. Mourad, F., Snoussi, H., Abdallah, F., Richard, C.: Model-free interval-based localization in manets. In: IEEE 13th Digital Signal Processing Workshop and 5th IEEE Signal Processing Education Workshop, 2009. DSP/SPE 2009, pp. 474–479. IEEE (2009)
15. Mourad, F., Snoussi, H., Richard, C.: Interval-based localization using RSSI comparison in MANETs. IEEE Trans. Aerosp. Electron. Syst. **47**(4), 2897–2910 (2011)
16. Waltz, D.L.: Generating semantic descriptions from drawings of scenes with shadows (1972)
17. Fruchterman, T.M.J., Reingold, E.M.: Graph drawing by force directed placement. Softw.: Pract. Exp. **21**(11), 1129–1164 (1991)
18. Kamada, T., Kawai, S.: An algorithm for drawing general undirected graphs. Inf. Proc. Lett. **31**(1), 7–15 (1989)

19. Ellson, J., Gansner, E., Koutsofios, L., North, S.C., Woodhull, G.: Graphviz—open source graph drawing tools. In: Mutzel, P., Jünger, M., Leipert, S. (eds.) GD 2001. LNCS, vol. 2265, pp. 483–484. Springer, Heidelberg (2002). https://doi.org/10.1007/3-540-45848-4_57
20. Eren, T., et al.: Rigidity, computation, and randomization in network localization. In: INFOCOM 2004, Twenty-third AnnualJoint Conference of the IEEE Computer and Communications Societies, vol. 4, pp. 2673–2684. IEEE (2004)
21. Čapkun, S., Hamdi, M., Hubaux, J.-P.: GPS-free positioning in mobile ad hoc networks. Cluster Comput. 5(2), 157–167 (2002)

Low Energy-Efficient Clustering and Routing Based on Genetic Algorithm in WSNs

Ranida Hamidouche[1,2]($\boxtimes$), Zibouda Aliouat[1], and Abdelhak Gueroui[2]

[1] LRSD Laboratory, University Ferhat Abbes Setif 1, El Bez, Setif, Algeria
{ranida.hamidouche,zaliouat}@univ-setif.dz
[2] LI-PaRAD Laboratory, University of Paris Saclay, University of Versailles,
Saint-Quentin-en-Yvelines, Versailles, France
mourad.gueroui@uvsq.fr

Abstract. To accommodate the limited resources of sensors and specially energy capacity, researchers are increasingly interested in their improvement by developing new aware energy protocols to relay data to the concerned application. Finding near optimal solutions for the energy problem is still an issue in Wireless Sensor Networks (WSNs). A new era is opened with algorithms inspired by nature, which are meta-heuristic imitating living systems, to solve optimization problems. For this purpose, the Low Energy-Efficient Clustering and Routing Based on Genetic Algorithm (LECR-GA) mechanism is proposed. LECR-GA aims to prolong the WSN life-time and enhance its quality of service (QoS). Extensive simulations of the proposed solution were performed and their results were compared with those of literature.

Keywords: Wireless Sensor Networks · Bio-inspired
Genetic algorithm · Clustering · Routing

1 Background and Motivation

Wireless Sensor networks (WSNs) are used in many applications, such as healthcare, environment, industry, environment monitoring surveillance in military battle field and so on. Scientists have the mission to find an efficient way in order to influence their future. They must overcome the major problems which WSNs are facing today, such as routing information in the network or the rapid depletion of energy [1].

According to literature, there are many routing schemes in WSN. Network structure can be flat or cluster-based [2]. Grouping sensor nodes into clusters provides an efficient and scalable network structure [3]. Various distributed cluster based routing protocols were proposed for WSNs. LEACH (Low Energy Adaptive Clustering Hierarchy) [4] is one of the wellknown of them. In this

© Springer Nature Switzerland AG 2019
E. Renault et al. (Eds.): MSPN 2018, LNCS 11005, pp. 143–156, 2019.
https://doi.org/10.1007/978-3-030-03101-5_14

protocol, at each round CHs are selected in arbitrary manner. Farther node can be selected as CH and this may lead to both CH and its members dissipate their energy quickly which constitutes a real weakness. Other centralized cluster based algorithms have also been developed for WSNs. As an example, LEACH-Centralised (LEACH-C) [5], a version of LEACH where selection of CHs is done by BS. After selection phase of CHs, BS inform all nodes about clustering. Thus, in large scale networks, that leads to energy exhaustion. That's why centralized approaches are applied only in small networks.

However, the classic solutions for cluster based routing protocols are not reliable for a large scale network because that requires a significant treatment to find the optimal solution. An efficient solution is using meta-heuristic approaches such as genetic algorithm (GA). GAs are based on the biological mechanisms such as the laws of Mendel and the fundamental principle of selection of Charles Darwin [6], the methods of evolutionary programming developed by Fogel [7] and the evolutionary strategies developed by Rechenberg [8] and Schwefel [9]. There are many GA based approaches for clustering in WSNs. A mechanism called "Economic Control Couverture Algorithm" (ECCA) [10], inspired by the multi-objective genetic algorithms (MOGAs) [11]), is used to maintain full coverage by optimizing the number of active nodes. Bhondekar et al. [12] proposed a low energy dissipation solution. The GA decide the selected active sensors, choose CHs and adjust the non-CH nodes transmission capacity. Contrariwise, the algorithm does not use intra-cluster multi-hop communications. Ferentinos and Tsiligkaridis [13] presented an "Adaptive design optimization of wireless sensor networks using genetic algorithms" (ADOGA). It has sophisticated features that make it capable to decide the activity/inactivity of the sensors. It manages the different roles of the sensors in function of their wireless signal. Bayrakli and Erdogan [14] proposed the algorithm GABEEC (Genetic Algorithm Based Energy Efficient Clusters). In this protocol, GA is applied to maximise time duration of network by finding the optimal number and location of CHs in each round. However, clusters number are fixed during the network lifetime. This leads to an unbalanced clusters. Hussain et al. [15] proposed an intelligent energy-efficient hierarchical clustering protocol named HCR-GA. It is applied only in small networks and it is not scalable. Song et al. [16] proposed a flat GA for energy-entropy based multipath routing in WSNs (GAEMW). In this solution, all nodes have equal functions and responsibilities. Every sensor is a transceiver/receptor in the same time, which may deplete its energy very quickly. Mohammed et al. [17] presented a new Genetic Algorithm-based Energy-Efficient adaptive clustering hierarchy Protocol (GAEEP) to preserve node's energy by finding the best CHs using GA. Thus, GAEEP improves the stable period and maximizes the lifetime of WSNs.

However, none of the above algorithms consider the multipath intra-cluster data routing. Even, none of them except [16] combined the advantages of hierarchical distributed mechanisms with multipath transmissions. The present paper is distinguished with regards to others in the literature by the following issues.

1. It deals with both GA based clustering and routing algorithms whereas literature considers only one of them based on GA.
2. Proposed GA based clustering saves energy using residual energy of nodes and the density criterion.
3. Proposed GA based routing performs data delivering using intra-cluster multipath transmissions.

The novelty of this work stands in the development of a new Low Energy hierarchical Clustering and Routing protocol based on Genetic Algorithm (LECR-GA) to efficiently maximize the lifetime and to improve the WSNs quality of service (QoS). The proposed clustering algorithm takes into account new parameters to optimize the mechanism of CHs selection. The improved algorithm introduced two characteristics including energy and the weight of a node (i.e. number of neighbours of the neighbours). By using the GA, the entire space of research was explored to arrive at a desired optimization (best number and location of the CH), therefore, an economy of energy. The routing mechanism finds out the optimum path from all members of the cluster to the CH by choosing the most beneficial route, going through sensors having more energy and less distance to achieve data. The LECR-GA is divided into rounds. Each round begins with a clustering (set-up) phase where the optimum number of CHs is found and non-CH nodes join the nearest CH. Followed by a routing (steady-state) phase, where the sensed data are transferred to the end user. Finding good values to genetic parameters is sometimes a delicate problem. However, the efficiency of these algorithms depends strongly on the choice of genetic operators used during the process of the population diversification and in the exploration of the solutions space. The performance of the LECR-GA is compared with protocols of literature using Network Simulator 2 (NS2) simulation.

Table 1 summarizes the properties of some classical and based GA protocols to save energy.

Table 1. Summary of properties of energy saving protocols.

Clustering Schemes	Authors	Connectiv	Energy efficiency	Load balancing	Scalability	Coverage	Topology	Distribution	Path	Method	Complexity
LEACH	Chandrakasan et al. (2000)	Low	Very poor	Medium	No	Poor	Hierarchic	Distributed	Unique	Classic	Low O(n)
LEACH-C	Heinzelman et al. (2002)	Low	Poor	Medium	No	Poor	Hierarchic	Centralized	Unique	Classic	Low O(n)
ECCA	Jia et al. (2009)	High	Medium	Medium	Yes	High	Hierarchic	Distributed	Unique	Based on GA	High $O(n^2)$
/	Bhondekar et al. (2009)	High	Medium	Medium	Yes	High	Hierarchic	Distributed	Multi-hop inter-cluster	Based on GA	High $O(n^2)$
ADOGA	Ferentinos and Tsiligkaridis (2007)	High	Medium	Medium	Yes	High	Hierarchic	Centralized	Unique	Based on GA	High $O(n^2)$
GABEEC	Bayrakli and Erdogan (2012)	Low	Medium	Poor	No	Poor	Hierarchic	Distributed	Unique	Based on GA	Low O(n)
GAEMW	Song et al. (2015)	Low	Poor	Poor	No	Poor	Flat	Distributed	Multi-path inter-cluster	Based on GA	Low O(n)
GAEEP	Sabor et al. (2014)	High	Medium	Medium	Yes	High	Hierarchic	Centralized	Unique	Based on GA	Low O(n)
HCR-GA	Hussain et al. (2007)	Low	Medium	Medium	No	Poor	Hierarchic	Centralized	Unique	Based on GA	Low O(n)

2   LECR-GA: Low Energy-Efficient Clustering and Routing Based on Genetic Algorithm

A presentation of our GA based algorithm is now given. It takes place in "rounds" which have approximately the same predetermined time interval. As shown in Fig. 1, each round consists of a clustering phase and a routing phase. Figure 2 is the detailed steps of the members organization in layers.

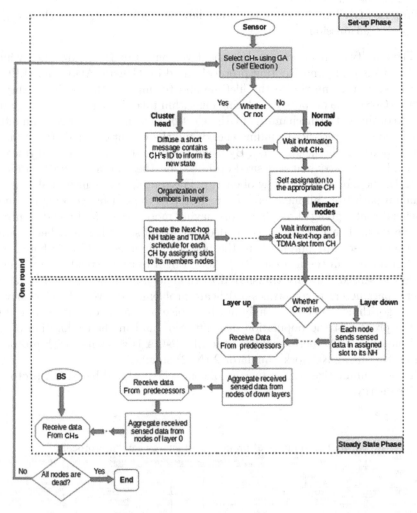

Fig. 1. Flow Chart of the proposed LECR-GA protocol

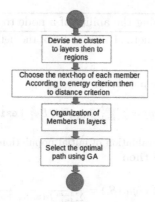

Fig. 2. Flow chart of organization members in layers

In the proposed LECR-GA protocol, the following assumptions about network model are fixed:

- The BS is not limited in terms of energy, memory and computing power.
- The BS is located outside the WSN.
- All sensor nodes and the BS are stationary during all the simulation.
- All sensors have a device to determine location.
- The WSN includes homogeneous sensor nodes.
- Initially, all nodes sensors have the same amount of energy.

2.1 Proposed Clustering Algorithm Based on GA

Our main focus is to maximize the network lifetime. This objective depends on the selection parameters of CHs and the cluster formation. Best number and positions of CHs are attended using the appropriate genetic parameters and energy of sensor nodes is minimised by choosing the nearest CHas performed by Algorithm 1.

Chromosome Representation: The chromosome is represented as a set of genes. Each gene is the concatenation of the values of the residual energy and the distance between the node and its neighbours. This explains our use of the real encoding genes. The number of live nodes indicates the size of the chromosome.

Initial Population: A set of chromosomes (all the living nodes of the network) is generated to create the initial population.

Algorithm 1. Determining the ability of a node to operate as a CH

Data: A population of N normal alive nodes of the network
Result: CHs nodes
begin

    A. Initialization of the population
    for *Each node* **do**
        1- Calculate $E(avg) = \sum_{i=1}^{i=N} E_{S_i} N$ //E_{S_i} `Residual energy of the`
        `node`
        B. Performances evaluation of initial population
        if $E_{S_i} >= E(avg)$ **then**
            C. Selection
            1- Calculate $Weight(S_i) = \frac{E_{S_i}}{\sum_{d=n}^{d=m} D(S_i,S_n)+...+D(S_i,S_m)}$
            2- Sort the list of $Weight$ in descending order //`Insertion sort`
            D. Performance evaluation of selected individual's
            if *If Node is in the 70% of the first cases of $Weight$* **then**
                1- Calculate $SNL(S_i) = \frac{Neigh_{S_i}}{N}$ //$Neigh_{S_i}$ `is the number of`
                `neighbours of the node` S
                if $(SNL(S_i) >= T_n)$ and (random number $< T_n$) **then**
                    F. Best individual //`Stop the algorithm`
                    Choose the node as CH
                end
            end
        end
    end
end

- The calculation of the average energy $E(avg)$: It is done using formula 1.

$$E(avg) = \frac{E_{S_1} + E_{S_2} + E_{S_3} + ... + E_{S_N}}{N} = \frac{\sum_{i=1}^{i=N} E_{S_i}}{N} \qquad (1)$$

where E_{S_i} is the residual energy of the node and N is the number of living nodes.

- Performances evaluation of initial population: After selecting the initial population, we must evaluate it according to energy criterion. If the residual energy of the node is greater than the average energy of the Network, the node can be a CH.

Selection: Once the performance evaluation of initial population step completed, the primary population on which another selection is made according to new criteria, is obtained. We look for all the nodes in the neighbourhood of the node S_i. Then we calculate the distance separating these nodes and S_i. At this level, we will introduce a new parameter, which we will call the *weight* of the node S_i described by formula 2:

$$Weight(S_i) = \frac{E_{S_i}}{\sum_{d=n}^{d=m} D(S_i, S_n) + ... + D(S_i, S_m)} \qquad (2)$$

where D is the distance between the node S_i and its neighbors and E_{S_i} is the residual energy of the node S_i. The *weight* list is sorted in order to facilitate its manipulation.

Performance Evaluation of Selected Individual's: After the list is sorted, the node in the 70% of the first cases in the *weight* list will participate in the new population for replacement.

- The computation of SNL_{S_i} (Neighboring-Life of node Sensor S_i) is made by introducing a new formula (3). It creates a relationship between the number of neighbors and the number of living nodes. More the SNL_{S_i} result is large, more likely, the node S_i will be a CH.

$$SNL_{(S_i)} = \frac{Neigh_{S_i}}{N} \tag{3}$$

where $Neigh_{S_i}$ is the number of neighbors of the node S and N is the number of the living nodes. The objective *Fitness* is described by formula (4). To be the best node elected as CH, the *fitness* function must be maximized. Obviously, the nodes having the maximum *weight* value, means that the transmission of data is more beneficial using these nodes. They need less energy and have more neighbours.

$$Fitness = max(weight) + max(SNL_{(S_i)}) \tag{4}$$

Mutation and Crossover: During the application of our algorithm, we will not need either crossover or mutation since we will reach the optimum the first time. In this case, the probability p_c and p_m are very small and can be neglected.

Best Individual: Finally, after computing the node's SNL_{S_i}, the result is compared to that obtained by the function $T(n)$.

$$T(n) = \begin{cases} \frac{p}{1-p*[rmod(\frac{1}{p})]} & n \in G \\ 0 & n \notin G \end{cases} \tag{5}$$

where **p** is the probability of CH in each round, which is the ratio of the total number of CH and nodes, **r** is the current round number, **G** is the set of nodes that have not been selected recently in $\frac{1}{p}$ of the rounds. If SNL_{S_i} is strictly greater than $T(n)$, the node is CH in this round. All elected nodes must inform the other nodes of the network of their decisions, using a maximum transmission radius to be heard by all the nodes. After receiving all warning packets, non-CH nodes join the best CH (nearest CH).

2.2   Proposed Routing Algorithm Based on GA

After cluster formation, the cluster space was divided into four layers over the cluster area (Circle centered by the CH with a radius equal to the distance of the furthest node from the CH). This will enable us to choose the next hop according to the distance criterion. Each layer was then divided into regions (North-east, North-west, South-East...) for choosing the next hop according to the energy criterion. Once this grouping is completed, we can apply our GA by Algorithm 2 to obtain the best paths as shown in Fig. 3.

Algorithm 2. The optimal Path according to the GA

Data: Next hops of node N_i (according to the distance and the energy criterion)
Result: Best path
begin
   1- Initialization of the population
   `//Having the Distance Path and Energy Path`
   if $DistancePath = EnergyPath$ **then**
     | Optimal-Path = Distance Path
   else
     2- Calculate Distance, Hop and Energy values
     3- Performance evaluation
     if $fitness_{(DistancePath)} < fitness_{(EnergyPath)}$ **then**
       | Optimal-Path = Distance Path
     else
       | Optimal-Path = Energy Path
     end
     if $Hop_{(DistancePath)} == Hop_{(EnergyPath)}$ **then**
       $Emp = 1$
       while $Emp < ((length[DistancePath]) - 1)$ **do**
         4- Crossover at one point at location Emp
         5- Performance evaluation
         if $(fitness_{(CrossedPath)} < fitness_{(EnergyPath)})$ and $(fitness_{(CrossedPath)} < fitness_{(DistancePath)})$ **then**
           | Optimal-Path = Crossed Path
         else
           6- The mutation
           if $(fitness_{(MutatedPath)} < fitness_{(EnergyPath)})$ and $(fitness_{(MutatedPath)} < fitness_{(DistancePath)})$ **then**
             | Optimal-Path = Mutated Path
           end
         end
         $Emp = Emp + 1$
       end
     end
   end
end

Layer Cluster Division: One of the most striking features of large scaling network is managing energy consumption. It should be noticed that the communication in clusters with a large number of nodes, quickly exhaust the CH battery. To solve these problems, a new concept called "Tree Trunk Approach"

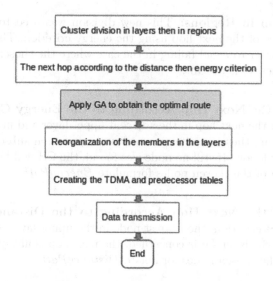

Fig. 3. Path construction with GA

was introduced. After determining the optimum number of CH and their locations, as well as the clusters formation, the "Tree Trunk Approach" will be applied. A layered network is formed and the members of the cluster are placed in these layers as illustrated in Fig. 4. In this case, each node of the cluster knows exactly the nodes that are placed in the upper and lower layers and communicates with them. It can be noticed that the center of our tree trunk is represented by the CH. The "Nearest Node" is the closer node to the CH and "min" is its distance, and the "Farthest Node" is the further node from the CH and "max" is its distance. Based on their positions, the cluster was cut into four layers. The option of this number of layers was made to have several hops, necessary for the application of our GA. To do this, the distance between each member node and the CH was computed. Next, each node was assigned to its layer by referring to Table 2 where A is calculated using the following formula 6.

$$A = (max - min)/4 \tag{6}$$

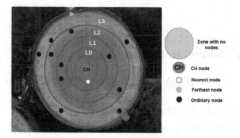

Fig. 4. Layer cluster division

Table 2. Interval layers

Layers	Layer 0	Layer 1
Interval	$[min,$ $(A+min)[$	$[(A+min),$ $(2A+min)[$
Layers	Layer 2	Layer 3
Interval	$[(2A+min),$ $(3A+min)[$	$[(3A+min),$ $max]$

Cluster Division in Regions: This new division was used to make a more appropriate choice of the next hop using the energy criterion. This second division is made in order to avoid falling in the case where the chosen node (having the maximum energy) is distant.

Calculation of the Next Hop According to the Energy Criterion: The idea is to look for the next hop in the adjacent upper layer and in the same area. If no node verifying these conditions was found, we search subsequently in the upper layers that follow. If still no node was found, the CH will be the next hop. The combination of the chosen nodes formulate *EnergyPath*.

Calculation of the Next Hop According to the Distance Criterion: With the distance criterion, the nearest node in the upper layer is chosen as the next hop. When the layer $L0$ is concerned, the next hop is always the CH. The combination of the chosen nodes formulate *DistancePath*.

Application of the GA: After finding the next hop of each node (according to both criteria), the GA can be applied to find the optimal (beneficial) route. The proposed algorithm for routing from cluster members to CH is now presented.

Gene Representation: A gene is represented by a string determining the member nodes. Each gene represents the identity of the node (using the real coding). A group of nodes including the CH represent a set of genes (chromosome). The number of hops indicates the size of the chromosome.

Initial Population: At this step, each node has two ways (chromosomes) to route the data to the CH. One is according to the energy criterion, the other is according to the distance. These two paths will be our initial population (two parents). Moreover, the probability of crossover is equal to $p_c = 0.99$ and the probability of mutation is equal to $p_m = 0.01$ or $p_m = 0$ (no mutation).
   - Calculation of Distance, Hop and Energy:
Distance is the distance traveled along this path, Hop is the number of hops and Energy is the total energy of the nodes forming the route.

   - Performance evaluation:
To evaluate the performance of the two routes that we obtained in the initialization phase, the *fitness* function is introduced in formula 7:

$$fitness = (0.04 * Distance) + (0.02 * Hop) + (0.94 * Energy) \qquad (7)$$

where 0.04, 0.02, and 0.94 are fixed constants for the entire simulation. Several coefficients have been tested and these one chosen gave us a better simulation results than others. We will try to minimize this function, since $Min(fitness)$ shows that the packet travelling along this path, travels less distance, passes through a reduced number of hops and has a very high energy. The energy coefficient is large since the energy criterion is favoured.

- Crossover:

If the number of hops is equal for both routes, a 1-point crossover is applied as shown in Fig. 5. Crossover at 1-point will create two children from both parents so that each child has a part of each parent chromosome. For this, we choose an integer i as i $\in [1, n[$, the first child will copy the genes 1, ..., i of the parent 1 and the genes i + 1, ..., n of the parent 2, and reciprocally for the second child. When there are a number of different hops, the optimal route is necessarily one of the two initial routes.

- Mutation:

The mutation is applied only if the *fitness* of the crossover is greater than the *fitness* of the two initial routes. An illustrative example is shown in Fig. 6. Mutation here consists of performing a random alteration of one gene of the chromosome.

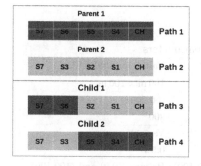

Fig. 5. Crossover at 1 point $(i = 2)$

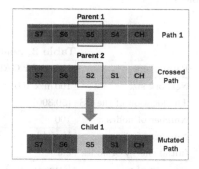

Fig. 6. Mutation at one 1 point $(i = 3)$

Reorganization of the Members in the Layers: After obtaining the optimal routes, each node will know its next hop. It can happen that a node, located in layer $L3$, will have its next hop in layer $L1$. In order to avoid synchronization problems, the layers were reorganized.

Creating the TDMA and Predecessor Tables: When each node has found its place in the layers, the TDMA table can be constructed by concatenating the lists $L3$, $L2$, $L1$ and $L0$. The distant members will transmit first. Having already assigned to each node its next hop, the table of predecessors can be structured.

Data Transmission: The CH remains in a sleep mode until the turn of the nodes in $L0$ for transmission arrives. When the nodes have received the tables (TDMA, predecessor and next hop), each one will use the Duty-Cycle technique to program the time of its sleep and its awakening. The Duty-Cycle is a technique used by the node sensor to save energy by switching periodically between the sleep mode "sleep" and the active mode "awake". The main idea is to reduce the unnecessary activity time of the node, the sensor wake up only in the time of the transmission or reception of data. The functions of data transmission to the upper layer and to the CH aggregate the data after each reception. When the CH received the data from all the members of $L0$ with the data of their predecessors, it will transmit them to the BS with a single hop.

3   Simulation Results and Analysis

In this section, simulations using NS2 were performed to analyse and evaluate the performance of the proposed Protocol. To eliminate the experimental error caused by randomness, each experiment was run for 10 different times and the average was taken as the final result. The parameters used are described in Table 3.

Table 3. Simulation parameters

Parameters	Values for GAEEP	Values for GABEEC
Network size	100 m x 100 m	100 m x 100 m
The location of the BS	(50,300)	(50,200)
Number of nodes	100	200
Number of clusters	Variable	Variable
Initial energy of nodes	0.5 J	0.5 J
Position of nodes	Between (0,0) and (100,100)	Between (0,0) and (100,100)
Round time	20 s	20 s
Transmission radius	30 m	30 m
Simulation time	3600 s	3600 s
Packet size	2000 bits	2000 bits

In Fig. 7 the performance of the GAEEP and LECR-GA protocols was evaluated in terms of the number of dead nodes. From this Fig. 7, it is noticed that the of first node death (FND) after 1000 s and all nodes died after 1175 s in GAEEP. However in LECR-GA protocol, the FND after 490 s and all nodes died after 1980 s. The LECR-GA prolongs the network lifetime by 35% compared to the GAEEP protocol, because the residual energy of sensors nodes in the proposed protocol decreases more slowly. This is related to the fact that the LECR-GA protocol always selects the nodes having higher energy than the average energy of the network to be CHs.

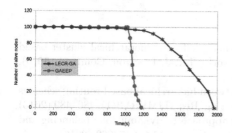
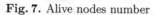

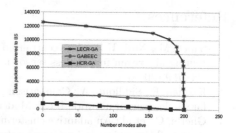

Fig. 7. Alive nodes number

Fig. 8. Packets number function of alive nodes number

Different network configurations are used in this simulation, for example the BS is located out of the network area (200 meters away) and their are 200 nodes (scalability) dispersed randomly in 100×100 m^2 area. Figure 8 shows the amount of data received by the BS according to the number of alive nodes for the GABEEC, HCR-GA and LECR-GA protocols. The main purpose to compare HCR-GA and GABEEC was to know if our protocol LECR-GA keeps the same efficient performance even in large scale networks. We note that with 200 nodes, the number of data packets received was 70000 using LECR-GA, only 12000 using GABEEC and 2000 using HCR-GA. As the number of living nodes decreases, the BS continues to receive a phenomenal number of data packets until reaching 125000 data packets using LECR-GA, corresponding to the total extinction of the nodes. At the moment when the variation of the number of data packets received was only between 15000 and 20000 data packets for the GABEEC protocol, and between 8000 and 10000 data packets for the HCR-GA protocol, at the end of the simulation. It can be noticed that LECR-GA protocol have more data rate than HCR-GA and GABEEC protocols. Distributed systems are favored when it comes to large scale networks, where generally centralized systems fail to control a very large number of nodes.

4   Conclusion

Wireless sensor networks, that proliferate many applications which can be critical such as health-care and surveillance of military battle field, face the challenge of limited energy capacity. To achieve an efficient energy consumption, a distributed protocol based on genetic algorithm, namely LECR-GA, is proposed. Adopting the right choice of chromosome representation, fitness function and GA operations have led to longer system operability and maximum data rate with low complexity. The experimental results showed that the performance of the proposed algorithms is better than GABEEC and GAEEP, in terms of energy consumption and throughput.

Acknowledgement. This research work is supported in part by PHC-Tassili, Grant Number 18MDU114.

References

1. Sabet, M., Naji, H.R.: A decentralized energy efficient hierarchical cluster-based routing algorithm for wireless sensor networks. Int. J. Electron. Commun. **69**(5), 790–799 (2015)
2. Krishan, P., Siddiqua, A.: Comparison between hierarchical based routing schemes for wireless sensor network. Int. J. Modern Eng. Res. (IJMER) **3**(1), 486–489 (2013)
3. Gherbi, C., et al.: An adaptive clustering approach to dynamic load balancing and energy efficiency in wireless sensor networks. Energy **114**, 647–662 (2016)
4. Miao, H., et al.: Improvement and application of leach protocol based on genetic algorithm for WSN. In: IEEE 20th International Workshop on Computer Aided Modelling and Design of Communication Links and Networks (CAMAD), Guildford, UK, pp. 242–245. IEEE, September 2015
5. Heinzelman, W.R., et al.: An application-specific protocol architecture for wireless microsensor networks. IEEE Trans. Wirel. Commun. **1**(4), 660–670 (2002)
6. Darwin, C.: On the Origin of Species. John Murray, London (1906)
7. Fogel, L.J., et al.: Artificial Intelligence Through Simulated Evolution. Wiley, Hoboken (1967)
8. Rechenberg, I.: Evolution Strategy: Optimization of Technical Systems According to Principles of Biological Evolution, vol. 86. Frommann-Holzboog, Stuttgart (1973)
9. Schwefel, H.P.: Numerical Optimization of Computer Models. Wiley, Hoboken (1981)
10. Jia, J., et al.: Energy efficient coverage control in wireless sensor networks based on multi-objective genetic algorithm. Comput. Math. Appl. **57**(11–12), 1756–1766 (2009)
11. Srinvas, N., Deb, K.: Multi-objective function optimization using non-dominated sorting genetic algorithms. Evol. Comput. **2**(3), 221–248 (1994)
12. Bhondekar, A.P., et al.: Genetic algorithm based node placement methodology for wireless sensor networks. In: The International Multi Conference of Engineers and Computer Scientist (IMECS), China, Hong Kong, vol. 1, pp. 1–7 (2009)
13. Ferentinos, K.P., Tsiligiridis, T.A.: Adaptive design optimization of wireless sensor networks using genetic algorithms. Comput. Netw. **51**(4), 1031–1051 (2007)
14. Bayrakli, S., Erdogan, S.Z.: Genetic algorithm based energy efficient clusters (GABEEC) in wireless sensor networks. The 3rd International Conference on Ambient Systems. Networks and Technologies (ANT), vol. 10, pp. 247–254. Istanbul, Turkey (2012)
15. Hussain, S., et al.: Genetic algorithm for energy efficient clusters in wireless sensor networks. In: The 4th International Conference on Information Technology (ITNG 2007), Las Vegas, NV, USA, pp. 147–154. IEEE, April 2007
16. Song, Y., et al.: A genetic algorithm for energy-efficient based multipath routing in wireless sensor networks. Wirel. Pers. Commun. **85**(4), 2055–2066 (2015)
17. Sabor, N., et al.: A new energy-efficient adaptive clustering protocol based on genetic algorithm for improving the lifetime and the stable period of wireless sensor networks. Int. J. Energy Inf. Commun. **5**(3), 47–72 (2014)

IoT Service QoS Guarantee Using QBAIoT Wireless Access Method

Ahmad Khalil$^{(\boxtimes)}$, Nader Mbarek, and Olivier Togni

University of Bourgogne Franche-Comté, Dijon, France
{Ahmad.Khalil,Nader.Mbarek,
Olivier.Togni}@u-bourgogne.fr

Abstract. Nowadays, providing Internet of Things (IoT) environments with service level guarantee is a challenging task. We describe in this paper a service level based IoT architecture that enables an IoT Service Level Agreement (iSLA) achievement between an IoT Service Provider and an IoT Client. This IoT SLA specifies the requirements of an IoT service in a specific application domain (e-health, smart cities, etc.). In order to guarantee these requirements, QoS mechanisms should be implemented within the IoT architecture. Thus, we propose an adaptation of the IEEE 802.15.4 slotted CSMA/CA mechanism to ensure the requirements of an IoT e-health service. Our approach called QBAIoT (QoS based Access for IoT) consists in creating different contention access periods corresponding to different specified traffic classes. Each of these periods within the QoS based adapted IEEE 802.15.4 superframe is specific for a traffic type. A QoS based contention access period called QoS CAP is configured with a number of slots during which only IoT objects belonging to the same QoS class can send data.

Keywords: IoT · e-health · IEEE 802.15.4 · Slotted CSMA/CA
Service level agreement

1 Introduction

Internet of Things (IoT) is nowadays an evidence in our everyday life. Indeed, billions of connected objects exist with an average of two devices per human on earth resulting in creating the IoT environment [1]. The future growth of IoT will lead to an important usage of technology in our daily life in order to facilitate everyday tasks. To ensure better user experience and improve the usage of IoT applications, a certain service level should be offered for IoT services. Consequently, we have to specify QoS mechanisms enabling the guarantee of this service level. In this context, the IEEE 802.15.4 standard is used as a base for different communication technologies in the IoT environment and specifically in the e-health domain. Thus, we specify a novel QoS based wireless access method for IoT environments called *QBAIoT* as an enhancement of the slotted CSMA/CA technique, used by the IEEE 802.15.4 standard. The objective of the proposed enhancement is to guarantee QoS parameters corresponding to the requirements of an e-health IoT service. These requirements are specified into a specific SLA called IoT SLA (*iSLA*). In this paper, we aim to present the design details and

© Springer Nature Switzerland AG 2019
É. Renault et al. (Eds.): MSPN 2018, LNCS 11005, pp. 157–173, 2019.
https://doi.org/10.1007/978-3-030-03101-5_15

performance evaluation of our proposed *QBAIoT* access method and its usage in an IoT architecture in order to satisfy the requirements of an e-health service according to a proposed iSLA. The reminder of the paper is organized as follows. We present in Sect. 2 the state of the art concerning the IoT environment and we introduce the important characteristics of the IEEE 802.15.4 technology. Section 3 describes the QoS motivations in the IoT as well as our service level based IoT architecture along with the proposed *iSLA* and its establishment. Then, we specify in the same section our proposed method enabling QoS based access for IoT environments. Section 4 presents a detailed performance evaluation of our novel access method along with a comparison with the standard IEEE 802.15.4 access method. Finally, we conclude the paper in Sect. 5 and present future works.

2 State of the Art

2.1 Internet of Things

IoT is considered as a heterogeneous system formed by subsystems of interconnected objects that communicate using different communication technologies. The all over system includes self-management capabilities in order to automatize the management process. The IoT uses external resources for the processing and the storage of huge amount of data such as cloud and fog computing. Cloud computing functionalities enhance reliability and efficiency of IoT service provision [2], whereas fog computing decentralize the computing capacities and distribute the operations on network extremities [3]. Furthermore, the IoT environment is used in different application domains like e-health, smart cities, smart building, vehicular networks, etc. [4]. Among these application domains, we focus on the one concerning e-health. The latter combines public health and ICT (Information and Communication Technologies) in order to provide humankind with novel health services [5]. These services are varied and can be as simple as a remote health management of patients or complex as a remote performed operation. Thus, connected objects can be sensors deployed on the patients to monitor their vital signals remotely and storing the corresponding data in the cloud for further analyses. Furthermore, objects can be connected robots performing the remote operation and managed by distant surgeons.

To interconnect objects, different communication technologies are used in conformance with IoT requirements (limited energy consumption and CPU utilization). These various technologies could be grouped into mobile technologies (LTE, 4G, NB-IoT, 5G, etc.) [6] and wireless technologies (IEEE802.15.4 [7], LoRaWAN [8], ZigBee [9], 6LoWPAN [10], etc.). For the e-health domain, different technologies, solutions and research works use ZigBee to interconnect the corresponding IoT objects. In [11], a ZigBee based wireless healthcare monitoring system is presented in order to provide real time information about the health condition of patients. The authors in [12] developed a continuous patients monitoring system based on ZigBee protocol. Furthermore, ZigBee, 6LoWPAN and other communication technologies use IEEE 802.15.4 as a foundation for their lower layers. Therefore, we describe in the following the most important characteristics of this standard.

2.2   IEEE 802.15.4

IEEE 802.15.4 is a standard for Low Rate Wireless Personal Area Network (LR-WPAN). It specifies the Physical (PHY) and Medium Access Control (MAC) layers to define essential parameters like data rate, control functions, data management format and the usage of the slotted CSMA/CA (Carrier-Sense Multiple Access with Collision Avoidance) access method. It provides also some management features like access to medium, synchronization, etc. [7]. Standards and technologies based on IEEE 802.15.4 use its PHY and MAC layers and add their specificities through higher layers.

Beacon-enabled mode of IEEE 802.15.4 uses a superframe structure consisting of an active part known as the Superframe Duration (SD) and can be followed by an inactive period. The SD is equally divided on 16 time-periods known as slots. The slots form a Contention Access Period (CAP) and an optional Contention Free Period (CFP). During the CAP period, nodes compete to gain access to the shared channel. On the other hand, during the CFP period, objects are allocated guaranteed time slots. At the Beacon Interval (BI) corresponding to the end of the superframe, the coordinator sends a beacon frame to all nodes in the WPAN. The Beacon is used to allow the coordinator to identify its WPAN, to synchronize the nodes and to communicate the values of the Beacon Order (BO) and the Superframe Order (SO). BO and SO are used by the nodes to calculate the BI and the SD according to Eqs. (1) and (2) respectively.

$$BI = BSFD * 2^{BO} \tag{1}$$

$$SD = BSFD * 2^{SO} \tag{2}$$

Base Superframe Duration ($BSFD$) corresponds to the minimum duration of a superframe, when $SO = 0$. It is fixed to 960 symbols of 4 bits. In addition, BO and SO should respect the inequality $0 \leq SO \leq BO \leq 14$ [7]. Three variables are used in the slotted CSMA/CA algorithm:

- Backoff Exponent (BE) used to compute the backoff delay observed by a node before performing the Clear Channel Assessment (CCA) on the shared medium. The value of BE is chosen randomly by the algorithm between 0 and ($2^{BE} - 1$).
- Contention Window (CW) corresponds to the number of backoff periods during which the channel must be idle before accessing the channel. It has a default value of 2.
- Number of Backoffs (NB) is the number of backoff executed before channel access. It is initialized to 0 and compared to a maximum value, $macMaxCSMABackoffs$ by default equal to 5. If the value of NB is greater than the maximum value, a failure occurs.

The slotted CSMA/CA algorithm is used for each transmission of a packet (See Fig. 1).

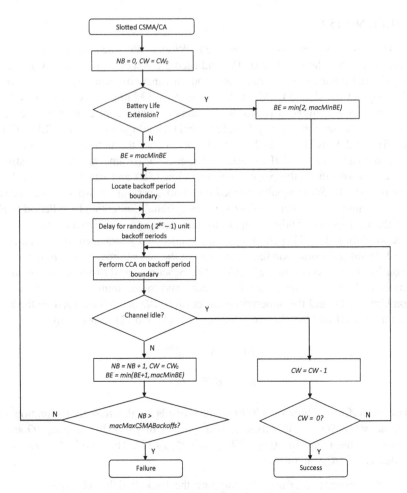

Fig. 1. Slotted CSMA/CA algorithm [7]

3 QoS Guarantee Within Internet of Things Environment

We have to deploy various QoS mechanisms at different layers of the IoT architecture in order to provide IoT objects with service level guarantee. We describe in the following QoS challenges and motivations in IoT environment. Then, we present our service level based IoT architecture and we specify our QoS adaptation of the slotted CSMA/CA access method used in IEEE 802.15.4.

3.1 QoS Motivation and Challenges in IoT

QoS guarantee is a challenging task in the IoT environment due to the increasing number of connected objects leading to a greater amount of data with different characteristics. Consequently, IoT traffic performance will be affected and especially the performance of QoS constrained data streams during congestion periods. In order to avoid performance degradation when delivering critical data, an effective and optimized management of the available resources is necessary to guarantee a certain service level in the IoT environment. This service level guarantee is possible thanks to the specification of QoS mechanisms in different layers of the IoT architecture in order to satisfy different QoS requirements and parameters such as delay, jitter, bandwidth and packet loss ratio for various traffic types [13]. Indeed, these QoS mechanisms must take into consideration different components of the IoT environment (sensing, gateway, network and cloud) in order to achieve an End-to-End service level guarantee for IoT services.

3.2 IoT Service Level Based Architecture

In order to allow an IoT Service Provider (*IoT-SP*) to deliver an IoT service to an IoT Client (*IoT-C*) in conformance with a global IoT-SLA (*iSLA*), we propose a service level based architecture with a usage scenario concerning an e-health service (see Fig. 2).

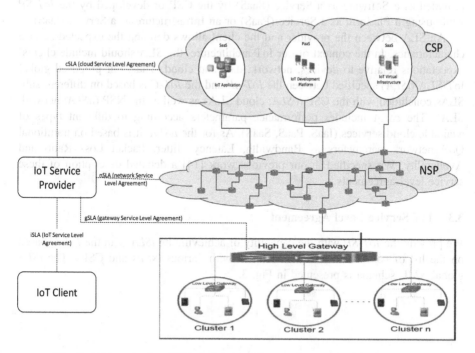

Fig. 2. IoT service level based global architecture for an e-health application

The proposed architecture is based on different entities with specific roles:

- The *IoT-C* requests a service from the IoT Service Provider and can use an IoT objects infrastructure provided by the *IoT-SP* or its own infrastructure.
- The *IoT-SP* offers IoT services for the *IoT-C*. It has its own cloud infrastructure or subscribes specific SLAs with different Cloud Service Providers (CSPs). The cloud infrastructure is used to store the huge amount of data created, for computation capabilities and for applications hosting. In addition, the *IoT-SP* subscribes SLAs with different Network Service Providers (NSPs) to interconnect the IoT objects infrastructure with the cloud infrastructure.

The IoT service is divided into an application part and an objects infrastructure part. The objects infrastructure retrieve information or execute orders. It is managed by High Level Gateways (*HL-Gws*) to ensure minimal bandwidth consumption while transmitting data to the cloud (data aggregation) and offers fog computing capacities to process data for non-delay tolerant services. In addition, Low Level Gateways (*LL-Gws*) ensure data classification for differentiation and manage object clusters. On the other hand, the application part allows object monitoring for orders execution or information processing. It is usually hosted on the cloud infrastructure and can be provided as a Software as a Service (SaaS) by the CSP or developed by the *IoT-SP* while using a Platform as a Service (PaaS) or an Infrastructure as a Service (IaaS).

An SLA between the provider and the client allows defining the expected service characteristics. In the context of our IoT architecture, the SLA should include clients' expectations relative to devices, network, data and cloud. Thus, our proposed global IoT-SLA (*iSLA*) specified between the *IoT-SP* and the *IoT-C* is based on different sub-SLAs concluded with the CSP (*cSLA*: cloud SLA) as well as the NSP (*nSLA*: network SLA). The *cSLA* includes performance parameters according to different types of available cloud services (IaaS, PaaS, SaaS). As for the *nSLA*, it is based on traditional QoS network parameters as Bandwidth, Latency, Jitter, Packet Loss Ratio and Availability. We specified in our previous work [14] a detailed description of these service level agreements.

3.3   IoT Service Level Agreement

We provide the *IoT-SP* with the capability of achieving an *iSLA* with the *IoT-C* based on the list of *cSLAs* and *nSLAs* concluded with various NSPs and CSPs. The *iSLA* global XML schema is presented in Fig. 3.

Fig. 3. XML global schema for iSLA

The *iSLA* contains a Service Identification attribute to specify the IoT service from the source side by a list of client IP addresses and for the destination side by an application ID, an application Interface IP along with the port number as well as the ID of the *HL-Gw* and *LL-Gws*. Furthermore, the *iSLA* contains an IoT Service Performance Parameters attribute describing the IoT Sensing Characteristics as well as IoT Application Characteristics and IoT QoS Parameters. Thus, the IoT Sensing Characteristics part of the *iSLA* includes all the characteristics of the gateways (*HL-Gw, LL-Gw*) and the IoT smart objects group. Then, the IoT Application Characteristics part of the *iSLA* includes parameters related to the *cSLA* such as Application ID, the maximum number of users, the mean number of requests per second per user, Time of Support and the Storage parameters. Finally, the IoT QoS parameters part of the *iSLA* is classified into qualitative and quantitative parameters. The qualitative characteristics define the application type by specifying the QoS class of the data generated (*RTMC*: Real Time Mission Critical, *RTNMC*: Real Time Non Mission Critical, Streaming and *NRT*: Non Real Time). The quantitative QoS parameters include the End-to-End Delay, Availability, Lifetime and Data Quality (Standard Deviation, Sensing Frequency and Data Error Ratio).

Financial elements are essential in *SLAs*. Therefore, the *iSLA* contains an IoT Business Parameters attribute. The latter includes an IoT Service Cost part as well as IoT Violations and Penalties part where we specify thresholds and the monitoring interval time for each IoT QoS parameter.

As a usage case, we consider an e-health service belonging to the Real Time Mission Critical class and we describe how to establish the corresponding *iSLA* within our IoT architecture in order to satisfy the requirements of such application. In this context, we present a Message Sequence Chart that illustrates the interactions that occur between the different components of our architecture (see Fig. 4).

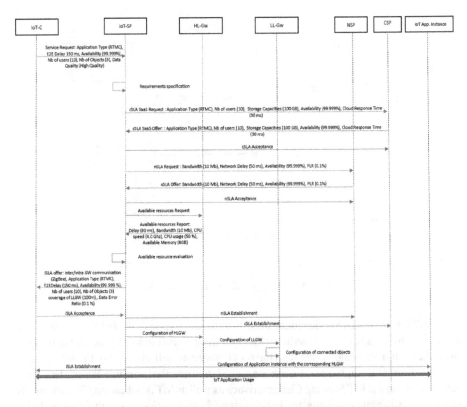

Fig. 4. IoT components interaction for e-health application iSLA establishment

The e-health application is a Real Time Mission Critical application that requires a limited End-to-End Delay (150 ms) with high Availability (99.999%) and a high Data Quality. The End-to-End Delay declines into IoT Application Response Time (Cloud), the IoT Sensing Response Time (Objects) and the Network Delay. As shown in the MSC (see Fig. 4), the *IoT-C* initiates the *iSLA* establishment by sending a request concerning the desired IoT service with its requirements. Then, the *IoT-SP* will classify the requirements in three types; the cloud requirements, the network requirements and the gateways and sensing requirements. After the classification, the *IoT-SP* chooses among the best offers available from CSPs and NSPs to serve the *IoT-C*. The *IoT-SP* initiates a *cSLA* request to the corresponding CSP and waits for his proposal. If the proposed *cSLA* meets the specified requirements, a *cSLA* Acceptance will be sent by the *IoT-SP*. Similarly, an *nSLA* request is initiated by the *IoT-SP*. The corresponding NSP should send its proposal and the *IoT-SP* accepts it if it meets the requirements. Afterwards, the *IoT-SP* evaluates the available resources on the corresponding *HL-Gw* to be used by the *IoT-C* requested service. A report about gateway resources' availability will be collected by the *IoT-SP*. Based on this report, the *IoT-SP* concludes an internal SLA called gateway SLA (*gSLA*) with the existing *HL-Gw* or with a new implemented one. Thus, the *IoT-SP* has the capability to propose an *iSLA* to the *IoT-C* based on the *cSLA*, *nSLA* and *gSLA*. If this offer is accepted by the *IoT-C*, the *IoT-SP* concludes the *cSLA* and *nSLA* with the CSP and NSP, configures the *HL-Gw*, *LL-Gw*, nodes and the application instance. Finally, the e-health IoT service is available for usage by the *IoT-C* users.

3.4   QBAIoT: QoS Based Access for IoT

In order to guarantee the negotiated values of the QoS parameters in the *iSLA* of our e-health usage case illustrated by the MSC of Fig. 4, we propose in this paper a novel QoS mechanism concerning the sensing layer of our IoT architecture. Indeed, we specify a QoS based wireless access method called *QBAIoT* enabling the communication between the IoT objects and the Low Level Gateway of our IoT architecture. The proposed QoS mechanism is an adapted IEEE 802.15.4 slotted CSMA/CA process in order to allow a traffic differentiation while satisfying the QoS requirements of each traffic type (i.e. minimal delay for delay sensitive applications, etc.).

Our *QBAIoT* method uses the IEEE 802.15.4 superframe while adapting its structure to satisfy the requirements of different traffics. Indeed, we can take into consideration up to four QoS classes that we define in our *iSLA* quantitative characteristics (*RTMC, RTNMC*, Streaming and *NRT*). Real Time (*RTMC* and *RTNMC*) traffics are highly sensitive to delay, whereas Streaming traffic is highly sensitive to jitter variation and the *NRT* traffic is a best-effort QoS class. To adapt the structure of the superframe to these QoS classes, we specify different CAPs within the standard IEEE 802.15.4 superframe. Each CAP is specific for one QoS class and it is called a *QoS CAP*. Our adapted superframe structure contains up to 4 *QoS CAPs* (see Fig. 5). The number of *QoS CAPs* configured in the adapted superframe within our Low Level Gateway (*LL-Gw*) depends on the number of QoS classes specified in the iSLAs where the considered *LL-Gw* is concerned. Furthermore, we do not use neither CFP nor inactive part in the superframe. The removal of the inactive part results in minimizing the delay for Real Time buffered data. Figure 5 represents a comparison between the structure of the standard IEEE 802.15.4 superframe and our *QBAIoT* adaptation.

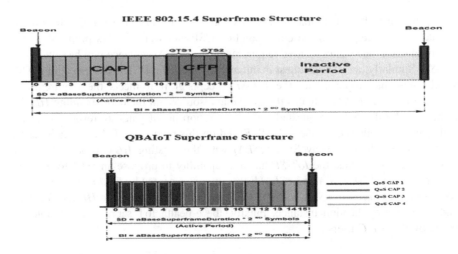

Fig. 5. IEEE 802.15.4 and QBAIoT superframe structure

During each *QoS CAP*, only objects belonging to the corresponding QoS Class can compete to gain access to the shared medium. Each *QoS CAP* is allocated a number of slots. The slots configuration and the fixed values of *BO* and *SO* depends on the number of available QoS classes and the number of Real Time QoS classes. If only one QoS Class exists, the normal IEEE 802.15.4 superframe structure will be used in our architecture but without CFP and inactive periods, as a single *QoS CAP* exists. In the case of multiple QoS classes, *BO* and *SO* will be initialized to a value equal to 2 if there is at least one Real Time QoS Class and to a value equal to 3 if there is no Real Time QoS classes. The value of *BO* and *SO* allows computing the superframe duration, consequently, the slot duration and the delay that the objects have to wait to be in their corresponding *QoS CAP*. Our *QBAIoT* access method is implemented on the Low Level Gateway (acting as a coordinator) as well as the IoT objects. Therefore, we describe in the following the design details of the proposed wireless access method not only for the IoT Gateway by also for the IoT objects.

3.5   IoT Gateway QoS Based Access Method

The IoT Low Level Gateway of our architecture adopts the proposed *QBAIoT* mechanism as a QoS based access method enabling QoS guarantee for IoT objects according to an achieved *iSLA*. We specify in Fig. 6 the Finite State Machine that illustrates the *QBAIoT* process within the *LL-Gw*.

In state 0, the *LL-Gw* determines the number of QoS classes available in its WPAN as well as the number of Real Time classes. If there is only one QoS class, the *LL-Gw* passes to state S1 then it sets *BO* and *SO* to 14, while creating one *QoS CAP*. After sending the beacon, *LL-Gw* is in state S2 where it receives data and sends beacon at each *BI*.

If during state S0, *LL-Gw* does not recognize any Real Time QoS Classes, it will pass to state S3 by setting *BO* and *SO* to 3 and the slots configuration to 9 slots for the first *QoS CAP* and 7 slots to the second *QoS CAP*. When the *LL-Gw* sends the beacon, it reaches state S4 where it receives data and sends beacon at each *BI*.

If a *LL-Gw* in state S0 recognizes at least one Real Time QoS class, it passes to state S5 by setting the *BO* and *SO* to 2. Based on the number of QoS classes and on the number of Real Time classes, the *LL-Gw* can pass to one of the following states:

- State S6: corresponds to 4 QoS Classes. In this state, the *LL-Gw* sets the slots configuration to 6 slots for RTMC, 5 for RTNMC, 3 for streaming, 2 for NRT.
- State S7: corresponds to 3 QoS classes including 2 Real Time QoS classes. In this state, the *LL-Gw* sets the slots configuration to 7 slots for RTMC, 6 for RTNMC and 3 for the other QoS class.
- State S8: corresponds to 3 QoS classes including 1 Real Time QoS class. In this state the *LL-Gw* sets the slots configuration to 9 slots for the Real Time QoS class, 4 for the Streaming class and 3 for the NRT class.
- State S9: corresponds to 2 Real Time QoS classes. In this state, the *LL-Gw* sets the slots configuration to 9 slots for the RTMC class and 7 for the RTNMC class.
- State S10: corresponds to 2 QoS classes including 1 Real Time QoS class. In this state, the *LL-Gw* sets the slots configuration to 12 slots for the Real Time QoS class and 4 for the other QoS class.

After setting the values of *BO*, *SO* and slots configuration in one of the states described above (S6 to S10), the *LL-Gw* passes to state S11 when it sends the beacon and will receive the data. Then, at each *BI* the *LL-Gw* sends the beacon.

In case of changes occurrence concerning the existence of QoS classes, the gateway reconsiders the values of *BO*, *SO* as well as slots configuration and sends an updated beacon at the BI. Considering the changes automatically corresponds to self-configuring capability. In addition, self-optimizing capability could be specified within the Low Level Gateway in order to reallocate non-used slots in certain *QoS CAPs* to other ones. Self-configuring and self-optimizing capabilities are out of the scope of this paper.

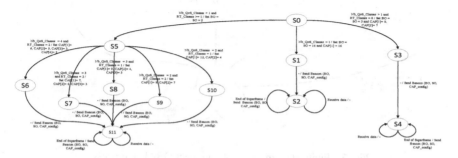

Fig. 6. Finite state machine of a gateway QBAIoT process

3.6   Class Based Access for IoT Objects

We specify in Fig. 7 the Finite State Machine that illustrates the *QBAIoT* process within an IoT object (i.e. a node). In state S0, an IoT object receives the gateway beacon specifying the configuration of *BO*, *SO* and *QoS CAPs*. Based on its QoS Class, the IoT object configures its Object_CAP$_{Start}$ and Object_CAP$_{End}$ and then passes to state S1. At state S1, if the IoT object determines that its *QoS CAP* has not started yet (i.e. Current slot < Object_CAP$_{Start}$), then it will remain in state S1 and waits for its *QoS CAP* in the current superframe. On the other hand, if the node determines that its *QoS CAP* had ended (i.e. Current slot < Object_CAP$_{End}$), then it will remain in state S1 and waits for its *QoS CAP* in the next superframe after receiving a new beacon. Finally, if the node determines that its *QoS CAP* is effective (i.e. Object_CAP$_{Start}$ < Current slot < Object_CAP$_{End}$), then it passes to state S2. At S2, an IoT object evaluates the remaining time in its *QoS CAP* in order to send a packet. If there is sufficient time, the node executes the CCA. An idle channel induces CW to be decremented and compared to 0. If CW is greater than 0, the CCA should be executed again, whereas a CW equal to 0, enables the node to send its data to the *LL-Gw* and to get back to state S1. Then, it waits for the beacon or tries to send another data packet.

On the other hand, if the channel is not idle, *NB* is compared to *macMaxBackoffs*. A value of *NB* greater than *macMaxBackoffs* leads to a MLME (MAC sublayer Management Entity) status set to "Channel Access Failure" and the node gets back again to state S1 where it waits for the beacon or tries to send another data packet. If *NB* is lower than *macMaxBackoffs*, the *NB* value will be incremented and CCA should be executed again while the node remains at state S2.

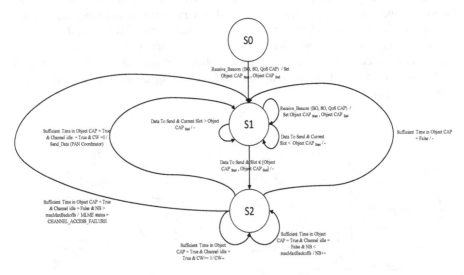

Fig. 7. Finite state machine of an object QBAIoT process

4 QBAIoT Performance Evaluation

We describe in the following the performance evaluation details of our proposed QoS based wireless access method used within the sensing layer of the IoT architecture in order to guarantee QoS parameters for Real Time Mission Critical traffic corresponding to an e-health service. We use OMNeT++ to implement and simulate our *QBAIoT* access method according to several scenarios in order to evaluate the performance of our proposal. To do so, we adapt an IEEE 802.15.4 model available for OMNeT++ [15]. The adaptation consists not only in removing the CFP and inactive parts of the standard superframe but also in creating different *QoS CAPs* in the same superframe. We conduct different simulation scenarios with common simulation parameters specified in Table 1. In addition, Table 2 shows the number of objects per QoS Class in each scenario with the corresponding slots configuration. Indeed the first scenario corresponds to an IoT e-health service with 3 RTMC nodes resulting in allocating the 16 slots to the 3 nodes. The second scenario corresponds to an IoT e-health service requiring the same 3 RTMC nodes but the gateway environment includes 3 additional RTNMC nodes. Based on our algorithm implemented on the *LL-Gw* and defined in Sect. 3.5, 9 slots are allocated to RTMC nodes and 7 to RTNMC nodes. The third scenario corresponds to 9 nodes (3 RTMC, 3 RTNMC and 3 Streaming) resulting in 7/6/3 respectively for the slots configuration. The last scenario (i.e. scenario 4) corresponds to the existence of 12 nodes (3 of each QoS class) resulting in a slots configuration of 6/5/3/2. The slots configuration is based on our *QBAIoT* mechanism described in Sect. 3.5.

Table 1. Common simulation parameters

Parameter	Value
Bit rate	250 Kbps
Simulation time	100 s
Mac payload size	50 Bytes
Data generation interval time	0.25 s
Number of generated data packets	400
Topology	Star
Number of coordinators per WPAN	1

Table 2. Number of objects by QoS class in each scenario

	RTMC objects	RTNMC objects	Streaming objects	NRT objects	Slots configuration
Scenario 1	3	0	0	0	16
Scenario 2	3	3	0	0	9/7
Scenario 3	3	3	3	0	7/6/3
Scenario 4	3	3	3	3	6/5/3/2

To evaluate the performance of *QBAIoT* according to the specified scenarios, we take into consideration the QoS parameters included in the *iSLA* specified in Sect. 3.3. First, the average delay refers to the average time experienced by a generated packet from the IoT object to be received by the Low Level Gateway. It is computed by dividing the sum of received packets delays by the number of received packet. Then, the Packet Delivery Ratio (PDR) evaluates the reliability degree achieved by the *QBAIoT* based sensing layer in terms of successful transmissions. It is computed by dividing the number of received packet by the number of generated packets. Figures 8, 9, 10 and 11 show the performance evaluation comparison between our *QBAIoT* approach and the traditional slotted CSMA/CA according to scenarios 1, 2, 3 and 4 correspondingly.

Figure 8 presents the delay and PDR evaluation corresponding to scenario 1 with only one QoS class traffic (*RTMC*). We can deduct that for one QoS class, *QBAIoT* acts like the traditional slotted CSMA/CA as one QoS class is allocated the totality of the slots. Indeed, the obtained results in terms of average delay and PDR are very close for the two approaches. In our approach, we can observe that we have a difference of 7 ms resulting from testing if the current slot is in the *QoS CAP*, which is not necessary in the traditional approach.

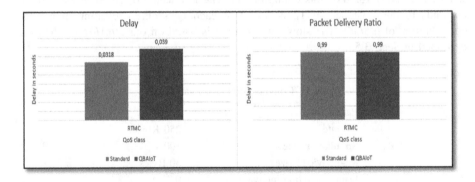

Fig. 8. Delay and PDR evaluation for scenario 1

The obtained results in Fig. 9 show that for 2 QoS classes *QBAIoT* ensures a better delay for *RTMC* and an identical delay for *RTNMC* comparing to the standard. Allocating 2 more slots for RTMC compared to RTNMC results in 10 ms better average delay for this QoS class. For the PDR evaluation, *QBAIoT* ensures better values for *RTMC* (99%) and *RTNMC* (98%) than the standard approach (56% and 55% respectively). Our approach enables these performance results in terms of PDR, as only objects of the corresponding QoS class can compete to access the channel during the slots of a *QoS CAP*. Thus, our class-based access will avoid collisions between different traffics generated by objects belonging to different QoS Classes.

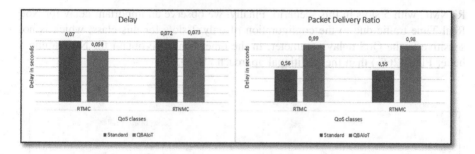

Fig. 9. Delay and PDR evaluation for scenario 2

Figure 10 shows the evaluation performance corresponding to scenario 3. The obtained results shows a better delay, while using *QBAIoT*, for RTMC and RTNMC traffic compared to the standard. With our QoS based access method, 7 Slots are allocated to the RTMC traffic and 6 for RTNMC traffic, resulting in better delays: 33 ms less than the standard for RTMC and 16 ms less as for RTNMC. Similarly, we obtain with our approach a better PDR for this scenario, as the number of collisions is lower. Indeed, the PDR for the RTMC traffic with *QBAIoT* is equal to 98.5% whereas it is equal to 26% with the IEEE 802.15.4.

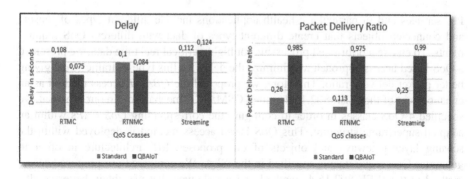

Fig. 10. Delay and PDR evaluation for scenario 3

The obtained performance results in terms of PDR and delay corresponding to scenario 4 where the *LL-Gw* configures 4 QoS classes are illustrated by Fig. 11. In this scenario, we observe that *QBAIoT* enables better delays for *RTMC* (90 ms) and *RTNMC* (106 ms) traffics compared to the IEEE 802.15.4 standard access method (115 ms for RTMC and 123 ms for RTNMC). Moreover, we observe better PDR for all QoS classes (>96% for 3 classes) using our approach compared to the standard (<20% for all classes). Indeed, for the IEEE traditional approach, all QoS classes will be served similarly and in the same time, resulting in more collisions and approximatively 4 slots for each QoS class; whereas our *QBAIoT* access method enables different *QoS CAPs* to minimize collisions and configures RTMC with 6 slots and

RTNMC with 5 slots in this scenario. Finally, we observe an important delay for Non Real Time traffic due to the configuration of only 2 slots for this class, which is not sensitive to the QoS delay parameter. In the other hand, we obtain for NRT traffic a better PDR (26%) than the traditional approach (16%).

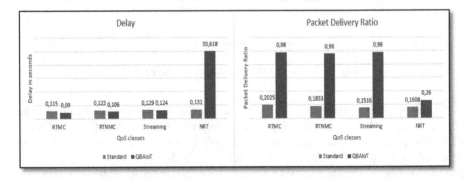

Fig. 11. Delay and PDR evaluation for scenario 4

5 Conclusion

IoT services and in particular e-health applications include different types of sensors and connected objects that create different types of data with different QoS requirements. To ensure a prioritized processing for highly critical real time data, we presented a QoS based access approach to minimize the delay for this type of traffic while giving better packet delivery ratio. Therefore, we proposed the *QBAIoT* access method as an enhancement of the IEEE 802.15.4 slotted CSMA/CA mechanism. In our proposal, we specified 4 QoS classes in order to configure the corresponding *QoS CAPs* within an adapted superframe structure. This QoS based access method is deployed within the sensing layer gateways and objects of our proposed IoT architecture in order to guarantee QoS requirements specified in the iSLA. We compared our proposed access method to the IEEE 802.15.4 standard and we showed that we obtain better results: reduced delay for Real Time traffics as well as a greater PDR for all QoS classes.

As ongoing work, we are implementing self-management capabilities within the IoT gateway in order to adapt the superframe configuration according to the IoT environment and the slots usage variation within each *QoS CAP*.

References

1. Nordrum, A.: Popular internet of things forecast of 50 billion devices by 2020 is outdated. IEEE Spectrum, August 2016
2. Mell, P., Grance, T.: The NIST definition of cloud computing, 2 p. NIST, July 2009. (Version 15)

3. Banafa, A.: Definition of fog computing. IBM, August 2014. https://www.ibm.com/blogs/cloud-computing/2014/08/fog-computing. Accessed 17 Mar 2018
4. ISO/IEC JTC 1, Internet of Things, Preliminary Report 2014, 17 p.
5. Question 28/16 – Multimedia framework for e-health applications, International Telecommunication Union. http://www.itu.int/ITU-T/studygroups/com16/sg16-q28.html. Accessed 17 Mar 2018
6. 4G Americas: Cellular technologies enabling the internet of things. Whitepaper (2015)
7. IEEE Standard for Local and Metropolitan Area Networks, Low-Rate Wireless Personal Area Networks, 311 p. IEEE Computer Society, September 2011
8. LoRa Alliance: A technical overview of LoRa® and LoRaWAN™ (2015)
9. Nath, S., Aznabi, S., Islam, N., Faridi, A., Qarony, W.: Investigation and performance analysis of some implemented features of the ZigBee protocol and IEEE 802.15.4 Mac specification. Int. J. Online Eng. (iJOE) **13**, 19 (2017)
10. Thubert, P., Bormann, C., Toutain, L., Cragie, R.: IPv6 over low-power wireless personal area network (6LoWPAN) routing header. In: IETF RFC, 37 p., April 2017
11. AlSharqi, K., Abdelbari, A., Abou-Elnour, A., Tarique, M.: ZigBee based wearable remote healthcare monitoring system. Int. J. Wirel. Mobile Netw. (IJWMN) **6**, 15 (2014)
12. Fernandez-Lopez, H., Afonso, J.A., Coreeia, J.H., Simoes, R.: ZigBee-Based Remote Patient Monitoring, 6 p.
13. Gubbi, J., Buyya, R., Marusic, S., Palaniswami, M.: Internet of things (IoT): a vision, architectural elements, and future directions. Futur. Gener. Comput. Syst. **29**, 16 (2013)
14. Khalil, A., Mbarek, N., Togni, O.: Service Level Guarantee Framework for IoT Environments, 8 p. (2017)
15. Kirsche, M.: IEEE 802.15.4-Standalone. https://github.com/michaelkirsche/IEEE802154 INET-Standalone. Accessed 17 Mar 2018

Recognition Over Encrypted Faces

Hervé Chabanne[1,2(✉)], Roch Lescuyer[1], Jonathan Milgram[1],
Constance Morel[1], and Emmanuel Prouff[3]

[1] Idemia, Paris, France
{herve.chabanne,roch.lescuyer,jonathan.milgram}@idemia.com
[2] Télécom Paristech, Paris, France
[3] ANSSI, Paris, France
emmanuel.prouff@ssi.gouv.fr

Abstract. Neural Networks (NN) are today increasingly used in Machine Learning where they have become deeper and deeper to accurately model or classify high-level abstractions of data. Their development however also gives rise to important data privacy risks. This observation motives Microsoft researchers to propose a framework, called Cryptonets. The core idea is to combine simplifications of the NN with Fully Homomorphic Encryptions (FHE) techniques to get both confidentiality of the manipulated data and efficiency of the processing. While efficiency and accuracy are demonstrated when the number of non-linear layers is small (e.g. 2), Cryptonets unfortunately becomes ineffective for deeper NNs which let the privacy preserving problem open in these contexts. This work successfully addresses this problem by combining several new ideas including the use of the batch normalization principle and the splitting of the learning phase in several iterations. We experimentally validate the soundness of our approach with a neural network with 6 non-linear layers. When applied to the MNIST database, it competes with the accuracy of the best non-secure versions, thus significantly improving Cryptonets. Additionally, we applied our approach to secure a neural network used for face recognition. This problem is usually considered much harder than the MNIST hand-written digits recognition and can definitely not be addressed with a simple network like Cryptonets. By combining our new ideas with an iterative (learning) approach we experimentally show that we can build an FHE-friendly network achieving good accuracy for face recognition.

1 Introduction

Neural networks (NN) aim to solve a so-called *classification problem* which consists in correctly assigning a label to a new observation, on the basis of a *training set* of data containing observations (or instances) whose labelling is known [20].

C. Morel and E. Prouff—This work has been done when the author was working at Safran Identity and Security (now Idemia).

A preliminary version of this work has been presented at Real World Crypto 2017.

It may also be viewed as the problem of approximating unknown (complex) functions that can depend on a huge number of inputs and are generally unknown.[1] NN, for instance, play a central role in face recognition [29], image classification [18] or speech recognition [12], and are thus widely deployed.

Machine learning algorithms are often applied on sensitive information such as medical data. The privacy protection of these sensitive data has been the subject of several articles during the last five years. They may be classified according to the learning algorithms which are involved: linear regression training or prediction [26,30], linear classifiers [3,4,11], decision trees [4] or neural networks [1,10,27,33,34].

All the previously mentioned Machine learning algorithms are composed of two stages: the *training phase* from a labelled database and the *classification* of new data. The training phase essentially aims at inferring the algorithm parameters from a labelled (or classified) database by optimizing some training objective (recognize/classify digits, faces, objects, etc.). The classification of a new datum then simply consists in applying the trained algorithm to it. Like in [10,31], where Cryptonets' solution is introduced, our article deals with the privacy-preserving problem for the classification (aka *matching*) processing in the context of deep Neural Networks. More precisely, we focus on *Convolutional Neural Networks* (CNN) which are very popular to address problems where the classification does not reduce to a simple linear separation. Readers not familiar with the basic concepts of NN may refer to [13] or to Sect. 2.

The problem addressed in this work is the following: A client has his data X. A server has a trained (deep) neural network. The client obtains the classification (aka label) of his data X from the server, and this classification must not reveal information about the trained neural network. The server obtains nothing (no information about the client input or labelling).

Our proposal follows an idea originally introduced in [10] where data are first encrypted by the client thanks to a fully homomorphic encryption (FHE) scheme. These encrypted data are then handled in the encrypted domain by the server to get its classification result. Finally, the server sends the encrypted label to the client for decryption.

Since Gentry's breakthrough work [9], numerous FHE schemes have been introduced in order to make it practical. Despite the significant progress in this area, no efficient scheme exist for all generic functions. However, for some specific applications, very efficient FHE schemes can be designed. Our solution is built upon the SEAL library [5] for performing homomorphic calculations. The SEAL library implements the Ring-LWE scheme introduced by Fan and Vercauteren [8]. Homomorphic schemes based on the Ring-LWE framework are the most efficient homomorphic schemes up-to-date.

For many FHE schemes, the feasibility of the encryption depends on the algebraic nature of the algorithm to be handled, and more precisely on its multiplicative depth, which is the maximum number of consecutive multiplications

---

[1] A classical simple example (*e.g.* detailed in [25, Chap. 1]) is the recognition of handwritten digits.

that must be computed during the processing of the algorithm to get the output. In our case, the main challenge is therefore to adapt the classification algorithm to render it compatible with homomorphic encryption while maintaining good accuracy.

1.1 Cryptonets Solution [10]

Cryptonets solution consists in replacing the high multiplicative depth layers (ReLU and max pooling) by low multiplicative depth polynomial layers into the CNN, without degrading too much the accuracy of the classification. To achieve this goal, the authors suggest replacing the ReLU function by the square function $x \mapsto x^2$ and replacing the max-pooling by the sum-pooling which has a null multiplicative depth. The proposal is tested in a small CNN (9 layers with only 2 activation layers) which is applied on the MNIST database [21]. They obtained an accuracy of 98.95% (the state of the art accuracy for this database is 99.77% according to http://yann.lecun.com/exdb/mnist/). The multiplicative depth of the CNN is equal to 2 and thus the classification with FHE (i.e. privacy preserving) is efficient.

Without getting deeper, the accuracy cannot be improved. Unfortunately, as actually acknowledged by the authors themselves, the squaring activation function has a derivative which is unbounded, which leads to unstable training, and hence important accuracy loss, when the CNN is deep. This observation about the incompatibility of the approach with deep CNN seems to strongly limit the practical interest of Cryptonets. At least it shows that more investigation is needed to make it practical for deep learning. To quote [7] written by the authors of Cryptonets one year later: "An interesting research problem is to extend the approach taken in [10] to more complicated neural networks, e.g., to ones with medical or financial applications." We hereafter extend [10] to the more complicated neural networks needed for faces recognition.

1.2 Our Contributions

To maintain the accuracy of our system, we make minor modifications in the CNN for the training step compared to state of the art CNNs. Namely, we keep the ReLU activation function which seems to be a key function in the current CNN performances and we replace the max-pooling by the average-pooling (this has only a small impact on the accuracy and has the advantage of replacing a step which is not FHE-friendly by a step with null multiplicative depth). For the CNN used in the matching, we propose to start with the trained CNN and to replace the ReLU functions by low degree approximations (hence reapplying the same basic idea as in CryptoNets). To deal with the fact that the ReLU function is a high degree polynomial and thus cannot have a good low degree polynomial approximation on the entire $\mathbb{R}$, our key innovation is to combine the polynomial approximation of the ReLU with a batch normalization layer [15]. Namely, before each ReLU layer, we add a batch normalization layer in order to have a restricted stable distribution at the entry of the ReLU, thus limiting our need of an accurate polynomial approximation to a small part of $\mathbb{R}$ around the point 0. To avoid high accuracy degradation between the training and the classification phases due to too many modifications into the CNN, the batch normalization layers will be added to the CNN for the training and the classification steps.

2 Convolutional Neural Network (CNN)

A convolutional neural network is a stack of layers that transforms an input layer, holding data to classify, into an output layer, holding the label scores. Each element of one layer (except the input layer) is the output of a function applied on components of the previous layer. A few distinct kinds of layers are commonly used such as the fully connected layer, the convolutional layer, the activation layer and the pooling layer.

Fully Connected Layer. Each neuron of this layer is connected to each neuron of the previous layer. The weight on the connection between the j-th neuron of the $(\ell - 1)$-th layer and the k-th neuron of the ℓ-th layer noted is denoted by ω_{kj}^{ℓ}. The bias of the k-th neuron of the ℓ-th layer is denoted by β_k^{ℓ} and its output x_k^{ℓ} equals $\beta_k^{\ell} + \sum_j \omega_{kj}^{\ell} x_j^{\ell-1}$, which is a simple inner product.

Convolutional Layer. Convolutional layers are based on convolutional filtering. The weights within the filter are the weights to learn during the training step. In addition, several filters are performed on the same layer in order to extract different kinds of characteristics. Hence, each layer is a three-dimension layer: a two-dimension matrix is obtained from each filter and then the result of each filter is put into a stack to obtain a three-dimension result. In addition, the filter is also in three dimensions in order to take into account the three dimensions of the previous layer. For instance, if n filters are applied on a layer containing $w \times h \times d$ neurons, then each filter contains $s \times s \times d$ weights where s is the filter size and the output layer contains $w \times h \times n$ neurons.

Activation Layer. A neural network containing only fully connected and convolutional layers can only classify data linearly. To solve more complex classification problem, the activation layer has been introduced. The same non-linear function called the activation function is applied to each neuron of the previous layer to obtain one neuron of the current layer: $x_{i,j,k}^{\ell} = f(x_{i,j,k}^{\ell-1})$ where f is the activation function. Therefore, an activation layer contains the same number of neurons as its previous layer. The two most common activation functions are the ReLU function $f(x) = \max(0, x)$ and the sigmoid function $f(x) = (1 + e^{-x})^{-1}$. Activation layers are usually used after convolutional or fully connected layers.

Pooling Layer. This layer reduces the spatial size in order to reduce the amount of neurons. This layer partitions the neurons of the previous layer into a set of non-overlapping rectangles and performs a function on each sub-area in order to obtain the value of one neuron of the current layer. Common pooling functions are the max-pooling which outputs the maximum values within the sub-area and the average-pooling which outputs the average of the values of the sub-area. In addition, the pooling layer operates independently on every depth slice of the previous layer. Pooling layers are usually used immediately after activation layers.

Common Architectures. The main block of a convolutional neural network is a convolutional layer (denoted $CONV$) directly followed by an activation layer (ACT), noted $CONV \rightarrow ACT$. The convolutional layer extracts locally information from the previous layer thanks to filters and the activation layer increases the complexity of the learned classification function thanks to its non-linearity. After some $CONV \rightarrow ACT$ blocks, a pooling layer ($POOL$) is usually added to reduce the number of neurons: $[CONV \rightarrow ACT]^p \rightarrow POOL$. This new block is repeated in the neural network until obtaining a layer of reasonable size. Then some fully connected layers (FC) are introduced in order to obtain a global result which depends of the entire input. A common convolutional network can be summarised in the following formula: $[[CONV \rightarrow ACT]^p \rightarrow POOL]^q \rightarrow [FC]^r$.

A neural network can be viewed as a function taking as inputs some parameters (weights and biases) and one data and which outputs the probability of each label for this data: for instance, if the neural network learns how to recognize handwritten digits, then its input layer will have as many neurons as pixels in image to classify and its output layer will contain ten neurons, one per possible digits. During the training step, the weights and biases will be learned in order to recognize as well as possible handwritten digits. The ten neurons in the output layer will contain the probability for each digit. The position of the highest neuron of the output layer indicates the digit of the input image.

3   Approximation of ReLU by Polynomials

The accuracy of our solution is strongly linked to the quality of the polynomial approximation of the ReLU function on the output distribution of the batch normalization layer (see [15, Algorithm 1]). The goal of this batch normalization is to ensure that the distribution of the input of non-linear layers remains stable as the network is trained. During the training, the mean and variance are computed from different batches of data. In fine, we want with these batches to iteratively compute an estimator of the expectation and variance of the testing set. These estimators are then used in the classification phase, where the batch normalization layer is simply an affine transformation with fixed parameters that comes right after a convolutional layer. Thus, according to the central limit theorem, the input distribution of the batch normalization layer is normal, and hence the output distribution is the standard normal one (Fig. 1).

To compute the polynomial approximation of the ReLU on this standard normal distribution, we used the polynomial regression function *polyfit* from the Python package *numpy*. This function inputs a set $X = (X_1, \ldots, X_N)$, a

Input: Values of x over a mini-batch: $\mathcal{B} = \{x_{1...m}\}$;
Parameters to be learned: γ, β
Output: $\{y_i = BN_{\gamma,\beta}(x_i)\}$

$$\mu_{\mathcal{B}} \leftarrow \frac{1}{m}\sum_{i=1}^{m} x_i \qquad \text{// mini-batch mean}$$

$$\sigma_{\mathcal{B}}^2 \leftarrow \frac{1}{m}\sum_{i=1}^{m}(x_i - \mu_{\mathcal{B}})^2 \qquad \text{// mini-batch variance}$$

$$\widehat{x}_i \leftarrow \frac{x_i - \mu_{\mathcal{B}}}{\sqrt{\sigma_{\mathcal{B}}^2 + \epsilon}} \qquad \text{// normalize}$$

$$y_i \leftarrow \gamma\widehat{x}_i + \beta \equiv BN_{\gamma,\beta}(x_i) \qquad \text{// scale and shift}$$

Fig. 1. Batch normalization [15, Algorithm 1]

set $Y = (Y_1, \ldots, Y_N)$ and a polynomial degree n and outputs the coefficients of the polynomial $P(X) = c_0 + c_1 X + c_2 X^2 + \ldots c_n X^n$ such that the square error $\varepsilon = \sum_{i=1}^{N}(P(X_i) - Y_i)^2$ is minimized. We applied this function on the set $\{(X_i, ReLU(X_i))\}$ where the X_i are randomly picked up from a standard normal distribution (see Table 1 and Fig. 2).

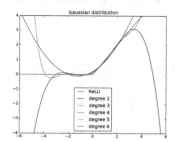

Fig. 2. Approximation of the ReLU function by polynomials on the standard normal distribution

We can observe that, for our method, the polynomials of odd degree $2n + 1$ approximate similarly as the polynomial of even degree $2n$. The same trend can be mathematically observed from a Taylor series around the point 0 of a smooth approximation of the ReLU function called softplus $ln(1 + e^x)$: $ln(1 + e^x) = ln(2) + \frac{x}{2} - \frac{x^4}{192} - \frac{17x^8}{645120} + \frac{31x^{10}}{14515200} + O(x^{12})$. Thus we only used the even degree polynomial approximations in our solution.

With the standard normal distribution, 99.73% of the values belong to $[-3, 3]$. When the degree of the polynomial approximation increases, our polynomial approximation brightens on $[-3, 3]$ but deteriorates outside $[-3, 3]$.

Table 1. Approximation of the ReLU function by polynomials on the standard normal distribution

Degree	Polynomials
2	$0.1992 + 0.5002X + 0.1997X^2$
3	$0.1995 + 0.5002X + 0.1994X^2 - 0.0164X^3$
4	$0.1500 + 0.5012X + 0.2981X^2 - 0.0004X^3 - 0.0388X^4$
5	$0.1488 + 0.4993X + 0.3007X^2 + 0.0003X^3 - 0.0168X^4$
6	$0.1249 + 0.5000X + 0.3729X^2 - 0.0410X^4 + 0.0016X^6$

4   Experiments on a Light CNN

To begin, we tested our solution on a light CNN (see Fig. 3) with the characteristics given in Fig. 3:

1. Convolutional layers Conv1 and Conv2 have respectively 20 and 50 feature maps and their filter sizes are respectively $(1 \times 5 \times 5)$ and $(20 \times 5 \times 5)$.
2. Average pooling layers have (2×2) window size.
3. The fully connected layers (FC1 and FC2) have respectively 500 and 10 outputs.
4. A batch normalization layer (BN) is present just before the ReLU layer.

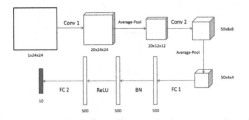

Fig. 3. Our light CNN

4.1   Accuracy Evaluation

We train this light CNN with Caffe framework [16] on the MNIST database with the following parameters: base learning rate b_{lr} equal to 0.01, learning rate policy equal to $b_{lr} * (1 + 10^{-4} * iter)^{-0.75}$, momentum equal to 0.9, weight decay equal to 0.0005, max iter equal to 10^4 and solver type equal to SGD. We obtained an accuracy of 97.95% which is far from the state of the art for the digit recognition problem (99.77%). That is due to the small size of our light CNN. The goal of this light CNN is to validate our solution by proving that our solution respects the accuracy requirement. Thus we would like to prove that the replacement of the ReLU layer by a low degree polynomial layer leads to a low accuracy degradation. To limit the accuracy degradation due to this activation layer modification, the polynomial has to approximate very well the ReLU function on the output distribution of the batch normalization layer. To do that, we firstly analyzed the output distribution of the batch normalization layer (see Fig. 4).

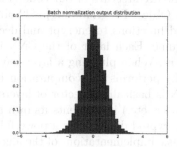

Fig. 4. Output distribution of the batch normalization layer

As expected, this distribution is close to a standard normal distribution. Then we replaced the ReLU functions by our polynomial approximations and obtained the accuracy of the Table 2.

Table 2. Classification accuracy for the light CNN

Degree	Accuracy
2	97.55%
4	97.84%
6	97.91%

As expected, the performances obtained with the private classification (FHE friendly classification with polynomial activation layer) are similar to the accuracy of 97.95% obtained with the non-private classification (with the ReLU activation layer). Thus, our solution on this light CNN respects the accuracy requirements. In addition, the multiplicative depth with this light CNN is equal to $\log_2 deg$ where deg is the degree of the polynomial approximation. Thus our solution applied on this light CNN respects the three requirements: privacy (thanks to FHE), efficiency (with a multiplicative depth of 1, 2 or 3 according to the polynomial approximation degree) and accuracy (thanks to the batch normalization and the proficient polynomial approximation on a standard normal distribution).

4.2   Efficiency Evaluation

We implement our light CNN architecture for evaluating CNN computations in the encrypted domain with the SEAL library, version 2.3 [5]. Our code is written in C++.

First Implementation. The architecture of our code is the following. The base object (in the sense of the Object Programming) is "Volume", embedding a volume of double values, and functions to encrypt and decrypt these values. The input of a CNN is a Volume. Each layer of the CNN is also itself a Volume, aka, the output of the layer. When plugging a layer, say L_1, as input to a next layer, say L_2, the layer L_2 performs the computation it implements with the layer L_1 as input. A CNN is basically a vector of layers. Each layer (ConvolutionLayer, AveragePoolLayer, etc.) implements its own algorithm, either in the plain domain or in the encrypted domain. As a powerful property of the homomorphic computations, basic implementations of the algorithms in the plain and in the encrypted domain are in fact the same, following the Template-oriented programming model in C++, except that they take different objects as input, respectively "double" and "Ciphertext".

We choose $n = 2^{13}$ and $t = 2^{47}$ as parameters for the SEAL library [5]. This means that the plaintext space is the polynomial quotient ring $\mathbb{Z}_t[X]/(x^n + 1)$. Note that this is the minimal size of n for having the noise level handled correctly, aka being able to decrypt. This version of the SEAL library implements the Fan-Vercauteren encryption scheme [8]. The ciphertext space is included in $R = \mathbb{Z}_q[X]/(x^n+1)$, where q is the coefficient modulus. We take the default parameter of SEAL for the q modulus. The encryption of a message m under the public key h is $[\lfloor q/t \rfloor m + e + hs]_q \in R$ where e and s are two small error polynomials.

We work in balanced base 3 which means that coefficients belong to $\{-1, 0, 1\}$ and have different signs. Taking back an example of [7], 25 is retrieved as $P(3)$ where $P(X) = X^3 - X + 1$.

In our implementation, a particular attention is taken on the representation of floats in the encrypted domain. It is worth noting that the CNNs we consider impose to perform computations involving thousands of weights with a precision of 5 digits after the decimal point. As in standard computations in the plain domain, there is a need for a float representation when computing with floats. The SEAL library comes up with a standard float representation, called "fractional". We allocate 50 coefficients to the integral part and 100 to the fractional part. That means that a real number $y = y^+.y^-$ where y^+ denotes the balanced base 3 digits $t_{I+}t_{I+-1}\ldots t_1 t_0$ and y^- stands for $t_{-1}t_{-2}\ldots t_{-I-}$, is encoded as the plaintext polynomial $\sum_{i \leq I+} X^i t^i - \sum_{0 < i \leq I-} X^{n-i} t^{-i}$.

We refer to [5] for further details on how the SEAL library works and the choice of its other parameters (including security parameters, see Sect. 8 of [5]).

Overall, the classification for $(28, 28, 1)$ input images is done in 2 hours and a half. If we restrict ourselves to $(12, 12, 1)$ image size, meaning that input images of the light CNN are cropped and resized from $(28, 28, 1)$ to $(12, 12, 1)$, the accuracy of the CNN is 93.14%, but it takes around 15 min to classify an image.

In the latter case, micro benchmarks are the following:

1. The encryption takes 1.3 s.
2. Applying a 5×5 filter inside the first convolution layer is done in 13.1 s.
3. Applying the first average pool layer to 20 input channels is done in 8.6 s.
4. The first fully connected layer is computed in 85.5 s.
5. The activation layer is computed in 67.3 s.
6. The last fully connected layer is computed in 27.3 s.
7. The decryption takes 31 ms.

The micro timings above are in line with those reported in Cryptonets [10].

The convolution layer is the main bottleneck regarding the efficiency. Computing both convolution layers takes 74% of the whole time. In fact, this layer involves a large number of additions and plain multiplications. Note that there are not two consecutive multiplications and the multiplicative depth stays at one. That implies that there is few noise loss for this layer. To the contrary, the activation layer has a larger multiplicative depth and thus, needs greater parameters to avoid the noise loss. However, it is rather efficient.

No bootstrapping is required as we choose to implement leveled homomorphic encryption where the parameters are chosen in order to not need this bootstrapping step.

This development has been partially funded by the H2020 European project TREDISEC, (see acknowledgements). As part of this project, a catalogue of primitives is proposed, including our primitive for extracting features in the encrypted domain (see http://www.tredisec.eu/primitives-catalogue).

Second Implementation. In a second implementation, we take advantage of the batching property following the recent work of Gazelle [17].

The batching property of homomorphic encryption enables SIMD (single instruction multiple data) addition, SIMD multiplication and permutations of several integers packed in a single ciphertext. In the SEAL library, batching slots are represented as a $2 \times (n/2)$ matrix, where $X^n + 1$ is the polynomial modulus. We then are able to pack n integers modulo t into a single plaintext, where t is the plaintext modulus.

The authors of Gazelle show how to pack convolution layers and fully connected layers into few ciphertexts, leading to huge improvements in terms of efficiency. For instance, the evaluation of the first layer of our light CNN, with 20 filters all packed in a single ciphertext, takes 1.3 s in our implementation, whereas it takes 23 min when we have one ciphertext per pixel.

We refer to [17] for a description of these techniques. Following the same ideas we implemented the activation layer – this is straightforward once we use our polynomial approximations – and the average pool layer.

Unfortunately, with the use of batching, we lose the fractional float representation (see above) when a single float is stored per ciphertext, since batching slots are integers modulo the plain modulus. Hence the encoding of floats we use is the scaling of real numbers to integers. Moreover, the negative number $-i$ is encoded as $t - i$.

These encodings lead to some restriction when evaluating several layers. In particular, the multiplication of scaled real numbers lead to big numbers that do not fit in the space modulo t. As introduced in SecureML [23], we tried to use the possibility of truncating the last bits of scaled real numbers to bound the fractional part. Unfortunately, this procedure introduces sometimes some errors that make the overall computation fails. A solution would be to use the garbled solutions for truncation of MiniONN [22], but we did not investigate this further. At this time of writing, we only decrypt and re-encrypt between layers, without sharing of intermediate values.

Micro benchmarks for our second implementation are the followings:

1. The encryption takes 14 ms.
2. Applying the 20 filters of the first convolution layer is done in 1.4 s.
3. Applying the first average pool layer to 20 input channels is done in 21.8 s.
4. The first fully connected layer is computed in 20.8 s.
5. The activation layer is computed in 27 ms.
6. The last fully connected layer is computed in 31.3 s.
7. The decryption takes 7 ms.

Applying the whole light CNN to a 12×12 image input is done in 92.5 s., instead of 15 min. with our first implementation.

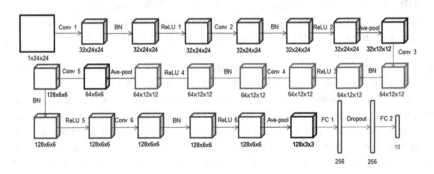

Fig. 5. Our CNN for hand-digit recognition

5   Experimentation on a Deeper CNN

In this section, we tested our solution on a deeper CNN (see Fig. 5) with more hidden layers and more activation layers in order to be closer to state of the art CNN. This CNN, which contains 24 layers and 6 ReLU activation layers, has the following characteristics:

1. In each convolutional layer, the filter size is $(n \times 3 \times 3)$ with n the number of feature maps of the input layer.
2. Conv1 and Conv2 have 32 feature maps, Conv3 and Conv4 have 64 feature maps, Conv5 and Conv6 have 128 feature maps.

3. Average pooling layers have (2×2) window size.
4. The fully connected layers (FC1 and FC2) have respectively 256 and 10 outputs.
5. A batch normalization layer (BN) is present just before each ReLU layer.
6. A dropout is used during the training step only to select 50% of the neurons

Firstly, we trained this CNN with the Caffe framework [16] on the MNIST database with the following parameters: base learning rate b_{lr} equal to 0.02, learning rate policy equal to $b_{lr} * (1 + 10^{-4} * iter)^{-0.75}$, momentum equal to 0.9, weight decay equal to 0.0005, max iter equal to 10^5 and solver type equal to SGD. We obtained an accuracy of 99.59% which is similar to state of the art accuracy (99.77%). Then we replaced the ReLU functions by our polynomial approximations and evaluated the accuracy of these FHE friendly classifications (see Table 3).

Table 3. Classification accuracy on our CNN

Degree	Accuracy
2	59.14%
4	97.91%
6	36.94%

The accuracy degradation is higher than on our light CNN. This degradation can be explained by the number of activations layers in our CNN. During the private classification, some errors appear after the first activation layer due to the replacement of the ReLU functions by our polynomial approximations. These errors lead to a low distortion of the output distribution of the next batch normalization layer. Our polynomial approximations are not perfectly suited for this new distribution and thus more and bigger errors appear after the second activation layer. The errors spread and strengthen from one layer to the next layer. To visualize the distribution distortion, we plotted the output distribution of the 6-th batch normalization layer with the degree 2 or 4 polynomial approximations (see Fig. 6).

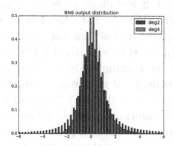

Fig. 6. Output distribution of BN6 with the degree 2 and 4 polynomial approximations

The distribution with the degree 4 polynomial approximation is closer to the standard normal distribution than the distribution with the degree 2 polynomial approximation. That explains the accuracy difference between this two approximations. These two distributions are closed to a normal distribution with a standard deviation slightly greater than 1. To improve our accuracy, we suggest building new polynomial approximations learned from a distribution closer to the output distribution of the batch normalization (for instance on a normal distribution with a standard deviation slightly higher than 1). Table 4 sums up our results with these new polynomial approximations. We limited our polynomial approximations to degree 2 and 4 to respect the efficiency requirement. Our solution has a multiplicative depth of 6 with degree 2 polynomial approximation and a multiplicative depth of 12 with degree 4 polynomial approximation. Both multiplicative depths are reasonable with respect to FHE.

Table 4. Classification accuracy with our new polynomial approximations

Degree	Normal distribution	Accuracy
2	$\mu = 0,\ \sigma = 1.1$	87.12%
2	$\mu = 0,\ \sigma = 1.2$	90.70%
2	$\mu = 0,\ \sigma = 1.3$	82.61%
4	$\mu = 0,\ \sigma = 1.1$	98.18%
4	$\mu = 0,\ \sigma = 1.2$	97.75%

To be closer to the non secure accuracy 99.59%, we adapted the CNN weights to our polynomial activation function. To do that, we started with the CNN trained with the ReLU activation function. We replaced the ReLU functions by our degree 2 polynomial approximations learned on a normal distribution with $\mu = 0$ and $\sigma = 1.2$. Finally we continued the CNN learning with a low learning rate (10^{-5}). With these new learning weights, we obtained an accuracy of 99.28%. Unfortunately this method does not work with degree 4 polynomial approximations because the last training with degree 2 polynomial activation layer is unstable.

As the distribution after each batch normalization layer depends on the polynomial approximations used, it is difficult to build a polynomial approximation which perfectly fits this distribution. Thus we decided to consider the polynomial approximation coefficients as learning weights in the last training step. In more detail, as previously, we started with the CNN trained with the ReLU activation function. Then we continued the learning after the replacement of the ReLU functions by our degree 2 polynomial approximation (learned from a normal distribution with $\mu = 0$ and $\sigma = 1.2$) where its coefficients belong to learning weights. With this solution, we achieved an accuracy of 99.30% which is very close to the accuracy from the non private classification (99.59%).

These experiments prove that our solution respects the accuracy requirement. In addition, our last private classification employs only degree 2 polynomial approximations. Thus it respects the efficiency requirement (with a multiplicative depth of 6). Hence, our solution respects the three requirements.

6   Application to the Face Recognition Problem

To more easily make the comparison with Cryptonets original work [10], we tested in previous section our new ideas on the classical MNIST database where handwritten digits have to be classified. It is well known that the underlying classification problem is relatively easy to solve and hence does not need very deep learning algorithms (which explains the good accuracy achieved in [10] with a single non-linear layer). In this last section, we focus on a much more difficult unconstrained problem: the face recognition. For our experiments, we assumed that the images at input had dimension $96 \times 96 \times 3$. To keep the CNN processing reasonably small (necessary to combine with FHE) we fixed the number of convolutional layers to 4 with 3×3-dimensional filters and a number of filters per layer respectively equal to 8, 32, 128 and 512. As described in Sect. 2, each CONV layer was followed by a ReLU non-linear layer and a 2×2 average pooling layer; the output of the last internal layer of the CNN (and hence the input of the last fully connected layer) is therefore of dimension $6 \times 6 \times 512$. With this architecture, our CNN contains roughly 10 millions parameters (aka weights) to train[2] and involves the processing of 294912 ReLU functions (*versus* 64512 for the CNN we used for the MNIST problem). The training of our CNN has been done with a private database composed of 3.5 millions images taken over around 30000 different persons. The matching accuracy of our CNN has afterwards been tested on the public database[3] Labeled Faces in the Wild (LFW) [14].

Before replacing the ReLU functions by polynomial approximations, our CNN achieved 96.5% accuracy. This is far from the accuracy achieved by the most recent best algorithms (*e.g.* FaceNet achieves 99.6% accuracy) but this is the counterpart of our choice of a light (and hence faster) CNN. For comparison, our accuracy is comparable with that of the DeepFace network proposed by FaceBook in 2014. The interested reader will find a comprehensive survey of the performances achieved on LFW database in [19]. After the replacement, the accuracy loss is very large (accuracy equal to 87.1% and therefore a loss of 9.4%) and performing a second training (with the polynomial approximations of the ReLU instead of the ReLU itself) did not allowed us to regain the accuracy (as it was the case for the MNIST experiments). This failure may be explained by the fact that we significantly increased the number of ReLU approximations compared to what we did for the MNIST example.

To overcome the problem above, we followed an iterative approach. First, we only replaced the ReLU functions after the first CONV layer and we re-trained the weights of the subsequent layers to compensate the accuracy loss; we then succeeded to get an accuracy of 96.4%). Secondly, we repeat the process to the

---

[2] For comparison, the CNN used by Google in FaceNet [29] has around 140 millions parameters to train.

[3] Note that this database and the private one have no identity in common.

second layer of ReLU functions and we master to keep an accuracy of 95.3% after the re-training (against 85% before the re-training). Applying the same approach to the third and fourth non-linear layers, we eventually got a CNN (with all the ReLU replaced by polynomial approximations) achieving an accuracy of 91.8% on the LFW database, that is with a loss of only 4.7% when compared to the initial accuracy of our CNN. Even if this accuracy does not compete those of the most recent algorithms, it is comparable to the state of the art 5 years ago (*e.g.* the classifier Tom-vs-Pete published in 2012 [2]) and stays efficient when combined with FHE (since the multiplicative depth is limited to 4).

7 Related Work

The problem of privacy-preserving neural networks has been widely studied since the beginning of the century. All existing methods are based on secure multi-party computation (SMC) or homomorphic encryption (HE) or a combination of those methods. The efficiency of these solutions strongly depends on the complexity of the neural network seen as a classification function.

Besides Cryptonets [10] (see also Sect. 1.1), there are other contributions of interest. In 2006, Barni *et al.* [1] proposed a privacy preserving neural network classification algorithm based on secure multi-party computation and homomorphic encryption. Their neural networks are composed of a succession of scalar products which are secured on the basis of homomorphic encryption and activation functions (threshold or sigmoid) secured with protocols based on secure multi-party computation. To securely evaluate each *threshold activation function* processing, Yao's solution to the millionaire's problem [32] is suggested. To securely evaluate the sigmoid activation function, firstly the sigmoid is approximated by a low degree polynomial and then the polynomial is evaluated with private polynomial evaluation [24]. Finally, the values of all intermediate outputs of scalar products and activation functions are revealed to the client. The authors noted this issue and promised to address it in a future work.

Orlandi *et al.* [27] enhanced the protocol [1]: intermediate results are no longer revealed to the client. To evaluate scalar products, they use the same protocol as Barni *et al.* with two improvements. Firstly they replace Paillier's cryptosystem by its extension by Damgård and Jurik [6]. Secondly, the scalar product results are masked before delegating the evaluation of the activation functions to the client. Unfortunately, this protocol has a similar computation/communication complexity to that of Barni *et al.* solution.

Recently, Liu *et al.* [22] introduce MiniONN, where they transform an existing neural network into an oblivious form in order to support privacy-preserving predictions. Sadegh Riazi et al. [28] introduce Chameleon, which improves over MiniONN. Mohassel and Zhang [23] introduce SecureML, a two-server solution for training models on joint data using two-party computations. Juvekar et al. [17] introduce Gazelle, a framework we investigate in Sect. 4.2. While the approaches of these works is new and noteworthy, they do not show how it behaves when applied to real life deeper networks as we do in Sects. 5 and 6.

8 Conclusion

Today, CNN (especially deep NN) provide the best classification methods in computer vision. The main difficulty here is to simultaneously respect the following three requirements: privacy, efficiency and accuracy. Our proposal is FHE friendly, efficient with a low multiplicative depth of 6 and accurate.

To achieve the accuracy requirement, we firstly test our solution on a light CNN in order to prove the low accuracy degradation between the non private classification (97.95%) and the private classification (97.91%). Then we test our solution on a deeper CNN with 24 layers. We get a private classification accuracy of 99.30% which is better than Cryptonets (98.95%) and close to the non private accuracy on the same CNN 99.59%. We also experimentally validate the soundness of our approach on the face recognition problem, which is considered much harder than the MNIST one. In this context, we propose to combine our previous ideas with an iterative retraining approach and we showed that this leads to the design of a FHE-friendly CNN for face recognition which achieves an accuracy of 91.8% on the public LFW database.

Acknowledgment. This work was partly supported by the TREDISEC project (G.A. no 644412), funded by the European Union (EU) under the Information and Communication Technologies (ICT) theme of the Horizon 2020 (H2020) research and innovation programme. This work has also been supported in part by the CRYPTOCOMP french FUI17 project.

References

1. Barni, M., Orlandi, C., Piva, A.: A privacy-preserving protocol for neural-network-based computation. In: Proceedings of the 8th Workshop on Multimedia & Security, MM&Sec 2006, pp. 146–151 (2006)
2. Berg, T., Belhumeur, P.N.: Tom-vs-Pete classifiers and identity-preserving alignment for face verification. In: Bowden, R., Collomosse, J.P., Mikolajczyk, K., (eds.) British Machine Vision Conference. BMVC 2012, 3–7 September 2012, pp. 1–11. BMVA Press, Surrey (2012)
3. Bos, J.W., Lauter, K.E., Naehrig, M.: Private predictive analysis on encrypted medical data. J. Biomed. Inform. **50**, 234–243 (2014)
4. Bost, R., Popa, R.A., Tu, S., Goldwasser, S.: Machine learning classification over encrypted data. IACR Cryptology ePrint Archive, vol. 2014, p. 331 (2014)
5. Chen, H., Han, K., Huang, Z., Jalali, A., Laine, K.: Simple encrypted arithmetic library v2.3.0 (2017). https://www.microsoft.com/en-us/research/project/simple-encrypted-arithmetic-library/
6. Damgård, I., Jurik, M.: A generalisation, a simplification and some applications of Paillier's probabilistic public-key system. In: 4th International Workshop on Practice and Theory in Public Key Cryptography Public Key Cryptography. PKC 2001, pp. 119–136 (2001)
7. Dowlin, N., Gilad-Bachrach, R., Laine, K., Lauter, K.E., Naehrig, M., Wernsing, J.: Manual for using homomorphic encryption for bioinformatics. Proc. IEEE **105**(3), 552–567 (2017)

8. Fan, J., Vercauteren, F.: Somewhat practical fully homomorphic encryption. IACR Cryptology ePrint Archive, p. 144 (2012)
9. Gentry, C.: A fully homomorphic encryption scheme. Ph.D. thesis, Stanford University (2009). crypto.stanford.edu/craig
10. Gilad-Bachrach, R., Dowlin, N., Laine, K., Lauter, K.E., Naehrig, M., Wernsing, J.: Cryptonets: applying neural networks to encrypted data with high throughput and accuracy. In: Proceedings of the 33nd International Conference on Machine Learning. ICML 2016, pp. 201–210 (2016)
11. Graepel, T., Lauter, K., Naehrig, M.: ML confidential: machine learning on encrypted data. In: Kwon, T., Lee, M.-K., Kwon, D. (eds.) ICISC 2012. LNCS, vol. 7839, pp. 1–21. Springer, Heidelberg (2013). https://doi.org/10.1007/978-3-642-37682-5_1
12. Graves, A., Mohamed, A., Hinton, G.E.: Speech recognition with deep recurrent neural networks. In: IEEE International Conference on Acoustics, Speech and Signal Processing. ICASSP 2013, pp. 6645–6649 (2013)
13. Hastie, T., Tibshirani, R., Friedman, J.: The Elements of Statistical Learning. Springer Series in Statistics. Springer, New York (2001). https://doi.org/10.1007/978-0-387-21606-5
14. Huang, G.B., Ramesh, M., Berg, T., Learned-Miller, E.: Labeled faces in the wild: a database for studying face recognition in unconstrained environments. Technical report 07-49, University of Massachusetts, Amherst, October 2007
15. Ioffe, S., Szegedy, C.: Batch normalization: accelerating deep network training by reducing internal covariate shift. In: Proceedings of the 32nd International Conference on Machine Learning. ICML 2015, pp. 448–456 (2015)
16. Jia, Y., et al.: Caffe: convolutional architecture for fast feature embedding. arXiv preprint arXiv:1408.5093 (2014)
17. Juvekar, C., Vaikuntanathan, V., Chandrakasan, A.: Gazelle: a low latency framework for secure neural network inference. Cryptology ePrint Archive, Report 2018/073 (2018). https://eprint.iacr.org/2018/073
18. Krizhevsky, A., Sutskever, I., Hinton, G.E.: Imagenet classification with deep convolutional neural networks. In: Advances in Neural Information Processing Systems 25: 26th Annual Conference on Neural Information Processing Systems 2012. Proceedings of a Meeting Held 3–6 December 2012, Lake Tahoe, Nevada, United States, pp. 1106–1114 (2012)
19. Learned-Miller, E., Huang, G.B., RoyChowdhury, A., Li, H., Hua, G.: Labeled faces in the wild: a survey. In: Kawulok, M., Celebi, M.E., Smolka, B. (eds.) Advances in Face Detection and Facial Image Analysis, pp. 189–248. Springer, Cham (2016). https://doi.org/10.1007/978-3-319-25958-1_8
20. LeCun, Y., Haffner, P., Bottou, L., Bengio, Y.: Object recognition with gradient-based learning. Shape, Contour and Grouping in Computer Vision. LNCS, vol. 1681, pp. 319–345. Springer, Heidelberg (1999). https://doi.org/10.1007/3-540-46805-6_19
21. LeCun, Y., Cortes, C.: MNIST handwritten digit database (2010). http://yann.lecun.com/exdb/mnist/
22. Liu, J., Juuti, M., Lu, Y., Asokan, N.: Oblivious neural network predictions via MiniONN transformations. In: Thuraisingham, B.M., Evans, D., Malkin, T., Xu, D. (eds.) Proceedings of the 2017 ACM SIGSAC Conference on Computer and Communications Security. CCS 2017, pp. 619–631. ACM, New York (2017)
23. Mohassel, P., Zhang, Y.: SecureML: a system for scalable privacy-preserving machine learning. In: 2017 IEEE Symposium on Security and Privacy. SP 2017, pp. 19–38. IEEE Computer Society (2017)

24. Naor, M., Pinkas, B.: Oblivious transfer and polynomial evaluation. In: Proceedings of the Thirty-First Annual ACM Symposium on Theory of Computing, 1–4 May 1999, Atlanta, Georgia, USA, pp. 245–254 (1999)
25. Nielsen, M.A.: Neural Networks and Deep Learning. Determination Press (2015)
26. Nikolaenko, V., Weinsberg, U., Ioannidis, S., Joye, M., Boneh, D., Taft, N.: Privacy-preserving ridge regression on hundreds of millions of records. In: 2013 IEEE Symposium on Security and Privacy. SP 2013, 19–22 May 2013, Berkeley, CA, USA, pp. 334–348 (2013)
27. Orlandi, C., Piva, A., Barni, M.: Oblivious neural network computing via homomorphic encryption. EURASIP J. Inf. Secur. **2007**, 037343 (2007)
28. Riazi, M.S., Weinert, C., Tkachenko, O., Songhori, E.M., Schneider, T., Koushanfar, F.: Chameleon: a hybrid secure computation framework for machine learning applications. IACR Cryptology ePrint Archive, vol. 2017, p. 1164 (2017)
29. Schroff, F., Kalenichenko, D., Philbin, J.: FaceNet: a unified embedding for face recognition and clustering. In: IEEE Conference on Computer Vision and Pattern Recognition. CVPR 2015, pp. 815–823 (2015)
30. Wu, D., Haven, J.: Using homomorphic encryption for large scale statistical analysis. Technical report, Stanford University (2012). http://cs.stanford.edu/people/dwu4/FHE-SIReport.pdf
31. Xie, P., Bilenko, M., Finley, T., Gilad-Bachrach, R., Lauter, K.E., Naehrig, M.: Crypto-Nets: neural networks over encrypted data. CoRR, abs/1412.6181 (2014)
32. Yao, A.C.: Protocols for secure computations (extended abstract). In: 23rd Annual Symposium on Foundations of Computer Science, 3–5 November 1982, Chicago, Illinois, USA, pp. 160–164 (1982)
33. Yuan, J., Yu, S.: Privacy preserving back-propagation neural network learning made practical with cloud computing. IEEE Trans. Parallel Distrib. Syst. **25**(1), 212–221 (2014)
34. Zhang, Q., Yang, L.T., Chen, Z.: Privacy preserving deep computation model on cloud for big data feature learning. IEEE Trans. Comput. **65**(5), 1351–1362 (2016)

Location Assignment of Capacitated Services in Smart Cities

Gerbrich Hoekstra[1,2] and Frank Phillipson[1(✉)]

[1] TNO, The Hague, The Netherlands
[2] University of Groningen, Groningen, The Netherlands
frank.phillipson@tno.nl

Abstract. This paper introduces the Multi-Service Capacitated Facility Location Problem for assigning equipment to access points. Here multiple services should be offered to customers in a Smart City context. Purpose is to offer the total of services to fulfil the customer demand, given the coverage of the service and their capacity constraints. The problem is formulated and some practical results are presented solving the problem as an Integer Linear Programming Problem.

Keywords: Smart city · Planning · Facility Location · Optimization

1 Introduction

By successfully implementing communication applications in urban areas, "smart cities" arise in which data collection and provision can be used to improve the quality of life. The smart city concept is defined by many authors. In general terms, according to [7] it is intended to cope with or reduce problems like mobility, and energy supply which arise from urbanisation and population growth. Another common understanding of the various interpretations of the smart city concept is the use of Information and Communications Technologies (ICT) for various purposes.

The concept of smart city planning belongs to the stream in literature concerning the planning of access networks. In general, access networks connect users and their supplier with each other by means of cables, wires, and other technological equipment. Such networks are generally studied in the context of telecommunication networks.

The planning of access networks is studied by several authors. Smart City planning is related the most to Hybrid Fiber Optic and Wireless Networks (Fiber-Wireless, FiWi) planning. In [43], the Hybrid Wireless-Optical Broadband Access Network (WOBAN) is considered, of which the planning, and setup are studied. A WOBAN consists of both wireless and wired connections. The design of the topology of such a network is considered by [14]. However, here only the planning of wireless services is considered. Specific literature on smart city planning is relatively scarce. Most recent literature on smart cities consider the

© Springer Nature Switzerland AG 2019
É. Renault et al. (Eds.): MSPN 2018, LNCS 11005, pp. 192–206, 2019.
https://doi.org/10.1007/978-3-030-03101-5_17

general concept, the different definitions of this concept (e.g. [2]), the combination of the Internet of Things (e.g. [21]), or the big data challenges in smart cities (e.g. [40]). A complete system, including multiple types of service deployments, is proposed in [39]. It develops a system, which makes use of big data, for urban planning, and smart city evolution. However, their developed four-tier architecture does not show how the various services should be distributed. A planning model for FiWi networks is proposed in [36]. It takes into account scalability and uncertainty in the various time stages. However, it does not consider the joint deployment of various services.

In [49] the Multi-Service Location Set Covering Problem is introduced, in which multiple services are distributed over a set of locations, here lampposts. This is done such that all demand points are covered for all services at minimal costs. In this paper, this model is extended with capacity constraints resulting in the Multi-Service Capacitated Facility Location Problem (MSCFLP). The aim of the MSCFLP is to find a feasible and efficient distribution of services across an urban area such that the total costs, consisting of fixed opening and fixed service costs, are minimised without violating capacity restrictions while satisfying all demand requirements.

The remainder of this paper is organised as follows. In Sect. 2 a literature review on related problems, and smart city (planning) is provided. The problem formulation of the MSCFLP is given in Sect. 3. The experimental design is reported in Sect. 4, and the results of the computational experiments are discussed in Sect. 5. Finally, conclusions and suggestions for future work are provided in Sect. 6.

2   Literature Review

In this section, literature related to the Multi-Service Capacitated Facility Location Problem (MSCFLP) is reviewed. This problem can be seen as an extension of the extensively studied and well-known Facility Location Problem (FLP). When facilities have some upper bound on the amount of demand it can fulfil, the problem is referred to as Capacitated FLP (CFLP), which is NP-Hard [10, 27]. However there are similarities, the MSCFLP is neither a special case nor a generalisation of the CFLP, caused by the differences in the cost structures and the multiple services. In the MSCFLP, no individual costs are concerned with serving a customer from a location, only a fixed opening cost has to be incurred when at least one customer is served from a location. Nevertheless, the MSCFLP shares the most similarities with (extensions of) the CFLP compared to all other already existing problems. We therefore discuss key findings on the CFLP.

Numerous exact and heuristic methods for the CFLP have been proposed in literature, varying from branch and bound [1], branch and price [26], to Benders' decomposition [53]. The ADD heuristic designed by [28], and the DROP heuristic designed by [13] are generalised by [24] to solve CFLPs. An approximation algorithm is developed by [32] for both the UFLP and the CFLP. However, the most applied solution method is Lagrange Relaxation, see [31,46] for a review of the various solution techniques.

A special case of the CFLP is the Single Source Capacitated Facility Location Problem (SSCFLP) in which every customer is served from exactly one facility. In general, all decision variables in this problem are integers, which complicates the problem compared to the CFLP in which the supply variables are continuous. Several authors have devoted attention to the problem, including [5,16,22,25,37]. Lagrangian heuristics are a successful and commonly used approach to generate solutions to the SSCFLP, as stated by [41].

Another variant of the CFLP is the Multi-Commodity Facility Location Problem (MCCFLP). The MCCFLP extends the CFLP by including multiple commodities (e.g. services, products). The aim of the MCCFLP is to find for every commodity a set of locations, and their set of customers such that total costs, which consist of fixed opening costs and travelling costs, are minimised. In contrast to the MSCFLP, a customer (zone) can have demand for various commodities, and a customer can be served from any location. Moreover, no travelling costs and other costs per demand point are considered in the MSCFLP.

Among the first papers that consider multiple commodities in the context of location problems are [51] and [52]. [20] extend this research by including capacity limitations for both plants and distribution centers. After these studies, several studies have been conducted on variations and generalisations of the problem, including the work by [8,23,33,38]. Even more, [29] combined the CFLP with a multi-commodity Min-Cost Flow Problem, and more recently, [30] considered the Multi-Product FLP in a two-stage supply chain setting.

To a lesser extent the MSCFLP relates to the Set Covering Problem (SCP). As stated by [18], the literature on (S)CPs is substantial, and it is known to be NP-complete [19]. The problem can be applied in various practical applications considering a wide variety of problems, including crew scheduling [9,11,42], ship scheduling [6,15], vehicle routing problems [3,17], emergency facility locating [4,45,47], and street lighting allocation in urban areas [34]. For a review on SCPs we refer to [12,44].

3   Problem Formulation

In this paper we consider an urban area in which services need to be offered. For this multiple services boxes are placed across the area. A service box can provide only a single service, and has to be installed at a location. When a service box is opened at some location, the location is said to be a "service access point" of the service. Depending on the context in which it will be used, the term "service" is used either to refer to the service itself or to refer to one of the service access points. For each service it has to be decided at which locations to install service boxes in order to meet the service expectations of its users. A location on which at least one service is provided, is denoted by the term "access location". Such a location is said to be opened to be equipped with services.

Every service has its own (unique) set of points, which potentially have demand for the service. The geographical location of a potential user for some service is referred to as a "demand point" of the particular service. Services do not have an unlimited reach, in fact each service has some limited range in which it can serve demand points. Next to the limited range, a service (box) can only serve a maximum number of demand points. Hence, services are restricted in both range, and in the number of demand points it can serve.

When a demand point is served by a specific service box at some access location, it is said that a "connection" is made between the access location and the demand point. A connection can be made between the access location and the demand point when the service is present at the access location, and the demand point is located in the neighbourhood of the access location. The reason is that services do not have an unlimited reach, in fact each service has some limited range in which it can serve demand points.

Opening a location comes at some fixed positive cost, and installing a service on such an access location comes at some fixed positive cost as well. No costs are associated with connections. As the optimality criterion the combined fixed opening costs of the locations and the services is used.

For this problem we can define a mathematical formulation. In Table 1 an overview of the notation is presented. The problem consists of a set of demand points, locations, and services. Each demand point $i \in \mathcal{G}^u$ potentially has some demand d_i^u for service $u \in \mathcal{F}$. A demand point $i \in \mathcal{G}^u$ is characterised by its location and its demand for service $u \in \mathcal{F}$. Similarly, a location $j \in \mathcal{L}$ is characterised by its location, and its connected services. A service $u \in \mathcal{F}$ is characterised by its range and its capacity η_j^u, which is defined as the maximum number of connections it can release at the same time.

The integer linear program (ILP) for the MSCFLP is formulated as,

$$\min \sum_{j \in \mathcal{L}} \sum_{u \in \mathcal{F}} c_j^u x_j^u + \sum_{j \in \mathcal{L}} f_j y_j, \tag{1}$$

subject to

$$x_j^u \leq y_j \qquad\qquad \forall j \in \mathcal{L}, \forall u \in \mathcal{F}, \tag{2}$$

$$\sum_{i \in \mathcal{G}^u} s_{ij}^u \leq \eta_j^u x_j^u \qquad\qquad \forall j \in \mathcal{L}, \forall u \in \mathcal{F}, \tag{3}$$

$$\sum_{j \in \mathcal{L}} s_{ij}^u \geq d_i^u \qquad\qquad \forall i \in \mathcal{G}^u, \forall u \in \mathcal{F}, \tag{4}$$

$$s_{ij}^u \leq a_{ij}^u M \qquad\qquad \forall i \in \mathcal{G}^u, \forall j \in \mathcal{L}, \forall u \in \mathcal{F}, \tag{5}$$

$$s_{ij}^u \in \mathbb{N} \qquad\qquad \forall i \in \mathcal{G}^u, \forall j \in \mathcal{L}, \forall u \in \mathcal{F}, \tag{6}$$

$$x_j^u \in \{0, 1\} \qquad\qquad \forall j \in \mathcal{L}, \forall u \in \mathcal{F}, \tag{7}$$

$$y_j \in \{0, 1\} \qquad\qquad \forall j \in \mathcal{L}, . \tag{8}$$

Objective (1) minimises the total costs, which is defined as the sum of the opening costs of the services boxes and the opening costs of the access locations.

Table 1. Parameters, and decision variables for the MSCFLP.

General Notation	
$\mathcal{L}$	Set of all locations
$\mathcal{F}$	Set of all services
$\mathcal{G}^u$	Set of all demand points for service $u \in \mathcal{F}$
$|\mathcal{X}|$	Cardinality of the set $\mathcal{X}$
Indices	
i	Demand point, $i \in \mathcal{G}^u$ for service $u \in \mathcal{F}$
j	Location, $j \in \mathcal{L}$
u	Service, $u \in \mathcal{F}$
Parameters	
$a_{ij}^u = \begin{cases} 1, & \text{if demand } i \in \mathcal{G}^u \text{ can be served from location } j \in \mathcal{L} \text{ for service } u \in \mathcal{F} \\ 0, & \text{if not} \end{cases}$	
c_j^u	Costs of opening service $u \in \mathcal{F}$ at access location $j \in \mathcal{L}$, $c_j^u > 0$
f_j	Costs of opening location $j \in \mathcal{L}$, $f_j > 0$
d_i^u	Demand of demand point $i \in \mathcal{G}^u$ for service $u \in \mathcal{F}$, $d_i^u \in \mathbb{N}$
η_j^u	Max. number connections location $j \in \mathcal{L}$ can release for serv. $u \in \mathcal{F}$, $\eta_j^u \in \mathbb{N}^+$
M	A large number, $M > 0$
Decision variables	
s_{ij}^u	Number of connections made between location $j \in \mathcal{L}$, and dem. point $i \in \mathcal{G}^u$, $s_{ij}^u \in \mathbb{N}$
$x_j^u = \begin{cases} 1, & \text{access location } j \in \mathcal{L} \text{ is a service access point for service } u \in \mathcal{F} \\ 0, & \text{if not} \end{cases}$	
$y_j = \begin{cases} 1, & \text{if location } j \in \mathcal{L} \text{ is an access location} \\ 0, & \text{if not} \end{cases}$	

Constraint (2) ensures that services can only be installed at access locations. Capacity restrictions are taken into account by including constraint (3). It limits the number of connections an access location can release for a specific service, to be no more than the maximum number of connections the service can have. When a service is not installed at an access location, the capacity is set equal to zero, which ensures that for the service at this location no connections can be made. Constraint (4) ensures that demand is satisfied, and constraint (5) implies that a connection can only be made between demand point $i \in \mathcal{G}^u$ and access location $j \in \mathcal{L}$ for service $u \in \mathcal{F}$, when the demand point is located in the range of the service ($a_{ij}^u = 1$). Lastly, constraints (6) – (8) specify the solution space. The problem formulation consists of

$$2|\mathcal{L}||\mathcal{F}| + |\mathcal{G}|(|\mathcal{L}| + 1) \quad \text{constraints, and} \tag{9}$$

$$|\mathcal{G}||\mathcal{L}| + |\mathcal{L}|(|\mathcal{F}| + 1) \quad \text{variables.} \tag{10}$$

A less intuitive formulation of the same problem, but much efficient in solving is the following formulation. The difference lies in the modulation of the connection variables s_{ij}^u. In the given formulation, the variable s_{ij}^u is defined for all combinations of $i \in \mathcal{G}^u$ and $j \in \mathcal{L}$ subject to constraint (5). When a demand point is not within range of a service for some location, this constraint implies that the solution space of the corresponding variable s_{ij}^u consist of the single element 0. Hence, it is reasonable to define s_{ij}^u only for those combinations of demand points and locations for which the demand point is within range of the location implying that the solution space of the corresponding connection variable consists of both elements 0, and 1.

In mathematical terms this implies the following. For some demand point $i \in \mathcal{G}^u$ having demand for service $u \in \mathcal{F}$ let the set of locations $j \in \mathcal{L}$, for which i is within the range, be denoted by $\mathcal{L}_i^u$. That is, let the set $\mathcal{L}_i^u$ be defined as,

$$\mathcal{L}_i^u = \{j | a_{ij}^u = 1\}, \tag{11}$$

for some demand point $i \in \mathcal{G}^u$ having demand for service $u \in \mathcal{F}$. Then define s_{ij}^u only for those combinations for which $a_{ij}^u = 1$, leading to the change in Eq. (4):

$$\sum_{j \in \mathcal{L}_i^u} s_{ij}^u \geq d_i^u \quad \forall i \in \mathcal{G}^u, \forall u \in \mathcal{F},$$

By this, constraint (5) becomes redundant and can be deleted from the problem formulation.

This problem formulation has

$$2|\mathcal{L}||\mathcal{F}| + |\mathcal{G}| \quad \text{constraints, and} \tag{12}$$

$$\sum_{u \in \mathcal{F}} \sum_{i \in \mathcal{G}^u} \mathcal{L}_i^u + |\mathcal{L}|(|\mathcal{F}| + 1) \quad \text{variables.} \tag{13}$$

Compared to the formulation of Eqs. (1)–(8) this problem formulation reduces the number of variables by $|\mathcal{G}||\mathcal{L}| - \sum_{u \in \mathcal{F}} \sum_{i \in \mathcal{G}^u} \mathcal{L}_i^u$ variables, and the number of constraints by $|\mathcal{L}||\mathcal{G}|$ constraints.

4   Experimental Design

In this section we discuss the experimental design of the various conducted experiments. In Sect. 4.1 we describe the software, and hardware that are used to implement and solve the problems. An overview on the various input parameters is given in Sect. 4.2. We present the set of locations, the set of studied services, and the demand point selection. In Sect. 4.3 the various test instances are discussed.

4.1   Software and Hardware

The problem has been implemented in, and the experiments are conducted by MATLAB version R2016b. It is a programming language published by Math-Works, which allows for a wide range of computations, and other data processing. The problems are solved by use of the external solver CPLEX. IBM ILOG

CPLEX Optimisation Studio (COS) is a solver developed by IBM. It is an optimisation software package for solving linear programs, mixed integer programs, and quadratic programs. The free student 12.7.1 version of the package has been used to generate the results. The experiments are performed on a DELL E7240 laptop with an Intel(R) Core(TM) i5-4310U CPU 2.00 GHz 2.60 GHz processor. The laptop is operational on a 64-bit operating system.

4.2 Input Parameters

In this section all parameter values and the various characteristics of the test instances will be discussed. We describe the parameter settings for the locations, services, and the demand points.

Locations. As described in Sect. 1, the lighting system is used as a network in which different locations can be opened. Every lamppost is a candidate access location which can be equipped with services. Data on the locations of lampposts is publicly available for many cities of the Netherlands. It is accessible via Dataplatform, which is an initiative of Civity. The test instances describe various subareas of the city of Amsterdam. The fixed opening costs of a location are taken to be equal to $f_j = 5,000$ for every location $j \in \mathcal{L}$. A mapping of all locations of some small subarea of the city of Amsterdam can be found in Fig. 1.

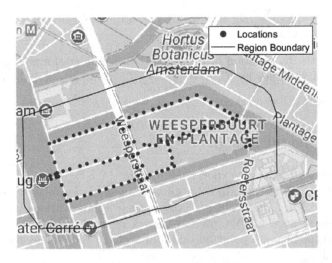

Fig. 1. Mapping of all access locations in some small subarea of the city of Amsterdam.

Services. In total three services will be considered for the test instances. The various services and their parameter values are based on the works of [48,50]. As previously stated, a service is characterised by its range and its capacity. The capacity is defined as the maximum number of connections it could release at the same time. It is assumed that every service has a circular coverage area. Given the range, the coverage matrix with elements a_{ij}^u can be filled. For every service, information is provided in Table 2 on the range, capacity, and opening costs of the service. The first service is a WiFi service. It has a range of 100 m, can serve up to a maximum of 30 demand points, and its opening cost is equal to 300. The second service is a Smart Vehicle Communication (SVC) technique, which aims at providing data to drivers. It has a range of 200 m, a capacity of 15 connections, and an opening cost of 300. The last service is an Alarm service, which has an unlimited capacity. This service has a range of 300 m, and opening cost equal to 150. The Alarm service aims at providing a loud signal to warn humans about dangers. As the service provision is independent on the number of humans within the range of the access location, the capacity of the service is unlimited.

Table 2. Overview of the considered services for the test instances.

Service	Range	Capacity η_j^u	Costs c_j^u
$u = 1$: WiFi	100	30 $\forall j \in \mathcal{L}$	300 $\forall j \in \mathcal{L}$
$u = 2$: SVC	200	15 $\forall j \in \mathcal{L}$	350 $\forall j \in \mathcal{L}$
$u = 3$: Alarm	300	∞ $\forall j \in \mathcal{L}$	150 $\forall j \in \mathcal{L}$

Demand Points. Every demand point requires service for only one service, and in turn every service has its own disjoint set of demand points. Although sets of demand points differ across the various test instances, every set is generated by the same procedure. The demand points are generated within the boundary that specifies the test area. An overview of all demand points classified per service in some small subarea of the city of Amsterdam is given in Fig. 2.

For the WiFi service, the home addresses located inside the boundary are taken as demand points. All houses are assigned a demand of one. As the second service is a SVC technique, which aims at providing data to drivers, the demand points are generated on the roads inside the boundary. In contrast to the WiFi service, not every road point has a demand of one. In fact, a demand point is assigned a demand 1, 2, or 3, depending on its characteristics. Demand points referring to so called "A-roads" are assigned a demand of 3, simulating the fact that these important highways are in general congested. These roads are labelled as motorways, and freeways in the original documentation (OpenStreetMap). Less important roads, are national and regional roads. These roads are labelled primary, and secondary roads, and a demand of 2 is assigned to demand points on such roads. All other roads are of least importance, and in turn are assigned a demand equal to one.

The last service is the Alarm service. As it has an infinite capacity, serving its demand points can be approached as a covering problem instead of some capacitated supply problem. In line with this approach, the demand points of the alarm are intersections of a grid. It is indicated in [35] that this approach works best with regard to computational efficiency. For more information on the generation of the grid, we refer to Sect. 6.3 of [50]. Similar to the WiFi service, a demand of one is assigned to every demand point. However, the optimal solution is the same for other demand values, as the Alarm service has an unlimited capacity. Hence, for efficiency reasons, a demand of one is assigned.

Note that the demand points, that are not located in range of at least one location, are excluded from the set of demand points. That is, when there is no location in the neighbourhood of a demand point, it is deleted from the set of demand points.

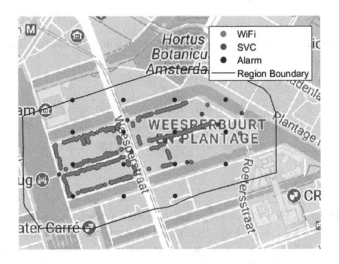

Fig. 2. Plot of the demand points per service of some small area in Amsterdam.

4.3   Test Instances

The MSCFLP will be solved on a number of test instances, as shown in Table 3. These test instances are small subareas of the city of Amsterdam. In total, 9 test instances are considered, of which instance 1 to 7 are the small instances.

5   Computational Results

In this section the computational results will be discussed. First, we look at the impact of the capacity constraints on the calculation time. Next we address the added value of the multi-service planning approach compared to a multiple single service planning approach.

Table 3. Overview of the test instances.

Inst.	No. locations $|\mathcal{L}|$	No. demand points $|\mathcal{G}^1|$	$|\mathcal{G}^2|$	$|\mathcal{G}^3|$	Tot. $|\mathcal{G}|$
1	33	47	3	9	59
2	77	73	8	15	96
3	99	260	9	13	282
4	102	462	8	15	485
5	400	111	20	25	156
6[a]	782	21	93	104	218
7	516	1,241	42	46	1,329
8	6,079	8,106	397	326	8,829
9[a]	6,981	10,122	528	431	11,081

[a]For these two test instance some demand points requiring WiFi or SVC service are excluded from the initial set of demand points, as these demand points could not be served from any location. Per service at most 5 demand points were deleted.

5.1 Impact of Capacity Constraint

First, the uncapacitated problem of [50] was solved on some test instances. This problem is similar to the MSCFLP without the capacity constraint. Then the MSCFLP is solved on the same test instances, but the capacity limitations taken to be greater than the total number of demand points. That is, the capacity constraints could never become binding in any of the feasible solutions. These two experiments on the two "uncapacitated" problems showed an increasing gap in the computation times. Hence, even without limiting capacity bounds, the computation times of the CPLEX solver increase due to the inclusion of the connection variables.

For the other instances of the MSCFLP in this paper, we use a stopping criterium. Two stopping criteria have been implemented. The solver is terminated when the gap between the objective value of the best solution found and the best lowerbound (using the Branch & Bound) is less than or equal to 5%, and for $\max_I$ iterations no improvement of the current solution has been made, where $\max_I$ is defined by Eq. (15). Besides this stopping criteria, a maximum running time duration of 43,200 s (i.e., 12 h) has been implemented

$$\max_I = 50,000 + \left\lceil \frac{\text{No. of Constraints} + \text{No. of Variables}}{10,000} \right\rceil \cdot 500 \qquad (14)$$

$$= 50,000 + \left\lceil \frac{|\mathcal{G}| + |\mathcal{L}|(3|\mathcal{F}| + 1) + \sum_{u \in \mathcal{F}} \sum_{i \in \mathcal{G}^u} \mathcal{L}_i^u}{10,000} \right\rceil \cdot 500 \qquad (15)$$

Table 4. Running times of the MSLSCP and the "uncapacitated" version of the MSCFLP.

Inst.	MSLSCP			MSCFLP with $\eta_j^u = \infty$		
	Obj.	Gap (%)	Time (s)	Obj.	Gap (%)	Time (s)
1	5,800	0.0	0.0	5,800	0.0	0.0
2	16,400	0.0	0.0	16,400	0.0	2.4
3	21,700	0.0	0.0	21,700	0.0	14.4
4	27,350	0.0	0.0	27,350	0.0	31.7
5	27,850	0.0	0.1	27,850	0.0	40.4
6	99,850	0.0	0.1	99,850	0.0	416.4
7	92,800	0.0	1.2	103,900	14.7	43,200.0
8	678,700	3.7	43,200.0	914,550	37.8	43,200.0
9	853,250	4.3	43,200.0	1,137,850	40.88	43,200.0

NB. In 5 instances the solver was terminated after 43200 s (i.e., 12 h).

5.2   Results

Next, it is worthwhile to investigate whether the multi-service planning approach does yield some cost reduction compared to the approach in which the distribution of the different services is optimised for each service individually. This last approach implies that multiple, but less complicated optimisations need to be performed, which may yield a lower overall running time. To this approach will be referred as the single service planning approach.

The following discussion will focus on the running time of the solver, and the objective value of the best solution found by the solver. In order to get a distribution network of the different services out of the single service planning approach, the solutions of the single service planning approach will be combined. However, the objective of the combined solution for all services is not simply equal to the sum of the single objective values for the single service planning approach. The reason is that a location can be opened in multiple solutions, but in reality it only needs to be opened for the first installed service. Data on the objective value, and running time for both approaches, can be found in Table 5. The running time of the single service planning approach is the combined running times of the different single service optimisations.

From Table 5 we can conclude that the multi-service approach yields positive cost savings for all test instance. For instances 1–6 the running time of the multi-service approach exceeds the running time of the single service approach. In contrast, for instances 7–9 a reverse statement holds. For instances 8 and 9 the reason is that all single service optimisations have been terminated as the maximum running time had been reached. The higher running time of the single service approach for instance 7 is a result of the optimisation of the WiFi service, which took 948.6 s. This is most likely the result of the relatively large number of WiFi demand points compared to the first 6 test instances. Summarising,

Table 5. Objective values and corresponding running times of the solver for both the single service approach, and the multi-service planning approach.

Inst.	Single service		Multi-service				
	Obj.	Time (s)	Obj.	Gap	Time (s)	Cost sav. (%)
1	16,100	0.1	11,100	0.0	1.1	31.1
2	31,700	0.2	21,700	0.0	22.1	31.5
3	63,550	0.6	48,200[1]	3.7	4.9	24.2
4	100,650	0.8	85,650[1]	4.0	6.4	14.9
5	58,150	1.4	38,150[1]	9.9	43,200.0	34.4
6	164,250	118.9	100,200	0.0	171.8	39.0
7	270,600	984.5	231,600[1]	2.5	316.6	14.4
8	2,007,950[1]	129,600.0	1,718,450[1]	7.6	43,200.0	14.4
9	2,494,950[1]	129,600.0	2,192,800[1]	9.8	43,200.0	12.1

[1]The optimisation has been terminated according to the stopping criteria of the previous section. For instances 8 and 9 all single service optimisations have been terminated.

although the multi-service optimisation has been terminated for almost all test instances in contrast to the single service approach, the multi-service approach outperforms the single-service approach according to the optimality criterion. In Table 6 additional information on the number of opened services, and the number of opened locations can be found for both approaches.

Table 6. Single service and multi-service results of the MSCFLP problem.

Inst	Single service				Multi-service			
	WiFi	SVC	Alarm	No. op. loc	WiFi	SVC	Alarm	No. op. loc
1	2	1	1	3	2	1	1	2
2	4	1	1	6	4	1	1	4
3	9	1	1	11	9	1	1	9
4	16	2	1	19	16	2	1	16
5	6	3	2	11	6	3	2	7
6	10	14	9	31	11	15	11	18
7	43	6	4	51	43	8	6	43
8	308	48	25	379	310	69	42	319
9	371	66	37	471	386	83	53	408

6 Discussion

In this paper, we optimised the distribution of multiple services in urban areas. For this optimisation problem, we introduced and defined the Multi-Service Capacitated Facility Location Problem (MSCFLP). It aims at optimising the distribution of multiple services simultaneously in some urban area, such that the total costs are minimised, while satisfying all demand requirements. For this problem an integer linear program (ILP) was formulated. A solver is used to solve this problem, and a stopping criteria has been introduced. The solver yields (near-)optimal solutions for only the small instances. The conducted experiments show that large cost reductions are obtained when the joint distribution of the services is optimised simultaneously.

Several opportunities exist for future work in this research area. First, some heuristic approaches can be developed to improve the calculation time for larger problem sizes. Second, one could extend the base model by allowing for multiple services boxes of the same service on one access location. For this extension, next to determining which locations should be equipped with services, it has to be decided how many service boxes should be opened per service on these locations. Third, a partial covering extension could be made, in which not all demand points have to be covered.

References

1. Akinc, U., Khumawala, B.: An efficient branch and bound heuristic for the capacitated warehoues location problem. Manage. Sci. **23**(6), 585–594 (1977)
2. Albino, V., Berardi, U., Dangelico, R.M.: Smart cities: definitions, dimensions, performance, and initiatives. J. Urban Technol. **22**(1), 3–21 (2015)
3. Balinski, M., Quandt, R.: On an integer program for a delivery problem. Oper. Res. **12**, 300–304 (1964)
4. Bao, S., Xiao, N., Lai, Z., Zhang, H., Kim, C.: Optimizing watchtower locations for forest fire monitoring using location models. Fire Saf. J. **72**, 100–109 (2015)
5. Barcelo, J., Casanovas, J.: A heuristic lagrangian algorithm for the capacitated plant location problem. Eur. J. Oper. Res. **15**, 212–226 (1984)
6. Brown, G., Graves, G., Ronen, D.: Scheduling ocean transportation of crude oil. Manage. Sci. **33**, 335–346 (1987)
7. Calvillo, C., Sànchez-Miralles, A., Villar, J.: Energy management and planning in smart cities. Renew. Sustain. Energy Rev. **55**, 273–287 (2016)
8. Canel, C., Khumawala, B., Law, J., Loh, A.: An algorithm for the capacitated, multi-commodity, multi-period facility location problem. Comput. Oper. Res. **28**, 411–427 (2001)
9. Caprara, A., Fischetti, M., Toth, P.: A heuristic method for the set covering problem. Oper. Res. **47**(5), 730–743 (1999)
10. Cornuéjols, G., Nemhauser, G., Wolsey, L.: The uncapacitated facility location problem. In: Mirchandani, P., Francis, R. (eds.) Discrete location Theory, pp. 119–171. Wiley, New York (1990)
11. Desrochers, M., Soumis, F.: A column generation approach to the urban transit crew scheduling problem. Transp. Sci. **23**, 1–13 (1989)

12. Farahani, R., Asgari, N., Heidari, N.: Covering problems in facility location: a review. Comput. Ind. Eng. **62**(1), 368–407 (2012)
13. Feldman, E., Lehrer, F., Ray, T.: Warehouse location under continuous economies of scale. Manage. Sci. **12**, 670–684 (1966)
14. Filippini, I., Cesana, M.: Topology optimization for hybrid optical/wireless access networks. Ad Hoc Netw. **8**, 614–625 (2010)
15. Fisher, M., Rosenwein, M.: An interactive optimisation system for bulk-cargo ship scheduling. Nav. Res. Logist. **36**, 27–42 (1989)
16. Fisk, J.: A solution procedure for a special type of capacitated warehouse location problem. Logist. Transp. Rev. **13**, 305–320 (1978)
17. Foster, B., Ryan, D.: An integer programming approach to the vehicle scheduling problem. Oper. Res. Q. **27**, 367–384 (1976)
18. Gandhi, R., Khuller, S., Srinivasan, A.: Approximation algorithms for partial covering problems. J. Algorithms **53**(1), 55–84 (2004)
19. Garey, M.R., Johnson, D.S.: Computers and intractability: a guide to the theory of NP completeness. Comput. Intractability (1979)
20. Geoffrion, A., Graves, G.: Mutlicommodity distribution system design by benders decomposition. Manage. Sci. **20**(5), 822–844 (1974)
21. Georgakopoulos, D., Jayaraman, P.P.: Internet of things: from internet scale sensing to smart services. Computing **98**(10), 1041–1058 (2016)
22. Guastaroba, G., Speranza, M.: A heuristic for BILP problems: the single source capacitated facility location problem. Eur. J. Oper. Res. **238**, 438–450 (2014)
23. Hinojosa, Y., Puerto, J., Fernández, F.: A multiperiod two-echelon multicommodity capacitated plant location problem. Eur. J. Oper. Res. **123**, 271–291 (2000)
24. Jacobsen, S.: Heuristics for the capacitated plant location model. Eur. J. Oper. Res. **12**, 253–261 (1983)
25. Klincewicz, J., Luss, H.: A lagrangian relaxation heuristic for capacitated facility location with single source constraints. J. Oper. Res. Soc. **37**, 495–500 (1986)
26. Klose, A., Görtz, S.: A branch-and-price algorithm for the capacitated facility location problem. Eur. J. Oper. Res. **179**(3), 1109–1125 (2007)
27. Krarup, J., Pruzan, P.: The simple plant location problem: survey and synthesis. Eur. J. Oper. Res. **12**, 36–81 (1983)
28. Kuehn, A., Hamburger, B.: A heuristic program for locating warehouses. Manage. Sci. **9**, 643–666 (1963)
29. Li, J., Chu, F., Prins, C.: Lower and upper bounds for a capacitated plant location problem with multicommodity flow. Comput. Oper. Res. **36**, 3019–3030 (2009)
30. Li, J., Chu, F., Prins, C., Zhu, Z.: Lower and upper bounds for a two-stage capacitated facility location problem with handling costs. Eur. J. Oper. Res. **236**, 957–967 (2014)
31. Magnanti, T., Wong, R.: Decomposition methods for facility location problems. In: Mirchandani, P., Francis, R. (eds.) Discrete Location Theory, pp. 209–262. Wiley, New York (1990)
32. Mahdian, M., Ye, Y., Zhang, J.: Approximation algorithms for metric facility location problems. SIAM J. Comput. **36**(2), 411–432 (2003)
33. Melo, M., Nickel, S., Saldanha da Gama, F.: Dynamic multi-commodity capacitated facility location: a mathematical modeling framework for strategic supply chain planning. Comput. Oper. Res. **33**, 181–208 (2005)
34. Murray, A., Feng, X.: Public street lighting service standard assessment and achievement. Socio-Econ. Plan. Sci. **53**, 14–22 (2016)
35. Murray, A.T., O'Kelly, M.E., Church, R.L.: Regional service coverage modelling. Comput. Oper. Res. **35**(2), 339–355 (2008)

36. Peralta, A., Inga, E.: Hincapié: optimal scalability of fiwi networks based on multi-stage stochastic programming and policies. Opt. Soc. Am. **9**(12), 1172–1183 (2017)
37. Pirkul, H.: Efficient algorithm for the capacitated concentrator location problem. Comput. Oper. Res. **14**, 197–208 (1987)
38. Pirkul, H., Jayaraman, V.: A multi-commodity, multi-plant, capacitated facility location problem: formulation and efficient heuristic solution. Manage. Sci. **25**, 869–878 (1998)
39. Rathore, M.M., Ahmad, A., Paul, A., Rho, S.: Urban planning and buidling smart cities based on the internet of things using big data analytics. Comput. Netw. **101**, 63–80 (2016)
40. Rathore, M.M., Paul, A., Ahmad, A., Chilamkurthi, N., Hong, W.-W., Seo, H.: Real-time secure communication for smart city in high-speed big data environment. Futur. Gener. Comput. Syst. **83**, 638–652 (2017)
41. Rönnqvist, M., Tragantalerngsak, S., Holt, J.: A repeated matching heuristic for the single-source capacitated facility location problem. Eur. J. Oper. Res. **116**, 51–68 (1999)
42. Ryan, D., Falkner, J.: On integer properties of scheduling set partitioning models. Eur. J. Oper. Res. **35**, 442–456 (1988)
43. Sarkar, S., Yen, H.H., Dixit, S., Mukherjee, B.: Hybrid wireless-optical broadband access network (WOBAN): network planning and setup. IEEE J. Sel. Areas Commun. **26**(6), 12–21 (2008)
44. Schilling, D., Jayaraman, V., Barkhi, R.: A review of covering problems in facility location. Locat. Sci. **1**(1), 25–55 (1993)
45. Schreuder, J.: Application of a location model to fire stations in Rotterdam. Eur. J. Oper. Res. **6**, 212–219 (1981)
46. Sridharan, R.: The capacitated plant location problem. Eur. J. Oper. Res. **87**(2), 203–213 (1995)
47. Toregas, C., Swain, R., Revelle, C., Bergman, L.: The location of emergency service facilities. Oper. Res. **19**, 1363–1373 (1971)
48. Verhoek, M.: Optimising the placement of access points for smart city services with stochastic demand. Master's thesis (2017)
49. Vos, T., Phillipson, F.: Dense multi-service planning in smart cities. In: International Conference on Information Society and Smart Cities (2018)
50. Vos, T.: Using lamppost to provide urban areas with multiple services. Master's thesis (2016)
51. Warszawski, A.: Multi-dimensional location problems. Oper. Res. Q. **24**, 165–179 (1973)
52. Warszawski, A., Peer, S.: Optimizing the location of facilities on a building site. Oper. Res. Q. **24**, 35–44 (1973)
53. Wentges, P.: Accelerating Benders' decomposition for the capacitated facility location problem. Math. Methods Oper. Res. **44**(2), 267–290 (1996)

Network Slicing Architecture and Dependability

Andres J. Gonzalez$^{(\boxtimes)}$, Min Xie, and Pål Grønsund

Telenor Research, Fornebu, Norway
andres.gonzalez@telenor.com

Abstract. The next generation of cellular networks known as 5G promises to be a major step in the evolution of communications technology, due to its enhanced technical features and because it is planned for a much wider set of applications and scenarios. Network slicing provides the scalability and flexibility needed to support this vision, by enabling the provision of independent and isolated network segments tailored to specific uses and requirements. The aim of this paper is to present the current status of the slicing architecture and based on that, define policies that assure its dependability. Guaranteeing dependability in network slicing is a top priority since 5G networks will be a critical infrastructure in industry sectors such as energy, health, transport and traditional telecom itself. Moreover, some slices are expected to deliver Ultra Reliable Communication (URC) with reliability requirements above 99.999%. A dependability design should be based on the system architecture. However, a standardized and final architecture for network slicing is still work in progress. This paper studies the most relevant architectural components defined to date, and based on that, it describes the dependability policies that should be used on each of them. Finally, this paper presents some analysis of the overall challenges for the integration of the different slicing components.

1 Introduction

5G is proposed as the future generation of mobile networks providing key features such as data rates in the order of several gigabits per second, latency of very few milliseconds, higher density of connected devices (x1000), among others [1]. Many of these characteristics will be driven by the imminent traffic increase in mobile networks, but also by a set of new use cases targeted for the mobile networks, many of them with extreme requirements [2].

Network slicing is the concept that allows multiple tailored and customized services and use cases to simultaneously run on one single 5G network. A Network slice is basically a logical network running on top of the physical network. Each network slice can have different capabilities such as quality of service (e.g. throughput, latency with edge computing), security (e.g. level of monitoring), robustness (e.g. link and function redundancy) and service assurance (e.g. active measurements). Network slicing thus become the key tool for operators

© Springer Nature Switzerland AG 2019
É. Renault et al. (Eds.): MSPN 2018, LNCS 11005, pp. 207–223, 2019.
https://doi.org/10.1007/978-3-030-03101-5_18

to empower and foster innovation in new vertical industries and then to widen its own portfolio of services and customers.

The main objective of this paper is to provide an overview of the current status of the network slice architecture, and based on that provide an initial set of policies that will lead to enhance its dependability.

Realizing a dynamic and dependable network slicing in 5G needs to be addressed from the very beginning on its architecture. The network slicing architecture is designed from the foundation of the Network Functions Virtualization (NFV) architecture, integrated with Software Defined Networking (SDN) [3,4] and [5]. Various works have contributed toward this direction. Compared to NFV and SDN, network slicing architecture is emphasized with features like multiple slices across heterogeneous networks and clouds [6,7]. Due to the complexity in constructing network slices from shared infrastructure, the challenge is high for control and management. In [5,8,9], different views are described to distribute the lifecycle management of slices, infrastructure and the associated Virtual Network Functions (VNFs) and Network Services (NSs) between management and control plane. Up to now, there is no conclusive and unified proposition for the network slicing architecture.

Network slicing will be a critical infrastructure in itself and will likely become a part of other critical infrastructure in industry sectors such as energy, health and transport. In addition, some slices are expected to deliver Ultra Reliable Communication (URC) with reliability requirements above 99.999%, as it was explicitly stated in the 5G vision [1]. For this reason, the design of clear policies that enable highly dependable network slicing deployments is a top priority. Despite its importance, dependability in network slicing is a topic that is not mature, and hence several further studies are needed. Some of the efforts from the 5G community have an initial focus on the wireless part, where consideration in the time and space domain are analyzed, as well as the use of different radio access technologies and cognitive radio techniques [10,11] and [12]. Dependability in traditional transport networks is also a key component for the appropriate network slicing development. There are severals studies for the design of dependable and survivable generic transport networks, such as those presented in [13] and [14]. In addition, with the emergence of SDN, new policies that consider a reliable design that take into account the details of this new architecture are needed. For this reason, works like [15] and [16] (among others) address the design of dependable transport networks using SDN, having in mind the implications of separating the control-plane from the data-plane. Since NFV is one of the main components in network slicing, the efforts made by the ETSI-NFV Reliability Working Group [17] represent a valuable contribution and a solid starting point for the dependable design of slicing components. Related works on cloud computing reliability such as the works presented in [18,19], and [20] become a good contribution that provide clear guidelines on the respective parts that will address those topics. Finally, it is important to highlight that some studies that provide a holistic view on the dependability of network slicing are still needed, being this work one of the first contributions in this direction.

This paper is organized as follows. In Sect. 2 the main network slicing features and concepts are presented. Section 3 presents the most relevant network slicing architectural features existing to date. Successively, in Sect. 4 are presented relevant dependability policies of some of the defined network slicing architectural components and the mechanisms and challenges for their integration. Finally, Sect. 5 concludes the paper.

2 Network Slicing

Network slicing is a concept that proposes the splitting of common physical infrastructure and virtual resources in isolated sub-groups (slices), able to provide independent specific network capabilities by fulfilling specific requirements that can be tailored according to the needs. Each network slice is an isolated logical network tailored for different functional and performance requirements, running on a common virtual and/or physical infrastructure. The initial three basic slice types defined in [5] are: (i) enhanced Mobile Broadband (eMBB). (ii) massive Machine Type Communication (mMTC). (iii) Ultra-Reliable Low Latency Communication (URLLC). Today, the number of use cases that can be provided is not constrained to any specific number, since they depend more on specific business needs and context. However, their features may be associated with any of the three original slices previously presented [5].

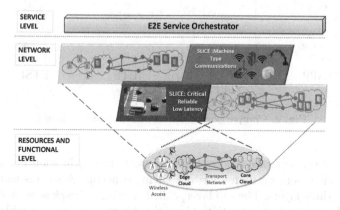

Fig. 1. A representation of network slicing.

Figure 1 illustrates a network slice example as follows. The bottom part, denominated as *resources and functional level* in [21] exemplifies the common physical infrastructure and virtual resources that are available to be assigned to the different slices. On top of them are presented the example of two slices, in the called *network level*; one for critical reliable low latency applications and the other for machine type communications. To each slice are assigned network, compute and storage resources, guaranteeing isolation and independence, even if they are allocated on top of common resources. Finally, on top is the *service level*, in charge of orchestrate and manage services, and keeping an updated an holistic view of the hole system.

Network slicing has been studied in different organizations, which gives different definitions. In general, the network slice is a composition of network functions, network applications, and the underlying cloud infrastructure that meets the requirements of a specific use case [1, 22]. A network slice usually covers all network segments including radio or wired access, core, transport and edge networks from end to end (E2E). To improve scalability and ease management, network slices are constructed in a recursive way as shown in Fig. 2 that summarizes the definitions of network slices given by 3GPP [22], NGMN [21], 5GPPP [4], IETF [5], and ETSI [23].

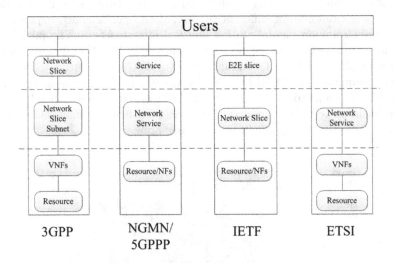

Fig. 2. Comparison of definitions of network slices

Despite of the separate studies from different standardization bodies, today there is an alignment on many network slicing concepts. A slice is usually constructed by three layers. The top layer, called *service*, *network slice* or *E2E slice*, corresponds to complete instantiated logical network that meets specific network characteristics required by customers. It is customer-oriented and responsible for the end-to-end (E2E) service orchestration[1]. In this sense, network slice is also called E2E slice in IETF. The bottom layer is resource- and infrastructure-oriented, including resources and network functions (NFs). The middle layer is often called *network slice* or *network slice subnet*. It is a set of NFs that execute certain network services but may not form a complete logical network.

---

[1] E2E service or slice orchestration can partially be considered traditional OSS (Operations Support System) task.

Network slicing requires isolation of logical network components from the underlying physical network resources, which can be achieved by technologies of abstraction, virtualization and softwarization. As a result, NFV and SDN are considered as important enablers for network slicing. Together they can provide the programmability and flexibility to efficiently operate multiple logical networks on one common network. SDN can provide the control plane that abstracts and dynamically configures the underlying forwarding plane according to specific slice requirements. NFV takes the role of managing the lifecycle of network slices, which is done by orchestrating the infrastructure resources, network services and VNFs in network slices. In combination, they pave the way to realize network slicing [9].

3   Network Slicing Architecture

Network slicing is an E2E concept and spans across cloud data centers and all network segments. As shown in Fig. 1, one network slice starts from the mobile edge, continues through the mobile transport up until the core network. The networks interconnect edge and core clouds that implement NFs. Furthermore, in order to support E2E network slicing, both management plane and control plane are required to coordinate with data plane NFs to complete the lifecycle of network slices, including preparation, instantiation, configuration and activation, running, and termination [8]. However, there is no conclusive consensus on how to distribute the tasks between the management plane and the control plane yet. The combined management and control plane should implement the creation and governance of both; the slicing infrastructure and the individual slices with their associated network functions and network services. More importantly, they should be capable of supporting automatic optimization and healing of slice instances.

3.1   Network Slicing Dimensions

Given the features and requirements of network slicing, we consider network slicing architecture from three dimensions: *network technology* such as access, core, and transport networks; *cloud* like edge cloud and core cloud; and *plane* including management plane, control plane and data plane, as illustrated in Fig. 3. This dimension diagram helps to position various network slicing components into a unified framework and is thus helpful to design the slicing architecture. For example, Cloud Radio Access Networks (C-RAN) can be realized in the mobile edge cloud as a radio access network technology, with control plane and data plane VNFs. As a core network function, virtual Evolved Packet Core (vEPC) spans the control plane (*e.g.*, PCRF) and the data plane (*e.g.*, packet gateway) and is deployed in the core cloud. SDN resides either inside clouds, referred to as Data Center (DC) SDN; or between clouds, known as WAN SDN. SDN is facilitated by transport networks such as front-haul and Multiprotocol Label Switching (MPLS).

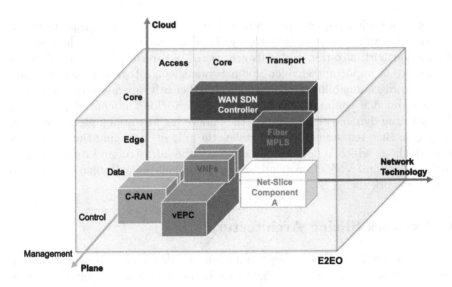

Fig. 3. Network slicing dimensions.

Figure 3 only demonstrates some typical slicing components for the sake of illustration. However, many components with cross multiple segments on the dimension diagram are hard to illustrate. Therefore, Table 1 presents additional details of such components. The NFV Management and Orchestration NFV-MANO is a management plane component and may be positioned in the edge cloud and core cloud. Moreover, as management is required in all networks, NFV-MANO could appear in access, core, and transport networks.

Table 1. Example of the dimensions of some network slice components

Component	Network technology	Cloud	Plane
C-RAN	Access	Edge cloud	Data and control plane
vEPC	Core	Core cloud	Data and control plane
Fiber MPLS	Transport	-	Data plane
WAN-SDN controller	Transport	Between	Control plane
DC SDN switches	Access/core	Edge/core cloud	Data plane
DC SDN controller	Access/core	Edge/core cloud	Control plane
MANO	Access/core/transport	Edge/core cloud	Management plane
E2EO	Access, core, and transport	Edge and core cloud	Management plane

Currently, NFV-MANO is often used to orchestrate network services (NSs). As shown in Fig. 2, an E2E slice is a higher level than NS and may consist of several NSs. Then, an additional E2E Orchestrator (E2EO) is expected to manifest the E2E network slicing. This E2EO is connected to all domain orchestrators or NS orchestrators (NSOs), as shown in Fig. 4. Note that the E2EO is responsible for not only the intra-slice E2E management but also the inter-slice management (*e.g.*, E2EO in [5] and Software-Defined Mobile Network Orchestrator (SDM-O) in [8]). Furthermore, the E2EO is a management component with a full coverage of the entire *Network Technology* dimension and *Cloud* dimension.

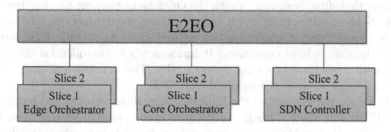

Fig. 4. An example of E2EO composed of edge cloud MANO, core cloud MANO and SDN controllers

Obviously, due to the tight coupling between network slicing and NFV/SDN, a network slicing architecture can be built on top of NFV and SDN architecture. NFV and SDN together form the three planes of network slicing to manage and control the lifecycle of network slices. One challenge of architecture design is to properly integrate NFV and SDN to realize network slicing. The other challenge is caused by the gap between NFV and network slicing, as exhibited in Fig. 2. ETSI NFV is more resource- and NS-facing while network slicing requires customer-facing [23]. To fill the gap, an E2EO is demanded to effectively coordinate NSOs for network slices and manage resources and NSs between network slices. Section 3.2 reviews existing work on network slicing architecture that addresses these two main challenges.

3.2   State of the Art of Network Slicing Architecture

The network slicing architecture aims to define, select and operate network slices simultaneously over a common network infrastructure. Although there is not yet a unified architecture that systematically describes how to realize network slices, a series of works have been done to define the requirements and propose architecture models, from academia, industry, and standardization organization (*e.g.*, [3,4] and [5]).

Standardization is necessary and critical to enable network slicing, whose success highly depends on the harmonized cooperation of different players, from infrastructure and VNF vendors to service providers. By far there is not a standardized architecture for network slicing. Many issues need to be agreed upon, such as the formal definition of network slice, what should be standardized, what NFs are independent of network slices, etc.

5GPPP describes the architecture from the perspective of the *plane* dimension, *i.e.*, *data, control,* and *management plane*[2] [8]. It focuses on integrating

---

[2] 5GPPP uses the term *layer*, which is equivalent to *plane* in our dimension diagram.

NFV and SDN. The management plane is based on the NFV MANO with NFV Orchestrator (NFVO), VNF manager (VNFM), and virtualized infrastructure manager (VIM), plus domain-specific application management and inter-slice resource broker that manages cross-slice resource allocation. It is the management layer that directly interacts with the Operations Support System/Business Support System (OSS/BSS) via a service management function. The control plane is responsible for governing the created slices to provide E2E services meeting the demands of customers. It includes SDN controller for data path control and other functions that connect NFs. The management and control layers coordinate to meet the required QoS/QoE.

In IETF [5], the focus is on the E2EO for E2E slices, constructed recursively as in 5GPPP and 3GPP. One high level slice is composed of several lower level slices (see Fig. 2), each of which is managed by network slice manager and domain orchestrator (DO). At the management plane, DOs interact with each other to exchange topology information exchange and/or convert protocols between domains. On top of network slice managers, there is an E2E Slice Orchestration that coordinates resources distributed across multiple domains and concatenate them into slices. DOs and E2EO jointly operate to manage the lifecycle of network slices. The DO is driven by the E2EO whereas the E2EO interacts with all DOs to coordinate the E2E orchestration. In addition, the E2E slice orchestration also protects the infrastructure from the side effect caused by multiple slice components running in parallel. Note that in IETF, the reconfiguration of logical resources is done by the E2E slice orchestration whereas in 5GPPP, it is the control layer that takes over the governance of the resources.

Given the recursive feature of network slices, a top-down approach was proposed to select and operate NFs from the *Network Technology* dimension and *Plane* dimension in [6]. The focus is on E2E slice orchestration. One slice is composed of an access network (AN) slice and a core network (CN) slice, bounded by network slice management. In the architecture, a CCNF (common control network function), positioned outside network slices, takes care of the network slice instance (NSI) selection, mobility management and authentication for all slices. Each network segment has its own CCNF, *e.g.*, AN-CCNF and CN-CCNF, and cooperate to realize the selection of an NSI. [6] considered two planes, *data plane* (DP) and *control plane* (CP). Both CP and UP functions can be shared between network slices. In the case that one UE is connected to multiple NSIs, slice-independent signaling and slice-specific signaling are requested to CCNFs and CP functions, respectively.

In [7], the network slicing architecture was presented from the *Cloud* and *Network Technology* dimension. In the multi-tenant environment, 5G slices are dynamically instantiated across clouds (MEC, NFV, SDN, C-RAN) and networks (convergence of multiple network technologies). The proposed slice architecture is built on top of ETSI MANO with VIM, VNFM, and NFVO. In addition, a multi-tenant slicing manager (MTSM) was added to manage both data plane network slices and management plane MANO. Furthermore, to meet the demand of network slicing across multiple domains, VIM is modified to orchestrate multiple SDN controllers and multiple distributed cloud data centers (edge, core, and public cloud). In an experiment, one SDN controller (OpenDayLight), one cloud controller (OpenStack) and one NFVO (OpenMANO) are integrated to form a simple slicing architecture.

In [9], an architecture is proposed based on the integration of NFV and SDN. This architecture is focused on the control plane and management plane with two type of SDN controllers added to the ETSI NFV architecture. One controller is called infrastructure SDN controller (IC) located at the infrastructure level to control and manage the resource of the underlay network to provide connectivity between the VNFs. The management of IC can be done by VIM. The other one is located at the tenant and thus called *tenant SDN controller* (TC). TC manages the pertinent VNFs in the overlay network used to realize the tenant's NSs. Combining IC and TC generates an abstract view of the connectivity-related components. Furthermore, the ETSI NFV MANO is reorganized into resource orchestrator (RO) and NSO. Individual slices are equipped with their own TC instances and NSO instances to allow for the required management isolation. RO, as an orchestrator for the entire infrastructure, plays an important role in assuring performance isolation between slices. It cooperates with slice-specific NSO to dynamically and flexibly allocate resources required by slices in real-time.

In summary, some work has been done to define network slicing and design the network slicing architecture, from the three dimensions we describe in Fig. 3. It is necessary to consolidate the relevant work and decide a unified architecture. Moreover, to make the architecture realizable, there is a demand to specify (i) how each dimension and components inside each dimension are defined and communicated; (ii) how components across dimensions communicate with each other; (iii) how components spanning dimensions coordinate between multiple dimensions. For example, at the management plane, DOs should communicate with each other to coordinate the resource sharing and allocation when infrastructure is provided by multiple vendors. DOs also communicate with E2EO to gain the E2E view. The E2EO not only involves multiple network technologies and multiple clouds but also probably manages the control plane and interacts with the data plane. It remains a challenge to standardize the dynamic and complex interactions between the dimensions and domains.

4   Network Slicing Dependability

Dependability is a crucial requirement for network slicing, where it is stipulated that even for some cases, the system reliability must be of 99.999% [1]. The previous section illustrated some of the most relevant architectural aspects of network slicing. In this section, we build on top of those concepts, to provide relevant policies that need to be considered for its dependability. First, we analyze related dependability policies in the access and transport networks. Then, we study the associated dependability aspects of cloud computing and the mobile core, where NFV and SDN play a considerable role. Since in the Network Slice architecture,

Management and Orchestration is fundamental to achieve the whole concept, we will provide here the respective dependability considerations in this regard. Finally, some relevant discussions and summary are provided at the end of this section.

4.1   Related Dependability Policies in the Access Network

Wireless access networks are those in direct contact with end-users devices, thus dependability is extremely important. Wireless access networks have a wide set of potential failures and related consequences, making it challenging for providers to be prepared against all the potential events that may occur. A good survey of the different wireless access networks failure features (severity, rate, dimension, duration and scope) and the failure causes (shadowing and fading, interference, congestion and node failure) is presented in [12].

Here, we present a set of considerations for the design of dependability in the wireless access networks according to the requirements expected from each use case (slice). The first important factor is the natural limitation posed by the potential number of users attached to one antenna, and the data rates offered to each of them. In [11] it is explained that the expected operating regions of 5G wireless systems depend on those two variables, and that the number of users and data rates required should not be very high in order to provide ultra-reliable communications. In addition to that, coverage is also a natural consideration in the design or a robust wireless access networks, where variables like multi-homing and multi-Radio Access Technology (RAT) should be added to the traditional and well known handover techniques, as explained for instance in [10], where ultra-reliable communications are studied in the space domain. Three traffic restoration techniques at the radio access level are presented in [24]: (i) load sharing protocols, (ii) dynamic channel allocation and (iii) adaptive channel quality protocols. One of the techniques that has been proposed to improve and guarantee the dependability in wireless access networks is Cognitive Radio. In [10] is explained how cognitive radios can use their inherent capabilities to implement efficient prevention and recovery mechanisms to combat failures and thereby provide reliable communications and consistent QoS under all circumstances.

Finally, one of the main approaches that will differentiate 5G networks is Cloud-RAN. It proposes to make more flexible, scalable and dynamic the base stations operations, by centralizing the BBU (Baseband units), which will be now known as BBU Pool that receives multiple high bandwidth connections from several RRHs (Remote Radio Heads) [25]. The RRH will be still in charge of tranceiving radio signal, amplification and power and A/D conversion duties, while the BBU pool will continue in charge synchronization, control, transport and processing of baseband signals, but this time it will be virtualized. The idea of following a cloud approach on the BBU allows a better scalability and distribution of loads at the radio access network (RAN), and enable the implementation of dependable architectures, which as it will be explained in Sect. 4.3. There are several considerations that needs to be taken in order to guarantee a dependable operation. However, this architecture has still many open challenges, where the realization of the Common public radio interface (CPRI) which interconnects the RRH with the BBU pool is the one that is taking most attention [26].

4.2 Related Dependability Policies in the Transport and Core Network

The resilience of the transport network may be defined as the ability of a network to automatically react to failures and to redirect the traffic from the paths affected to alternative failure-free paths. The enabling mechanisms are denoted as *recovery mechanisms*, which make use of the redundancy in the network topology. Those networks should be designed with at least two disjoint paths between any two nodes, and with enough spare capacity to be used when needed. A classification of the properties of those recovery mechanisms into five groups is presented in [13] as follows: (i) Resource usage: The resources may be reserved before the failure or not. (ii) Path setup: The recovery path may be set up before the failure, or determined after the failure (with the risk of not finding sufficient capacity). (iii) Operations Domain: The recovery mechanism may operate inside a single domain or it may be multi-domain. (iv) Recovery Scope: The recovery scope may be global for the end to end path, or local for only segments of the path. (v) Operation Layer: Single layer mechanisms or multi-layer mechanisms.

Protection is one of the most common strategies used to meet dependability requirements in transport networks. In this approach the network resources that provide connection between two points are planned in advance. For this, the use of predefined backups is a common policy. According to the protection scheme used, a network connection can be classified as dedicated and shared backup protected. Dedicated path protection is a scheme where the capacity used by the working and the backup path(s) is reserved exclusively for one connection. A network connection that uses dedicated backup goes down when any of the links of the working path fails, and the backup path is not available at that time, due to another failure already affecting it. Shared Backup Path Protection (SBPP) is a scheme where a connection may share bandwidth on its backup path with other connections. In that sense, each connection (e.g. tenant) will have a dedicated working path, and a shared backup path that can be used by several connections in case of failure. In this case, the offered availability not only depends on the network resources assigned to one connection, but also on the state of other connections. Since the backup path has certain probability of being occupied for this reason, when SBPP is used, the concept of Shared Risk Link Group (SRLG) has to be considered in order to enhance robustness. That means that the connections affected by one single failure on a dedicated working path, cannot share any backup resource, guaranteeing restoration at least for the case of single failures. Full details on the different protections and restoration mechanisms, as well as details on SBPP and SRLG can be found in [14].

It is an advantage to know the path to be used in advance of failures, when SLAs with availability requirements are specified. For instance, given that the path assigned to a connection is known, the end-to-end availability offered to that connection can be assessed. To make such assessment, the network provider has to characterize the dependability behavior of the elements that compound the network. Connection oriented networks allow a controlled planning of the resources to be assigned, the assessment of the availability to be offered, and thereby the definition of SLA requirements that can be met with a high probability [14].

Multiprotocol Label Switching (MPLS) networks are nowadays a common example of connection oriented networks. By means of an appropriate management, the previously presented policies can be executed in order to obtain the desired dependability level [27]. Today, SDN is taking the position as one of the best enabler of such policies, since it makes easier to integrate them into the coming 5G networks, as it is presented in [15] and [16].

4.3   Related Dependability Policies in the Cloud Computing

Availability is one of the main concerns of cloud computing. Here, we study some aspects that are relevant for cloud providers in order to keep the availability level expected for each of the services offered. As presented in [28], some initial considerations should be: (i) Redundancy and size of the computing center providing cloud services. (ii) Fault tolerance features of the virtualization platform. (iii) Policies for the efficient use of the cloud resources.

Regarding redundancy, it must start at the hardware level with redundant compute, storage and network. Best practices suggest the design of robust cloud computing environments with enough hardware redundancy. Based on the dynamics posed by the iteration of failure and repair processes, hardware resources may be classified as: active, spare, and on-repair. Here, the challenge is to allocate enough redundant resources to face potential failures, following a cost efficient plan as explained in [29].

Following with virtual resources, cloud computing uses the concept of *distributed load* in order to enhance the maximum performance of any running function/application, and at the same time enhance reliability. This is for instance, a common approach used in the design of the future virtual Evolved Packet Core (vEPC), and its associated virtual instances (VNFs) as presented in [30]. Having load balancing and redundant virtual machines/VNFs across multiple availability zones reduces the probability of downtime, since after the failure of one instance, the traffic may be easily redirected to one that is operating correctly. In this way, the different virtual machines/VNFs can act independently and in parallel. However, it is important to consider the case when the running function/application is state dependent (stateful). In such a case, provide the respective mechanisms that guarantee the synchronization of the state image among the different instances of the cluster is fundamental. An alternative approach to distributed load is the *Master-Slave* approach, where for example only one instance would be in charge of the execution of functions and synchronization duties (the master), while the backup VNFs (slaves) are used to provide fault tolerance and receive passively updates from the master. Additional details on virtual resources redundancy and fault tolerance can be found in [20,28].

A final consideration in cloud computing is the design of the datacenter network which has special features. With the introduction of 5G and NFV, datacenters will have a large number of servers. They will be organized into racks with a logical hierarchical network fabric overlaid on top of the servers, where the use of spine and leaf switches is common, which will be organized into racks with a logical hierarchy, as presented in [31].

In addition, the introduction of SDN technology has enhanced the programmability properties needed in such networks as is illustrated for instance in [32] and [18].

4.4   Related Dependability Policies in Orchestration and Management

When talking about the dependability of Orchestration and Management tools it is important to establish a division on the scope. First, their influence on the managed and orchestrated components. Second the dependability of the Management and Orchestration (M&O) platform itself.

For the dependability of the managed and orchestrated components, it is fundamental to use regular monitoring for detecting abnormal conditions and implement appropriate countermeasures. Monitoring all components and system layers may be demanding. In some cases, an event can trigger several related alarms, due to the multiple layers and complexity of the system structure, leading to an alarm storm which may consume significant system resources and delays. This can then create a negative impact on the dependability of the affected slices. One possible solutions to this issue includes the adequate isolation and segmentation of the monitoring tools, and the intelligent filtering of reported events. A successful monitoring should be followed by a proper failure management strategy. In network slicing there is a huge diversity of components and, hence, multiple approaches that need to be clearly defined and executed by the management and orchestration systems to guarantee the execution of a successful recovery. Finally, the slice manager should be aware of the state properties of the elements that it controls and guarantee the reliable state synchronization of stateful managed instances. Due to the huge diversity of components that need to be managed, the management and orchestration system should have the capacity to address such diversity, and have the modularity and clear mechanisms to include any new coming type of component that may come in future. Finally, it is important to elaborate mechanisms that verify the correctness of the execution of the management and orchestration actions. In other words, to verify that the commands are executed in the way they are meant to, and validate that their effect on the targeted components is the one expected. In addition, in case of detecting mis-operations, the management and orchestrator platform should be prepared with actions that correct undesired effect detected.

Regarding the dependability of the Orchestration and Management platform as such, their absence may put the system in a very vulnerable state that is prone to serious errors and failures. Some important policies in this regard are mentioned as follows.

The most fundamental policy is to avoid Single Point-of-Failure. It implies that the M&O platform cannot be implemented as an individual element, but it needs to be deployed in a robust way such that a failure does not produce unavailability of their functionalities. To this target, modularity and redundancy need to be considered, taking into account that the Orchestrator and Manager are composed of several components that may be stateless and stateful, and consequently different strategies for providing dependability should be considered. Particularly, the dependability of stateful subsystems/modules requires the implementation of reliable and distributed storage systems and their respective synchronization mechanisms, in addition to the redundant instances and failover mechanisms. The design of redundancy policies for stateful systems need to assess the delay implied in the synchronization, and keep the balance of consistency and performance, as it is addressed for instance in [19].

There are two methods for the design of virtual redundant instances, as explained before in the cloud computing section, but that become also relevant here. First, the cluster based approach called Distributed Load, which offers flexibility and the scalability, but since each unit acts independently, making consistent decisions based on a common global view is a challenge. On the other hand, there is the Master/Slave approach. The criteria for selecting a distributed-load or a master/slave approach will depend on the size of the domain that each of the modules need to manage and orchestrate, and to balance performance and consistency (as explained previously). Finally, the manager and managed systems must be allocated and designed in Failure-Independent Domains. Therefore, a failure in one of those, ideally must not imply downtime on the other, and vice versa.

4.5   Summary and Discussion

This Section presents a set of dependability policies on the access, core, transport, cloud, and management and orchestration components of network slicing, based on the architecture features presented in Sect. 2. Table 2 present a summary of them. In terms of *complexity*, it is important to highlight that a holistic control and coordination of each of those individual policies is needed, which represent a remarkable challenge that must be addressed. As explained previously on each individual part, a dependable scheme depends on the design of the adequate reaction mechanisms for recovery, based on accurate information of the occurring events and the current state of the system. However, due to the size and complexity of the network slice system, having opportune and reliable information demands smart mechanisms to efficiently detect and filter all the reported events, which is still an open issue.

Finally, isolation represents the most important feature of network slicing. In this context, the main challenge is the implementation of the orchestration and control tasks that harmonize the different isolation techniques in the different domains, in order to fulfill the requirements of each specific slice. Including the important task of avoiding failure propagation among slices and/or components.

Table 2. Summary of useful network slicing dependability policies

Network slice part	Dependability policies
Access networks	– Assess: shadowing, fading, interference, congestion, and node failure – Assess: number of users (UEs) and data rates to be offered – Coverage, multi-homing and multi-RAT considerations – Design: load sharing protocols, dynamic channel allocation, and adaptive channel quality protocols – Cognitive radio for implementing efficient prevention and recovery mechanisms to combat failures [12] – Dependable cloud-RAN design, including a resilient common public radio interface (CPRI)
Transport and core networks	– Assess: resource usage, paths setup, operations domain, and recovery scope – Dedicated path protection – Shared path protection – Restoration: finding a backup path on demand, when no previous reservation, or reserved resources are busy (no guarantee) – Local and global recovery planning.
Cloud computing	– Servers, storage and network redundancy planning – Design and implementation of independent availability zones – Distributed load and restoration mechanisms design – Datacenter network topology design (e.g. spine and leaf), management, control and programmability (e.g. SDN)
Orchestration and management	– Assessment in two different fronts: orchestrated/managed and orchestrator/manager components – Monitoring and effective alarm processing – Clear recovery policies defined for each of the managed/orchestrated parts (Network slice components) – Mechanisms to verify the correctness of the management and orchestration operations – Avoid single point of failure for all M&O components – Plan the synchronization mechanisms for stateful components of the M&O – Distributed load or master slave for the different M&O components – Failure-independent domains (i.e. different availability zones)

5   Concluding Remarks

Network slicing is currently in the top of the agenda of the telco industry as a whole. It is a concept that allows multiple tailored and customized services and use cases to simultaneously run on one single network. Though, the vision of network slicing seems to be agreed upon, we point to differences but somehow aligned views on architectures for network slicing across standardization bodies. Further, as the main contribution of this paper, we focus on the dependability design and policies for network slicing, which to our best knowledge so far is lacking focus in standardization and research literature.

We proposed a dimension model for network slicing architecture with three dimensions, *network technology*, *cloud*, and *plane*. All components of existing network slicing-related architectures can be properly positioned into this model. The model helps to reveal the synergy between existing architectures and thus can support unification of the existing and future architectures. It further clarifies what needs to be defined and standardized, such as the intra-dimension interfaces or the inter-dimension communications. Generally, it can be used as a reference to design network slice architecture.

Finally, we made a structured assessment of the design policies for dependability in network slicing, focusing on the main domains involved; access network, transport network, cloud computing, and orchestration and management. The integration of all of the potential policies from each of the different domains in order to achieve a common slice dependability is still an open challenge that needs to be addressed. The expected number of components that need to be individually managed and integrated into and E2E solutions, as well as the respective amount of information that needs to be processed and the inherent system complexity is huge. This, combined with the fact that current efforts to address those holistic dependability challenges are not enough, represent the main message and motivation of this paper, in order to encourage further studies in this regard.

References

1. 5GPPP: 5G Vision (2015). https://5g-ppp.eu/wp-content/uploads/2015/02/5g-vision-brochure-v1.pdf
2. 5GPPP: 5GPPP use cases and performance evaluation models (2016). https://5g-ppp.eu/wp-content/uploads/2014/02/5g-ppp-use-cases-and-performance-evaluation-modeling_v1.0.pdf
3. 3GPP Standard Organization: Network Slicing. 3GPP Use Case (2017). https://tools.ietf.org/id/draft-defoy-netslices-3gpp-network-slicing-02.html
4. 5GPPP Architecture Working Group: View on 5G Architecture (2017). https://5g-ppp.eu/wp-content/uploads/2018/01/5g-ppp-5g-architecture-white-paper-jan-2018-v2.0.pdf
5. IETF Network Working Group: Network Slicing Architecture (2017). https://tools.ietf.org/id/draft-geng-netslices-architecture-01.html
6. Yoo, T.: Network slicing architecture for 5G network. In: 2016 International Conference on Information and Communication Technology Convergence (ICTC), pp. 1010–1014, October 2016
7. Mayoral, A., Vilalta, R., Casellas, R., Martinez, R., Munoz, R.: Multi-tenant 5G network slicing architecture with dynamic deployment of virtualized tenant management and orchestration (MANO) instances. In: ECOC 2016; 42nd European Conference on Optical Communication, pp. 1–3, September 2016
8. 5G-PPP: View on 5G Architecture, December 2017. https://5g-ppp.eu/wp-content/uploads/2014/02/5G-PPP-5G-Architecture-WP-For-public-consultation.pdf
9. Ordonez-Lucena, J., Ameigeiras, P., Lopez, D., Ramos-Munoz, J.J., Lorca, J., Folgueira, J.: Network slicing for 5G with SDN/NFV: concepts, architectures, and challenges. IEEE Commun. Mag. **55**(5), 80–87 (2017)
10. Mendis, H.V.K., Li, F.Y.: Achieving ultra reliable communication in 5G networks: a dependability perspective availability analysis in the space domain. IEEE Commun. Lett. **21**(9), 2057–2060 (2017)
11. Popovski, P.: Ultra-reliable communication in 5G wireless systems. In: 1st International Conference on 5G for Ubiquitous Connectivity, pp. 146–151, November 2014
12. Azarfar, A., Frigon, J.F., Sanso, B.: Improving the reliability of wireless networks using cognitiveradios. IEEE Commun. Surv. Tutor. **14**(2), 338–354 (2012)
13. Cholda, P., Mykkeltveit, A., Helvik, B.E., Wittner, O.J., Jajszczyk, A.: A survey of resilience differentiation frameworks in communication networks. IEEE Commun. Surv. Tutor. **9**(4), 32–55 (2007)
14. Gonzalez, A.J.: Methods for guaranteeing contracted availability in connection oriented networks. Doctoral Thesis, NTNU (2013)

15. Nencioni, G., Helvik, B.E., Gonzalez, A.J., Heegaard, P.E., Kamisinski, A.: Availability modelling of software-defined backbone networks. In: 2016 46th Annual IEEE/IFIP International Conference on Dependable Systems and Networks Workshop (DSN-W), pp. 105–112, June 2016
16. Guan, X., Choi, B.Y., Song, S.: Reliability and scalability issues in software defined network frameworks. In: 2013 Second GENI Research and Educational Experiment Workshop, pp. 102–103, March 2013
17. Network Functions Virtualisation (NFV) ETSI Industry Specification Group (ISG): ETSI GS NFV-REL 001 V1.1.1: Network Functions Virtualisation (NFV); Resiliency Requirements, Technical Report, January 2015
18. Bari, M.F., et al.: Data center network virtualization: a survey. IEEE Commun. Surv. Tutor. **15**(2), 909–928 (2013)
19. Gonzalez, A.J., Nencioni, G., Helvik, B.E., Kamisinski, A.: A fault-tolerant and consistent SDN Controller. In: 2016 IEEE Global Communications Conference (GLOBECOM), pp. 1–6, December 2016
20. Bauer, E., Adams, R.: Reliability and Availability of Cloud Computing. Wiley-IEEE Press, Hoboken (2012)
21. NGMN P1 WS1 E2E Architecture Team: Description of Network Slicing Concept (2016). https://www.ngmn.org/fileadmin/user_upload/160113_network_slicing_v1_0.pdf
22. 3GPP: TR 28.801 V15.1.0: Study on management and orchestration of network slicing for next generation network, January 2018
23. ETSI: ETSI GS NFV-MAN 001: Network Functions Virtualisation; Management and Orchestration, December 2014
24. Tipper, D., Dahlberg, T., Shin, H., Charnsripinyo, C.: Providing fault tolerance in wireless access networks. IEEE Commun. Mag. **40**(1), 58–64 (2002)
25. Checko, A., et al.: Cloud RAN for mobile networks; a technology overview. IEEE Commun. Surv. Tutor. **17**(1), 405–426 (2015)
26. Hadzialic, M., Dosenovic, B., Dzaferagic, M., Musovic, J.: Cloud-RAN: innovative radio access network architecture. In: Proceedings ELMAR-2013, pp. 115–120, September 2013
27. Lam, K., Mansfield, S., Gray, E.: Network management requirements for MPLS-based transport networks. In: Internet Engineering Task Force (IETF), September 2010
28. Gonzalez, A.J., Helvik, B.E.: System management to comply with SLA availability guarantees in cloud computing. In: 4th IEEE International Conference on Cloud Computing Technology and Science Proceedings, pp. 325–332, December 2012
29. Gonzalez, A.J., Helvik, B.E.: The positive impact of failures on energy efficient virtual machines consolidation. In: 2014 IEEE International Conference on Communications (ICC), pp. 4307–4312, June 2014
30. Gonzalez, A., Gronsund, P., Mahmood, K., Helvik, B., Heegaard, P., Nencioni, G.: Service availability in the NFV virtualized evolved packet core. In: 2015 IEEE Global Communications Conference (GLOBECOM), pp. 1–6, December 2015
31. Jyothi, S.A., Dong, M., Godfrey, P.B.: Towards a flexible data center fabric with source routing. In: Proceedings of the 1st ACM SIGCOMM Symposium on Software Defined Networking Research, SOSR 2015, New York, NY, USA, pp. 10:1–10:8. ACM (2015)
32. Shen, H., Wang, H., Wieder, P., Yahyapour, R.: S-fabric: towards scalable and incremental SDN deployment in datacenters. In: Proceedings of the 2017 International Conference on Telecommunications and Communication Engineering, ICTCE 2017, New York, NY, USA, pp. 25–29. ACM (2017)

A Hierarchical *k*-Anonymous Technique of Graphlet Structural Perception in Social Network Publishing

Dongran Yu, Huaxing Zhao, Li-e Wang, Peng Liu[✉],
and Xianxian Li[✉]

Guangxi Key Lab of Multi-source Information Mining and Security,
Guangxi Normal University, Guilin 541004, China
yudran@foxmail.com, zhxing.vip@foxmail.com,
{wanglie,liupeng,lixx}@gxnu.edu.cn

Abstract. The structural information of social network data plays an important role in many fields of research. Therefore, privacy-preserving social network publication methods should preserve more structural information, such as the higher-order organizational structure of complex networks (graphlets/motifs). Therefore, how to preserve the graphlet structure information in a social network as much as possible becomes a key problem in social network privacy protection. In this paper, to address the problem of excessive loss of graphlet structural information in the privacy process of published social network data, we proposed a technique of hierarchical *k*-anonymity for graphlet structural perception. The method considers the degree of social network nodes according to the characteristics of the power-law distribution. The nodes are divided according to the degrees, and the method analyzes the graphlet structural features of the graph in the privacy process and adjusts the privacy-processing strategies of the edges according to the graphlet structural features. This is done, in order to meet the privacy requirement while protecting the graphical structural information in the social network and, improving the utility of the data. This paper uses two real public data sets, *WebKB* and *Cora*, and conducted experiments and evaluations. Finally, the experimental results show that the method proposed in this paper can concurrently provide the same privacy protection intensity, better maintain the social network's structural information and improve the data's utility.

Keywords: Social networks · Graphlet · Privacy protection
Hierarchical *k*-anonymity

1 Introduction

Currently, with the rapid development of science and technology and the increase of social platforms, the application of social networks has become increasingly more widespread, which has a profound impact on people's daily lives. Social networks such as Facebook, Twitter, Momo and Renren Network, bring convenience to people's daily lives, and most people choose to exchange and interact on these platforms. These behaviors will generate a lot of social networking related data. Social network analysis gradually become the hotspot in many fields.

© Springer Nature Switzerland AG 2019
É. Renault et al. (Eds.): MSPN 2018, LNCS 11005, pp. 224–239, 2019.
https://doi.org/10.1007/978-3-030-03101-5_19

The graphlet is the equivalent to a basic unit of a graph. It is a definite structure and characterizes many social phenomena. In the biological web, there are a large number of different graphlet structures in the nematode neural network that together control certain actions of nematodes [19]. In transportation networks, different graphlets represent different path reachabilities. There are also a large number of graphlets in the social network graph. For example, in the family network, they can represent kinship between family members. In the friendship network, friends of friends also tend to become friends, enemies of friends are friends, and so on. Therefore, the structures of graphlets is important in the analysis of social networking data. In the process of anonymity, the structures of graphlets are preserved as much as possible and the utility of the data will be greatly improved.

If the social networking is data released directly, then the user's personal information will be fully open on the network. Some user's do not want others know their information, such as personal diseases, account passwords and so on, which will cause privacy leak problems. To avoid the above problems, when publishing social network data and information, it is necessary to make corresponding privacy protections. Simply deleting the sensitive attributes of data can only provide simple anonymity protection, and simple anonymity can no longer be effective if attackers enhance their background knowledge. Over time, other privacy protection methods for social networks were proposed one after another, such as k-anonymity, random perturbation and differential privacy. This have become increasingly popular for meeting the privacy requirements and ensuring the data's utility.

Both random perturbations and differential privacy methods randomly add or delete the edges of the graph. The two randomized operations, although having a relatively small influences on the clustering coefficient of the graph, cause greater damage to the structure of the graph. However, the k- anonymous method adds more edges and deletes fewer edges of the graph. The effect of this kind of operation is opposite to the former two methods. In contrast, [13], the k-anonymous method has little structural perturbations for the graph. Therefore, in order to preserve the anonymous network structural information, the paper chooses k-anonymity to protect the social network.

The current k-anonymous method [7] considers only low-order connected organizational structures (such as nodes or edges) or uncertain structures (such as community structures [17]) in the privacy process. The nodes and edges of social network graphical data adopt a uniform privacy policy, and they do not consider whether the characteristics of the social network's node degrees obey a power-law distribution, this behavior both destroys the information of graphlet structure in social network data, can also causes the over-protection of some nodes. In short, it will reduce the value of social networking data.

In this paper, we use an undirected graph with no weight and no label, and assume that the attacker's background knowledge is the degree of the node. In view of the above research's insufficiencies, we propose a hierarchical k-anonymous technique of graphlet structural perception on social network publishing.

1.1   Contribution

In this paper, we defined the graphlet structure, which mainly refers to the triangular structure. Because triangle represents graphic clustering coefficient, it describes the probability of mutual recognition between any three users, which reflects the closeness of the user's acquaintance relationships in the entire social network. We assign weight to the social network graph according to the triangular structure in which the weight of the edge indicates the number of edges that participate in the triangle. In the privacy processing, we analyze the features of the graphlet's structure and adjust the edge privacy processing strategies according to their features. Therefore, we propose a hierarchical k-anonymous method of graphlet structural perception in social network publishing.

In this paper, according to the degree to which the social networking graphical node obeys the characteristics of a power-law distribution [16], we divide the degrees of nodes, and the divided nodes define the different privacy levels according to their practical means.

The remainder of this paper is organized as follow. Section 2 highlights the related works. Section 3 defines the research problems and states the method of solving the problem. We design an algorithm in Sect. 4, and we present our experimental settings and analyze the performance of our method in Sect. 5. Finally, we conclude this paper in Sect. 6.

2   Related Works

As we already mentioned, the methods for anonymizing social networks can be broadly classified into three categories: generalization by means of the clustering of vertices, the deterministic alteration of the graph by edge additions or deletions, and the randomized alteration of the graph by the addition, deletion or switching of edges.

In the first category, Hay et al. [1] propose to generalize a network by clustering the vertices and publishing the number of vertices in each partition together with the densities of the edges within and across the partitions. Campan and Truta [2] study the case in which vertices contain additional attributes, such as demographic information. They propose to cluster the vertices and reveal only the number of intra- and inter-cluster edges. Tassa and Cohen [3] consider a similar setting and propose a sequential clustering algorithm that issues anonymized graphs with higher utility than those issued by the algorithm of Campan and Truta.

Cormode et al. [4, 5] consider a framework where two sets of entities (e.g., patients and drugs) are connected by links (e.g., which patient takes which drugs), and each entity is also described by a set of attributes. The adversary relies upon knowledge of attributes rather than the graphical structure in devising a matching attack. To prevent matching attacks, their technique masks the mapping between vertices in the graph and real-world entities by clustering the vertices and the corresponding entities into groups. Zheleva and Getoor [6] consider the case where there are multiple types of edges, one of which is sensitive and should be protected. It is assumed that the network is published without the sensitive edges and the adversary predicts the sensitive edges based on the observed non-sensitive edges.

In the second category of methods, Liu and Terzi [7] consider the case that a vertex can be identified by its degree. Their algorithms use edge additions and deletions in order to make the graph k-degree anonymous. This means that for every vertex, there are at least $k - 1$ other vertices with the same degree. Casas-Roma et al. [14] constructs a *k*-degree anonymous network by the minimum number of edge modification. They consider the edge relevance in order to improve the data utility on anonymize network.

Zhou and Pei [8] consider the case that a vertex can be identified by its radius-one induced subgraph. Adversarial knowledge that is stronger than the degree is also considered by Thompon and Yao [9]. It is also considered that the adversary know the degrees of the neighbors, the degrees of the neighbors of the neighbors, and so forth. Zou et al. [10] and Wu et al. [11] assume that the adversary knows the complete graph, and the location of the nodes in the graph. Hence, the adversary can always identify a vertex in any copy of the graph, unless the graph has other vertices that are automorphically-equivalent.

In the third category of methods, Hay et al. [12] study the effectiveness of random perturbations for identity obfuscation. They concentrate on the degree-based re-identification of vertices. Given a vertex v in the real network, they quantify the level of anonymity that is provided for v by the perturbed graph as the belief probability.

Ying et al. [13] compare the random perturbation method to the method of *k*-degree anonymity [7]. They conclude that the approach for *k*-degree anonymity preserves the graphical structure better than random perturbation methods. Task et al. [18] proposed out-link privacy, which redefines the neighbor dataset by deleting or adding any node from the graph and all edges starting from that node. It also defines the *k*-out-link privacy, the definition of the neighbor graph is changed to: *k* nodes arbitrarily added or deleted from the graph and the edges starting from the node. By protecting the relationship between nodes, when calculating noise, it reduces the impact of high-degree nodes on the result.

3 Problem Statement

A graphlet is a kind of higher-order connected organization network structure. It is a basic interactive mode in the network and represents rich graphical structural information. A graphlet is a subgraph structure. It has many forms, such as triangles, quadrilaterals, and so on. In social networks, there are many relations where friends of friends tend to become friends themselves. Thus mapping in the social network graph will result in a large number of graphlet structures in the form of—triangles [20]. This structure can provide a lot of relevant information for analyzing a person's social circle. The transportation reachability network, the S. cerevisiae transcriptional regulation network, the Florida Bay food web, etc. [19] contain a large number of graphlet structures. In the transportation reachability network, the graphlet structure can determine which route is direct and which route is to be transferred, which helps the tour guide evaluate travel time. In the food web, different levels of energy flow in the network are discovered according to the structure of the graphlet. Therefore, the graphlet structure is gaining increasingly more attention in data mining and analysis.

The original graph $G = (V, E)$ is undirected, unlabeled and unweighted, in which V denotes a set of nodes, E denotes a set of edges, d_i denotes the degree of node i, and d_G denotes the original degree sequence in graph G. In the anonymous graph $G' = (V, E')$, E' denotes a set of anonymous edges, and $d_{G'}$ represents the anonymous degree sequence. The attacker's background knowledge is the degree of the target node, and in this paper it is mainly implemented to resist the identity of the target node being leaked. The node of the social networking graph represents the user and the edge represents the relationship. If the degree of the target node in the graph is unique, the attacker can uniquely identify the target node based on the existing background knowledge. If we assume that the identity of the target node is sensitive, then this will cause an identity privacy leak. For example, in a company's personnel network, the degree of a node indicates how many colleagues that position needs to contact with. If an attacker knows the degree of a target node and there are fewer nodes in the personnel network that have the same degree as the target node, then attacker could identify the target node with a high probability. To resist this kind of attack and preserve more structural information, we apply a hierarchical k-anonymous technique of the graphlet structural perception in social network publishing.

Definition 1. Graphlet: Locally connected subgraphs in social networks, which are also called motifs.

Definition 2. k-nonymity: Suppose G is an unweighted, unlabeled undirected social network graph, and G' is an anonymous graph. The attacker's probability of uniquely identifying the target node does not exceed $1/k$ for the published G'.

Definition 3. k-degree anonymity: If the social network $G (V, E)$ satisfies that at least one other $k - 1$ node and its degrees are the same for any arbitrary $u \in V$, then $G (V, E)$ is anonymous network.

Definition 4. Hierarchical k-degree anonymity: In the social network $G = (V, E)$, the nodes are classified according to their degrees, and each category sets the corresponding k value according to the sensitivity so that they meet k-degree anonymity respectively.

Definition 5. Diameter ($dist$): Diameter represents the shortest path between node u and node v in the social network.

The graphlet considered in this paper mainly refers to the triangle. The structure is as shown in Fig. 1, and the matrix representation is as is shown in the following formula (1).

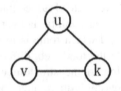

Fig. 1. Trangular structure

$$T = \begin{matrix} 0 & 1 & 1 \\ 1 & 0 & 1 \\ 1 & 1 & 0 \end{matrix} \tag{1}$$

In Eq. (1), 0 represents no edge between nodes, and 1 represents an edge between nodes.

Because the degrees of the nodes of the social network graph obey the power-law distribution, the nodes with high- degrees are fewer and the distribution is uneven. The nodes with low-degrees are numerous and distributed evenly. If the high-degree nodes are processed together with low-degree nodes, this can cause high-degree nodes overprotected, can produce more damage to the graphs, thus resulting in the utility of anonymous data being greatly reduced. Based on this, we first divide the nodes into two categories: The first is the high-degree nodes and the second is the low-degree nodes. Then we set different privacy levels k for each category in anonymous processing, and combine the two categories of anonymity sequences in descending order. Then, the value of the anonymous degree sequence is correspondingly subtracted from the value of the original degree sequence. According to the corresponding difference, we choose the node set with an increasing edge and the one with decreasing edge, and the two sets of nodes respectively addressed to obtain the added the edge and deleted edge candidate sets. Finally, according to the diameter, we select the appropriate edge from the added edge candidate set and add the appropriate edge to the graph. According to the edge weight, we remove the edge from the graph until the anonymous demand is met. See Sect. 4 for a detailed process of the algorithm.

Referring to the conclusion of Theorem 3.5 in [15] that divides the high-degree nodes and the low-degree nodes, the formula (2) is as follows.

$$d = E^{\frac{w-1}{w+1}} \tag{2}$$

Where d represents the degree of the node, E represents the number of edges in the graph, and w represents the index of matrix multiplication, $w < 2.376$.

If the degree of a node is greater than d, the node is defined as a high-degree node. Otherwise, it is defined as a low-degree node.

The given social graph G with the deleted quasi-identifiers is as shown in Fig. 2.

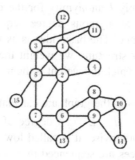

Fig. 2. Simple anonymous graph to delete quasi identifiers

Figure 3 shows the weighted graph.

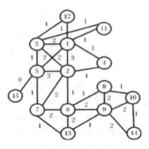

Fig. 3. Weighted graph

In the above graph, the degree sequence of the original node $d_G = \{6,6,5, 5,5,5,4,3,3,3,2,2,2,2,1\}$. Since the nodes with degree 4 and 1 are unique, the privacy leak will be caused after the graph is released. In this paper, we apply the hierarchical k-anonymous technique of the graphlet structural perception method. The degree sequence of the high-degree nodes is $\{6, 6, 5, 5, 5, 5, 4\}$, and the degree sequence of the low-degree nodes is $\{3, 3, 3, 2, 2, 2, 2, 1\}$. Set $kh = 3$ and $kl = 4$, and get the anonymous degree sequence merged into $d_{G'} = \{6,6,6,5,5,5,5,3,3,3, 3,2,2,2,2\}$. The difference between the two sequences is $dieta = d_{G'} - d_G = \{0,0,1,0,0,0,1,0,0,0,1,0,0,0,1\}$. Then, the set of nodes with increasing degrees is $VS+ = \{$'3', '7', '11', '15'$\}$ such that the added edge candidate set is ('3', '7'), ('3', '15'), ('7', '11'), ('7', '15'), ('15', '11'), which corresponds to the diameter *dist* as 2,2,3,2,3. According to the diameter, the added edge candidate sets can be divided into two categories. The first is ('7', '11'), ('15', '11' ('15', '11'), ('15', '11'), ('15', '11' '3', '7') and the second is ('3', '7'), ('3', '5'), ('7', '15'), ('15', '11'). Finally, the added edge set is ('15', '11'), ('3', '7').

4   Algorithms

In this paper, the original social network graph is weighted according to the triangular structure. Then apply the hierarchical *k*-anonymous technique of the graphlet structural perception is applied to divide the nodes into high-degree nodes and low-degree nodes in the weighted graph. We apply *k*-anonymity for the degree sequencing of the two respective categories, get the anonymous degree sequence, and modify the graph according to this degree sequence. The basic idea is as follows.

According to the triangular structure, we weight the original social network, and obtain a weighted graph G_w in which the weight is the number of participating triangles of the edge.

The degrees of all the nodes in the graph are calculated, and the nodes are divided into two categories according to $d = E^{\frac{w-1}{w+1}}$. If degree of a node is greater than d, it is called the high-degree node. Otherwise, it is called low-degree.

Two categories' node degrees are sequenced in descending order.

k values are given to the two respective kinds of degree sequences, and *k*-degree anonymous algorithms are performed.

In the k-degree anonymity algorithm, the first group allocates k nodes first, and subsequently calculates the first degree and the other degree difference in the group, which is called the costs. Then after the $k + 1$ element is merged into the first group, the same calculation is performed again, which is denoted as C_{merge}.

Calculate the costs from the $k + 1$ element to the $2k$ element, which is denoted as C_{new}.

If $C_{merge} < C_{new}$, they are merged, and otherwise they are not merged. Repeat steps 5 and 6 until the number of elements in each group is greater than or equal to k.

After dividing the group, the elements of each group are modified based on the median of the group and the degree sequence of anonymity was obtained.

The anonymity degree sequence obtained by the high-degree node is combined with the anonymity degree sequence obtained by the low-degree node and then sorted in descending order.

Subtract the originality sequence from the anonymity sequence, and choose the node set to be processed according to their difference. The node set that needs to be added edge is denoted as $VS +$, and the node set whose edge is deleted is denoted as $VS-$.

Use $VS +$, $VS-$ to obtain the candidate edge set. The candidate set that needs to be added to the edge is denoted as $add\_edge(VS + , VS +)$, and the candidate set that needs to delete the edge is denoted as $del\_edge(VS-, VS-)$.

The edges formed by $add\_edge(VS+, VS+)$ are divided into two categories according to their priorities: The first category is diameter $dist(u,v) \geq 3$ (that is, the number of the intersections of the set of neighbor nodes of node u and the set of neighbor nodes of node v is zero.). The second category is diameter $dist(u,v) < 3$ (that is, the number of intersections of the set of neighbor nodes of node u and the set of neighbor nodes of node v is not zero).

Modify the edges of the graph based on the candidate edge sets. Some edge operations may be added. First add operations to the first category's edges. If you still have nodes that do not meet the privacy requirements after processing the first category, select the second category's edges to add operations to until all nodes in $VS+$ satisfy the privacy requirement. In addition, some edge operations may be deleted. For edges formed by $del\_edge(VS-, VS-)$, priority is given to edge operations with small edge weights until all nodes in $VS-$ satisfy the privacy requirements.

4.1 Anonymous Algorithms Overview

Algorithm 1 Anonymity

Input: original $G(V,E)$, kh , kl
Output: k-anonymous graph G'
1: $d_{G'}$=hierarchical k degree(G); // Anonymous descendingdegree sequence
2: while new_degree $!= d_G$:
3:     call findcandidateOP(G, kh, kl); // Calculate candidate edge sets
4:     modify graph; // Add or delete edges based on candidate edge sets
5:     new_degree= G'.degree() ; // The descending order of the new graph
6: Return G' // Return anonymous graph

The algorithm modifies the graph, and uses the findcandidateOP module to get the candidate edge set. According to the add edge set *add_edge* and the delete edge set *del_edge*, original graph is modified, If the modified anonymous degree sequence is equal to the k anonymous degree sequence, then it returns the anonymous graph G'. Otherwise, it repeats the execution of rows 2 to 5 until the end is satisfied.

4.2   FindcandidateOP Algorithm

Algorithm 2 findcandidateOP

Input: $G(V,E),kh,kl$

Output: *add_edge,del_edge*

1: *add_edge*=∅; *del_edge*= ∅;   // Initialize the set

2: Calculate edge weights and get weighted graph G_w; // The number of edges involved in triangle

3: d_G=Degree sequence of nodes in G_w and descending order;// Original degree sequence

4: if $d_i > E^{\frac{w-l}{w+l}}$ then   // Node classification

5:    Put d_i and node i into H_node;

6: else

7:    Put d_i and node i into L_node中;

8: end if

9: $d_{G'}$=call hierarchical k-degree anonymity function(G_w, H_node, L_node,kh,kl);//
     Get anonymity sequence

10: $dieta$=$d_{G'}$-d_G

11: Place a node with a value greater than zero in the *dieta* into VS+ and less than zero into the VS-;

12: Take the elements in $VS+$, calculate the added edge candidate *listadd_edges*;

13: Calculate $dist(u,v)$, put *first_cluster* with value greater than 3, otherwise put into *second_cluster*;

14: Remove duplicate elements in the *first_cluster* set;

15: *add_edges*=*first_cluster*;

16: If *add_edges* node! = All nodes in $VS+$, select the largest diameter edge from the *second_cluster* set to add *add_edges*;

17: Take the elements in VS- and calculate the delete edge candidate set *listdel_edges*;

18: Delete duplicate elements in *listdel_edges*;

19:   If the node in *del_edges*! = In all nodes in VS-, select the edge with the smallest edge weight in the *listdel_edges* set into the *del_edges* set;

20:   Remove the edge from *listdel_edges*;

21:   Return *add_edge,del_edge*

The algorithm first preprocesses the original graph. It uses lines 2–3 to obtain the weighted graph and the initial degree sequence based on the triangle. Lines 4–8 divide the nodes into high-degree and low-degree nodes according to the threshold $d = E^{\frac{w-1}{w+1}}$. Lines 9–10 subtract the original degree sequence value from the anonymity degree sequence value of the corresponding node to obtain the difference set *dieta*. Lines 11 obtain VS+ and VS- node sets. Then, the value of the anonymous degree sequence is correspondingly subtracted from the value of the original degree sequence. If the difference is greater than zero, it indicates that the degree of the corresponding node needs to be increased. If the difference is less than zero, it indicates that the degree of the corresponding node needs to be decreased. Lines 12 calculate the added edges' candidate set, and combine the nodes that need to be added to the edges one by one. If the combined edges are not in the original graph, put them in the candidate edge set and traverse all nodes in VS+ all the time. Lines 13 divide the added edge candidate set into two categories: $dist(u,v) \geq 3$ is the first category, and $dist(u,v) < 3$ is the second category, Lines 14–16 give priority to the first category. If there are still nodes that do not meet the privacy requirements after processing the first category, select the second edge adding operation until all meet the privacy requirements in node VS+. Lines 17–20 calculate the deleted edges in the candidate set and traverse all nodes in VS−. If there are edges, put them in the edge candidate set until all nodes in VS− are traversed. The duplicated edge and the edge corresponding to the repeated processing node are deleted according to the weight value. The principle is that the edge with the smallest weight value is preferentially deleted, and then the edge with the smallest weight is removed cyclically until the condition is satisfied. In the lines 21 return *add_edge* and *del_edge*.

4.3   Hierarchical k-degree Anonymous Algorithm

Algorithm 3: hierarchical k-degree Anonymity

Input: original graph G(V,E), H_node, L_node, kh,kl

Output: Anonymous degree sequence $d_{G'}$

1: Calculate the degree of H_node and L_node respectively and sort them in descending order, get to high_degrees, low_degrees;

2: For high_degrees, the low_degrees degree sequence specifies the thresholds kh, kl , respectively, to obtain the corresponding anonymous degree sequence listh, listl;

3: Listl sequence is merged into the listh sequence to get the overall anonymous degree sequence $d_{G'}$:

4: Return $d_{G'}$ //Rrturn anonymous degree sequence

The hierarchical k-degree anonymous algorithm, traverses the degree sequence of all nodes, and the time complexity of the algorithm is O(n). The *FindcandidateOP* algorithm first traverses the difference sequence, and the time complexity required for the candidate node set is O(n). The process of forming the edge between the point and the point in the candidate node set requires traversing the candidate node set twice. Therefore, the algorithm's time complexity is O(n^2).

5 Experiments and Result Analysis

The experimental environment in this paper uses the Windows 7 operating system and Intel Core i5-6500 3.20 GHz CPU. The programming language is Python and the compilation environment is Python 2.7.6. The experiment uses two real data sets as follows.

The *WebKB* [22] dataset contains 877 scientific publications and the citation network consists of 1,608 links, which form a network graph with a total of 877 nodes and 1608 edges.

The *Cora* [22] dataset consists of 2708 scientific publications and the citation network consists of 5429 links. It consists of a network of 2708 nodes and 5429 edges.

In this paper, we better preserve the triangular structure of the graph concurrently with the privacy protection. To measure the information loss and structural changes of the social network graph before and after the anonymity, we use the average clustering coefficient and the one-dimensional structure entropy as the measurement standards.

Definition 6. The average clustering coefficient *ACC* describes the probability of mutual recognition between any three users, which reflects the closeness of the user's acquaintance relationships in the entire network. The formula is as follows.

$$C_i = \frac{2e_i}{k_i(k_i-1)} \tag{3}$$

$$ACC = \frac{1}{|V|} \sum_{i \in V} C_i \tag{4}$$

$|V|$ represents the number of nodes in the network, C_i is the clustering coefficient of node v_i, k_i represents the number of v_i neighbors, and e_i represents the number of undirected edges that actually exist among the k_i neighbors.

Definition 7. The one-dimensional structural entropy is the structural information changes used to measure the social network graph. The formula is as follows [21].

$$H^1(G) = H(p) = H\left(\frac{d_1}{2m}, \dots, \frac{d_n}{2m}\right) = -\sum_{i=1}^{n} \frac{d_i}{2m} . log_2 \frac{d_i}{2m} \tag{5}$$

In the social network graph $G = (V, E)$, V represents the node, E represents the edge, m represents the number of edges, n represents the number of nodes, d_i represents the degree of the node i, and $P_i = \frac{d_i}{2m}$.

This paper proposed hierarchical k-degree anonymous algorithm is compared with the high utility k-degree anonymous algorithm proposed by Casas-Roma et al. [14]. As shown in (a) and (b) of Fig. 4, the graphs describe the changes of the respective average clustering coefficients of the dataset *WebKB* and *Cora*, when kh is 2 and the kl value is 5, 10, 15, 20, 25, and 30.

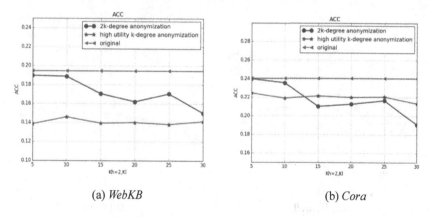

(a) *WebKB*   (b) *Cora*

Fig. 4. Average clustering coefficient (*ACC*)

In Fig. 4, the polyline of the connected circles represents the average clustering coefficient of the anonymous graph processed by the method of this paper. The polyline of the connected star represents the average clustering coefficient of the anonymous graph processed by the high utility *k*-degree anonymous method. The polyline of the connected triangles represents the average clustering coefficient of the original graph.

It can be seen from the change of the polyline in the figure that as the privacy level *kl* increases, the average clustering coefficient of the anonymous graphs processed by the two anonymous methods as a whole has a downward trend. The reason is that, when the degree sequences are grouped, as the *kl* value increases, the number of degrees in each group will increase. In addition, because the anonymous degree takes the median of the degrees in each group, the number of nodes to be modified will increase, then the structure of the original graph is destroyed more and the overall average clustering coefficient became smaller. Furthermore, it can be clearly seen from the experimental result graph that the average clustering coefficient of the anonymous graph obtained by the hierarchical *k*-anonymous technique of graphlet structural perception is closer to the original graph than the anonymous graph processed by the high utility *k*-degree anonymity method. This shows that the method of this paper causes less damage to the original network graph and has better utility.

As shown in (a) and (b) of Fig. 5, the graphs describe the changes of the structural information entropy of respective *WebKB* and *Cora*, when *kh* is 2 and the *kl* value is 5, 10, 15, 20, 25, and 30.

From the experimental results in Fig. 5, we can see that as the *kl* value increases, the one-dimensional structural entropy obtained by both methods also increases. The larger the value of the structural entropy is the greater the uncertainty of the graph. As the privacy level *kl* increases, the number of added or deleted edges increases, and the uncertainty of the graph increases. Therefore, the smaller the *kl* value, the smaller the disturbance to the structure of the social network and the greater the utility.

In this paper a hierarchical *k*-anonymous technique of graphlet structural perception in a social network is published according to the degree with which the social network nodes obeys the power-law distribution, and the technique assigns different privacy

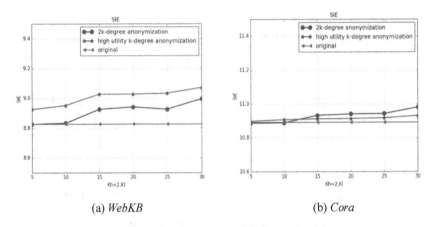

(a) *WebKB*   (b) *Cora*

Fig. 5. Structure information entyopy (*SIE*)

levels to the high-degree nodes and the low-degree nodes according to different sen-
sitivities. In the following, this paper compares the changes of the average clustering
coefficient and the one-dimensional structure entropy of two real data sets under different *kh* values, and then compares the influence of the values of *kh* on the two
evaluation criteria.

Figure 6(a) and (b) are the average clustering coefficient and one-dimensional
structure entropy of the *WebKB* dataset, respectively.

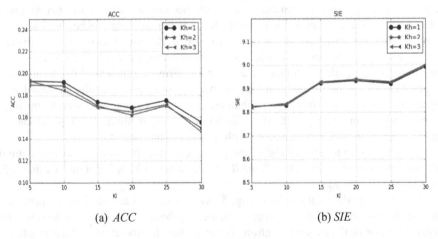

(a) *ACC*   (b) *SIE*

Fig. 6. *WebKB*

As seen from Fig. 6, with the increase of the *kl* value, the three polylines all show a
decreasing trend. When the value of *kh* is 1, the polyline is obviously above the other
two polylines. This is because the high-degree nodes have not been processed
anonymously, but only the low-degree nodes have been disturbed. For privacy, a value

of 1 for *kh* is not desirable. When the value of *kh* is taken as 2 and 3, the difference between the two polylines is not large, and, in the weighting of the privacy and utility, it is preferable that the values of *kh* be taken as 2 and 3.

From the figure, we can see that the one-dimensional structure entropy increases with the increase of the *kl* value, and the three polylines all show an upward trend. This is because as the level of privacy increases, the changes to the graph become larger, and thus the destruction of the structure is greater. Although the difference between the three polylines in the figure is not obvious, it can be seen that when the value of *kh* is 3, the value of the polyline is higher than when the value of *kh* is 1 or 2.

Figure 7(a) and (b) are the average clustering coefficient and the one-dimensional structure entropy of the Cora dataset, respectively.

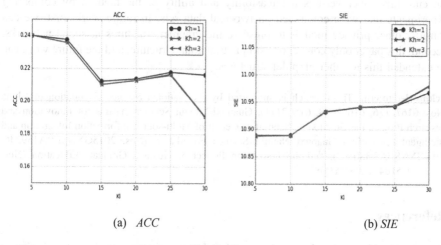

(a) *ACC*   (b) *SIE*

Fig. 7. *Cora*

From Fig. 7, we can see the result that for the data set *Cora*, the average clustering coefficient gradually decreases with the increase of the privacy level, and the one-dimensional structural entropy gradually increases with the increase of privacy level. The overall variations of the average clustering coefficient and the one-dimensional structural entropy are the same as that of the data set *WebKB*, and the reasons for the change trends are also the same. In this dataset, when the value of *kh* is 2 or 3, the two polylines are almost coincident and the difference is very small. Therefore, the value of *kh* has little effect on the two evaluation criteria here. For this data set, in terms of its availability and usability, when *kh* is 2 or 3, the effects are almost the same.

In summary, the parameters of the two datasets are changed. We establish the hierarchical *k*-anonymous technique of graphlet structural perception on social network publishing, and weigh the privacy and utility aspects. For relatively smaller data sets, the utility is better when the value of *kh* is taken as 2. For relatively larger data sets, when the value of *kh* is 2 or 3, the utility is the same.

6   Conclusions

The graphlet structure is a basic structural unit in the social network. It reveals the important behavioral features of the network. Based on this motivation, in this paper, we propose a hierarchical k-anonymous technique of graphlet structural perception on social network publishing. This technique considers the characteristics of social network nodes that obey the power-law distribution and divides the nodes according to the degree. We set corresponding privacy level for each category of nodes. In the process of privacy processing, we analyze the structural features of the graphlet. According to the characteristics of the graph, we adjust the privacy processing strategies of the edges, thereby protecting the graphlet structure information in the social network while satisfying the corresponding privacy requirements and improving the utility of the data. In the end, this paper verifies the feasibility and utility of the method by comparing experiments that were conducted on two real data sets. In future work, first, we can consider other privacy models to preserve the graphlet structures in social networks. Second, this paper only considers a simple triangular structure, and the future work can be extended this to other graphlet structures.

Acknowledgment. The research is supported by the National Science Foundation of China (Nos. 61672176, 61662008, 61502111), Guangxi "Bagui Scholar" Teams for Innovation and Research Project, the Guangxi Collaborative Center of Multi-source Information Integration and Intelligent Processing, Guangxi Natural Science Foundation (Nos. 2015GXNSFBA139246, 2016GXNSFAA380192), and the Innovation Project of Guangxi Graduate Education (Nos. YCSZ2015104, 2018KY0082).

References

1. Hay, M., Miklau, G., Jensen, D., Towsley, D.: Resisting structural re-identification in anonymized social networks. Proc. VLDB Endow. **1**(1), 102–114 (2008)
2. Campan, A., Truta, T.M.: Data and structural k-anonymity in social networks. In: Bonchi, F., Ferrari, E., Jiang, W., Malin, B. (eds.) PInKDD 2008. LNCS, vol. 5456, pp. 33–54. Springer, Heidelberg (2009). https://doi.org/10.1007/978-3-642-01718-6_4
3. Tassa, T., Cohen, D.: Anonymization of centralized and distributed social networks by sequential clustering. IEEE Trans. Knowl. Data Eng. **25**(2), 311–324 (2012)
4. Cormode, G., Srivastava, D., Bhagat, S., Krishnamurthy, B.: Class-based graph anonymization for social network data. PVLDB **2**(1), 766–777 (2009)
5. Cormode, G., Srivastava, D., Yu, T., Zhang, Q.: Anonymizing bipartite graph data using safe groupings. PVLDB **1**(1), 833–844 (2008)
6. Zheleva, E., Getoor, L.: Preserving the privacy of sensitive relationships in graph data. In: Bonchi, F., Ferrari, E., Malin, B., Saygin, Y. (eds.) PInKDD 2007. LNCS, vol. 4890, pp. 153–171. Springer, Heidelberg (2008). https://doi.org/10.1007/978-3-540-78478-4_9
7. Liu, K., Terzi, E.: Towards identity anonymization on graphs. In: SIGMOD Conference, pp. 93–106 (2008)
8. Zhou, B., Pei, J.: Preserving privacy in social networks against neighborhood attacks. In: ICDE, pp. 506–515 (2008)
9. Thompson, B., Yao, D.: The union-split algorithm and cluster-based anonymization of social networks. In: ASIACCS, pp. 218–227 (2009)

10. Zou, L., Chen, L., Özsu, M.T.: K-automorphism: a general framework for privacy preserving network publication. PVLDB **2**(1), 946–957 (2009)
11. Wu, W., Xiao, Y., Wang, W., He, Z., Wang, Z.: k-symmetry model for identity anonymization in social networks. In: EDBT, pp. 111–122 (2010)
12. Hay, M., Miklau, G., Jensen, D., Weis, P., Srivastava, S.: Anonymizing social networks. University of Massachusetts, Technical report 07-19 (2007)
13. Ying, X., Pan, K., Wu, X., Guo, L.: Comparisons of randomization and k-degree anonymization schemes for privacy preserving social network publishing. In: SNA-KDD, pp. 1–10 (2009)
14. Casas-Roma, J., Herrera-Joancomartí, J., Torra, V.: k-degree anonymity and edge selection: improving data utility in large networks. Knowl. Inf. Syst. **50**, 447 (2017)
15. Alon, N., Yuster, R., Zwick, U.: Finding and counting given length cycles. Algorithmica **17**(3), 209–223 (1997)
16. Faloutsos, M., Faloutsos, P., Faloutsos, C.: On power-law relationship of the internet topology. In: ACM SIGCOMM. ACM Press, Cambridge (1999)
17. Wang, H.: Research on anonymous method of effectively preserving the community structure for social network data publication. Guangxi Normal University, Guilin (2016)
18. Task, C., Clifton, C.: A guide to differential privacy theory in social network analysis. In: IEEE/ACM International Conference on Advances in Social Networks Analysis and Mining, pp. 411–417. IEEE (2013)
19. Benson, A.R., Gleich, D.F., Leskovec, J.: Higher-order organization of complex networks. Science **353**(6295), 163–166 (2016)
20. Wasserman, S., Faust, K.: Social Network Analysis: Methods and Applications, vol. 8. Cambridge University Press, Cambridge (1994)
21. Li, A., Pan, Y.: Structural information and dynamical complexity of networks. IEEE Trans. Inf. Theory **62**(6), 3290–3339 (2016)
22. http://linqs.umiacs.umd.edu/projects//projects/lbc/index.html

Arp Attack Detection Software Poisoning and Sniffers in WLAN Networks Implementing Supervised Machine Learning

Nicolas Ricardo Enciso[1], Octavio José Salcedo Parra[1,2(✉)], and Erika Upegui[3]

[1] Department of Systems and Industrial Engineering, Faculty of Engineering, Universidad Nacional de Colombia, Bogotá D.C., Colombia
{nricardoe, ojsalcedop}@unal.edu.co
[2] Faculty of Engineering, Intelligent Internet Research Group, Universidad Distrital "Francisco José de Caldas", Bogotá D.C., Colombia
osalcedo@udistrital.edu.co
[3] Faculty of Engineering, GRSS-IEEE/UD & GEFEM Research Group, Universidad Distrital "Francisco José de Caldas", Bogotá D.C., Colombia
esupeguic@udistrital.edu.co

Abstract. Nowadays, the growing number of mobile device users such as tablets and smart phones, has shown an increase of wireless network usage (Wi-Fi). At the same time, the number of attacks against this network has been growing too, taking advantage of vulnerabilities typical of protocols such as ARP and 802.11 as shown in a study done by Verizon on social network attacks. The proposal is to create a tool capable of detecting man in the middle attacks such as ARP poisoning/spoofing and network sniffers that use NICs in monitor mode. A machine learning algorithm is then generated which is trained with data from networks being attacked or neutral to later be able to classify incoming network data and catalog them as an attack alert or not.

Keywords: Supervised machine learning · MITM attacks · ARP table
NIC's monitor mode · Packages sniffers

1 Introduction

The increasing use of Wi-Fi networks has represented in the same way the increase in attacks coming from the use of WLAN networks, being the main form of computer attacks in the year 2017 [1], so what is needed then, an alternative that help reduce these attacks, focused on those of wireless type. Additionally, the current firewalls and antivirus programs are unable to keep pace with advance regarding the nascent new types of attacks, adding to the need, the ability to adapt to new types of attacks on the proposed tool.

1.1 Related Works

The use of machine learning has been studied in several fields in security. One of them focuses on the detection of intrusions from the analysis of network traffic to alert

© Springer Nature Switzerland AG 2019
É. Renault et al. (Eds.): MSPN 2018, LNCS 11005, pp. 240–250, 2019.
https://doi.org/10.1007/978-3-030-03101-5_20

mainly about malware on Android devices [2], implementing ML, effectively, with rates of more than 98% true alerts, as well as in big data analysis, using framework, in which traffic is analyzed with the use from ML [10]. The intrusion detection systems have gone implementing the use of ML to give the possibility of adaptation that is needed, as well as the implementation of network flow analysis, considering cases in which up to 3 types of attacks can be detected through machine learning analysis [11]. The analysis of network traffic patterns has been a field of great progress in the implementation of intrusion systems, with the methodologies of Bayes and K nearby neighbors as forms of classification of the data in attackers or neutrals [3], also in the field of Internet of Things (IoT) where its communications over wifi networks grant a constant vulnerability, which has been attacking through the study of the data generated by these devices [12], as well as methods in WLAN that use MAC address layers [14], As in Wi-Fi also, data mining has been implemented and ML in the detection search in own vulnerabilities of the most used WLAN network protocol, 802.11 [15]. With use of Deep Learning, it has also been possible to improve the intrusion detection systems, using neural networks recurrent [13], having important results.

It shows then that the analysis of network traffic is a possible alternative to the detection of certain types of intrusions. This article focuses on the attacks they use vulnerabilities inherent in the ARP protocol [5–7] and 802.11n. With study laboratories about these attacks [8], shows that it is possible to implement in a simple way MITM attack detectors of type ARP Poisoning in networks Ethernet, in addition to being able to create totally virtual networks, with the desire to have low costs, which also represents the shows that it is economical to have a simulated environment of attacks [9]. As for the detection of sniffers, it is presented a different scenario, due to the nature of these attacks, which are silent and in the vast majority of cases, undetectable One method [4], proposes the use of sending network messages to all possible hosts connected to the network, to waiting for response messages, which would confirm that a NIC is in monitor mode, clear sample of the existence of a sniffer in the network, since, the monitor mode is to put in total package receipt to the NIC, regardless of whether the packages are not for him, so this methodology is used of operation for the NIC to respond to a message without it being for him.

2 Materials

The software is developed in the programming language Python 3, due to its simplicity of use, compatibility with libraries and compatibility with multiple operating systems. Additionally, external software is used, such as NMAP that is compatible with Linux-based systems. The data set is generated locally, from multiple network simulations, which are subsequently labeled, organized and stored in plain text files. The data set is then made up of the results of the analysis done in the software, resulting in the variables studied, as well as the label of the class to which it belongs: attack or neutral.

Software and tests are built into the operating system Linux, Kali distribution, because it was developed with the purpose of providing a specialized tool in the computer security, including various tools for audit of networks and other security software. For such reason the software resulting from this article in its prototype works only on Kali operating systems Linux In the network infrastructure, a simple WLAN is used, only required an Access Point (AP) router, and two hosts: the analyzer with attack detection software, and the host attacker The magnitude of the network directly affects the network information collection times, because is done for all possible hosts connected or not to the network WLAN that is being analyzed. The router must use the IEEE 802.11n wireless communication protocol and use the spectrum bands of 2.4 GHz.

3   Methodology

The software follows a development in two moments; both embedded in single py extension software in Python 3, so you have a monolithic architecture, because the software is not very extensive, each moment is explained follow:

3.1   Collection and Analysis of Network Data

The collection of network information includes the use of system terminal, for the information request of the device. First, network interface selection is made which is being used, so that the IP address is obtained and the network mask of the device. With this information, calls for pen testing software in NMAP networks, using the sniffers detection script [4], which makes use of the IP and network mask of the device that is connected to the wireless network as arguments. The command is executed sending 7 network messages to each possible host on the network, and wait for the answer from them, if it is given, mark a 1, the output of for each host will be a string of length 7 characters, 1 if received return, or "_" if nothing was answered. These answers are taken from a text file which stores the results of the executed command. Subsequently, the continuous review part of the ARP table of the device for changes, which indicate spoofing of the MAC addresses with the IP [8] is evaluated multiple times in order to determine a measure of cases positive, for further evaluation and analysis. The general results of the evaluation are stored in an output file in plain text, in the same location in which is the Python file.

3.2   Analysis of Results

The second module corresponds to the analysis of the previous data collection. The basis is in the algorithm of machine learning, which was previously trained, that is, first many compilations of information were created, with the difference would be to know which corresponded to an attack, and which, no, with the idea of developing two groups of points located in graph, which are grouped naturally in a special area, showing the tendency to classification. The training is therefore the classification of those areas that distinguish between different groups, in this case, the group of data corresponding to those of an attack, and the group of points that correspond to those of a normal, neutral network. Then, a classification is made by two methods: k neighbors and subdivision of the area. The first is that, given a point, we measure the 3 or 5 points closest to this, to make a vote of those closest points, on what is the majority representative of classification group, the point then it is cataloged as a class, if the majority of its neighbors belong to that class. The second uses so similar to the previous method, but, instead of evaluating a point, he is drawing a line as he calculates distances between groups of different classes, it is done with a large number of iterations, until a situation is reached stationary, where the line stops moving through the graph, and completely divides the two groups, thus helping with both methods to classify incoming points and finalize the classification.

When a program execution is finished then it is they collect the data, then they go to the machine algorithm previously trained learning, and then give as output if you have an attack alert or not. With more test data to training mode, you will have a more precise mode of evaluate the situation of the network, also giving way to subsequent software improvements, such as the implementation of more analysis variables, or new machine learning methods.

3.3   Machine Learning Classification Algorithm

The algorithm must respond to the ability to evaluate by some criterion of approximation to previously given data and evaluated in the space that is being worked on. For them, uses a simple ML-supervised algorithm, such as the one the neighboring K This algorithm needs two variables, two values since, the algorithm makes the study of the criterion of approximation for how close you are to a point in the Two-dimensional space, through the calculation of distance Euclidean, which is the square root of the sum of the square of the subtraction of each point of the same variable [16]:

The algorithm in its training phase consists of the spatial location of the same, knowing the class to which each point belongs, so it can be said that it is supervised, previously the algorithm knows the type to which each class belongs In the dimensional area, in the case of software application two corresponding variables are used to the two outputs that gave the data analyzes previously collected, where each variable corresponds to a type of attack that is being evaluated. The data is then translated into points that are located in the space of two dimensions. The concept of K neighbors uses the idea that, the points that behave in a similar way locate an area space-specific, that is, the points that belong to the same class behave in a similar way, so it is they will group in a space of the two-dimensional graph. With that idea, then there will be two groupings approximated in the graph, which correspond to the two types of cases that can be had: neutral or under attack. Once then the points of the cases already studied put in the graphic, it can be said that the algorithm is already trained, because it already has well differentiated the two classes that they want to classify.

Later, when the software is running, and collects data from the first phase, the table review ARP and sending messages in search of sniffers, the results are passed to numerical values so that the point is put in the two-dimensional graph. Then K is executed neighbors, where the new point measures its Euclidean distance with all the points that you have nearby, taking the calculation from the distance an odd number of neighbors, to later to make a vote, where it is reviewed to that class belong the neighbors who calculated as the most close, and, the class that has the most representatives, is what determines the class of the point that entered as new, so, the point will be classified in a class based on the proximity you have regarding your neighbors, making use of the idea that the approximation of point with other points corresponds to the points that belong to the same class, behave in a way similar, so, the point that corresponds to the current execution of the software, will give a result based on your classification of whether the team that performs the execution is under attack, or it is neutral, that is, it has no risk.

The algorithm depends to a large extent on the input data, the training, because based on them, is that classification, in that order of ideas, they should be multiple data or training cases, the more data training, the better the classification of the incoming points corresponding to new analyzes of the software, varying according to the previous results the value of the neighbors that are going to be evaluated.

4 Design

The software is composed of two fundamental modules of Data collection and analysis. The design is formed from the data entry, which are the status of the network, the table ARP of the device, and the sending and possible receipt of messages to the entire WLAN network looking for possible NICs in monitor mode. Then the composite analysis of the algorithm machine learning that classifies the variables of the given data, to output an alert or not to the device.

As you can see in Fig. 1, the design of the general model is based on collecting data and analyzing them with the algorithm of machine learning to know the answer. The data collection is made up of two parts, one for each type of attack: ARP Poisoning/Spoofing and detection of sniffers. The ARP part consists of multiple revisions, a odd number of revisions, with which it is determined from continuously in a time range the ARP table of the device, comparing constantly each iteration the previous table that was had with the current one, in search of modifications that indicate possible changes by attack of Poisoning the ARP table, pretending to be an attacking host by the router, thus intercepting communications. It makes a Odd number of times to avoid draw situations.

$$d(\bar{x}, \bar{y}) = \|\bar{x} - \bar{y}\| = \sqrt{(x_1 - y_1)^2 + \ldots + (x_n - y_n)^2}$$

Fig. 1. Euclidean distance equation in a vector space Authorship [16].

The model in Fig. 2 exemplifies the collection of responses of messages sent to all hosts in the network, looking for answers by mistake sent by the NICs that are in monitor mode, confirming possible sniffer in the network. He starts with the selection of the network interface with which you are connected to the network that you want to review, giving the possibility to the user to choose it manually or, to be done in a automatic, to then obtain the IP of the device with its network mask, needed as arguments for the command that sends the messages, using NMAP. Then, regarding the revision of the ARP table and the changes, only a call is made to the terminal, which shows the current ARP table, this is saved in a text file, to later make another revision, compare it with the saved in the text and then save it again, in each iteration then compare the current and the previous one (Fig. 3).

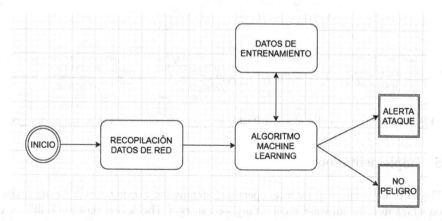

Fig. 2. Scheme general model software operation of attack detection.

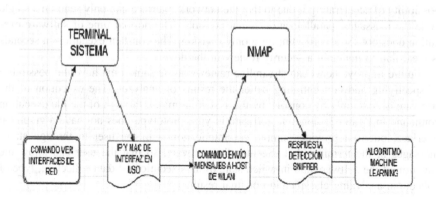

Fig. 3. Network sniff detector operating model WLAN.

The comparisons are made searching if for the given IP previously the same MAC is maintained, in each of the listed devices, since, a typical ARP attack, consists of impersonate a MAC, that of the router by the device of the attacker. Finally, both revisions are finalized in a file of text that is then classified by the machine algorithm learning (Fig. 4).

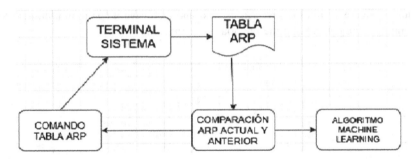

Fig. 4. Operation model reading ARP table and constant comparison in search of changes.

5   Implementation

The software is intended for local operation, alerting the existing attacks on the device on which runs the software, so, it is only local margin. The device must run Kali Linux as operating system in its version 4 and have Python 3. The software is designed for WLAN networks of size medium to small in number of connected hosts, due to that, in detecting sniffer due to the need to send 7 messages to each host, and wait for their return, makes it have very large execution times for large host quantities, without the possibility of accelerating it due to that the network interface can only send on a single node the messages, parallelization is not possible. The normal time of software execution does not exceed 10 min, for a only revision. The constant execution in seconds is ideal flat, to maintain a security review in the device.

Future improvements can streamline reviews at the same time have the possibility of specifying and concentrating better the results of analyzes. The execution of the software is done only by console, by the system terminal, through of the file execution command in Python3, since the software in your prototype does not have a graphical interface, but if it provides simple communication with the user to through status messages in the terminal that executes the software, so that the user can know the situation of the software and in which state of the execution is: data collection, type of collection, analyzing classification or final result.

6   Results Evaluation

After several consistent tests in the two types of cases that can be had: under attack or neutral, it was obtained for 20 tests made for each type of case, it has an effectiveness of 60%, where more than 14 cases were analyzed by the software correctly, which demonstrates the effectiveness of the use of machine learning and the basic classification method used, as was the classification by K neighbors. The wrongful cases were consolidated as causal cases extremes of either the attack case or the neutral case, that is, additional to the error margin of the software and its tools associated, the training data plays a role fundamental, because they are the ones that make the way in which the cases that are given are classified and by consequently the alert classification that can be had when the user runs the software. It can additionally note that the number of hosts that can be have for the range of network addresses is directly proportional to the time required by the software to do the analysis. For networks with more than 100 hosts, possible addresses assignable for the given network address and network mask, times begin to grow exponentially in the completion of the scanning of the network and its subsequent analysis, so that the software is capable of solving problems of Intrusion security through packet sniffer and attacks by ARP poisoning effectively in networks with less than 100 hosts in its range of assignable addresses in the WLAN.

7   Results Discussion

The software gives its outputs after the analysis made through messages in the terminal where the software is running, and for where the dialogue with the user is given. In a first instance the user is welcomed and given a display of the network interfaces that you have in use user's device so that it is he who enters the current interface that you have in use (Fig. 5).

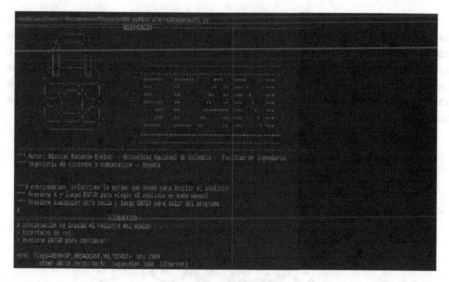

Fig. 5. Terminal display when running the software, Welcome to the user and initial menu.

The user is provided with a menu where he enters the interface, you are provided with the IP address display and network mask that will be used in the analysis, obtaining as results the alert or not of being in a possible attack, and you provide the rate of possible sniffer intrusions in both Cases: attack and neutral. In the case of attack, if you have an attack with ARP poisoning the user is shown the MACs of the devices that may have been the ones that are attacking the user. The used files are consigned in the same folder where the user has saved the software to allow the option that the user can review the complete execution of the software (Fig. 6).

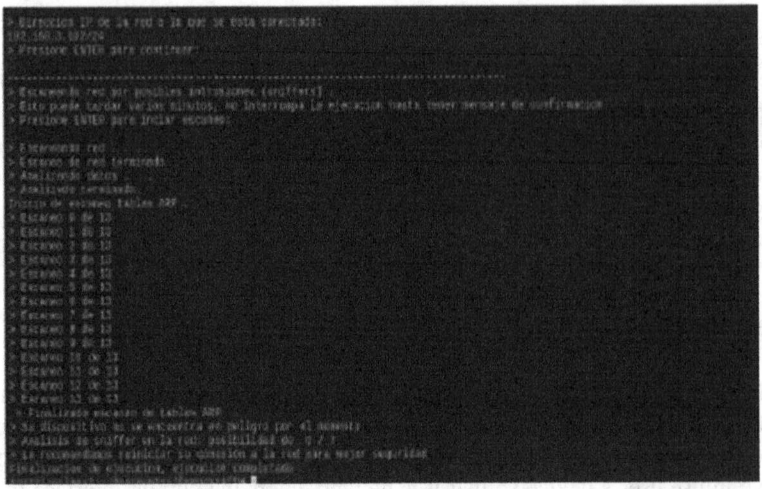

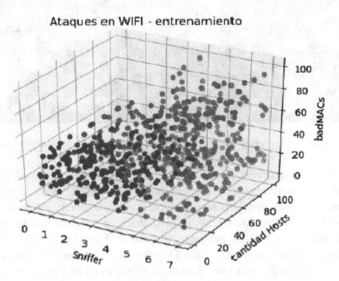

Fig. 6. Display of software execution status with an analysis of the state in which it is.

The software shows the user additionally a three-dimensional graphic where you can see the data used for training, being the points of color red corresponding to the attack cases, and in blue the cases corresponding to neutral cases. The current case, that is, the one being analyzed, the current situation of the user is shown in the graph in green, so that can have a better idea of the proximity of the case to the that you have training and you have a better dimensionality of how far or near you are to some of the cases that you have for classification (Fig. 7).

Fig. 7. Visualization of training cases and Current: red attack case, blue neutral case, green case current. (Color figure online)

The classification is made with 7 points close to the encouragement to have a significant precision with respect to given data. With the data shown and the user obtaining the result, it is suggested to restart the connection to the Wi-Fi router so this is a measure that can help you to rule out cases where the software could not alert of an attack (Fig. 8).

```
root@localhost:~/Documentos/ProyectoGR# python alertaAtaqueswifi.py
> Su dispositivo esta bajo ataque, reinicie la conexion a su red
> Analisis de sniffer en la red: positivo para posible intrusion con grado de 7 / 7
Finalizacion de ejecucion, ejecucion completada
```

Fig. 8. Visualization of the result of one of the cases tested, where it is alerted of a possible attack.

8 Conclusions

The use of machine learning for computer security results in a powerful tool with the capabilities of ideal adaptation and precision, which can help significant to combat attacks on Wi-Fi wireless networks. For cases of very large networks, it is proposed to continue with the study of the possibility of using the software by modules or sections of the same network, to specify analyzes and not enter very long execution times. The possibility of increasing the capacity of others is presented operating systems to make use of the software, such as possibility of improvement of the present product the article: the software.

Additionally, the possibility of power is visible add more forms of wireless network analysis, way to help improve the accuracy of analyzes, and the coverage of the large number of different types of attacks that exist, besides being able to add more modules that make use of the different classification alternatives and study that are part of machine learning and that can significantly improve the amount of real alerts attack.

It has as a key idea the possibility of improving very important the accuracy of the data, using the same software product of the article, taking a dataset with many more cases, that is, it determines that the amount of cases that are studied, can improve the accuracy of software are the need to add modules to the software, because the data is what determines the classification made, with a much larger dataset and with many cases studied as training, they need better results in the detection of attacks.

References

1. Verizon 2017 Data Breach Investigations Report, DBIR (2017). http://www.verizonenterprise.com/verizon-insights-lab/dbir/2017/. Accessed 23 Oct 2017
2. Kumar, S., Viinikainen, A., Hamalainen, T.: Machine learning classification model for network based intrusion detection system. In: 11th International Conference for Internet Technology and Secured Transactions (ICITST) (2016)
3. Limthing, K., Tawsook, T.: Network traffic anomaly detection using machine learning approaches. Computer Engineering Department, Bngkok University (2015)

4. Sanai, D.: Detection of promiscuous nodes using ARP packets (2002). A white paper from http://www.securityfriday.com
5. Fleck, B., Potter, B.: 802.11 Security Securing Wireless Networks. O'Reily, New York (2015)
6. McClure, S., Scambray, J., Kurtz, G.: Hacking Exposed 7: Network Security Secrets & Solutions. McGraw Hil, New York (2016)
7. Van, N.T., Thinh, T.N., Sach, L.T.: An amomaly-based network intrusion detection system using deep learning. In: International Conference on System Science an Engineering (ICSSE) (2017)
8. Xu, Yuan, X., Yu, A., Kim, J.H., Kim, T., Zhang, J.: Developing and evaluating a hands-on lab for teaching local area network vulnerabilities. In: 2016 IEEE Frontiers in Education Conference (FIE), Erie, PA, USA, pp. 1–4 (2016). https://doi.org/10.1109/FIE.2016.7757364
9. Fukuyama, K., Taniguchi, Y., Iguchi, N.: A study on attacker agent in virtual machine-based network security learning system. In: IEEE 4ta Conferencia de electronica de consume, Universidad de Kink, Osaka Japón (2015)
10. Casas, P., Soro, F., Vanerio, J., Settanni, G., D'Alconzo, A.: Network security and anomaly detection with Big-DAMA, a big data analytics framework. In: 2017 IEEE 16va Conferencia internacional Cloud Networking (CloudNet), República Checa, Praga (2017)
11. Kakihata, E.M., et al.: Intrusion detection system based on flows using machine learning algorithms. IEEE Latin América Trans. **15**, 1988–1993 (2017)
12. Aminanto, M.E., Choi, R., Tanuwidjaja, H.C., Yoo, P.D., Kim, K.: Deep abstraction and weighted feature selection for Wi-Fi impersonation detection. IEEE Transactions Seguridad y forense de información **PP**, 1 (2017)
13. Yin, C., Zhu, Y., Fei, J., He, X.: A deep learning approach for intrusion detection using recurrent neural networks. IEEE Access **PP**, 1 (2017). Laboratorio de ingeniería matemática y computación avanzada, Zhengzhou, China
14. Alotaibi, B., Elleithy, K.: A majority voting technique for wireless intrusion detection systems. In: Conferencia de tecnología y aplicaciones en sistemas LISAT IEEE Long Island (2016)
15. Kolias, C., Kambourakis, G., Stavrou, A.: Intrusion detection in 802.11 networks: empirical evaluation of threats and a public dataset. IEEE Encuestas de comunicaciones y tutoriales **18**, 184–208 (2015). Universidad del Egeo, Samos, Grecia
16. Facultad de Ciencias UNAM: Espacios métricos. Universidad Nacional Autónoma de México, Facultad de ciencias, área de sistemas (2017)

VISECO: An Annotated Security Management Framework for 5G

Tran Quang Thanh[1,2(✉)], Stefan Covaci[2], and Thomas Magedanz[1]

[1] Fraunhofer FOKUS, Berlin, Germany
thanh.quang.tran@fokus.fraunhofer.de
[2] Technical University Berlin, Berlin, Germany

Abstract. A novel security management framework is presented in this paper leveraging the current ETSI NFV MANO architecture and taking into account Software Defined Security principles. Specifically, the proposed VISECO framework allows developers, service providers to consider security across lifecycle: from embedding of security properties in the source code, parsing and interpreting for automatic deployment to active responding during operation. Mobile operator can use VISECO to secure its infrastructure and to provide "Security-as-a-Service" solution to potential customers such as IoT service providers. As an illustration, a framework prototyping and an IoT use case application are implemented and discussed.

Keywords: 5G · IoT · MANO · NFV · Security management

1 Introduction

The cloud-based security service market is continuously growing reaching 5.9 billion USD in 2017 (21% from 2016 and close to 9 billion USD by 2020) [1]. Such growth presents opportunities and also challenges for service providers to deliver cost-effective, high-quality managed security services to customers. Diverse types of security functions, lack of standard interfaces to control and monitor, mixed integration of both virtualized and physical security functions, the demand to control security function dynamically, the need for automation to assure high quality and speed of security management, are some of key challenges [2–4] that service providers need to take into account when offering security management and orchestration services.

Mobile network architecture evolution is continuing toward the fifth generation (5G). Still, the 5G networks are expected to have a very high-speed data transfer, extremely low latency and ubiquitous connectivity support. However, additional key driving factors will enter the scene including the convergence of mobile network and Cloud Computing or the support of Internet of Thing (IoT) applications from vertical industries (e.g., automotive, healthcare, energy). In addition to that, to support new requirements, mobile operators are currently considering "network softwarization" for their network infrastructures by investigating several enabling software-related technologies such as Network Functions Virtualization (NFV), Software Defined Network (SDN). With NFV, applications that were previously coupled to proprietary hardware

É. Renault et al. (Eds.): MSPN 2018, LNCS 11005, pp. 251–269, 2019.
https://doi.org/10.1007/978-3-030-03101-5_21

can now be virtually instantiated and deployed on generic commercial off-the-shelf (COTS) computing hardware.

Obviously, the current 3GPP security architectures and measures cannot simply re-applied to the new networks as they are tied to the traditional operator-subscriber trust model and basic IP/telecom services. To support emerging requirements, new security concepts are required to take into account novel technological approaches (e.g., network virtualization, software-defined principles) with particular interests on built-in (by-design), flexible and automation. New innovative solutions for security management and monitoring are key to achieve and ensure the highest level of security as demand for the 5G networks [5]. In addition to that, supporting IoT applications represents incredible potential but also great risk. Because of least resistance, IoT devices (machines) are becoming the new targets of the fraudsters/hackers and many incidents were reported. Hundreds of stolen SIM cards of smart light devices in Johannesburg were discovered too late [6] (the damage was not only losses caused by using these SIM for making malicious calls but also the traffic jam and the accidents). Botnets are growing larger and smarter than ever by exploiting poorly-secured IoT devices (e.g., CCTV cameras) to launch DDoS attack [7]. According to Gartner, by 2019, the amount of mobile malware will be one-third of the total malware reported (up from 7.5%) [8].

In this paper, a novel security management framework is presented that leverages the current NFV MANO architecture, enables mobile operator not only to secure its network infrastructure but also to provide efficient and secure "As-a-Service" solution to potential customers. The remainder of the paper is organized as follows: Sects. 2 and 3 present the related works as well as our motivation and framework design principles. Section 4 describes the framework architecture and operation. An implementation of the framework and an evaluation IoT use case application have been discussed in Sect. 5. Section 6 concludes the paper.

2 Related Works

In the recent effort, the security management integration is investigated and being improved by the ETSI NFV Security group. Some important ideas have been introduced including the security management framework [3]. However, similar to other ETSI NFV specifications, the current ETSI SEC specification provides only the concept, still at a high level, and will need further efforts from related ETSI NFV groups in order to reach the desired detail-level required by implementers. The IETF Interface to NSF devices (I2NSF) work proposes to standardize a set of software interfaces and data modules to control and monitor the physical and virtual NSFs [9]. At this moment, the I2NSF only focuses on the flow-based NSFs and how to control and monitor NSFs at a functional implementation level. For the I2NSF capability layer, the I2NSF work proposes an interoperable protocol that passes NSF provisioning rules and orchestration information between an I2NSF client on a network manager and I2NSF agent on an NSF device.

A security orchestrator is proposed by Nokia [10], acting as an overarching function for the MANO orchestration enabling the direct control of the security service deployed in the physical networks as well as the through the OSS to the virtual security-related functions. The Security Orchestrator proposed is a holistic component having a full perspective on the system and enhancing the network service descriptors with security-related items. The approach is still at a high level, and no further works were reported. The Open Security Controller Project (OSC) [11] is a new open source project of the Linux Foundation. The mission of the project is to support the collaboration of development of software to centralize security services orchestration for multi-cloud environments. OSC interacts with different components to automate and orchestrate the virtualized security functions. OSC supports OpenStack, works with SDN controller and security functions through plugins, but the current version does not support NFV MANO. Commercial solutions from product vendors such as [12] tend to deploy mono-vendor security functions in a network segment. Several European research projects were and are ongoing to provide different types of security services, toolkits and evaluate them in various use cases and domains (e.g., T-NOVA, ENSURE, SONATA, SHIELD and ANASTACIA) [13–17]. Many common security services are provided by every cloud providers (e.g., Amazon AWS [18], Google GCP [19] and OpenStack [20]) or open source community (e.g., Cloud Native Computing Foundation [21]).

This work shares some common ideas with existing works such as policy-based, standard-align. As targeting 5G mobile operators, the framework design leverages the current NFV MANO reference architecture. Moreover, to automate the security management activity and simplify the policy specification and enforcement, different types of security-related metadata can be provided across application lifecycle not only at deployment time (proper security policies) but also during software component development (source code annotations).

3 Motivation and Design Principle

3.1 Software Defined Security (SDSec)

According to [22], SDSec is an architectural approach to protection and compliance that decouples and abstracts controls away from physically-oriented elements (e.g., hardware, topology, or physical location). Based on five principles, SDSec can provide security orchestration and automation in any infrastructure environment being protected and at any scale. Security abstraction means all controls must be completely non-dependent on specific hardware, topologies, or physical location of the environment being protected. Security automation means that any control (e.g., firewall policies, configuration vulnerability scans, intrusion detection, multi-factor authentication) can be deployed and managed with minimal human intervention. Security orchestration maintains alignment between security requirements, changing application dynamics, and control implementation through automated workflows, provisioning, and change management. Automatic scalability expresses that security and compliance control capacity must scale up or down dynamically and without human intervention. API enablement expresses that security monitoring and enforcement control functions should be fully accessible via open application programming interfaces (APIs).

3.2   ETSI NFV Security Management Framework

NFV is set of de-facto standards and technologies that enable network managers running their infrastructure in an efficient manner by moving network functions out of dedicated hardware devices into the software. To leverage NFV technology, the European Telecommunications Standards Institute (ETSI) has defined a standard reference framework for VNF management and orchestration (NFV MANO) [23]. In the initial phase, network service deployment is automated by NFV-MANO without explicitly considering security management requirement. As security protection of NFV network services necessitates security functions like Virtual Security Functions (VSFs) and NFVI-based Security Functions (ISFs), as well as Physical Security Functions (PSFs). For managing and monitoring those security functions with a certain level of automation, NFV Security Management (NSM) functionality is required to cope with inherent complexity, separation of domains and consistency challenges of security management for network services across these domains. The shaded areas in Fig. 1 show the high-level Security Management Framework as a logical extension to the current NFV MANO framework. The major difference of NSM from NFV-MANO is the clear focus on security tasks including security functions realized in the physical network part, i.e., NSM manages not only the security functions in virtualized network but also security functions in the traditional physical network to enhance the overall protection level.

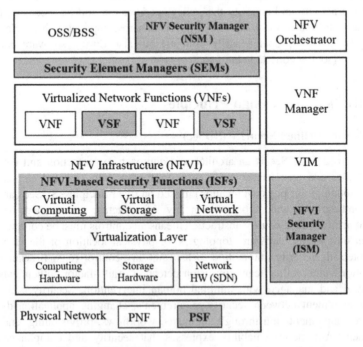

Fig. 1. ETSI NFV security management framework

3.3   Source Code Annotation

Annotations are a form of metadata that provide data about a program that is not part of the program itself. The developer of an application should annotate its code with required metadata information. Annotations can be included within the source code and supported by modern programming languages such as Java, C# and be properly translated before building the executable, as well as externally accompany the executable and be properly translated by other components of the architecture during executable's placement and runtime. From the software engineering perspective, annotations are practically a special interface. Such an interface may be accompanied by several constraints such as the parts of the code that can be annotated (it is called @Target in Java), the parts of the code that will process the annotation, etc. An example of an annotation declaration using Java is presented in Fig. 2.

@*Metric*

(*name*="unauthorizedRequestRate",

description = "numbers of unauthorized requests per minute",

unitofmeasurement = "min",

valuetype = ValueType.SingleValue,

maxvalue = "1000",

minvalue = "0",

higherisbetter = false)

Fig. 2. Sample Java annotation

4   Framework Architecture

In this section, a policy-based context-aware security management framework (VISECO) is presented to support the security management of NFV-based application (network service) over its entire lifecycle. Authorized users can secure their applications by integrating available security functions/enablers into the applications (by design) and security metadata to be automatically interpreted, provisioned and configured to support security requirements across the application lifecycle. Security functions can be provided by different vendors/operators: either as infrastructure-based services or embedded virtual security functions/agents. The high-level architecture is shown in Fig. 3 with different components (functional blocks). Its design has been realized considering the current ETSI NFV reference architecture [23] as well as the IETF Security Controller architecture [9].

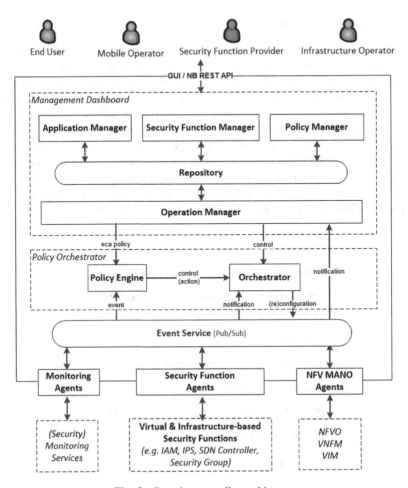

Fig. 3. Security controller architecture

4.1 Main Actors

There are four main actors in the VISECO: End User, Security Function Provider, Mobile Operator, and Infrastructure Operator.

- *End User:* It is the entity (customer) that uses the framework platform to create, deploy and operate his applications (network services). Thus, an end user can be a private person or an account on behalf of an organization (e.g., enterprise, service provider, mobile operator). To protect such application, user can use any available security services on the platform (offered by mobile operator).
- *Security Function Provider:* It is the entity that provides security functions and required agents/element managers (SEM). Following the framework information model, during the development phase, the SEM is annotated with the required

qualitative and quantitative metadata/properties that can be used by policy orchestration engine to simplify the policy definition and activation. Such annotations can be included within the source code and be properly translated before building the executable, as well as accompany the executable and be properly translated by other components of the architecture during executable's placement and runtime.

– *Mobile Operator:* It is the main entity responsible for the operation of the framework platform. The mobile operator manages all security functions/agents, makes them available for end users and maintains a smooth and secure operation.
– *Infrastructure Operator:* It is the entity that operates the physical infrastructure, including computation, communication, storage resources as well as available security supported functions/services. Most probably but not necessarily, the Infrastructure Operator will be the same as the Mobile Operator.

4.2 Components

The Security Controller architecture, as shown in Fig. 3, contains several subcomponents/functional blocks and interfaces. In the upper level (management dashboard) is a set of available components for design, deploy and manage NFV applications. The *"Policies Manager"* enables users to define policies and associate them with a running application/network service record (NSR). The *"Security Function Manager"* manages all security functions to make them available to authorized users and the similar to the *"Application Manager"*. The *"Operation Manager"*, the main component in the upper layer, supports the deployment and operation of the application with policies. It communicates with other components in the lower level to collect runtime information to perform required functionalities. Defined policies are sent to the framework event-based *"Policy Engine"*. The *"Orchestrator"* component receives reactions/controls from *"Policy Engine"* or *"Operation Manager"*, prepares the (re)-configurations for the *"NFV MANO Agent"* (e.g., life-cycle action command) or *"Security Function Agents"* (e.g., configuration update towards security functions).

To avoid vendor lock-ins, a flexible architecture is taken into account using different types of agent (Monitoring, Security Function, and NFV MANO). The *"Monitoring Agent"* (MON) communicates with any available monitoring service to provide monitoring events to the *"Policy Engine"*. Such monitoring events can be any from common monitoring metrics (e.g., CPU/memory usage, received TCP/UDP packets/flows) or security-specific metrics (e.g., IPBlacklist reported event from a fraud/intrusion detection system). The *"NFV MANO Agent"* consumes available NBI (Northbound Interface) APIs/SDK provided by related NFV MANO solutions. It can, in one hand, execute MANO lifecycle commands/controls (e.g., NS/VNF START, STOP), on the other hand, collect supported runtime information/events from the MANO solution. The *"Security Function Agent"* (or Security Element Manager by ETSI - SEM) implements control interfaces towards real security functions. Depending on how to implement security functions, there are two types of agents: Generic and

Wrapper. The former can manage all newly developed security functions (using common RESTful API), following the proposed annotation-based context model. The latter applied to any existing solutions. Different wrapper agents are required to implement to manage such legacy security functions. Users can interact with the framework through a central management dashboard, and northbound APIs are provided to interested parties.

4.3   Information Model

To be compliant with the current NFV MANO solutions, our framework adopts current NFV Information Model [24]. Network Service Descriptor (NSD) is the deployment template for a network service including several VNFs and description of their connectivity through virtual links. It is used by the NFV Orchestrator (NFVO) for deploying network services (as a combination of multiple VNFs). Virtual Network Function Descriptor (VNFD) is a deployment template which describes any VNF regarding its deployment and operational behavior requirements and its parameters. JSON and TOSCA compliant Network Service Template [25] are the two common data formats for NSD and VNFD.

The event information is based on a simple Next Generation Service Interface (NGSI) context model using the notion of context entities. It was first specified by Open Mobile Alliance (OMA) [26] and was adopted and extended by FIWARE [27]. As seen in Fig. 4, an entity represents a thing, i.e., any physical or logical object (e.g., a sensor, a person, a device, a service). Each entity has an entity id and entity type. Each entity is uniquely identified by the combination of its id and type. Also, meta-data is used to describe further the information contained in the attributes. In NGSI specification, besides a data model for context information, there are also two different interfaces: a context data interface for exchanging information using query, subscription, and update operations (NGSI 10) and a context availability interface for exchanging information on how to obtain context information (NGSI 9).

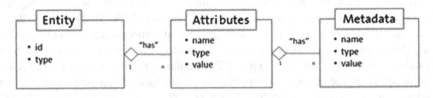

Fig. 4. NGSI context information model

In VISECO, entity types are used as the event name, and the ids are the event source. Context attributes can contain all kind of data structures as well as multi-value sets. The events are functionally grouped into four categories, and different prefixes are used to distinguish them (see table below) (Table 1).

Table 1. Event types

Event prefix	Description
MONS	Monitoring events generated by (security) monitoring agents (e.g. MONS_SynFlood, MONS_UDPFlowsFromSource, MONS_Blacklist, MONS_UnauthorizedHTTPRequest)
CONF	Configuration events generated by the Orchestrator include lifecycle actions towards MANO component and configuration updates towards Security Functions (e.g., CONF_MANO, CONF_SEM)
MANO	NFV MANO lifecycle events generated by MANO agents. (e.g. MANO_NSR_INSTANTIATE_FINISH, MANO_VNFR_START, MANO_VNFR_STOP)
REGS	Registration events generated by three types of agents (REGS_MANO, REGS_MON, REGS_SEM)

For the action (control) part, we took into account current evolving OpenC2 (Control and Command) model by the international standards body OASIS. OpenC2 was designed to focus on the actions that are to be executed to thwart an attack, mitigate some vulnerability, or otherwise address a threat. OpenC2 can be implemented in a variety of systems to perform the secure delivery and management of command and control messages in a context-specific way. In the OpenC2 language, three distinct types of messages have been specified: Command, Response, and Alert. Control (or Action) information can use OpenC2 Command with following form and the actual encoding can leverage pre-existing conventions and notations such as XML, JSON, TLV, etc (Table 2).

```
(
        ACTION = <ACTION_TYPE>,
        TARGET (
        type = <data-model>:<TARGET_TYPE>,
        <target-specifier>
        ),
        ACTUATOR (
        type = <data-model>:<ACTUATOR_TYPE>,
        <actuator-specifier>
        ),
        MODIFIERS (
        <list-of-modifiers>
        )
)
```

Table 2. OpenC2 command field description

Types	Description
ACTION	Required. The task or activity to be performed (i.e.the 'verb')
Data-model	Required. The data model for the TARGET
TARGET	Required. The object of the action. The ACTION is performed on the TARGET
Type	Required. The TARGET type will be defined within the context of a target data model
Target-specifier	Optional. The specifier further describes a specific target, a list of targets, or a class of targets
ACTUATOR	Optional. The subject of the action. The ACTUATOR executes the ACTION on the TARGET
Type	Required if the actuator is included, otherwise not applicable. The ACTUATOR type will be defined within the context of an actuator profile
Data-model	Required if the actuator is included, otherwise not applicable. The data model for the ACTUATOR
Actuator-specifier	Optional. If the actuator is included, otherwise not applicable. The specifier further describes a specific actuator, a list of actuators, or a class of actuators
MODIFIERS (<list-of-modifiers>)	Optional. Provide additional information about the action such as date/time, periodicity, duration, and location

The "Event-Condition-Action" (ECA) policy model is selected to represent policies. An event is an important occurrence in time of a change in the system being managed, and/or in the environment of the system being managed. A condition is defined as a set of attributes, features, and/or values that are to be compared with a set of known attributes, features, and/or values in order to determine whether or not the set of actions can be executed or not. Policy Rule is often made up of three Boolean clauses: an Event clause, a Condition clause, and an Action clause. A Boolean clause is a logical statement that evaluates to either TRUE or FALSE. It may be made up of one or more terms; if more than one term, then a Boolean clause connects the terms using logical connectives (i.e., AND, OR, and NOT). It has the following semantics:

```
IF <event-clause> is TRUE
    IF <condition-clause> is TRUE
        THEN execute <action-clause>
    END-IF
END-IF
```

4.4   Main Activities

Annotated Security Function

One of the challenges for a centralized security management solution is how to automatically update/reconfigure security functions by different vendors that might have various features and different management interfaces. In VISECO, to address such challenge and simplify the policy definition process, each security function is required to be annotated either implementing from scratch or extending the control part. An annotation library is provided during Security Functions/Manager Agents development for the inclusion of a set of required metadata at the software level.

In VISECO, the annotations are functionally grouped into three main categories (identification, configuration, and metric). The configuration-based annotation can be used to describe the capability of security function/service as well as to control such capability by updating its value at runtime (e.g., activate/deactivate). The metric-based annotation can be used to provide component-specific monitoring information. Before making available to end-users, all security functions/agents are needed to register. During the submission, the system performs a set of validations to check the logical validity of the provided annotations. When the component passes the validation phase, a specific parser undertakes the task to transform the arguments of the annotations to a serialized format and store in the repository and can be used later to define policies. Figure 5 depicts the data format of the framework metric-based annotation.

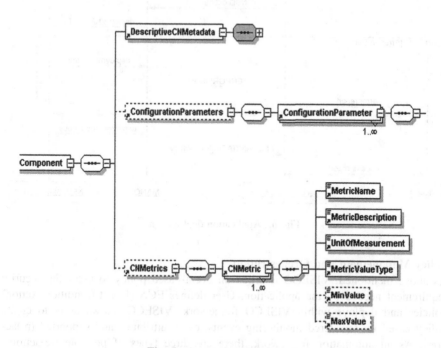

Fig. 5. Annotation data format

Application Deployment

VISECO supports authorized users to select available security functions/agents from the repository to deploy with their applications. The current network/application service descriptor (NSD) will be updated to include selected security functions. Users can deploy such NSD any time. Such activities are described in Fig. 6.

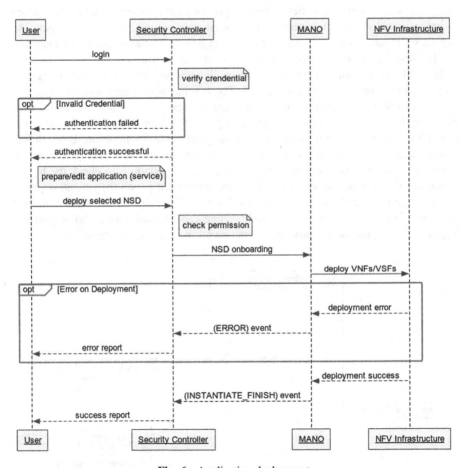

Fig. 6. Application deployment

Policy Management and Orchestration

As above mentioned, VISECO is relied on event-based policy to tailor the security requirement needed by the application. User defines ECA (Event-Condition-Action) policies and deploys within VISECO framework. VISECO allows users to create policy based on registered monitoring events, event attributes and supported (re)actions. As an automation framework, there are three types of possible (re)actions: Notification (e.g., display in the dashboard, send/forward to admin or interested parties), Configuration Update (e.g. update the value of related configuration parameter that can be handled by SF agents to trigger proper responses) or MANO lifecycle controls (e.g. start/stop a VNF instance).

5 Implementation and Proof-of-Concept Use Case

5.1 Framework Implementation

In this section, a prototype of the proposed framework is briefly presented based on several open source solutions. OpenBaton [28] (version 5.0), developed by our colleges at TU Berlin, is selected to provide MANO functionality. It is an open source project that implements the current ETSI MANO framework, supports OpenStack VIM, provides a generic VNFM and an NFVO. The module design architecture is flexible to extend its functionalities as well as integrate with external components through provided APIs/SDK. Figure 7 gives an overview of OpenBaton architecture framework release three implementations with all developed components (core and extension)

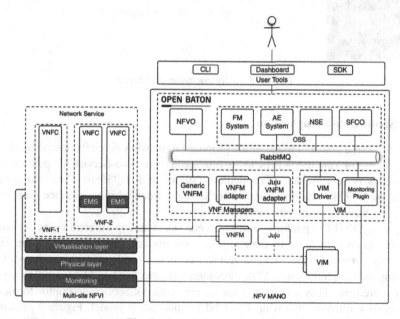

Fig. 7. OpenBaton architecture

Another open source solution, Orion Context Broker [29], is adopted to provide event service (PubSub) functionality including required NGSI9/10 APIs. For the policy engine, two Java-based solutions are taken into account: EasyRules [30] and Drools [31] (to support more complex policies). Other components are implemented using Java Spring Boot framework [32]. Spring is a very popular Java-based framework for building web and enterprise applications and Spring Boot project makes it easy to create stand-alone, production-grade Java-based applications/microservices. A MANO agent software component has been developed using OpenBaton SDK. The annotation library was developed by UBITECH team in the context of our previous ARCADIA project [33]. Figure 8 gives an overview of current Dashboard implementation. Further information about the capability of the framework is presented in the next section.

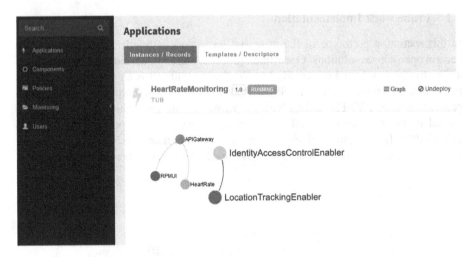

Fig. 8. Security controller dashboard

5.2   Securing IoT Application

In this section, a potential usage of the proposed framework is briefly described. A (5G) mobile operator can use VISECO to provide Secure-As-a-Service to potential IoT customers/service providers. For demonstration, an IoT "Heart Rate Monitoring" application (HRM) was implemented including a frontend user interface component (UI) and a backend heart rate service (CB).

By using VISECO platform, customers can select among different types of security functions to include them in their applications/services. For example, in the HRM application, to protect the backend service, customer needs to deploy a firewall. As accessing the backend though APIs, customers can select an "API Gateway" to support such requirement. They can extend the current network service descriptor to include such security function following ETSI NFV information model. Figure 9 presents a brief view of the new NSD with three VNFs (the Frontend UI, the Backend CB and the new API Gateway AF) following current TOSCA standard data format [25]. Customers can make use of other external supported services to protect their applications. As seen in Fig. 8, two such services are introduced: Location Tracking Enabler and Identity Access Manager Enabler. The former is a software component, developed in another project, to support tracking device location and to report potential malicious activities. The latter, also developed by us, is required (by the API Gateway and the Location Tracking Enabler) to provide identity and access control service.

```
tosca_definitions_version: tosca_simple_profile_for_nfv_1_0
description: NS for HRM
metadata:
  ID: :HRM
  vendor: AG
  version: beta
relationships_template:
  rel1:
    parameters:
    - private
    - private_floatingIp
    source: af
    target: ui
    type: tosca.nodes.relationships.ConnectsTo
  rel2:
    parameters:
      - private
    source: cb
    target: af
    type: tosca.nodes.relationships.ConnectsTo
topology_template:
  node_templates:
    private:
      type: tosca.nodes.nfv.VL
    CP1:
      properties:
        floatingIP: random
      requirements:
        - virtualBinding: VDU1
        - virtualLink: private
      type: tosca.nodes.nfv.CP
    CP2:
      properties:
        floatingIP: random
      requirements:
        - virtualBinding: VDU2
        - virtualLink: private
      type: tosca.nodes.nfv.CP
    CP3:
      properties:
        floatingIP: random
      requirements:
        - virtualBinding: VDU3
        - virtualLink: private
      type: tosca.nodes.nfv.CP
```

Fig. 9. Network service descriptor in TOSCA

As aforementioned, during the development of security functions, different security-related annotations are included in the source code (e.g., specific metrics, configuration parameters). Table 3 describes some implemented metric (M) and configuration (C) annotations. For example, the "iamEndPoint" configuration annotation is used to activate/deactivate the policy-based access control capability of the API Gateway by updating its value.

Table 3. Security annotations

Name (type)	Component
isRunning (M)	All
unauthorizedRequest (M)	API Gateway
errorRequest (M)	API Gateway
iamEndPoint (C)	API Gateway
user-account (C)	Identity Access Control Enabler
distance (M)	Location Tracking Enabler
is-roaming (M)	Location Tracking Enabler

Security policies can be specified leveraging such context information using the Policies editor. Figure 10 describes an ECA policy where the security monitoring event is triggered by the "Location Tracking" enabler (user/device change location/distance), the reaction is handled by the "Identity Access Control" enabler (add new user-account policy to deny the access) and the enforcement is provided by the "API Gateway" (check access policy before grant user access).

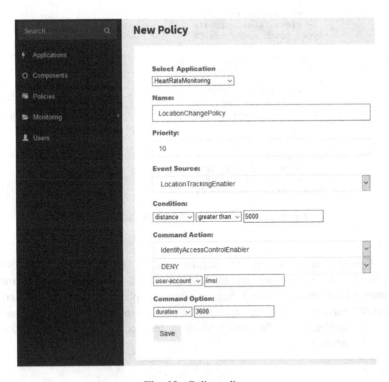

Fig. 10. Policy editor

Moreover, common monitoring data (e.g. component CPU/Memory usage, Sent/Received packets) can also be used to define policy. For example, an auto-scaling policy can be defined to support the high availability of new security function "API Gateway". Based on the report of received packets (a common monitoring metric), the Security Controller can request, through the "NFV MANO agent, to start a new instance (scale out) or remove one of the running instances (scale in). Figure 11 visualizes the average received packet per each "API Gateway" instance. We can see that the number of received packets per component start decreasing at the scale-out event.

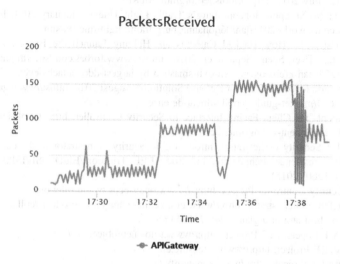

Fig. 11. API Gateway auto scaling

6 Conclusion

In this paper, a novel context-aware security management framework in NFV environment has been proposed. It allows developers, service providers to consider security across application/service lifecycle: from embedding of security properties in the source code, parsing and interpreting for automatic deployment to active responding during operation. The framework design leverages current NFV MANO architecture, and its components can be integrated with existing solutions to provide security management functionality. The implementation of the framework and demo application are also discussed.

Acknowledgment. The research leading to these results has partly received funding from the European Community's Horizon 2020 Framework Programme (ASTRID project [34] under grant no. 786922).

References

1. Gartner Forecasts Worldwide Cloud-Based Security Services to Grow 21 Percent in 2017. http://www.gartner.com/newsroom/id/3744617
2. I2NSF Problem Statement and Use Cases. https://tools.ietf.org/html/draft-ietf-i2nsf-problem-and-use-cases-16
3. ETSI NFV Security Management and Monitoring. http://www.etsi.org/deliver/etsi_gs/NFV-SEC/001_099/013/03.01.01_60/gs_NFV-SEC013v030101p.pdf
4. 5G-PPP Phase 1 Security Landscape. https://5g-ppp.eu/new-security-group-5g-ppp-white-paper-phase-1-security-landscape/
5. IETF Interface to Network Security Functions (I2NSF) RFC 8192: Problem Statement and Use Cases, July 2017. https://tools.ietf.org/html/rfc8192
6. Smith, D.: No Stopping Johannesburg's Traffic Light Thieves, January 2011. http://www.guardian.co.uk/world/2011/jan/06/johannesburg-traffic-light-thieves-sim
7. Fox-Brewster, T.: How Hacked Cameras are Helping Launch the Biggest Attacks the Internet has Ever Seen, September 2016. https://www.forbes.com/sites/thomasbrewster/2016/09/25/brian-krebs-overwatch-ovh-smashed-by-largest-ddos-attacks-ever/
8. Market Guide for Mobile Threat Defense Solutions, August 2017. https://www.gartner.com/doc/3789664/market-guide-mobile-threat-defense
9. Requirements for Client-Facing Interface to Security Controller. https://tools.ietf.org/html/draft-ietf-i2nsf-client-facing-interface-req-03
10. Jaeger, B.: Security orchestrator: introducing a security orchestrator in the context of the ETSI NFV reference architecture. In: 2015 IEEE Trustcom/BigDataSE/ISPA, Helsinki, pp. 1255–1260 (2015)
11. Open Security Controller Project. https://www.opensecuritycontroller.org
12. Cisco Defense Orchestrator. http://www.cisco.com/c/dam/en/us/products/collateral/security/defense-orchestrator/at-a-glance-c45-736943.pdf
13. T-NOVA European FP7 Project. http://www.t-nova.eu/objectives/
14. 5G ENSURE Project. http://www.5gensure.eu
15. 5G SONATA Project. http://www.sonata-nfv.eu
16. SHIELD Project. https://torsec.github.io/shield-h2020/
17. ANASTACIA Project. http://www.anastacia-h2020.eu
18. Cloud Security, Identity & Compliance with AWS. https://aws.amazon.com/products/security/
19. Google Cloud Platform Security. https://cloud.google.com/security/
20. OpenStack Security Guide. https://docs.openstack.org/security-guide/
21. Cloud Native Computing Foundation. https://www.cncf.io/
22. What CSOs Need to Know About Software-Defined Security. http://itsecurityleaders.com/wp-content/uploads/2015/03/Cloud-Passage-What-CSOs-Need-To-Know-About-SDSec.pdf
23. ETSI NFV MANO Specification. http://www.etsi.org/deliver/etsi_gs/NFV-MAN/001_099/001/01.01.01_60/gs_NFV-MAN001v010101p.pdf
24. ETSI GR NFV-IFA 015: Management and Orchestration; Report on NFV Information Model, January 2017. http://www.etsi.org/deliver/etsi_gr/NFV-IFA/001_099/015/02.01.01_60/gr_NFV-IFA015v020101p.pdf
25. TOSCA Simple Profile for NFV, March 2016. http://docs.oasis-open.org/tosca/tosca-nfv/v1.0/csd03/tosca-nfv-v1.0-csd03.pdf
26. Open Mobile Alliance: Next Generation Service Interfaces Architecture, May 2012. http://www.openmobilealliance.org/release/NGSI/V1_0-20120529-A/OMA-AD-NGSI-V1_0-20120529-A.pdf

27. FIWARE-NGSI v2 Specification. http://fiware.github.io/context.Orion/api/v2/stable/
28. OpenBaton, http://openbaton.github.io
29. FIWARE Orion Context Broker GE. https://fiware-orion.readthedocs.io
30. A Simple Yet Powerful Java Rules Engine. https://github.com/j-easy/easy-rules/wiki
31. Drools - Business Rules Management System. https://www.drools.org/
32. Spring Framework: The Source for Modern Java. https://spring.io
33. H2020 ARCADIA Project. http://www.arcadia-framework.eu
34. H2020 ASTRID Project. https://www.astrid-project.eu

Use of KRACK Attack to Obtain Sensitive Information

Luis Felipe Epia Realpe[1], Octavio José Salcedo Parra[1,2(✉)],
and Julio Barón Velandia[2]

[1] Department of Systems and Industrial Engineering, Faculty of Engineering,
Universidad Nacional de Colombia, Bogotá D.C., Colombia
{lepiar, ojsalcedop}@unal.edu.co
[2] Faculty of Engineering, Universidad Distrital "Francisco José de Caldas",
Bogotá D.C., Colombia
{osalcedo, jbaron}@udistrital.edu.co

Abstract. This project presents an implementation of the recent KRACK attack for hacking WPA2 networks and obtaining sensitive information such as passwords, credit card numbers, messages, pages visited by the victim, etc., this attack works against any current modem, and depending on the operating system, and configuration of the network, you can inject or modify information. This project will show its operation for a Linux operating system laptop that connects to a Wi-Fi network encrypted with WPA2 protocol, and you will obtain sensitive information through KRACK attacks. Additionally, it will explain how to identify if you are being victim of this attack.

Keywords: WPA2 · Network security · Hacking

1 Summary

WPA2 is a protocol and security certification program designed for secure wireless communication (WiFi), which arose in response to the WEP protocol that had several security flaws and was relatively easy to break. This protocol uses a much more robust encryption system (AES-CCMP) than its WPA and WEP hearers, which is still extremely difficult to break, so if we tried to break a password by brute force, it would take a certain amount of time astronomical, but the Wifi protocol itself has a vulnerability just brought to light, making any WPA2 implementation sensitive to the attack described in this document. The attack that will be used in this document takes advantage of the "4-way handshakeüsed" by the WPA2 protocol, which is executed when a client wants to connect to a WiFi network and is used to confirm that both the access point and the client have the correct credentials (such as the password saved by the client) [1, 2].

© Springer Nature Switzerland AG 2019
É. Renault et al. (Eds.): MSPN 2018, LNCS 11005, pp. 270–276, 2019.
https://doi.org/10.1007/978-3-030-03101-5_22

2 Background

WiFi network audits are carried out with other types of attacks that exploit weaknesses of different types, with the WEP protocol being the most affected, due to the number of weaknesses that it presents [3].

Currently the security in 802.11 standard WiFi networks, is managed by an algorithm called TKIP for signature, and WPA2 uses the AES CCMP algorithm which is much more robust and eliminates security failures such as "Beck-Tews attack.°r. ° higashiMorii attack". The recommendation is to eliminate TKIP support if possible, although to this day the attacks are not sufficiently extended [4].

3 Related Works

3.1 Café Late Attack

This attack is not made directly to the source, but a particular client. The reason for its name is because it can be done in a matter of 5 min, which is how long it takes to have a coffee, and it works as follows:

The attacker creates a Wi-Fi hotspot with an ES-SID exactly the same as one that has the victim saved with WEP security but with a different password since we do not know it. Although the attacker and the victim have different encryption keys, the WEP encryption allows to reach the customer's association phase to the access point.

In the process of client authentication is done through a challenge that is nothing more than the encrypted Wi-Fi key. The client will respond, and the false access point will tell you that it is correct, even if it is false, sending a correct authentication message.

Once associated with the victim, she will try to obtain an IP address, but it will not be possible to assign one because it is a false point and does not have DHCP, so it will be assigned a static IP and will start sending ARP's informing of the static IP.

The last step is made from the fake AP, from the ARP the AP will begin to make IP requests that will be answered by the client creating enough traffic to crack the WEP network.

3.2 Chop Chop Attack

The chop chop attack can not get the key directly but through the attack we can get the necessary information to obtain the key. The good thing about this attack is that it deciphers the WEP package without knowing the key. Rather than deciphering the term would be to enter by brute force by the nature of the attack. The objective is to intercept the modification in the WEP scheme and allow the attack to be manipulated to obtain the key.

This type of attack takes advantage of the way in which the data is transmitted: The packages used in the WEP protocol have two main parts: the encrypted part, and the ICV (Integrity Check Value), where the latter is used to determine if the data has suffered any error or corruption.

The first step of the chop chop attack is to capture the packet in the air and proceed to the elimination of the last bit before the ICV. The attack then replaces the bit with the value it should. Possible values range from 00 to FF in alphanumeric format making this a maximum of 256 attempts. The package, with this bit already modified, is sent to the Access point, if the option is correct it will be accepted, if it is not correct it will be rejected, once this bit is found, it is passed to the next bit and so until the value is found. every bit.

Once found about 10,000 valid packages and we can use a tool like Aircrack to start cracking the password and in a matter of few to get it.

3.3   REAVER Attack

Some routers have a weakness called WPS, (Wi-Fi Protected Setup) is a standard promoted by the Wi-Fi Alliance for the creation of secure WLAN networks. In other words, WPS is not a security mechanism per se, it is the definition of various mechanisms to facilitate the configuration of a secure WLAN network with WPA2, designed to minimize user intervention in domestic environments or small offices (SOHO). Specifically, WPS defines the mechanisms through which different devices in the network obtain the credentials (SSID and PSK) necessary to initiate the authentication process [5].

The vulnerability occurs in the authentication process that allows an attacker to reduce the number of attempts and checks in a brute-force attack to discover the network access password used by the AP in the WPS protocol. Brute force attack is the way to recover a key by trying all possible combinations until finding the one that allows access. The attack is possible, because the WPS protocol does not implement the possibility of limiting the number of possible attempts. In addition, the detected vulnerability reduces the time necessary to perform this type of attack, at a time interval of 4 to 10 h [6].

The vulnerability has been detected in the EAP-NACK messages sent by the Registrar (AP) to the client and/or device linked to the first and second half of the PIN, when initiating an external authentication using a PIN code.

This form of authentication dramatically reduces the number of attempts needed to find out the PIN, reducing the number from 100,000,000 to approximately 20,000 [7].

3.4   Pixie Dust Attack

This attack, like the attack with REAVER, is aimed at the WPS protocol, and focuses on capturing the exchange of packets between the victim router and the attacker, to subsequently crack the PIN offline. This attack takes advantage of the way in which pseudo-random numbers are generated, since the algorithm used has very little entropy, and allows brute force over the options (Do not confuse with REAVEN) [8].

3.5 Bruce Force Attack

This attack as its name indicates is done trying to enter the network by brute force, in other words, testing passwords until you find the correct one. To start the attack, we must capture a Handshake [9].

What Is a Handshake?
The handshake is the first package that sends a device when connecting correctly with an AP, this package is necessary to be able to perform dictionary attacks. One of the ways to force a handshake is by launching a de-authentication attack but it does not always work.

There are also several software's that can perform dictionary attacks using our hashing or our graphics cards, so no dictionary is needed, and it increases the number of keys that can be tested per second, but we will require a powerful graphics card to do it [10].

4 Methodology

Ubuntu 17.04 will be used to execute the script provided by WhiteHat to obtain information that an android 6.1 cellphone, Asus makes through the WiFi network. The vulnerability is especially powerful in Linux and Android because the operating system can be tricked into re-installing a zero-key encryption key to obtain sensitive information that would normally be virtually impossible to crack.

For the other desktop systems (Windows and MAC), a large number of packages are required to crack them, but it can be achieved. However, due to the great ease that these systems have for obtaining updates, this vulnerability, as long as the systems are up to date and supported versions are used (Windows 7, 8, 10, MAC OS 10.8 or greater) should not represent a threat in the medium and long term and even short term due to the speed at which critical security updates are released in these systems.

Android phones are especially susceptible to this attack because manufacturers do not usually release updates after a year that the cell phone has gone to the market, causing security bugs to remain in cellphones without support, and the same happens with IoT, since to generate updates for the great variety of electronic articles that use this protocol is not viable for the manufacturers due to its great diversity.

5 Implementation

5.1 Preparation of the Network

An 802.11n Wi-Fi network will be created using as a point of access a computer running Ubuntu Gnome 17.10, with the software installed by default for this purpose, this network has the name testnetwork, and password "ZXCvbnm1234#*", as it can be seen it has a secure password according to general Internet standards: it has several numbers, letters and special characters.

5.2 Preparing the Attack for Android

The Python code provided by WhiteHat is executed, adding as argument the network controller, the name of the network to attack and the MAC address of the device to be attacked (only a specific device can be attacked).

The tool starts the search for the protected WiFi network objective and clones that network in a different channel, this in order to manipulate reliably the recognition messages (handshake) that is required for the use of the weakness discovered in WPA2.

Then it ensures that the user of the Android device can access the internet through our cloned network. Additionally, we execute the tool textbf sslstrip that will try to remove the additional protection textit https from incorrectly configured websites (as in the case of textit uk.match.com).

Wireshark will be used to capture all the data that the client will be transmitting.

5.3 Choosing with Page Will Visit the Cellphone

To show the theft of information, a web page with an additional layer of security that can be observed by the extra notice in the URL bar will be used, however the identification of this network has been incorrectly configured, allowing another desauthentification attack to deactivate that barrier.

5.4 Running the Android Attack

Turn on the Android phone and start the WiFi connection and initially try to connect to the original network which is not the purpose of the attack, which is resolved by sending special WiFi telegrams to the Android device which forces it to change the channel making it connect to our cloned network. Eston allows us to reliably manipulate the messages and carry out the key reset attack against the 4-way handshake (see Annex 1).

Normally after executing the reinstallation of the key, the Android device will reuse nonces (arbitrary numbers) when encrypting data frames and this allows us to recover the encrypted data, however due to an implementation error Android reinstalls an encryption key in zero which makes it trivial to intercept and decipher the transmitted data. Now if we observe by Wireshark captured packages are perfectly readable (usually encrypted) and if from the Android device is accessed with username and password to uk.match.com, such sensitive information is perfectly visible only by viewing the packages without having the password of the WiFi network (see Annex 2).

6 Blindage

This implementation error is easily soluble in computer systems as long as the operating system is kept up to date and the system version has support. In the case of Android systems due to the lack of updates, there are two options: Use mobile networks or wait for the Internet service provider to apply a firmware solution in the access points. Until then use a mobile network or a computer for processes that require sending sensitive information through the network, such as initial session on a bank's website, etc. Currently many companies are solving this weakness in all their devices, or at least those that have active support; the complete list can be found at http://www.zdnet.com/article/here-is-every-patch-for-krack-wi-attack-available-right-now/.

7 Results

In general, the tools used to audit networks and execute the attacks described in the related jobs "section are not effective in the WPA2 protocol", or they do not work most of the time, and when they do they take a very high amount of time in breaking the security, and initially get the password of the network to then get sensitive information.

The KRACK attack, however, demonstrates an extremely high effectiveness under relatively common circumstances (using an Android 6.0 phone or higher without support), and is able to obtain sensitive in formation even without knowing the password, and in real time.

References

1. https://github.com/vanhoefm/krackattacksscripts
2. https://techcrunch.com/2017/10/16/hereswhat-you-can-do-to-protect-yourself-from-thekrack-wi_-vulnerability/
3. https://www.krackattacks.com/
4. Vanhoef, M.: Key Reinstallation Attacks: Forcing Nonce Reuse in WPA2
5. Li, Y.: No-Match Attacks and Robust Partnering Definitions—Defining Trivial Attacks for Security Protocols is Not Trivial

6. http://home.bt.com/techgadgets/computing/windows-7/windows-7-support-end-1136408131 5419
7. https://en.wikipedia.org/wiki/MacOS
8. InteropNet Labs: What's Wrong With WEP?
9. http://www.zdnet.com/article/here-is-everypatch-for-krack-wi-_-attack-availablerightnow/
10. SANS Institute InfoSec Reading Room, Wireless Network Audits using Open Source tools

Adaptive ARMA Based Prediction of CPU Consumption of Servers into Datacenters

Fréjus A. R. Gbaguidi[1,3], Selma Boumerdassi[1(✉)], Ruben Milocco[2],
and Eugéne C. Ezin[3]

[1] Conservatoire National des Arts et Métiers/CEDRIC, Paris, France
selma.boumerdassi@inria.fr
[2] Universidad Nacional Comahue, Buenos Aires 1400, 8300 Neuquén, Argentina
[3] Université d'Abomey Calavi/IMSP, Cotonou, Benin

Abstract. The optimization of the energy consumed by data centers
is a major concern. Several techniques have tried in vain to overcome
this issue for many years. In this panoply, predictive approaches start to
emerge. They consist in predicting in advance the resource requirement
of the Datacenter's servers in order to reserve their right quantities at the
right time and thus avoid either the waste caused by their over-supplying
or the performance problems caused by their under-supplying. In this
article, we explored the performance of ARMA models in the realization
of this type of prediction. It appears that with good selection of parameters, the ARMA models produce reliable predictions but also about 30%
higher than those performed with naive methods. These results could be
used to feed virtual machine management algorithms into Cloud Datacenters, particularly in the decision-making of their placement or migration for the rationalization of provisioned resources.

Keywords: Datacenter · ARMA · Prediction · Energy consumption

1 Introduction

The march of the world to the all-digital does not stop. All the vital sectors of
the economy to sport and health are transformed day after day on the common
base of computer technologies. With the emergence of social Internet and mobile
terminals, big data and the Internet of things, there is almost no limit in men's
quest to improve their everyday lives with ever more sophisticated tools. To
curb this non-stop evolution, virtualization technologies and cloud computing
have been improved to meet the need for speed and handling of large amount
of data. Starting in the past with enterprise computing in which many servers
and storage arrays are deployed for each specific needs of the business, cloud
computing introduces novels ways of hosting information systems based on virtualization. Based now in single datacenters, the computing of many companies from the least sensitive to the most demanding, Cloud operators therefore

© Springer Nature Switzerland AG 2019
É. Renault et al. (Eds.): MSPN 2018, LNCS 11005, pp. 277–288, 2019.
https://doi.org/10.1007/978-3-030-03101-5_23

inherit obligations to ensure the satisfaction of users' quality of service requirements while minimizing the amount of resources deployed. The virtualization techniques in perpetual evolution bring a part of the solution to this equation. In the face of increasing demand for cloud services, operators generally undertake to virtualize all or part of the deployed infrastructure, starting from switches to servers via storage devices and firewalls. Hypervisors, Network Function Virtualization (NV/NFV) and Software Defined Network (SDN) have all significantly improved the design of hosting systems and enabled the success of cloud computing services. However, the legitimate requirements of users to operate their online services without the risk of disconnection require operators to oversize the infrastructure and thus minimize the congestion factors of servers or storage spaces. Unfortunately, this engineering constraint seems to be very expensive in terms of the amount of energy deployed to power some non-use or underutilized infrastructure. Experts are increasingly concerned about an explosion in the energy demand of the cloud computing industry, which could surpass that of aeronautics by 2020 if suitable solutions are not provided [6]. From then on, new techniques were invented to optimize the quantities of resources deployed to satisfy their users' needs. Some methods involve monitoring underutilized resources and turning them off manually. Others automate this task by setting high and low resource occupancy thresholds from which an action is triggered to readjust their affectations. It is also possible to implement more dynamic methods consisting on observing trends in traffic arriving on servers and defining the corresponding mathematical formulas in order to determine in a timely manner the necessary reassignment plans. This last category of strategy called the predictive approach has already produced quite satisfactory results. It is a question of finding, on the basis of an analysis of the trends in solicitation of the hardware resources of the servers, the distribution plans of virtual machines which best prevent the under-consumption and thus generating energy losses, or over-consumption which may lead to unavailability of services and violation of SLAs. Several methods compete for this purpose. Their choice depends strongly on the type of problem, the objectives pursued and the types of data available. The simplest method is the naive method of transferring the previous value as a prediction to the immediate horizon. Although it produces acceptables results, we choose here to implement a more robust method based on ARMA models. It is then necessary to demonstrate the adaptability of this method for the case of our study and formalize the approach of it's implementation. This will enable us to develop a reliable technique for predicting future CPU consumption on virtuals servers within Datacenters and to anticipate the decision to adjust their placement and then rationalize the consumption of the supplied electrical power. We will also demonstrate the reliability of the results of our model in comparison with those obtained with the naive method. The rest of this article is as follows: We will present in the second section the similars works to ours, then we will discuss the theoretical framework of ARMA models in Sect. 3 before presenting in Sect. 4 the approach of implementation of our method, followed by simulations and results in Sect. 5 and finally, we'll conclude this work.

2   Related Works

The predictive models are used in many cases. In the field of cloud computing these methods are increasingly sought in particular for the prediction of resource requests to the servers in order to improve their planning. In the goal of maximization of the use of server resources, [10] showed that it is possible to use the prediction of traffic using the HoltWinters and Box Jenkins autoregressive models and develop a system that assess the number of servers to maintain in operation during the night. A resource planning solution based on the prediction was also developed by [5]. Based on the prediction of resources demand they achieve a dynamic algorithm consolidation of servers and resource allocation to reduce the number of physical servers in operation. [2] also use ARIMA and Holt models to predict the traffic and energy consumption for the prevention of peaks and supplies improving.

To overcome the shortcomings of autoscalling, [1,8] tested the impact of ARMA type models on resource planning and established that by this means, allowances and resources deallocation plans are respecting the QoS constraints. All these papers while pursued the same goal with ours, did not handle real Datacenters dataset but generally generate synthetics workloads to validate their assumptions. Our approach is to test the reliability of a so popular statistics tools ARMA on Google cluster data. The interest is to perform these experiments on data coming from a real data center to qualify the result to generalization. We process approximately 29 days of data on five of the most requested servers to catch maximum resource consumption trends as part of our future work.

3   Theoretical Framework

3.1   AR Process

An autoregressive process is a process where an observation at time t is written as a linear combination of past observations plus some white noise [9]. The time series $\{X_t : t \geq 0\}$ is an autoregressive process $AR(X)$ of order p with $(p > 0)$ if it can be written in the following form:

$$x_t = \sum_{k=1}^{p} a_k x_{t-k} + \epsilon_t \tag{1}$$

where $a_k (k = 1, 2, \cdots, p)$ are the parameters of the model and ϵ_t is an arbitrary input sequence of the $AR(x)$ process. Using the forward shift operator Z, where $x_{t+1} = Z x_t$, it can be written as,

$$A(Z)x_t = \epsilon_t \tag{2}$$

with

$$A(Z) = 1 - a_1 Z - a_2 Z^2 - \cdots - a_p Z^p$$

3.2 MA Process

We say that the sequence $\{x_t : t \geq 0\}$ is a moving average process $MA(\epsilon)$ of order q with $(q > 0)$ if it can be written in the following form:

$$x_t = \sum_{k=1}^{p} b_k \epsilon_{t-k} + \epsilon_t, \tag{3}$$

where the $b_k (k = 1, 2, \cdots, q)$ are the parameters of the model. In this case we write, [7]

$$x(t) = MA(Z)\epsilon_t \tag{4}$$

with

$$B(Z) = 1 + b_1 Z + b_2 Z^2 + \cdots + b_q Z^q.$$

3.3 ARMA Models

- Definition: The combination of both the autoregressive and the moving average processes is called $ARMA(p, q)$ where p and q are the orders of the AR and MA components respectively. In terms of prediction, $ARMA$ models are frequently used in particular because of their adaptability to a wide range of data types, [3] and [4]. A process is called ARMA (p, q) if there exist real sequences $\{\varphi_k\}$ and $\{\epsilon_k\}$ such that

$$x_t = \sum_{k=1}^{p} a_k x_{t-k} + \epsilon_t + \sum_{j=1}^{q} b_j \epsilon_{t-j}, \tag{5}$$

where $\{\epsilon_t\} \sim N(0, \sigma_\epsilon^2)$ is a white sequence. We can also use the polynomials $\varphi(B)$ and $\theta(B)$ to rewrite this model under the form:

$$A(Z)x_t = B(Z)\epsilon_t.$$

- Model order: Determining the best value of p and q is called model order identification. There are several error criteria used for model identification, they aim at determining the best model that is the model minimizing an error criterion. We can cite the most frequently used that are the Akaike's Information Criterion (AIC) and the Bayesian Information Criteria (BIC). These criteria apply a log-likelihood function and penalize more complex models having a great number of parameters. More precisely, let $\log L$ denote the value of the maximized log-likelihood objective function for a model with k parameters fit to n data points, we have:

$$AIC = -2\log L + 2(p+q)$$

$$BIC = -2\log L + \log n(p+q)$$

AIC is used when the observation size is small relative to the model dimension, usually $n/(p+q) < 40$. For the BIC criterion, the penalty is also function of the sample size. The models providing the smallest values of the selected error criterion are chosen. These indicators will be used to analyze the optimum ratio $(p+q, w)$, with w the size of the sliding horizon of past samples, for this type of application by using typical records.

- Parameters identification of an ARMA model: Let us assume the following quadratic cost over an horizon of t past samples:

$$V_t = \frac{1}{2} \sum_{i=1}^{t} \epsilon_i^2 \tag{6}$$

where ϵ_t is the prediction error given by

$$\epsilon_t = x_t - p_t \tag{7}$$

where p_t is the prediction using the $ARMA(p,q)$ model with parameters vector $\theta_t = [a_{1,t}, \ldots, a_{p,t}, b_{1,t}, \ldots, b_{p,t}]^T$ that minimizes V_t, where T means transposed. The parameters vector θ_t is unknown and it is estimated by using the well-known Recursive Prediction Error Method (RPEM). To this end, the Gauss-Newton recursive algorithm over the cost function is used. The algorithm and its properties are given by the following theorem: **Theorem:** Consider the cost function V_t to be minimized, with respect to the parameter vector θ_t, by the following Gauss Newton recursion:

$$\epsilon_t = x_t - p_t \tag{8}$$

$$M_t = M_{t-1} - \frac{M_{t-1}\epsilon_t'\epsilon_t'^T M_{t-1}}{1 + \epsilon_t'^T M_{t-1}\epsilon_t'} \tag{9}$$

$$\theta_t = \theta_{t-1} + M_t\epsilon_t'\epsilon_t'^T \tag{10}$$

where t is the iteration step, M_t is a square matrix of dimension $(p+q)$; and ϵ_t' is a column vectors derivative of ϵ_t with respect to the parameters in θ_t. Then, the following holds: θ_t converges as $k \to \infty$ with probability 1 to one element of the set of minimizers.

$$\left\{ \theta | \sigma'^2 = 0 \right\} \tag{11}$$

where σ'^2 is the derivative of the prediction error variance with respect to θ. Proof: See L. Ljung, T. Soderstrom, (1983). Theory and Practice of Recursive Identification. MIT Press. 1987.

The initial values are as follows: $t = 1$, M_0 is the identity matrix and ϵ_t is a vector of zeros. θ_0 is obtained by doing the least squared estimation from data. This recursive algorithm can be repeated several times over the observation window where the parameters obtained in the previous stage are used as initial values of the new stage. In the convergence vector optimal parameters are obtained at each step t.

- Sliding window strategy: To improve the accuracy of the predictions, we propose to use an adaptive $ARMA(p,q)$ model: at each time t, the parameters of the $ARMA(p,q)$ model are computed on a sliding window of size w. More precisely, at time $t - 1$, the $ARMA(p,q)$ model predicts the value of the time series at time t according using the w last observations in the window $[t - w, t - 1]$ to compute the vector parameter θ of the $ARMA(p,q)$ model. This principle is illustrated in Fig. 1. Then, the sliding window moves one step ahead, starting at time $[t - w + 1]$ and ending at time t, the parameters are computed using the observations in this window, and the prediction for time $t + 1$ is given. Notice that the models order (p, q) is fixed, whereas the computation of parameter vector θ is done at each time t using an iterative parameter estimation algorithm. That is why the $ARMA(p,q)$ model is said adaptive.

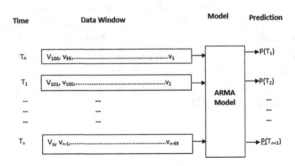

Fig. 1. Sliding windows scheme

4   Problem Statement

Within Datacenters, manufacturers now provide physical servers with large CPU, memory, or disk resources to enable the creation of high volumes of virtual servers. These machines receive the many quick queries that come from users whose needs do not stop. Virtual servers concurrently share physical machine resources and common reserved values of them are usually underused or overused. Underutilization of resources results in under-consumption of the electrical energy supplied to the physical machine since most server power supplies provide their rated power regardless of the utilization rate, while overuse may cause violation of service level agreements often established between Cloud operators and their customers. Our objective is therefore to monitor the futures needs of resources by virtual servers in order to ensure that they will be provided and consumed at optimally. To do so, it is essential to plan in advance the occupancy rates of these resources. Several methods exist. We try to use statistical methods based on ARMA models to predict at a given time the probable values of the needs of the resources of physical servers within Datacenters. In this framework, we use the historical data from a Google Datacenter, from which we extract the processor consumption values on 5 servers during 29 days of data collection. The graphs of CPU usage on these servers are presented in Fig. 2.

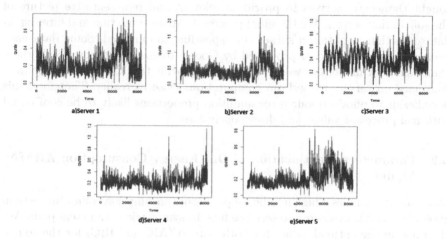

Fig. 2. Processor consumption of 5 Google Datacenters servers during 29 days

On this data we sampled per hour of use, we determine the corresponding ARMA model and then we calculate a prediction of consumption over the next hour. This result is then compared with that obtained on the same data by applying the "naive" method.

5   Simulations and Results

5.1   Dataset Description

The data used in the context of this work comes from traces recently published by Google [11]. These data refer to traffic collected for 29 days in a Datacenter containing approximately 12000 servers with various features. These traces are a rare one which provide traffic data from real data centers of significant size that can afford to make relevant analyzes and draw credible conclusions. All data can be divided into 3 categories namely: (i) information and events on servers, including the creation, modification and deletion of virtual servers in the data center; (ii) data on requests and tasks performed by servers and (iii) information on resource consumption of all servers throughout the data collection period. It is on this latter category of data that we focus our analysis. The folder task_usage indeed contain a collection of amounts of CPU (processor), RAM, disk space etc. consumed by the various tasks performed on each server in the data center. Because of the number of servers involved, the duration of collection (every 5 min for 29 days) and the volume of traffic processed in the Datacenter, the folder task_usage proves very large size (160 gigabyte) and therefore requires enormous computing power to processing and analysis.

We are particularly interested in processor quantities consumed on the most sought Datacenter servers to provide a relevant and representative picture of the solicitation servers. We therefore proceed to some extraction and filtering on data collection to obtain a subset corresponding to our need. Some data have been deliberately elided or processed by Google to ensure privacy. While these changes do not hinder our work, they do not provide true CPU values resources consumed on servers to perform computations close to reality. Therefore, this is sufficient to obtain resource consumption proportions likely to be confronted with real processor values and draw conclusions.

5.2 Parameters Identification of Our Energy Consumption ARMA Model

Our data file includes a high number of processor consumption values (more than 8000 per server), we choose to test the first 15 symmetric parameters pairs. We then obtain the optimal values for both criteria (AIC and BIC) for the couple $p = q = 14$. With these values, we apply in a sliding window our model to the dataset to obtain a prediction based on the $w = 100$ previous observations through a recursive algorithm. Using the proposed adaptive $ARMA$ prediction method to the five servers data both data and predictions are shown in Fig. 2.

5.3 Accuracy of Resources Consumption Prediction

The prediction errors are contained in an interval $[-0.2, 0.2]$ with a centering on 0 as shown in the histograms of the residuals, ϵ_t in Fig. 3. Thus, the estimations are not biased and almost gaussian distributed. Also they are uncorrelated as shown in Fig. 4 which means the predictions are optimal.

In order to have a comparison with a benchmark, we will compare the performance of our ARMA(14,14)-predictor with the naive predictor. The naive method is just to use the measurement x_{t-1} as prediction of x_t. In Table 1 it is presented the comparative metric of prediction errors obtained as the ratio between the standard deviation of predictions and the standard deviation of observations, which is in fact the squared root of the Mean Squared Error, MSE, as follows:

$$MSE^{1/2} = \sigma(x_t - p_{t+1})/\sigma(x_t)$$

of the prediction with the two methods on the 5 servers (Figs. 5 and 6).

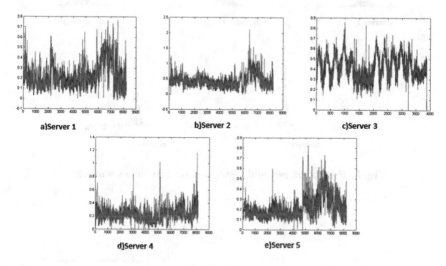

Fig. 3. Processors consumption prediction

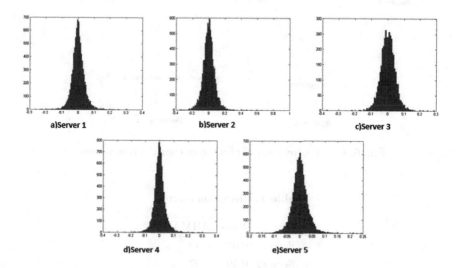

Fig. 4. Prediction residual histogram

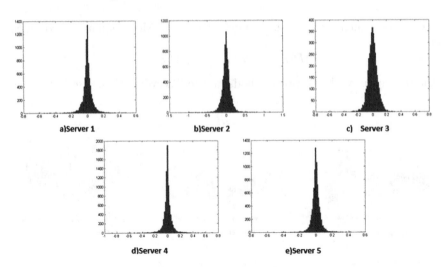

Fig. 5. Prediction residual histogram on 100 values windows

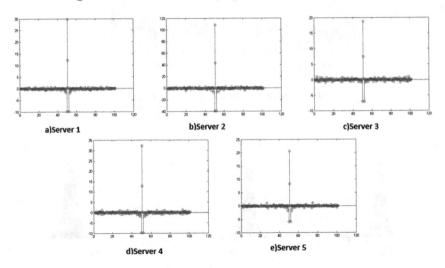

Fig. 6. Cross correlation of processors consumption values

Table 1. Prediction errors

Server	Naive	ARMA
Server1	0.64	0.40
Server2	0.59	0.37
Server3	0.58	0.36
Server4	0.69	0.43
Server5	0.50	0.31

6   Conclusion

The search for solutions to optimize the use of resources within Datacenters deserves to be deepened on the understanding that the energy needs in the future will not decrease and above all, that energy is still not an extensible resource at infinity. Techniques compete to achieve this goal. However, it remains a challenge to establish models that can be applied to different scenarios and adapt to the real-time constraints and huge amount of data that cloud computing imposes. Through this article, we have tried to explore the possibility of adopting a predictive approach to mastering the resource requirements of a Datacenter over time in order to develop on this basis the best supply plans for these resources. Our work consisted in developing an ARMA model adapted to the type of data that is processed within Datacenters relative to the consumption of processor resources and to realize real-time predictions of their future needs. To do this, we relied on a data collection from a Google Datacenter in which we extracted, on 5 servers, the averages of processor consumption over 5 min over a total of 29 days. We then realized sliding windows of 100 data which allow us each time to predict the needs of processor resources in the horizon of one hour. Our results clearly show that the ARMA models, when the parameters are well determined, constitute a reliable means of predicting this kind of data since the residual is containing into $[-0.2, 0.2]$ interval. This proves that most predictions are very close to the real values of consumption. The other contribution of this work was to compare our predictions based on the ARMA model with those made using the naive method. The results confirm once again the performance of our ARMA model, with predictive accuracy of about 30% higher than the naive method. Overall, predictive methods could significantly improve efficient use of physicals resources within Datacenters and thus promote the optimization of energy resources. The achievement of these results with the ARMA models and a real Datacenters experiment situation, is a good opening towards achieving this goal, since it could be integrated in the algorithms of virtuals machines placement or migrations allowing the optimization of electric power supplied.

References

1. Davis, I., Hemmati, H., Holt, R.C., Godfrey, M.W., Neuse, D., Mankovskii, S.: Storm prediction in a cloud. In: 2013 ICSE Workshop on Principles of Engineering Service-Oriented Systems (PESOS), pp. 37–40. IEEE (2013)
2. Hao, M.C. et al.: A visual analytics approach for peak-preserving prediction of large seasonal time series. In: Computer Graphics Forum, vol. 30, pp. 691–700. Wiley Online Library (2011)
3. Hibon, M., Makridakis, S.: ARMA models and the Box-Jenkins methodology (1997)
4. Hoff, J.C.: A Practical Guide to Box-Jenkins Forecasting. Lifetime Learning Publications, Belmont (1983)
5. Huang, Q., Shuang, K., Xu, P., Li, J., Liu, X., Su, S.: Prediction-based dynamic resource scheduling for virtualized cloud systems. J. Netw. 9(2), 375–383 (2014)

6. Kellner, I.L.: Turn down the heat. J. Bus. Strategy **16**(6), 22–23 (1995)
7. Robinson, P.M.: The estimation of a nonlinear moving average model. Stoch. Process. Their Appl. **5**(1), 81–90 (1977)
8. Roy, N., Dubey, A., Gokhale, A.: Efficient autoscaling in the cloud using predictive models for workload forecasting. In: 2011 IEEE International Conference on Cloud Computing (CLOUD), pp. 500–507. IEEE (2011)
9. Yule, G.U.: On a method of investigating periodicities in disturbed series, with special reference to Wolfer's sunspot numbers. Philos. Trans. R. Soc. Lond. Ser. A **226**, 267–298 (1927)
10. Vondra, T., Sedivy, J.: Maximizing utilization in private iaas clouds with heterogenous load through time series forecasting. Int. J. Adv. Syst. Meas. **6**(1–2), 149–165 (2013)
11. Wilkes, J.: More Google cluster data. Google research blog, November 2011

Congestion Control in a Location Service for VANETs

Kim van Gulik[1,2], Frank Phillipson[1(✉)], and Hacène Fouchal[3]

[1] TNO, The Hague, The Netherlands
frank.phillipson@tno.nl
[2] Erasmus University, Rotterdam, The Netherlands
[3] CReSTIC, Université de Champagne-Ardenne, Reims, France

Abstract. Vehicular ad-hoc networks are self-organized networks to provide communication between the vehicles. It is challenging to determine a routing protocol for the communication between the vehicles since the vehicles are moving in different speeds and directions, which causes a rapidly changing network topology. Other approaches in literature assign traffic to the best available path, possibly causing congestion in the network. In this paper, we determine the optimal route of intersections based on a penalty function to obtain load balancing in the network.

Keywords: VANET · Location based routing · Congestion control

1 Introduction

Vehicular ad hoc networks (VANETs) are self-organized networks in which the vehicles are the mobile nodes in the network. They are used to provide communication between vehicles, the nodes in the network. A VANET is a specific type of Mobile Ad Hoc Networks (MANET). Communication between vehicles will happen through multiple hops if vehicles cannot directly communicate with each other. The message will then be relayed by other vehicles until it is received by the destination vehicle. Since vehicles are moving at different speeds and in different directions, the network topology changes rapidly. Therefore, it is challenging to design a routing protocol for the communication between vehicles. In addition to the high mobility of the vehicles, the broadcast transmission range is also limited. Thus, it is preferred to have enough vehicles on the road to ensure the connection. The data package can get lost if there is no possibility to relay the package or if the connection is disrupted.

The special characteristics of VANETs make it hard to use specific topology-based routing protocols for MANETs. However, the possibility to work with GPS systems within the nodes/cars makes it possible to use position based routing protocols like GSR [5], GPSR [4], A-STAR [7], GyTAR [3] and IDTAR [1].

Routing of packets is very important for the success of VANETs, it will make the difference whether network and application requirements will be met. In [6] a location service is proposed for the routing protocol to provide communication

© Springer Nature Switzerland AG 2019
É. Renault et al. (Eds.): MSPN 2018, LNCS 11005, pp. 289–293, 2019.
https://doi.org/10.1007/978-3-030-03101-5_24

between the vehicles. They assume that vehicles are equipped with an on board unit (OBU), these OBUs can communicate with other OBUs (vehicle-to-vehicle communication) or with road side units (vehicle-to-infrastructure communication). The road side units (RSUs) are located at each intersection and they have a limited coverage range and bandwidth. They keep track of the information of the vehicles that are positioned in its coverage range, which includes their location, direction and velocity. Each vehicle knows its information since they are equipped with GPS (Global Positioning System). The RSUs can communicate with location servers which keep track of the information on all vehicles. An illustration of the network is shown in Fig. 1.

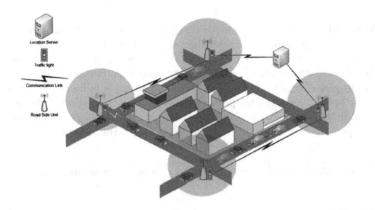

Fig. 1. An illustration of the communication network, in which the communication between the vehicles, the road side units and the location server is shown. Adapted from "A Realistic Location Service for VANETs" by [6].

In the routing algorithm of [6], the optimal route, which consists of a sequence of intersections, will be determined. Improved greedy forwarding [3] will be used to relay the message by the vehicles which are on the path of the sequence of the intersections. When a vehicles wants to send a message to another vehicle, it will send a route request to the nearest RSU. This is possible since it is assumed that each vehicle has a static digital map of all locations of the RSUs. The RSU will send the route request to the location server, which will return the optimal route of intersections. This route reply will then be sent to the source vehicle, which can then relay its message to the destination vehicle by forwarding the message to vehicles that are along the optimal route of intersections. The location server will determine the optimal route of intersections based on the length and the connectivity of the route. If the route was already determined previously, it will return the route that is saved in the routing table.

A drawback of the approach is that most data is transmitted on certain roads with higher connectivity, which can lead to data congestion on these roads. Roads that can also provide a good connection to forward the messages are not used since these roads are not the most dense. Another drawback is that the method does not take into consideration that the traffic density of the roads changes over time, since the best found path between intersections is not updated. In this paper we propose an improvement of the method by [6], by modifying the determination of the optimal route of intersections and frequently updating the selection of the optimal route.

2 Contribution

In the current implementation of the Location Service [6], the best path of intersections is determined based on the normalized length of the path and the connectivity of the path. Dijkstra's shortest path algorithm [2] is used to determine the optimal path. We introduce a penalty cost that is assigned to roads that were selected in recent time to avoid congestion of the network.

Let $G = (V, E)$ be the graph with vertex set V and edge set E. The network consists of vertices (the intersections) and edges (the roads), where an edge (i, j) is represented by the nodes i and j. The cost of edge (i, j) can be defined as

$$cost_{(i,j)} = \alpha \cdot L_{(i,j)} + \beta \cdot LC_{(i,j)} + \gamma \cdot P_{(i,j)}, \tag{1}$$

where $L_{(i,j)}$ is the normalized length of edge (i, j), $LC_{(i,j)}$ is the link connectivity and $P_{(i,j)}$ is the penalty which will be assigned for a certain time to a road when it is used for forwarding a message.

The normalized length L is defined as

$$L_{(i,j)} = \frac{length_{(i,j)}}{max(length_{(i,j)} \mid \forall (i,j) \in E)}, \tag{2}$$

in which the length of edge (i, j) is divided by the maximum road length in the graph set V, having a value in the interval $[0, 1]$.

The link connectivity function LC that is introduced in [6] to provide a solution to decrease the probability of package loss, also takes a value between zero and one and it represents the average of the remaining communication distance between consecutive vehicles on a road. The link between the vehicles represents the remaining distance in which they are able to communicate with each other. The link between vehicles v_m and v_n is defined as

$$Link(v_m, v_n) = \begin{cases} R_{tr} - distance(v_m, v_n), & \text{if } distance(v_m, v_n) \leq R_{tr} \\ 0, & \text{otherwise,} \end{cases} \tag{3}$$

where R_{tr} is the range of transmission. The mean link is the average of the link values for the all N vehicles on edge (i, j). It is formulated as

$$ML_{(i,j)} = \frac{Link(J_a, v_1) + \sum_{m=1}^{N-1} Link(v_m, v_{m+1}) + Link(v_N, J_b)}{N + 1}, \tag{4}$$

where J_a and J_b are the intersections on the sides of edge (i, j). The connectivity metric LC of edge (i, j) is then defined as

$$LC_{(i,j)} = 1 - \frac{ML_{(i,j)}}{R_{tr}}. \tag{5}$$

The penalty of edge (i, j) is expressed as

$$P_{(i,j)} = \frac{\text{package bytes sent in the last period along edge (i, j)}}{\text{channel capacity}}, \tag{6}$$

in which the total number of package bytes that are selected to be forwarded along edge (i, j) in the last time period, is divided by the channel capacity, also defined on the interval $[0, 1]$.

3   Simulation Results

We simulated the two approaches, the original of [6] and our adjusted version, by creating a Manhattan grid of 1500×1500 meters and 144 intersections. The positions of the vehicles are randomly drawn from the uniform distribution. To make a distinction between connectivity for the roads, each road has a possibility to have no vehicles on the road, to have a low density, a normal density or a high density. The location of the vehicles will be drawn each 50 ms, whereas the density of the roads will be drawn each 2000 ms.

The cost function parameters in Eq. 1 are set to $\alpha = 0.4$, $\beta = 0.3$ and $\gamma = 0.3$. The simulation is ran for sending 10,000 messages, in which every 50 ms a message is sent with a package size of 512 bytes. The bandwidth capacity is equal to 2000 bytes. Figure 2a shows how often a road is selected when the route selection is based on the length and the connectivity of the path. In Fig. 2b congestion control is performed using the penalty function. The figure shows that the load is more balanced over all the roads.

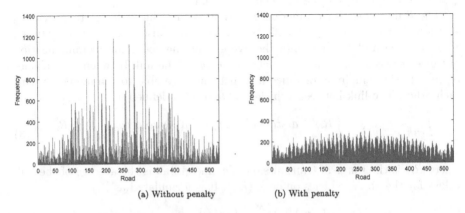

(a) Without penalty   (b) With penalty

Fig. 2. The number of times a road is selected for forwarding the message

The average length of the paths is not affected by the inclusion of the penalty function. The average link connectivity of the used links however decreases with about 19.0%.

4   Conclusion

In this paper an improvement of the method by [6] was proposed. We introduced congestion control in the communication network by assigning a penalty cost to the roads that were selected in the previous time period. This makes sure that the load will be balanced over the roads. The results show that the load is more balanced over the roads without affecting the length of the routes. Extensive simulations need to be done to examine how the alteration of the method by [6] influences the packet delivery ratio and the end-to-end delay.

References

1. Ahmed, A.I.A., Gani, A., Ab Hamid, S.H., Khan, S., Guizani, N., Ko, K.: Intersection-based distance and traffic-aware routing (IDTAR) protocol for smart vehicular communication. In: 2017 13th International on Wireless Communications and Mobile Computing Conference (IWCMC), pp. 489–493. IEEE (2017)
2. Dijkstra, E.W.: A note on two problems in connexion with graphs. Numer. Math. 1(1), 269–271 (1959)
3. Jerbi, M., Senouci, S.M., Rasheed, T., Ghamri-Doudane, Y.: Towards efficient geographic routing in urban vehicular networks. IEEE Trans. Veh. Technol. 58(9), 5048–5059 (2009)
4. Karp, B., Kung, H.T.: GPSR: greedy perimeter stateless routing for wireless networks. In: Proceedings of the 6th Annual International Conference on Mobile Computing and Networking, pp. 243–254. ACM (2000)
5. Lochert, C., Hartenstein, H., Tian, J., Fussler, H., Hermann, D., Mauve, M.: A routing strategy for vehicular ad hoc networks in city environments. In: IEEE Proceedings of the Intelligent Vehicles Symposium, 2003, pp. 156–161. IEEE (2003)
6. Nebbou, T., Fouchal, H., Lehsaini, M., Ayaida, M.: An urban location service for VANETs. In: Concurrency and Computation: Practice and Experience, pp. 1–14. Wiley (2017)
7. Seet, B.-C., Liu, G., Lee, B.-S., Foh, C.-H., Wong, K.-J., Lee, K.-K.: A-STAR: a mobile ad hoc routing strategy for metropolis vehicular communications. In: Mitrou, N., Kontovasilis, K., Rouskas, G.N., Iliadis, I., Merakos, L. (eds.) NETWORKING 2004. LNCS, vol. 3042, pp. 989–999. Springer, Heidelberg (2004). https://doi.org/10.1007/978-3-540-24693-0_81

Latency and Network Lifetime Trade-Off in Geographic Multicast Routing for Multi-Sink Wireless Sensor Networks

Lucas Leão[✉] and Violeta Felea

FEMTO-ST institute, Univ. Bourgogne Franche-Comté, CNRS, DISC,
16 route de Gray, 25030 Besançon, France
{lucas.leao,violeta.felea}@femto-st.fr

Abstract. The deployment of multiple sinks in Wireless Sensor Networks may provide better reliability, timely communication and longevity, depending on the routing strategy. Moreover, geographic routing is a powerful strategy to avoid the costs related to maintaining high network knowledge. In this paper, we present a Geographic Multicast Routing solution (GeoM), focused on the latency and network lifetime trade-off. Our solution considers a linear combination of network metrics during the decision process of the next hop. Packets are forwarded to all sinks, and duplications are defined on the fly during the forwarding. The network lifetime is addressed with an energy balance strategy and a trade-off between progress and energy cost. We make use of the maximum energy consumption as an indication of the network lifetime. Simulation results show that GeoM has an overall better performance than the existing solutions, with improvements of approximately 11% for the average latency, and 54% for the maximum energy consumption.

Keywords: Multi-Sink Wireless Sensor Networks · Routing
Multicast · Latency · Network lifetime · Geographic routing

1 Introduction

A Wireless Sensor Networks (WSN) is defined as a network composed of small wireless devices with limited capacity in terms of memory, processing and communication range. They share a common task of collecting and forwarding sensed data from various sources to a base station (sink) [2]. Applications of WSN may include environment monitoring in smart buildings and smart cities, military surveillance, planetary exploration etc.

The design of a WSN may consider different techniques for communication optimization, as for instance, the deployment of multiple base stations. A Multi-Sink WSN (MS-WSN) provides an immediate performance gain in terms of latency reduction [12]. Depending on the routing strategy, the deployment of multiple sinks also increases the network reliability, since packets may be forwarded to multiple different destinations.

© Springer Nature Switzerland AG 2019
É. Renault et al. (Eds.): MSPN 2018, LNCS 11005, pp. 294–310, 2019.
https://doi.org/10.1007/978-3-030-03101-5_25

In MS-WSNs, the final application drives the way communications take place. The information may be collected and forwarded following different models in order to cope with the application objective and requirements. As for instance, in order to meet a specific requirement such as reliability, the communication scheme may be designed as a many-to-many (any multiple sinks), or a many-to-all (all sinks) solution. These models require different routing specifications and strategies.

The routing perspective of the communication schemes are:

- **Unicast:** once the path towards a sink is defined, the route is reused until a predefined objective is no longer satisfied. As for instance, in real-time applications routes may change only when the maximum tolerable delay is surpassed.
- **Anycast:** information is addressed to a group of sinks. It can be 1-anycast, when information is forwarded to anyone of the sinks in the group, or k-anycast when information must reach any k sinks. The anycast routing may be applied to either increase network reliability (k sinks) or extend the network lifetime (any one sink).
- **Multicast:** information is addressed to all sinks in the network. The information of a single sensor node must be replicated and forwarded to each one of the sinks. Multicast approaches are focused on network reliability.

In this work we are interested in the case of MS-WSN with Multicast communication scheme, where packets must be forwarded to all sinks in the network. For that, we propose a Geographic Multicast Routing solution (GeoM), focused on reducing latency and increasing the network lifetime. Our algorithm differs from the literature by combining techniques to reduce latency and balance the energy consumption with multicast communication scheme and geographic routing. In geographic routing there is no need for routing tables or a setup phase, since routes are constructed on the fly based on the location information. In our solution, the next hop decision is taken using a linear combination of network metrics along with predefined weights. Based on the amount of consumed energy, the paths are constantly changed during the lifetime of the network, which balances the energy consumption. We also combine and adapt two different void handling techniques, making use of the right-hand rule and the passive participation [4].

The remainder of this paper is organized as follows. Section 2 presents a brief discussion on the existing works in MS-WSN routing. Section 3 describes our assumptions and the system model. Our solution is detailed in Sect. 4, along with the testing scenarios and the discussion of the performance evaluation in Sect. 5. We conclude the paper in Sect. 6 with the future perspectives.

2   Related Work

There are few examples of works treating the many-to-all case. Most of the MS-WSN solutions are designed as unicast and 1-anycast routing protocols, dealing with the many-to-one and many-to-any cases. However, a unicast routing protocol could be used as a many-to-all solution if we assume that packets are duplicated at source and forwarded in sequence. The problem is that the energy consumption rises dramatically, since the number of packets forwarded individually is increased as a function of the number of sinks in the network. On the other hand, k-anycast solutions could be used as a multicast routing protocol if we assume that k equals the amount of sinks in the network. Because of that, in this section we describe both multicast and k-anycast solutions.

2.1 Multicast

In [5] the objective is to relay the messages from multiple sources to multiple sinks while reducing the number of links used to forward the messages. The strategy considers maximizing the overlap of paths from sources to sinks. This way, the same sub-routes, from the point of aggregation up to the splitting point, are used from different sources to forward messages to sinks. The next hop is defined by selecting the neighbors with more path overlaps and serving more sinks. The algorithm also considers a process of changing routes, which is an iterative mechanism that periodically triggers a search for new sub-routes.

The objective in [9] is to identify a routing tree connecting all sources to all destinations with the minimal number of links. The solution applies a searching method to identify an initial non optimal tree, which is improved by consecutive search iterations. The routes are initially constructed based on the hop distance to the sink. Each source has an independent path to each sink. Then, the algorithm tries to merge the independent paths from a source to all sinks, reusing as much as possible the same path. Later, the merge takes place with the sources, trying to determine a point of aggregation and replication. The convergence node is responsible to aggregate the message from the sources and re-split it to the sinks.

Although the works in [5] and [9] describe distributed solutions for multicast routing, they rely on heavy network knowledge in order to perform all the paths optimizations. They are also focused on data aggregation as a method to reduce energy consumption, and not explicitly oriented to latency minimization.

2.2 K-Anycast

The authors in [3] propose RelBAS, a data gathering algorithm with a fault recovery scheme specially designed to assure reliability. The algorithm considers the construction of disjoint trees, rooted at each sink. However, the sensor nodes serving as forwarders are also disjoint, meaning that a node serves as forwarder to exactly one tree. In order to improve reliability, the solution considers forwarding the packet to exactly k sinks, which are decided in advance. The nodes are always part of exactly k trees, in order to forward the packet to the k sinks.

In [8] we find RPKAC, a routing protocol for Rechargeable MS-WSN designed to reduce network latency and optimize the energy consumption, but focused on assuring the delivery by forwarding the packets to k sinks. The authors establish strategies to forward the packets to at least k sinks, at most k sinks and exactly k sinks. The algorithm builds spanning trees rooted at the source node, with nodes sending route request messages in order to define the routing path. The neighbor nodes reply with their cost to reach a sink, and the current node decides to join an existing path with the lowest cost. The cost is calculated based on the linear combination of metrics: hop count, latency, energy cost and energy replenish rate.

The main objective in KanGuRou [14] is to guarantee the packet delivery to exactly k sinks and at the same time reduce the overall energy consumption. The strategy considers a geographic routing towards a set of sinks. The path is constructed in a greedy way. The current node builds a spanning tree to k sinks with minimum cost. The next hop is decided based on the cost of the energy-weighted shortest path (ESP). The solution assumes an adaptable transmission range in order to reduce the energy cost. At each hop, the algorithm calculates the cost over progress and decides to duplicate the packet towards different paths in order to reach k sinks. When a packet is duplicated, it is targeted to a set of specific sinks, in order to assure the delivery. The case of network void areas inherent to geographic routing is handled using a recovery mode with face routing, so packets can be forwarded out of the problematic area.

Routing solutions [3] and [8] are based on the hop-count distance, so the packets are forwarded to the neighbor with the lowest hop-count distance to the sink. This strategy implies either higher network topology knowledge or an important setup phase, with nodes discovering their hop-count distance to each sink. In [14] the focus is on reducing the energy consumption, favoring transmissions to closer nodes. Since the transmission range is variable, the energy cost to transmit a packet to a closer node is reduced. However, the amount of hops is increased and consequently the latency.

3   System Model and Assumptions

We represent a MS-WSN as a graph $G = (V, E)$, where V represents the set of all nodes and E the set of existing wireless links. Each $e \in E$ corresponds to a pair of nodes (i, j) as long as i and j, with $i \in V$ and $j \in V$, are within each other's transmission range (symmetric link). The set of neighbors of i is represented by V_i. We also specify that $V = S \cup N$ where S represents the set of sink nodes and N the set of sensor nodes, with $S \cap N = \emptyset$. The number of sinks is denoted by $|S|$.

We assume that every node is aware of its own geographic position and the geographic position of all sinks. For simplification, the geographic positions are represented by the Cartesian coordinates (x, y), and the distance is always the euclidean distance represented as $|ij|$ with $i, j \in V$. We also assume that packets are generated by sensor nodes only. For the energy consumption, we follow the radio model in [10], defining the consumed energy during transmission:

$$E_{T_x} = E_{elec} \times p + \epsilon_{amp} \times p \times d^2 \tag{1}$$

and the consumed energy during reception:

$$E_{R_x} = E_{elec} \times p \tag{2}$$

where E_{elec} is the dissipated energy for the transmitter/receiver electronics, ϵ_{amp} is the dissipated energy for the transmit amplifier, p is the amount of bits of the message and d is the transmission distance.

We consider two types of networks: with void areas and without void areas. A network with void areas is defined by the existence of a specific node out of the transmission range of a particular sink and for which there is no other neighbor node that presents a better geographic progress towards that sink than the node itself. In summary, $\exists\{n, s_i\}, n \in V, s_i \in S, (n, s_i) \notin E$ such that $|ns_i| < |v_j s_i|$ for all $v_j \in V_n$. Thus, the void area definition is for a node in relation to a sink. Because of that, in a MS-WSN it is possible for a node to be in the void area in relation to one or more sinks.

4   Geographic Multicast Routing

GeoM is a geographic routing protocol for Multi-Sink Wireless Sensor Networks that is capable of forwarding a generated packet to all available sinks in the network using a multicast communication scheme. It is focused on finding the trade-off between latency and the network lifetime. The next hop is selected by the current node based on the calculation of weighted metrics, and the highest intersection among forwarder candidates and sinks. The algorithm can be divided into two steps: filtering and selection. The first step is responsible for filtering the neighbor nodes in order to create a list of candidate forwarders. The filtering takes place by eliminating the neighbor nodes with negative progress and neighbors in void areas. If no neighbor is found, the recovery mode is triggered and a neighbor is selected using a void handling technique. At the same time, a broadcast message is sent to inform the neighbor nodes that the current node is in a void area. The second step is dedicated to effectively selecting the forwarders. The candidates are evaluated based on the weighted metrics, and a forwarder is selected based on the largest intersection of sinks. We also consider a metric called deviation factor, which increases the possibility of intersections by relaxing the constraints of the weighted metrics. Although GeoM does not require massive network knowledge, broadcast messages are used to periodically advertise the existence of neighbor nodes, their void area status and the amount of consumed energy.

4.1   Filtering Process

The filtering process starts with the reception of a packet. The first step is to check if the current node n is a target sink itself. In this case, the node must be removed from the list of destination sinks (S_r), since the packet has reached a

---

Algorithm 1. $GeoM(n, V_n, H, packet)$ - Run at the current node.

Input: n: current node, $packet$: packet to be forwarded, V_n: set of neighbors of n, H: set of neighbor nodes in void areas for a set of sinks

1: $S_r \leftarrow get\_sinks(packet)$ /* Set of target sinks */
2: $p \leftarrow get\_progress(packet)$ /* Progress of the previous hop */
3: **if** $n \in S_r$ **then**
4:      $S_r \leftarrow S_r \backslash \{n\}$
5: **end if**
6: **if** $S_r = \emptyset$ **then**
7:      **return**
8: **end if**
9: $L \leftarrow \emptyset$ /* Set of pairs [candidate, sink] */
10: /* Check if the current node offers a positive progress towards the sinks */
11: /* A negative value means that the packet is in recovery mode */
12: $p_{new} \leftarrow ProgressTowards(n, S_r)$
13: **if** $p_{new} < p$ **then**
14:     /* Select a candidate with the recovery mode using right-hand rule */
15:     $L = Recovery(n, V_n, S')$ /* In this case L has a single candidate */
16:     $ForwardersIntersec(n, L, S_r, packet)$
17:     **return**
18: **end if**
19: /* Look for the neighbors closer to the sinks than the current node */
20: $S' \leftarrow \emptyset$ /* Set of found sinks */
21: **for all** $v_j \in V_n$ **do**
22:     **for all** $s_i \in S_r$ **do**
23:         **if** $dist(n, s_i) > dist(v_j, s_i)$ **and** $\{[v_j, s_i]\} \notin H$ **then**
24:             $L \leftarrow L \cup \{[v_j, s_i]\}$
25:             **if** $S' \cap \{s_i\} = \emptyset$ **then**
26:                 $S' \leftarrow S' \cup \{s_i\}$
27:             **end if**
28:         **end if**
29:     **end for**
30: **end for**
31: **if** $0 < |S'| \leq |S_r|$ **then**
32:     $ForwardersIntersec(n, L, S', packet)$
33: **end if**
34: /* Check if a forwarder was found to all sinks */
35: $S'' \leftarrow S_r \backslash S'$
36: **if** $|S''| > 0$ **then**
37:     /* Notify neighbors about the existence of a void area */
38:     $SendVoidNotification(n, V_n, S'')$
39:     $L = Recovery(n, V_n, S'')$ /* In this case L has a single candidate */
40:     $ForwardersIntersec(n, L, S'', packet)$
41: **end if**
42: **return**

---

target sink (Algorithm 1, line 4). The list of target sinks must be composed of a set of unique and identifiable entities. This is important in order to assure that all packets are delivered to different sinks. If instead we had only a number of target sinks to reach, we would risk delivering all the packets to the same sink, because of the distributed aspect of our solution.

The second step is to check the progress of the current node in relation to the previous hop. If the current node (n) progress to the set of remaining sinks (S_r) represents a negative value compared to the value from the previous hop (line 12), it means that the packet was in Recovery Mode and no positive progress was yet found. In this case the packet must keep the Recovery Mode status and the forwarder candidate is selected using the right-hand rule [4]. The recovery strategy follows the same principles of the works in [11,13] and [14]. In this case, only one node is selected and the packet is directly forwarded to this neighbor.

If the current node presents a positive progress towards the target sinks, the filtering step starts. Based on the neighbor list (V_n) of the current node, the algorithm creates a new list of candidate forwarders (L). The solution selects the neighbor nodes with a positive progress to at least one sink, and excludes the neighbors that have already announced being in a void area (line 23). The H list represents the set of pairs $[v_j, s_i]$ in which v_j is the neighbor node in a void area for the sink s_i. At the same time, a second sink list (S') is created in order to store the found sinks (line 26). If the number of found sinks is smaller than the amount of available sinks, it means that the algorithm could not find a suitable candidate to all sinks (line 35). In this case, the recovery mode is again activated in order to complete the list of candidates. A broadcast message (void announcement) is sent in order to inform the neighbors nodes that the current sink is in a void area (line 38). This strategy is important in order to allow future packets to avoid going through the void area.

4.2   Selection Process

The selection process is called when a forwarder candidate has to be selected. It is responsible for evaluating the list of candidates based on the weighted metrics and searching for the maximum intersection of candidates and sinks in order to avoid duplications. The first step is to calculate the weighted metrics to all candidates in relation to the sinks (Algorithm 3, line 1). The aggregated decision metric W represents the value of the calculated weighted metrics to all candidates in relation to all available sinks.

The calculation process considers three network metrics and it is described in Algorithm 2. The first is the relative distance from the candidate node and the target sink (line 13). The second metric is related to the energy cost for sending a packet from the current node to the candidate forwarder (line 14). The combination of these two metrics provides a balance between the progress towards the sink and the energy cost of that progress. Finally, the third metric is the total consumed energy of the candidate forwarder (line 15). This metric is used as a way to distribute the load over all the nodes and balance the energy consumption in order to avoid the early depletion of the battery. The total consumed energy of the neighbor is obtained from the received broadcast messages.

Algorithm 2. $W = CalculateMetric(n, S_r, L)$

Input: n: current node, S_r: list of remaining sinks, L: set of pairs [candidate, sink]
with positive progress
Output: W: a matrix $[|S_r|, |V|]$ that stores the calculated weighted metrics
1: /* α: weight for the distance metric, β: weight for the energy cost metric, */
2: /* δ: weight for the consumed energy metric */
3: $W \leftarrow \emptyset$
4: **for all** $v_i \in \{v_i | [v_i, s] \in L\}$ **do**
5:      **for all** $s_j \in S_r$ **do**
6:          $D[v_i, s_j] \leftarrow dist(v_i, s_j)$
7:      **end for**
8:      $E[v_i] \leftarrow EnergyCost(n, v_i)$
9:      $C[v_i] \leftarrow ConsumedEnergy(v_i)$
10: **end for**
11: **for all** $s_j \in S_r$ **do**
12:     **for all** $v_i \in \{v_i | [v_i, s] \in L\}$ **do**
13:         $x \leftarrow \alpha \times \frac{D[v_i, s_j] - Min(D[*, s_j])}{Max(D[*, s_j]) - Min(D[*, s_j])}$ /* for the distance between v_i and s_j */
14:         $y \leftarrow \beta \times \frac{E[v_i] - Min(E)}{Max(E) - Min(E)}$ /* for the energy cost from n to v_i */
15:         $z \leftarrow \delta \times \frac{C[v_i] - Min(C)}{Max(C) - Min(C)}$ /* for the energy consumption of neighbor v_i */
16:         $W[s_j, v_i] = x + y + z$
17:     **end for**
18: **end for**
19: **return** W

The second step is related to the pre-selection of candidates based on their aggregated decision metric (Algorithm 3, line 3). The algorithm fixes a sink and calculates the mean and the standard deviation to all candidates having that sink in their list. Later, a new list (C) is created having all the candidates that passed the pre-selection step for each sink. The pre-selection eliminates the candidates that have their aggregated decision metric with a value higher than the mean plus a factor (γ) of the standard deviation (line 9). By using a factor for the standard deviation the algorithm increases the forwarding angle, allowing non optimal nodes to be selected. This strategy is important to increase the possibility of intersections among candidates from one sink to another.

The third step of the selection process is responsible for calculating the largest intersection among the pre-selected candidates. This strategy tries to avoid early duplications, which translates to fewer packets being individually forwarded. In order to start the process, the closest sink (s) to the current node is selected (line 16) and all its candidates are inserted in the list $(P[p_k].nodes)$. The sink s is removed from the list of remaining sinks (S_r) and included in the list of the already selected sinks (S_{used}). The algorithm searches for the next sink s by selecting the closest sink to an already selected sink (line 35). Later, the algorithm checks the list of candidates of the new s against the list of the already selected sink (line 27). If an intersection is detected, the sink s is added in the

Algorithm 3. $ForwardersIntersec(n, L, S_r, packet)$ - Run at the current node.

Input: n: current node, L: set of pairs [candidate, sink] with positive progress, S_r: list of remaining sinks, $packet$: packet to be forwarded

1: $W \leftarrow CalculateMetric(n, S_r, L)$ /* The matrix that stores the weighted metrics */
2: $C \leftarrow \emptyset$ /* The list that holds the structure having the candidate nodes */
3: **for all** $s_j \in S_r$ **do**
4:      $\mu_{W_{s_j}} \leftarrow mean(W[s_j, *])$
5:      $\sigma_{W_{s_j}} \leftarrow stdev(W[s_j, *])$
6:      **for all** $v_i \in \{v_i | [v_i, s] \in L\}$ **do**
7:          /* Check if the calculated metric of the node v_i for the sink s_j is smaller */
8:          /* than the mean of all other candidates plus a factor (γ) of the stdev */
9:          **if** $W[s_j, v_i] \leq \mu_{W_{s_j}} + \gamma \times \sigma_{W_{s_j}}$ **then**
10:             $C[s_j].nodes \leftarrow C[s_j].nodes \cup \{v_i\}$
11:         **end if**
12:     **end for**
13: **end for**
14: $P \leftarrow \emptyset$ /* P is the list that holds the intersection structure */
15: $S_{used} \leftarrow \emptyset$
16: $s \leftarrow ClosestSink(\{n\}, S_r)$ /* Get the closest sink to n */
17: **repeat**
18:     /* Go through P and search for intersection */
19:     **for all** $p_k \in P$ **do**
20:         **if** $P[p_k].nodes \cap C[s_j].nodes \neq \emptyset$ **then**
21:             $P[p_k].nodes \leftarrow P[p_k].nodes \cap C[s].nodes$
22:             $P[p_k].sinks \leftarrow P[p_k].sinks \cup \{s\}$
23:             $C[s].nodes \leftarrow \emptyset$
24:         **end if**
25:     **end for**
26:     /* If no intersection is found, a new entry is created (packet duplication) */
27:     **if** $C[s].nodes \neq \emptyset$ **then**
28:         $p \leftarrow |P| + 1$
29:         $P[p].nodes \leftarrow C[s].nodes$
30:         $P[p].sinks \leftarrow \{s\}$
31:         $C[s].nodes \leftarrow \emptyset$
32:     **end if**
33:     $S_{used} \leftarrow S_{used} \cup \{s\}$
34:     $S_r \leftarrow S_r \setminus \{s\}$
35:     $s \leftarrow ClosestSink(S_{used}, S)$ /* Get the closest sink to any selected sink */
36: **until** $S_r \neq \emptyset$
37: **for all** $p_k \in P$ **do**
38:     $v \leftarrow v_i \in P[p_k].nodes$ which minimizes $mean(W[P[p_k].sinks, v_i])$
39:     $SendPacket(P[p_k].sinks, v, packet)$
40: **end for**
41: **return**

P list corresponding to the intersection. Only the intersected candidates are kept in the $P[p_k].nodes$ list. However, if no intersection is detected, a new entry in the P list is created with the sink s and all its candidates. A new entry in P represents a duplication of the packet due to the impossibility of finding an intersection. The entire process is repeated iteratively for all sinks.

The final step considers that multiple candidates may still exist within an entry p_k of the P list, in the sense that a set of sinks $P[p_k].sinks$ may have more than one candidate forwarder $|P[p_k].nodes| > 1$. For that matter, the algorithm searches for the candidate forwarder that minimizes the mean considering the set of sinks $P[p_k].sinks$. This is the opposite view of the pre-selection step, where the mean was calculated on all candidates for a single sink. At this time, we calculate the mean on all sinks in $P[p_k].sinks$ for a given candidate $v_i \in P[p_k].nodes$. Once the candidate v_i is defined, the packet is sent.

5 Simulation and Results

GeoM protocol was developed using Contiki OS [6], which is a lightweight open source operating system designed for resource limited devices. Contiki OS is implemented in C programing language and provides portability to different platforms. We evaluated the performance of our solution through simulations using Cooja [6], which is a network simulator for the Contiki OS. Cooja is a Java-based application capable of emulating various sensor nodes [15].

The performance of our solution was compared to an existing approach (Kan-GuRou) [14], that was also adapted to Contiki OS and tested with Cooja under the same configurations. KanGuRou is a k-anycast solution, however it is capable of performing multicast routing, since k-anycast becomes multicast when k equals the amount of all sinks. The decision to use KanGuRou as a benchmark is related to the compatibility of assumptions. Both GeoM and KanGuRou are designed for geographic routing, which implies a small need of network knowledge, no routing table maintenance and no set up phase.

The simulation environment and details are outlined in Table 1. In order to keep a similar deployment density over all variations of $|V|$, we make the network area vary with the number of deployed nodes, as given by Eq. 3 in Table 1. We tested the solutions under different network topologies, varying the number of sensor nodes and the existence of void areas (10 simulations for each scenario).

The performance is evaluated by observing the average of all metrics for all simulations, and the results are presented with a confidence interval of 95%. The considered metrics include the Latency, defined by the average time a packet takes to be routed from the source to all sinks. It is calculated to each network considering the sum of all latencies divided by the number of received packets. We also analyze the Maximum Energy Consumption, which regards the node that consumed the largest amount of energy in the network at the end of the simulation. It gives an indication of the Network Lifetime, since it shows how far the node is from the entire depletion of its battery. As per explanation, we consider a network to be alive as long as all nodes have some energy. Therefore, network lifetime is considered to be the earliest moment at which a node's battery is completely depleted.

Table 1. Configuration for the simulations

Simulation settings	
Deployment density (d)	8 neighbors (on average)
Network area (variable)	$\frac{\pi \times r^2}{d} \times |V|$ (3)
Communication range (r)	50 m
# of Sensors ($|N|$)	50, 100, 150, 200, 250, 300
# of Sinks ($|S|$)	10% of the number of sensors
# of Generated networks	10 per scenario
# of Scenarios	6 scenarios with voids and 6 without voids
Packet size	240 bytes
Packet generation rate	20% chance at every minute for each sensor
Radio type	802.15.4
MAC protocol	CX-MAC, modified version of [1]
Execution time	120 min for each network

Two main network scenarios were considered: with void areas and without void areas. The results are presented the same way, and we vary the amount of sensors and sinks in order to evaluate the behavior of the solution when the network grows.

5.1   Networks Without Void Areas

As we can notice in Fig. 1, GeoM presents a better performance in terms of Maximum Energy Consumption, with gains varying from 23% to 53%. For both solutions, the value for the maximum energy consumption increases when the network grows. However, the increase in GeoM is much smoother compared to KanGuRou. This is explained by our energy balance strategy and the deviation factor that distributes the load among other neighbors instead of using the same path for every forwarding. We can confirm this observation with Fig. 2, that shows the evolution of the maximum energy consumption during the simulation for the scenario with 300 sensor nodes. We can see that GeoM has a much smoother increase compared to KanGuRou. At the end of the simulation, GeoM presents half of the value for the maximum energy consumption. In terms of longevity, the maximum energy consumption for KanGuRou translates into a faster depletion of the node's battery.

In Fig. 3 we present the distribution of nodes in terms of energy consumption at the end of the simulation for the scenario with 300 sensor nodes. For KanGuRou, we can see a huge concentration of nodes with a small energy consumption, and a small group of nodes with a high level of energy consumption. For GeoM, we can see a different configuration, with a concentration of nodes at the first half of the range, which shows a better balance of the energy consumption.

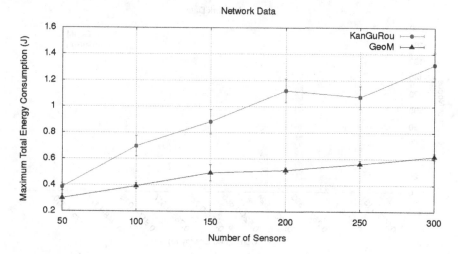

Fig. 1. Maximum Energy Consumption results with the network size varying from 50 to 300 nodes and sinks at 10% of the sensor nodes - networks without void areas.

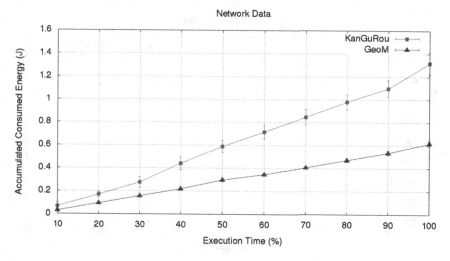

Fig. 2. Evolution of the maximum consumed energy. Results for 300 sensors and 30 sinks in a network without void areas.

The network may face many issues when a node's battery is completely depleted. The first one is the risk of disconnection, when part of the network is isolated and unable to forward packets to a sink. Even if a disconnection does not take place at a first moment, void areas may be created, since the depleted nodes are generally the ones within the sink neighborhood. The consequence of that is an increase of the latency and energy consumption, since a longer path is expected in order to bypass the void area. Another issue is related to the application, that faces a lack of coverage in the sensed field.

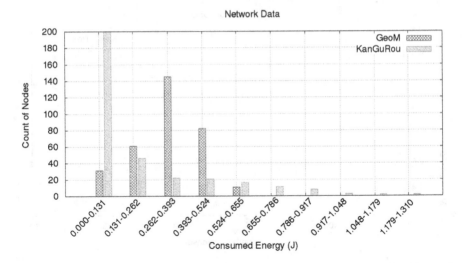

Fig. 3. Final State of the Network with the distribution of nodes in terms of consumed energy. Results for 300 sensors and 30 sinks in a network without void areas.

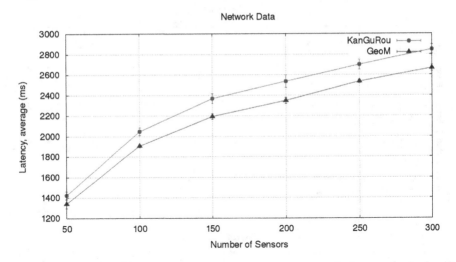

Fig. 4. Average Latency results with sensor varying from 50 to 300 nodes and sinks at 10% of the sensor nodes in a network without void areas.

The Latency results are presented in Fig. 4. We can notice that even with the energy balance strategy, GeoM presents a performance gain of around 7%. This as a positive indication, since the energy balance and the deviation factor strategies normally increase the path length. The performance gain can be explained by the fact that GeoM duplicates the packets a little earlier than KanGuRou, which speeds up the delivery. This is part of the trade-off between better energy consumption and latency.

5.2 Networks with Void Areas

The existence of a void area is a problematic and inherent issue in geographic routing. Strategies must be applied in order to handle the packets entering in a void area. GeoM deals with void areas using two existing techniques, the right-hand rule and the passive participation (void announcements) [4]. When a packet is in recovery mode, after being forwarded to a void area, the next hop decision does not consider the energy and latency optimizations. Normally, the path to exit the void area is always the same, regardless the amount of time it is used. In order to avoid this scenario, GeoM makes use of the void announcements as a way to prevent packets from entering in a void area, whenever it is possible. The simulation results show that GeoM is able to handle void areas and provide performance gains for both the energy and latency.

In Fig. 5 we can notice a performance gain varying from 5% to 26%. Even with the existence of void areas, GeoM is capable of distributing the loads and consequently reducing the maximum energy consumption. The network grow affects GeoM positively, with an increase in the performance gain in relation to KanGuRou. With the increase of the network size, the nodes in void areas may be avoided more easily, since both sink options and the possibility of candidate forwarder intersections are also increased.

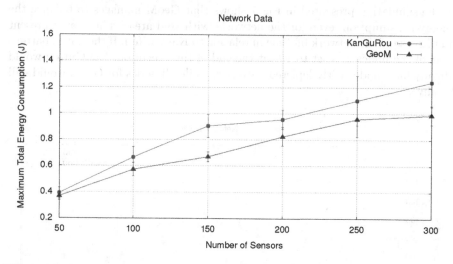

Fig. 5. Maximum Energy Consumption results with sensor varying from 50 to 300 nodes and sinks at 10% of the sensor nodes in networks with void areas.

We can see in Fig. 6, for the scenario with 300 sensor nodes, that GeoM and KanGuRou have a similar behavior in terms of energy consumption over time. However, GeoM has a slightly better curve compared to KanGuRou, reaching the end of the simulation with a level of energy consumption that represents less than 80% of the energy consumed by KanGuRou.

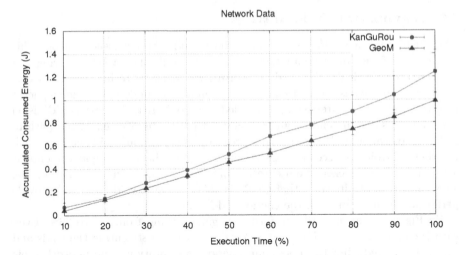

Fig. 6. Evolution of the maximum consumed energy. Results for 300 sensors and 30 sinks (network with void areas).

The distribution of the nodes in terms of energy consumption at the end of the simulation presented in Fig. 7 shows that GeoM manages to balance the energy consumption, even for the networks with void areas. This may represent an increase of the network lifetime in relation to KanGuRou. If the initial battery level of the nodes was set to $1J$, at the end of the execution, KanGuRou would already have nodes with depleted batteries, while all nodes for GeoM would still be alive.

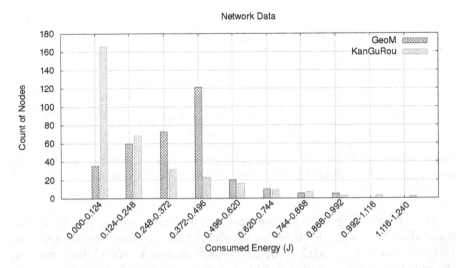

Fig. 7. Final State of the Network with the distribution of nodes in terms of consumed energy. Results for 300 sensors and 30 sinks in networks with void areas.

In terms of latency, GeoM presents a performance gain of around 10% in relation to KanGuRou, as displayed in Fig. 8. This can be explained by the void announcements strategy. When packets enter in void areas, the paths become longer as a consequence of the void handling technique to exit the void area. However, with the nodes announcing their void situation, neighbors try to forward packets to other directions, avoiding the problematic area.

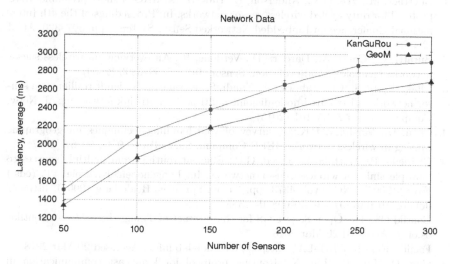

Fig. 8. Average Latency results with sensor varying from 50 to 300 nodes and sinks at 10% of the sensor nodes (network with void areas).

6 Conclusion

This paper presented a new Geographic Multicast Routing solution for Wireless Sensor Networks with multiple sinks. Our strategy makes use of weighted metrics to establish the list of forwarder candidates, and search for intersections among the sinks and candidates in order to avoid duplications. The main goal was to find a balance between Latency and Network Lifetime optimizations. We tested our solutions through simulations against another geographic routing strategy capable of forwarding packets to multiple sinks. The simulation results indicate that our solution has an overall better performance than the existing protocol, with maximum gains of approximately 11% for Latency and 54% for Maximum Energy Consumption.

As future work, we plan to execute real-life experiments for GeoM and Kan-GuRou using the testbed from the FIT IoT-LAB [7] and evaluate the performance of the solution under real conditions.

Acknowledgments. This work is partially supported by the Brazilian National Council for Scientific and Technological Development (CNPq). Computations have been performed on the supercomputer facilities of the Mésocentre de calcul de Franche-Comté.

References

1. Buettner, M., Yee, G.V., Anderson, E., Han, R.: X-MAC: a short preamble MAC protocol for duty-cycled wireless sensor networks. In: Proceedings of the 4th International Conference on Embedded Networked Sensor Systems, pp. 307–320. ACM (2006)
2. Buratti, C., Conti, A., Dardari, D., Verdone, R.: An overview on wireless sensor networks technology and evolution. Sensors **9**(9), 6869–6896 (2009)
3. Chakraborty, S., Chakraborty, S., Nandi, S., Karmakar, S.: Fault resilience in sensor networks: distributed node-disjoint multi-path multi-sink forwarding. J. Netw. Comput. Appl. **57**, 85–101 (2015)
4. Chen, D., Varshney, P.K.: A survey of void handling techniques for geographic routing in wireless networks. IEEE Commun. Surv. Tutor. **9**(1), 50–67 (2007)
5. Ciciriello, P., Mottola, L., Picco, G.P.: Efficient routing from multiple sources to multiple sinks in wireless sensor networks. In: Langendoen, K., Voigt, T. (eds.) EWSN 2007. LNCS, vol. 4373, pp. 34–50. Springer, Heidelberg (2007). https://doi.org/10.1007/978-3-540-69830-2_3
6. Contiki OS: The Open Source OS for the Internet of Things. http://www.contiki-os.org/. Accessed 20 Mar 2018
7. Facility FIT: FIT IoT-LAB. https://www.iot-lab.info/. Accessed 20 Mar 2018
8. Gao, D., Lin, H., Liu, X.: Routing protocol for k-anycast communication in rechargeable wireless sensor networks. Comput. Stand. Interfaces **43**, 12–20 (2016)
9. He, X., Kamei, S., Fujita, S.: Autonomous multi-source multi-sink routing in wireless sensor networks. Inf. Media Technol. **7**(1), 488–495 (2012)
10. Heinzelman, W.R., Chandrakasan, A., Balakrishnan, H.: Energy-efficient communication protocol for wireless microsensor networks. In: 33rd Annual Hawaii International Conference on System Sciences (HICSS), pp. 1–10. IEEE (2000)
11. Heissenbüttel, M., Braun, T., Bernoulli, T., Wälchli, M.: BLR: beacon-less routing algorithm for mobile ad hoc networks. Comput. Commun. **27**(11), 1076–1086 (2004)
12. Kim, D., et al.: On bounding node-to-sink latency in wireless sensor networks with multiple sinks. Int. J. Sens. Netw. **13**(1), 13–29 (2013)
13. Mitton, N., Simplot-Ryl, D., Stojmenovic, I.: Guaranteed delivery for geographical anycasting in wireless multi-sink sensor and sensor-actor networks. In: 28th Annual IEEE Conference on Computer Communications (INFOCOM), pp. 2691–2695 (2009)
14. Mitton, N., Simplot-Ryl, D., Voge, M.-E., Zhang, L.: Energy efficient k-anycast routing in multi-sink wireless networks with guaranteed delivery. In: Li, X.-Y., Papavassiliou, S., Ruehrup, S. (eds.) ADHOC-NOW 2012. LNCS, vol. 7363, pp. 385–398. Springer, Heidelberg (2012). https://doi.org/10.1007/978-3-642-31638-8_29
15. Osterlind, F., Dunkels, A., Eriksson, J., Finne, N., Voigt, T.: Cross-level sensor network simulation with COOJA. In: Proceedings of 31st IEEE Conference on Local Computer Networks, pp. 641–648. IEEE (2006)

Non-interfering Multipath Mechanism for Media Stream Transmission in Wireless Sensor Networks

Mohamed Nacer Bouatit[1], Selma Boumerdassi[1(✉)], and Ruben H. Milocco[2]

[1] Center for Studies and Research in Computer Science
and Communications - CNAM, Paris, France
`selma.boumerdassi@inria.fr`
[2] Department of the Electrical Engineering, National University of Comahue,
Neuquén, Argentina

Abstract. Potential applications of multimedia sensor networks cover a wide spectrum from military to industrial and from commercial to environmental monitoring. These applications require high bandwidth and are extremely delay sensitive. However, multipath routing is one of the appropriate solutions for multimedia data transmission, unlike traditional schemes using the shortest paths. Therefore, in this paper, we address the issue of interference in WMSNs and present an non-interfering multipath mechanism, integrated in our previous GMFT routing protocol. The proposed mechanism intervenes during path exploration phase in order to limit adjacent paths interactions.

Simulations results show a significant contribution and indicate that the proposed mechanism provides a higher data packets delivery rate.

Keywords: Wireless Multimedia Sensor Networks
Non-interfering paths · Multipath transmission · Geographic routing

1 Introduction

Multi-path transmission consists of building several routes between source-sink pair and uniformly sending data packets via these multiple paths in order to:

- Balance the load between nodes, which extends their life and that of the network;
- Improve the channel utilization rate;
- Reduce transmission delays;
- Tolerate possible failures and increase the level of security.

On the other hand, in order to have a high efficiency, we must take into consideration the characteristics and constraints of sensor nodes transmissions, notably the phenomenon of interference in CSMA/CA wireless environments. Indeed, the interference usually results from the geographical proximity of the

© Springer Nature Switzerland AG 2019
É. Renault et al. (Eds.): MSPN 2018, LNCS 11005, pp. 311–321, 2019.
https://doi.org/10.1007/978-3-030-03101-5_26

paths as shown in Fig. 1, where the node m which is in the transmission radius of the node j, interferes with the reception/transmission of the latter and causes data packets collisions, thus reducing the reliability rate of the routing protocol used.

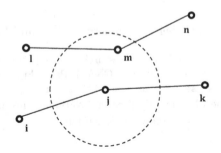

Fig. 1. Example of the interference phenomenon

The remainder of this paper is organized as follows: Sect. 2, presents network model. Proposed non-interfering multipath mechanism is described in Sect. 3. Results of extensive simulations are shown in Sect. 4. Finally, Sect. 5, concludes the paper.

2   Network Model

We consider a flat network architecture and the wireless sensor network is composed of N sensors, deployed in a static deterministic manner. Each sensor node being aware of its geographic location and its 1-hop neighbor nodes geographic locations. We assume that only source nodes knows sink nodes locations and all other sensor nodes know sink locations by receiving packets from source nodes. All nodes have the same transmission range and are homogeneous and are endowed with identical physical capabilities (detection and communication). Only bidirectional links are used to build paths. Each sensor node may be in one of the following states:

- Valid: ready to build a path;
- Active: already used in a path (locked for specific path);
- Blocked: no valid next-hop except its predecessor;
- Failed: damaged;
- Vulnerable: low-residual energy.

Each path is composed of a finite set of links, each node can belong to only one path, except source nodes and sink nodes. In GMFT [1], all generated routing paths are node-disjoint routing paths, which share no common nodes. The link cost function denoted by $f(x_k)$ is used by $node_k$ to select the best valid next-hop as mentioned in EGMFT [2] which is an extension of GMFT, taking into account node's residual energy.

3   Proposed Non-interfering Multipath Mechanism

The sensor nodes are deployed in areas of interest for various reasons, where event detections may occur either simultaneously or alternately in time intervals. Consider in this paper, the case where at an instant t, a single data stream is conveyed in the network on multipath between a source-sink pair and a set of intermediate nodes.

3.1   Description

During path construction phase, our non-interfering multipath mechanism tries to find the maximum number of node disjoint paths by minimizing interference between these adjacent paths as much as possible.

In fact, node disjoint paths do not share any common node and are of particular interest because they prevent some nodes from transmitting more packets than others and avoid the breakdown of several paths at the same time. In addition, in wireless communication, the bandwidth is shared between neighboring nodes, where a node can interfere with geographically close nodes, thereby degrading the delivery rate.

For this purpose, a node that is at one hop from an already constructed path as shown in Fig. 2, has the lowest priority as a candidate node for constructing other routing paths. This type of node is called *interfering node* and will not be chosen during construction process.

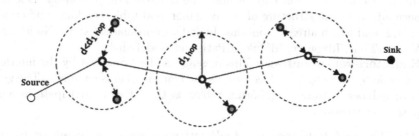

Fig. 2. Interferent nodes at one hop from a built path

However, the proposed mechanism ensures that most of the nodes belonging to the operational routing paths between the source and sink are at least two hops apart, which will logically reduce the loss of data due to collisions.

3.2   Messages and Function Used

Our mechanism is based on interfering nodes identification. To do this, we used two new messages in complement of our EGMFT routing protocol [2] and the overhearing functionality, which consists of receiving or listening packets that are not intended for the current node. Indeed, by sharing a wireless medium, transmitted data by a node can reach other nodes that are either in the transmission range of the transmitter/receiver as schematized in Fig. 3. When the node A transmits data to node B, the sending of A is on the listening of C and the reception of B is on the listening of D.

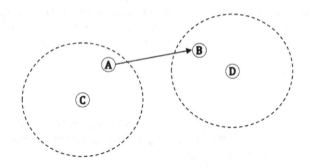

Fig. 3. Overhearing example

1. **Overhearing of optimization messages:** This feature allows us to identify nodes that are at one jump from a routing path. This is done following the over-listening by the non-concerned node of the optimization message, sent or received by an active node belonging to the constructed path.
2. **WarningInterference message:** As soon as an interfering node identifies itself, it broadcasts an interference warning message to its *Neighborset* to inform them that it is at one hop from a routing path. Upon receipt this message, neighboring nodes update their neighborhood tables by marking this interfering node. For this purpose, the Boolean *InterferingNode* field has been added to the structure of the neighborhood table previously described in [1,2] and which already contains: IdNode, Coordinates (X, Y), NodeState, ValidityTime, IdSource, IdSink, IdPath and NodeLabel.
3. **EndInterference message:** This message is also broadcast by the interfering node to its *Neighborset* as soon as the transmission is complete. The goal is to unblock it from neighboring tables so that it can participate in next paths construction.

The *WarningInterference* and *EndInterference* messages broadcast by the interfering node are added as new types in the format of the control message used during exploration phase and which already included: *GreedyForwarding*, *WalkingBack*, *Optimization* and *Liberation*.

Note that the sink does not process the *WarningInterference* messages sent by the interfering nodes because it is not affected by the discovery phase (*Greedy-Forwarding*). This minimizes the sending of unnecessary control messages and ensures rapid convergence of built routing paths.

In the case where the interfering node is adjacent to several routing paths, a counter is used to increment the number of its adjacent paths. At the end of data transmission on the different neighboring routes of the interfering node, the latter decrements its counter at each overhearing of release message. When the counter is reset, the interfering node broadcasts the *EndInterference* message to its *Neighborset*.

3.3   Progress

In the example of Fig. 4, the first exploited path linking the *source* to the *sink* is $ch1 = \{source, a, b, c, sink\}$. During the optimization phase of this path, the *sink* sends an *Optimization* message to node c, which transmits it to node b and from that node to node a. The node f which is in the transmission range of c listens to the optimization request and concludes that it is at one hop of a routing path being built via its distance which is less than the distance of one jump ($d_{fc} < d_{1jump}$). Nodes e and d also realize that they are at one jump from the 1st path.

Thus, the interfering nodes (d, e, f) broadcast the *WarningInterference* message to announce this information to their neighbors. As it happens (j, k) for the node f, (h, i, j) for the node e and ($source$, g, h) for the node d. These neighbors put them in their neighborhood tables as interfering nodes.

The other active nodes (a, b, c) also receive the warning message but are not concerned by the construction of the 2nd path.

During the construction of the 2nd routing path, the *source* does not choose the node d as next hop, although it is closer to the *sink* than the node g. Indeed, the node d is marked as an interfering node and therefore the *source* designates the node g as the next hop. With the same logic, the node j selects the node k instead of node f.

For this purpose, the 2nd built path is $ch2 = \{source, g, h, i, j, k, sink\}$. We find that the two routing paths built between the *source* and the *sink* are disjoint and their nodes are separated by two hops.

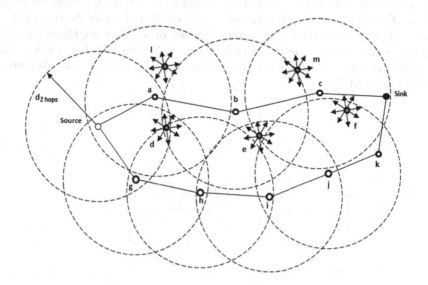

Fig. 4. Non-interfering paths

4 Evaluation

This section presents and discusses simulation results conducted on Tossim simulator [3], that relies on low-energy consumption operations using powerTossim plugin [4] and also due to its compatibility with real Imote2 [5] sensors, object of our second experimental step of small-scale on real testbed over TinyOS [6] platform.

We implemented both EA-TPGF [7] and AGEM [8], which are geographic routing protocols that bypass static holes during paths construction and use multipath transmission (Table 1).

Table 1. Main configuration parameters.

Parameter	Value
Network size	500 m × 250 m
Number of sensor nodes	253
Bandwidth	250 kb/s
Transmission range	25 m
Packet size	1024 bits
Data size	5.85 Mo
Number of path	5

In order to better present our interference management approach, we have increased network density to be in real conditions where the transmission range is 25 m. For this purpose, we preferred a grid configuration as shown in Fig. 5. Each node has 24 neighbors in its *NeighborSet*, of which 8 neighbors are at 1 hop (the empty nodes) and 16 neighbors are at 2 hops (the full nodes). The 24 neighbors are separated from the current node by the following distances: $d, 2d, d_1, 2d_1$ and d_2.

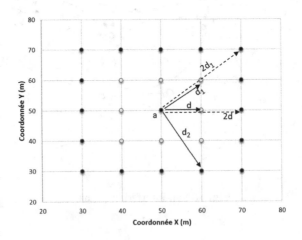

Fig. 5. Current node *ForwardingSet*

4.1 Used Metrics

1. *Delivery Ratio (DR):* Is the ratio between the Number of Received Packets (NRP) and the total Number of Sent Packets (NSP). This mectric reflects protocol reliability during packets transfer from source to destination.

$$DR = \frac{NRP}{NSP} \tag{1}$$

2. *Average End-to-end Delay (AED):* Is the sojourn time of packets in the network from source node, until their arrival at the sink.

$$AED = \frac{1}{Nrp} \sum_{i=1}^{Nrp} (T_{in_{sink}} - T_{out_{source}}) \tag{2}$$

3. *Receiving Rate (RR):* This metric measures receiving flow continuity at the sink (a high-receiving rate provides a good quality of multimedia stream). Otherwise, it is the average rate of received packets per unit of time.

$$RR = \frac{N_{rp}}{T_{rp} - T_1} \tag{3}$$

N_{rp}: Number of received packets, T_{rp}: Reception time of the last packet, T_1: Reception time of the first packet.

4.2 Simulation Results

Delivery Ratio: Figures 6 and 7 show that GNMFT records a significant difference in reliability over EA-TPGF and AGEM. Indeed, according to the histogram of Fig. 6, the success rates of EA-TPGF and AGEM show a clear deterioration by supplying respectively the 47% and 61%, when 5 nodes belonging to various paths fall into breakdowns (one node down per path).

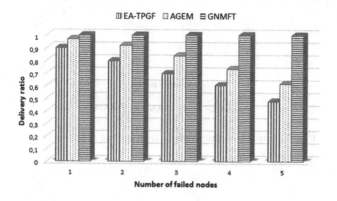

Fig. 6. Impact of the number of failed nodes on the delivery ratio

This is mainly due to the absence of paths maintenance policy face to dynamic holes (sensor failure during real-time data transmission) in the case of EA-TPGF and the lack of interfering path management strategy in AGEM. The latter, which uses only a smart greedy routing in reactive mode, records at the beginning (from 1 to 3 failed nodes) a satisfactory rate higher than 80% with an energy over-cost, but which degrades quickly after 4 and 5 nodes in breakdowns. However, we confirm the formula of the number of lost packets (NLP) described previously in [1,9] and we deduce that the larger the dynamic hole, the smaller the reliability rate.

We also note that above 100 p/s as shown in Fig. 7, the curves of the success rates of the three protocols decrease but those of EA-TPGF and AGEM drop significantly due to the large number of collisions due to channel access competition for adjacent nodes. In addition, the overflow of queues causes the congestion effect during transmissions in AGEM and has a considerable impact on its success rate. Operational paths reduction in EA-TPGF and the high throughput cause enormous loss where all data packets that have borrowed the faulty paths are a priori lost.

Our hybrid routing design used by GNMFT and previously described in [1,9], combined with the Fault Tolerance Mechanism (FTM) and the Non-interfering Multipath Mechanism (NMM), ensures better reliability of transmitted data. In fact, the FTM locally repairs breakdowns when communication links fails at transmission time while minimizing the NLP and the NMM considerably reduces interferences between adjacent paths, which increases routed packets success rate.

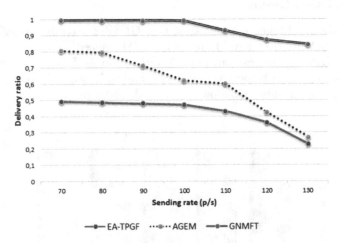

Fig. 7. Impact of the sending rate on the delivery ratio

Average End-to-End Delay: Figure 8, indicates that the average end-to-end delay is proportional to sending rate in AGEM and EA-TPGF. As the through-put increases, packets take longer in queues before being sent.

In fact, AGEM records the highest delays. Its reverse mode to rebuild the faulty path in case of failure or mobility, slows data packets sending. The same observation for EA-TPGF, where its curve is more proportional because of the length of the used paths, especially when the topology change. Furthermore, the lack of a maintenance strategy reduces operational paths number, which prolongs the stay of data packets in queues.

Moreover, maintained links by our curative mechanism are shorter in terms of hop number compared to AGEM and EA-TPGT path's, which positively reduces the average delay of all packets. On the other hand, the reparing technique used makes it possible to use more paths and lighten the queues. In addition, the access to transmission channel is faster in GNMFT compared to other proto-cols because of the low interference/overlap of radio channel for operational nodes belonging to parallel routing paths. For this purpose, packets collisions are reduced and media stream is more fluid.

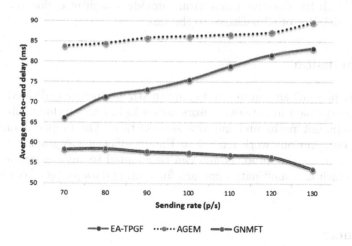

Fig. 8. Impact of the sending rate on the average end-to-end delay

Receiving Rate: The graph in Fig. 9, exhibits that up to 110 p/s, AGEM and GNMFT receiving rate have almost the same evolution, while EA-TPGF receiving rate is much lower due to high data packet loss caused by paths number reduction.

Beyond 110 p/s, we notice a significant regression of the receiving rate of the AGEM protocol, compared to GNMFT. Indeed, when the holes are detected, AGEM tries to bypass them in a reactive manner in real time, which further overloads nodes near these holes and causes interaction between the nearby routing paths. As a result, the routes used do not support the large stream broadcasted beyond a certain threshold and the queues overflow quickly. On the

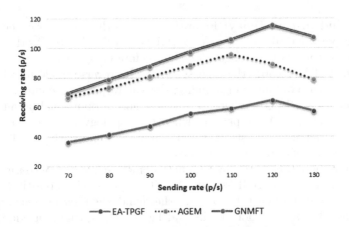

Fig. 9. Impact of the sending rate on the receiving rate

other hand, our non-interfering mechanism allows to build non-interfering paths, combined with the curative mechanism, provide a high reception rate as they ensure the delivery of all packages to the sink.

5   Conclusion

This paper presents an non-interfering multipath mechanism dedicated to media stream transmission in wireless sensors networks in order to limit interferences between adjacent paths and improve success rate. The proposed mechanism improves our previous work related to Energy-efficient Géographic Multipath Fault Tolerant routing protocol and can be adapted to any geographic routing protocol which uses multipath approach for routing data packets from source to sink.

References

1. Bouatit, M.N., Boumerdassi, S., Minet, P., Djama, A.: Fault-tolerant mechanism for multimedia transmission in wireless sensor networks. In: 84th Vehicular Technology Conference (VTC–Fall) (2016)
2. Bouatit, M.N., Boumerdassi, S., Djama, A., Milocco, R.H.: Energy-efficient preventive mechanism for fault tolerance in wireless multimedia sensor networks. In: Vehicular Technology Conference (VTC-Fall), vol. 86, pp. 1–5, September 2017
3. Levis, P., Lee, N., Welsh, M., Culler, D.: TOSSIM: accurate and scalable simulation of entire Tinyos applications. In: Proceedings of the 1st International Conference on Embedded Networked Sensor Systems, pp. 126–137 (2003)
4. Perla, E., Cath, A.O., Carbajo, R.S., Huggard, M., Goldrick, C.M.: PowerTOSSIM z: realistic energy modelling for wireless sensor network environments. In: Proceedings of the 3nd ACM workshop on Performance Monitoring and Measurement of Heterogeneous Wireless and Wired Networks (MSWIM), pp. 35–42. ACM (2008)

5. Crossbow. Imote2.Builder Kit Manual. Crossbow Technology, California, USA (2008)
6. Levis, P., Gay, D.: TinyOS Programming, 1st edn. Cambridge University Press, New York (2009)
7. Bennis, I., Fouchal, H., Zytoune, O., Aboutajdine, D.: An evaluation of the TPGF protocol implementation over NS-2. In: IEEE International Conference on Communications (ICC), pp. 428–433, June 2014
8. Medjiah, S., Ahmed, T., Krief, F.: AGEM: adaptive greedy-compass energy-aware multipath routing protocol for WMSNS. In: IEEE Consumer Communications and Networking Conference (CCNC), vol. 7, pp. 1–6. IEEE (2010)
9. Bouatit, M.N., Boumerdassi, S., Djama, A.: Experimental evaluation of fault-tolerant mechanisms over imote2 platform. In: IEEE Annual Consumer Communications Networking Conference (CCNC), vol. 15, pp. 1–4 (2018)

Wireless Fog-Mesh: A Communication and Computation Infrastructure for IoT Based Smart Environments

Shabir Ali$^{(\boxtimes)}$, Shashwati Banerjea, Mayank Pandey, and Neeraj Tyagi

Motilal Nehru National Institute of Technology Allahabad, Allahabad, India
{rcs1501,shashwati,mayankpandey,neeraj}@mnnit.ac.in

Abstract. Recently, the ideas of fog and edge computing have been proposed to move the computation near the end devices that produce or consume data. These ideas can easily be utilized in the context of IoT based smart environments. Generally, the practical implementations of smart environments rely heavily on cloud for data processing, analytics and decision making. The data captured by IoT devices is transferred via Internet towards cloud data centers which may introduce unwanted delay in real time scenarios. If we go by the popular predictions regarding number of active IoT devices, the best effort service provided by Internet may become a huge bottleneck. Further, to make the environment IoT friendly, a scalable communication infrastructure is needed which should be cost effective and can sustain the ever increasing number of devices. In this paper, we present our initial attempt to make a wireless mesh based fog computing infrastructure for IoT enabled smart environments. The important aspect of our approach is that, it can quickly be deployed for use-cases where smart environment is needed on a temporary basis, such as rock concerts, fairs, sporting events, etc. We have implemented a small scale prototype test-bed where mesh routers can also act as fog nodes. For resource discovery among fog nodes, we have utilized the concepts of Distributed Hash Table (DHT). This DHT also performs the role of distributed broker for data sharing among IoT devices. Further, we have performed simulations to test the scalability of our approach. Both implementation and simulation results are satisfactory and establish the applicability of our approach.

1 Introduction

The advances in pervasive and ubiquitous computing have enabled the researchers to envisage the idea of smart environments. According to Mark Weiser (who is also known as the father of ubiquitous computing), smart environment is "a physical world that is richly and invisibly interwoven with sensors, actuators, displays, and computational elements, embedded seamlessly in the everyday objects of our lives, and connected through a continuous network" [1]. The practical realization of smart environments has only become possible due to the advent of Internet of Things (IoT) technologies [2]. The IoT devices are

© Springer Nature Switzerland AG 2019
É. Renault et al. (Eds.): MSPN 2018, LNCS 11005, pp. 322–338, 2019.
https://doi.org/10.1007/978-3-030-03101-5_27

installed at the events like fairs, rock concerts, sporting, mass gathering places for information acquisition and subsequent analysis.

In 2013, Cisco gave a prediction that more than 50 billion devices are expected to be connected to the Internet by 2020 [3]. This predicted exponential growth in IoT devices has forced the researchers to think about modifications in existing network technologies and also to invent new network protocols. Existing Internet protocol stack is not able to handle such huge number of devices and more importantly huge amount of data generated by them. There are a number of issues that need to be resolved for building a resilient smart environment [4–10]. The issues are listed below:

– *Dependency over Cloud:* The data generated by IoT devices in smart environments are huge in size. The typical method used is to throw all data back to the cloud for storage, processing, and analytics. Though this appears to be a viable solution, continuous transfer of the entire data to the cloud is very costly and leads to wastage of Internet bandwidth. Further, not all the IoT applications can tolerate the latency which is introduced due to reliance on centralized cloud computing.
– *Non-Standardization:* The sudden proliferation of IoT devices has created the problem of a non-universal protocol stack. In practice, different vendors manufacture IoT devices for various domains e.g. vendors for IoT devices required for smart hospitals may be different from IoT devices needed in case of smart parking. Gradually, it resulted in the variety of protocols, utilized by different IoT devices in all layers of a protocol stack. Due to this non-conformity of standards, communication among IoT devices manufactured by different vendors is difficult.

In addition to the above issues, designing smart solutions for scenarios such as religious mass gatherings, rock concerts, sport related events etc. is even more challenging because wired communication infrastructure is limited. A typical example of such mass gathering is Kumbh Mela at Allahabad, India [11] where around 30 million people congregate for a period of around 40 days. On some auspicious days, the assemblage is more than the population of Sanghai. A dismantleable city in the outskirts of the city of Allahabad is setup with all the modern facilities such as temporary houses, police stations, ATMs, post offices etc. Crowd management and providing facilities such as clean lavatories, smart parking, monitoring the vicinity from disasters and stampedes remain a big challenge.

To resolve the above mentioned issues, we have proposed a wireless communication and computation framework that supports scalability with increasing number of IoT devices. Our proposed framework is self healing, self-configurable, cost effective and quickly deployable. We have utilized Wireless Mesh Network (WMN) [12], which is an elegant option for underlying network substrate in such scenarios [13,14]. The mesh access points/routers of WMN are utilized as IoT gateways to facilitate communication among IoT devices which use different protocols. Also, to reduce the latency caused by data transfer towards cloud for its analysis, we have used the concepts of fog computing [15]. Our approach augments the cloud based solution and the goal is to provide computing services near to the source of data generation. We have used WMN nodes (mesh access points/routers) as our fog nodes. These mesh access points and routers acting as fog nodes primarily provide routing services and we have utilized their unused CPU cycles for computation. It may be noted that different fog nodes may experience different routing load which changes dynamically as per the need and routing paths formed by WMN. This creates the challenge of finding fog nodes which are capable enough to provide computing services. We have utilized distributed hash table (DHT) [16] based peer-to-peer (P2P) [17] overlay of fog nodes for computing resource discovery in our approach.

Further, the data generated from data producers (sensors) need to be disseminated asynchronously to data consumers such as actuators (for taking actions) and fog nodes (for analysis). These producers and consumers require rendezvous for timely action. In traditional IoT architectures, event based solutions such as MQTT [18], AMQP [19] etc. are utilized for data dissemination. These event based architecture are generally based on centralized broker system. As already discussed, we have utilized a DHT based P2P overlay of fog nodes for computing resource discovery. The same overlay is utilized in our approach to act as distributed broker for dissemination of data among producers and consumers.

Our contributions can be listed as follows:

1. Design and implementation of WMN based network substrate capable of interconnecting IoT devices governed by different protocols.
2. Design and implementation of fog computing solution by utilizing computation and storage capabilities of wireless mesh access points/routers.
3. Design and implementation of resource discovery and event based data dissemination over DHT of fog nodes.

The organization of the paper is as follows. In Sect. 2, we have presented state-of-the-art which are close to our work. Section 3 presents our architecture which includes the description of utilizing existing technologies. The implementation details of our test-bed and simulation setup are described in Sect. 4. The results obtained from experiments are discussed in Sect. 5. Finally, Sect. 6 provides conclusion and some future directions.

2   Related Work

In recent years, some research efforts [20–23] have been made to utilize DHT, wireless technologies and fog computing in the context of IoT based smart environments. The approaches presented in [20–22] have used DHT for tackling discovery of resources and their access in large scale IoT environment. Here, the term resource is used for an IoT device or an IoT gateway which can provide information of interest. These approaches provide solution for integrating multiple IoT domains govern by different IoT networks. These approaches have focused on how to discover (and access) the IoT network and/or a resource in the network which can provide the desired information according to the application context. In [20], a DHT of different IoT gateways is proposed to design a federation of otherwise disjoint IoT networks. In [22], similar idea is utilized by proposing 2-tier DHT of IoT gateways for looking up multi-attribute resource queries. However, this work only tackles the resource discovery problem. In both [20] and [22], the term fog or edge computing could not be found. Apparently, they have assumed some dedicated and designated nodes to be used as IoT gateways. In [21], ideas similar to [20] and [22] are proposed. However, in this approach it is proposed to place IoT gateways in fog or edge nodes. Further, in [21], a standard interface for resource discovery and access is also proposed. The combination of fog computing and WMN is utilized in [23] for designing Mobile Mesh Social Network (MMSN). Here, the computing and networking resources in users' close vicinity are used to form fog network to improve the overall efficiency of MMSN.

Different from the approaches discussed above, our approach targets to utilize the underutilized CPU cycles of networking devices for computing purposes. We have used WMN as our underlying network (suitable for use cases where wired infrastructure is limited) and mesh access points and routers are utilized as fog nodes. The DHT of these fog nodes is used to discover appropriate computing resources (memory, CPU cycles) for task assignment. The computing resources on these fog nodes change dynamically depending on the routing load handled by them. The same DHT is also utilized to act as distributed mediator between data producers (sensors, cameras etc.) and data consumers (fog nodes, actuators etc.).

3   Proposed Architecture

Providing smart services in places where huge crowd gatherings are experienced on temporary basis remains an interesting application domain. Some of the popular crowd gatherings are Kumbh Mela in India and Hajj in Mecca, Saudi Arabia. These places remain crowded on some auspicious days and crowd management, parking, hygiene, sanitation, medical facilities, banking etc. are required for a short period of time. Rendering these services poses two major challenges. The first challenge is limited permanent basic communication infrastructure which restrict the hooking places for IoT devices. Moreover, Crowd-sensing [24] techniques, which can become potential forces in these scenarios, also suffer due to lack of fixed communication infrastructure. Installation of permanent communication infrastructure is not a cost effective solution as these events happen for a short span of time.

The second challenge is dependency over cloud. For instance, to design a smart emergency response system for Kumbh Mela at Allahabad [11] (where millions of pilgrims gather to take a holy dip in river Ganges) lots of CCTV cameras, sensors and actuators are required to be installed. This event happens in a large area of about $20\,km^2$. Relying over cloud computing solutions is not advisable because decisions based on data analysis have to be taken very quickly and cloud based systems may suffer from unwanted latency.

Our proposed architecture, Wireless Fog-Mesh is depicted in Fig. 1 can handle the above requirements. The architecture consists of four layers. Each layer is discussed next from bottom to top.

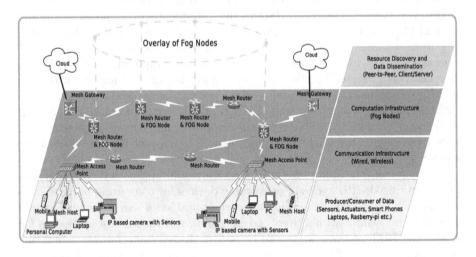

Fig. 1. Wireless Fog-Mesh

3.1 Layer-1 (Producer/Consumer of Data)

Layer-1 consists of IoT devices like actuators, sensors, CCTV cameras, smartphones, smart watches etc. The sensors (temperature, infrared, ultrasonic, touch, proximity, pressure, smoke, gas etc.) are producers of data whereas actuators (hydraulic, pneumatic, electric, mechanical etc.) are consumers of processed data which take further actions.

3.2 Layer-2 (Communication Infrastructure)

We have chosen Wireless Mesh Networks (WMN) [12] for communication among the devices described in layer-1. Wireless Mesh Network (WMN) can play an important role in providing robust wireless infrastructure for IoT applications which can be quickly deployed in an ad-hoc manner [13,14]. These networks are characterized by dynamic self-organization, auto-configuration, and self-healing capabilities [12]. Wireless Mesh Networks have mesh-access points, mesh-routers, and mesh-portals/gateways which communicate using IEEE 802.11 wireless MAC protocol. The gateways can also act as protocol translators to provide different vendor specific IoT devices. The interesting feature of this network is layer-2 routing which provides quick decision-making of route changes under constrained environment. Another feature which makes them suitable for a smart environment is that the mesh-routers, mesh-portals etc. can act as edge or fog nodes for local computing requirements.

3.3 Layer-3 (Computation Infrastructure)

Layer-3 utilizes the concepts of "Edge Computing" [15] or "Fog Computing" [25] for providing computation infrastructure for IoT devices. The notion behind both these concepts is to extend cloud-based services to the edge of the network. These technologies can be easily used in the context of smart environment for providing cloud-like services with less latency.

The fog computing architecture was introduced in [26] using the concepts of Virtual Machine (VM) based cloudlets. Afterwards, this architecture was popularized by Cisco as a complimentary resource-rich layer that sits between the edge device and the Cloud [27]. In [26], it is suggested that this layer can be one hop away from the edge devices to offer both low and predictable latencies to support IoT applications.

The entities like laptops, smartphones, wireless access points, routers can act as possible fog nodes [28]. In our approach we have utilized mesh routers described in layer-2 as fog nodes. Fog computing raises several challenges during its practical implementation. The first challenge is to provide an execution environment to run processes on fog nodes which are generally resource constrained. Containers and hypervisors [29] have capability to provide execution environment. We plan to use Docker [30] to provide an execution environment for running processes.

The second challenge is selection of adequate computing paradigm. Trivial distributed computing paradigms such as map-reduce [31] are used for batch processing and hence not suitable for analyzing stream data. Cisco has introduced Data in Motion (DMo) [32] concept which can act as an alternative. Similarly, HortonWorks Dataflow (HDF) [33] can be used as computation paradigm for real-time data processing. HDF is an integration of three tools; Apache NiFi [34], Apache Kafka [35] and Apache Storm [36] which are appropriate for handling continuous data flow from IoT devices.

3.4 Layer-4 (Resource Discovery and Data Dissemination)

This layer of our proposed architecture is responsible for following two important tasks.

1. Resource Discovery: As already discussed, the possible candidates to take the role of fog nodes can be devices which are already installed in the environment for other different purposes. These devices can be wireless access points, routers, laptops, desktops etc. The challenge is to harness the computing resources which remain underutilized when these devices perform their routine tasks. The amount of underutilization may vary dynamically depending upon usage of these devices. For example, in a WiFi network load on different wireless access points may be different depending upon the number of end devices connected to them.

In our approach, we propose to utilize available laptops and desktops as wireless mesh routers that can also act as fog nodes. To do this, a simple low cost USB based wireless mesh enabled Network Interface Card (NIC) is used.

These fog nodes form a DHT-based overlay on top of underlying wireless mesh network. This DHT-based overlay assist in locating a fog node having enough computing resource required for given task at given instance.

2. Data Dissemination Among IoT Devices: As already discussed in introduction section, we require a communication paradigm which can provide decoupling and asynchrony between producers and consumers of data. These producers and consumers are IoT devices working as sensors and actuators. To support this many protocols such as Message Queue Telemetry Transport (MQTT) [18], Data Distribution Service (DDS) [37], Advanced Message Queuing Protocol (AMQP) [38], Extensible Messaging and Presence Protocol (XMPP) [39] etc. exist. The common feature of these protocols is that they utilize variants of Publish/Subscribe communication paradigm [40] which provides decoupling and asynchrony among communicating entities. Generally, these protocols utilize a centralized broker on cloud for matching related publications and subscriptions. In our approach, we propose a DHT-based distributed broker architecture of fog nodes for this purpose.

4   Implementation Details

In this section, we present the implementation details of the test-bed of our proposed architecture for smart environments. The description is divided into three parts; (1) Setup of a wireless mesh network that act as communication infrastructure, (2) Utilization of mesh nodes as fog nodes followed by resource discovery among them, (3) Implementation of fog nodes as distributed brokers for data dissemination among IoT devices.

4.1   Implementation of Communication Infrastructure

Our implemented topology of wireless mesh network consists of ten mesh devices which are organized in the hierarchy shown in Fig. 2. Out of these ten mesh devices, six are mesh routers and rest are mesh access points. Mesh routers form a backbone network and forward the packets towards destination using default Hybrid Wireless Mesh Protocol (HWMP) [41]. The mesh access points are used to provide the connectivity to IoT devices, smart-phones etc. present in Layer-1 of our proposed architecture (Fig. 1).

We have used desktops and laptops running Linux (kernel version 4.8) to act as mesh-routers and mesh access points. A USB based mesh-enabled wireless NIC (TP-Link model no. TL-WN722N) is used to provide mesh connectivity. This NIC provides data rate of 54MBps transmission range of 100 m. The mesh-enabled interface uses default HWMP as a routing protocol. The mesh access points have two interfaces. One interface is 802.11 enabled to provide connectivity to end devices in infrastructure mode. Another interface is 802.11 mesh-enabled and connects to mesh routers in ad-hoc mode. We have installed and enabled a *hwmp daemon* in mesh access points and mesh routers for forwarding and routing. To avoid the collision, we have set mesh access points and routers

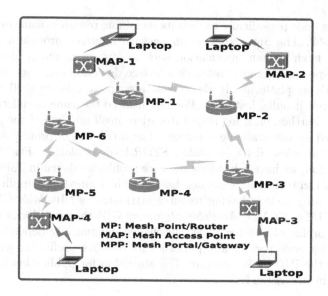

Fig. 2. Implemented wireless mesh network topology

on different channels. The mesh routers operate at channel no. "5" and mesh access points are set at channel no. "1".

The respective loads on these Linux boxes (mesh routers and access points) are synthetically set to be variable and dynamically changing with time. This is done by executing heavy programs (which take substantial CPU cycles and RAM) in periodic manner. Also, these mesh devices are made quasi-stationary (they leave the system very rarely, but they can do this once in a while). Our scripts ensure that available CPU percentage and RAM for each mesh node vary from 20–80% and 64–256 MB respectively.

As already discussed, we have utilized these mesh routers and access points as fog nodes. Whenever, the computing requirement is raised from the system, it is required to find a node (or set of nodes) with appropriate resources. The computing requirement includes the program and execution environment needed for task execution. This gives an idea of the required CPU cycles, RAM and storage. Afterwards, the required code and execution environment can be packed in a Docker [30] container which gets installed on appropriate fog node.

4.2 Resource Discovery

We have used topic-based publish/subscribe paradigm over DHT to find the fog nodes that have sufficient computational capability. Chord DHT [42] is used to form a structured P2P overlay of fog nodes. An open source distributed P2P application Open-Chord [43] is customized and installed on fog nodes. Topic-based publish/subscribe communication paradigm is implemented on top of this overlay for the discovery of desired resources.

Every fog node periodically records its remaining resources using open source Sigar API [44]. The Sigar application package interface provide a decoupled interface to fetch system information such as system memory, load average, uptime, per-process memory, network interface detection etc. regardless of different underlying platforms. It also consist a script to execute shell commands like df, du, free, ifconfig, iostat etc. We have utilized the same to collect fog node information. Further, each fog node categorizes itself into one of the predefined profiles based on the available resources. The attributes of profiles are defined as $<$CPU Utilization, RAM Available, STORAGE Available$>$. For the current implementation, we have taken four resource profiles as shown in Table 1. These profile types can be further extended based on the context and application. For instance, if a fog node is having resource attributes as (Available_CPU = 78%, Available_RAM = 256 MB, Available_Storage=3 GB) then it belongs to Profile-1. Further, profile of any fog node can change dynamically depending on the load. Each fog node periodically publishes its resource profile (or when profile changes) to the P2P broker overlay. The algorithm for publication installation is provided in Algorithm 1.

Table 1. Example resource profiles

Resource-profile	Available CPU %	Available RAM (MB)	Available storage (GB)
Profile-1	60–80	256	>= 2 GB
Profile-2	45–60	128	>= 2 GB
Profile-3	30–45	64	>= 1 GB
Profile-4	20–30	32	>= 1 GB

Algorithm 1. Publication Installation

1: **procedure** PUBLISH
2:     $Profile - ID \leftarrow hash(Resource - Profile)$ ▷ Resource-Profile is obtained from our Predetermined profile class
3:     $Fog - IP \leftarrow chord\_lookup(ID)$ ▷ lookup the fog node whose hash(IP) is immediate successor of Profile-ID
4:     Store the publication at returned Fog-IP

In Chord DHT [42], both node identifiers and resource identifiers are mapped to a single universal identifier space. A node identifier can be generated by hashing a unique attribute such as IP address whereas resource identifier can be generated by hashing its name or any other attributes of its meta-data. The resource information is stored on the first peer whose identifier is greater than or equal to the resource identifier in clockwise direction. This is done by a procedure $find\_successor()$ of Chord DHT in Algorithm 1.

Like publication installation, subscriptions can also be installed by hashing the profile name. Suppose an IoT application requires some computing on the data created, the data will be transferred to the nearest fog node. If that fog node is not able to provide the desired computing resources, it can subscribe for the resource profile which is required. It may be noted that same publication and subscription profiles rendezvous at atleast one fog node in the overlay. The rendezvous fog node takes the role of broker and notifies the subscriber about the fog node(s) that currently have the desired resource profile. In this way resources can be discovered among the fog nodes.

4.3   Data Dissemination Among IoT Devices

The interesting aspect of our design is that the DHT of fog nodes is also utilized for data dissemination among IoT devices. These IoT devices are producers/consumers of data described in Layer-1 of our proposed architecture in Sect. 3.

Normally, the IoT data dissemination protocols such as MQTT [18] use topic-based publish/subscribe communication paradigm. In MQTT, the topics are organized in hierarchy. For example, the temperature data from the thermal sensors installed in room no. 402 of fourth floor of a building can be published as "Temperature = 30 degree/Floor = 4/ Room = 402" where topic is Temperature and others are subtopics. Similarly, subscriptions can also be specified in similar manner.

The publications and subscriptions of IoT devices implementing MQTT are routed to a cloud based centralized broker where they are matched and notifications are generated. In our implementation, we have used the Chord DHT of fog nodes to route publications and subscriptions related to same topic to a rendezvous node. These publication and subscription topics are hashed using SHA-1. The rendezvous fog node then performs matching and forwards notifications towards subscriber devices. Depending upon the context, the notifications/publications/subscriptions can also be transferred to fog nodes that can provide appropriate computing environment and resources (discovered in resource discovery phase) for further analysis. This process is depicted in Fig. 3.

In our test-bed implementation, we have installed a MQTT client [45] in some computers which are connected to mesh access points. Further, we have coded and deployed a C program generating temperature data every 15 seconds. Some MQTT client act as a data producer (publisher), while others subscribe for the data (subscriber). Both the publisher and subscriber send their respective request to the nearest fog node. This fog node uses Open-Chord application which routes published/subscribed data to a rendezvous fog node using lookup procedure of Chord DHT. The broker application running at rendezvous node matches the publication and subscription according to topic and notifications are sent to subscribers.

Further, for comparison purpose with centralized brokering and computing system, we have utilized the private cloud server of our institute. In this case, the computers running MQTT clients send publications/subscriptions to a central

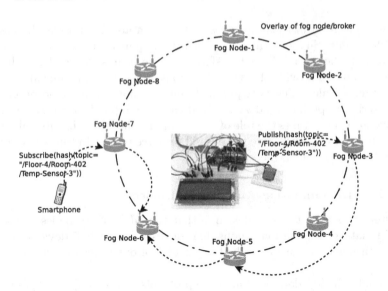

Fig. 3. Publication and subscription in overlay of brokers

broker. This centralized broker sends notifications to subscribers after performing matching operations. We have recorded both the results obtained from our infrastructure and centralized system.

4.4   Simulation Setup

To evaluate the performance of our approach in large scale settings, we have performed simulation also. As our test-bed is small and have few number of fog nodes, we attempted to check the applicability of proposed approach where number of IoT devices and fog nodes can increase up to a large scale. Our simulation platform comprises of an integrated framework consisting of OverSim [46], INET-MANET 2.0 [47] and OMNeT++ 4.6 [48]. The first challenge is to create a wireless mesh network. We have solved it using customized INETMANET package over OMNeT++ platform. Second, on top of this underlying wireless mesh network, we have to run P2P application for exchange of publication/subscription topics. To configure underlying networks for running P2P application, OverSim provides four types of underlay configurator: InetUnderlayConfigurator, ReaSE-UnderlayConfigurator, SimpleUnderlayConfigurator, SingleHostunderlayConfigurator. None of the configurator present in the OverSim is able to configure wireless network. We have build a WirelessUnderlayConfigurator to configure wireless network [49].

We have chosen the most referred structured overlay protocol, Chord [42] which builds a ring-based topology and uses a Distributed Hash Table (DHT) to perform routing of overlay messages across the ring. The Chord overlay uses an application named "PubSubTestApp" [46]. This is used to test the flow of messages based on publish/Subscribe communication paradigm among peers.

PubSubTestApp Application generates random key-value pair from a specific domain. These key-value pairs are stored in chord ring using DHT routing.

The performance of PubSubTestApp is evaluated over the WMN underlay which uses HWMP [41] for multi-hop routing. We have taken NoChurn model [46] in which the nodes only join the scenario periodically to realize the churn dynamics. Stationary Mobility model is used for simulating the wireless mesh network of fixed nodes. The important settings of simulation are summarized in Table 2. The certain characteristics of fog nodes such as continuously changing CPU and routing load have not been modeled due to the limitation of simulation framework.

Table 2. Simulation settings

Simulation parameter	Value
Simulation area	1000×1000 m^2
No. of nodes	10, 25, 50, 100, 200
Overlay protocol	Chord
Tier-1 application	Dummy
Tier-2 application	PubSubTestApp
Overlay routing	Iterative
Transport layer protocol	UDP
MAC layer	IEEE80211SMAC
Underlay routing protocol	HWMP (Layer-2)
Data rate	54 MB/s
Transmission range	100 m

5   Results and Discussion

In this section, we present test-bed results and simulation results of our proposed infrastructure. Also, these results are compared with cloud based centralized computing systems.

5.1   Test-Bed Results and Discussion

The authors in [50] had done a feasibility study of fog computing. They found that the latency varies from 30 milliseconds to 98 milliseconds in the case of cloud servers. However, when a server is placed at the edge of a network, the latency decreases and it ranges from 0–50 millisecond. We have also captured the latencies i.e. publication time, subscription time and notification delay. The *publication time* and *subscription time* are defined as the time taken by publishing/subscribing message to reach to the destination. Similarly, the *Notification Delay* is defined as the time taken by notify message to reach to the destination.

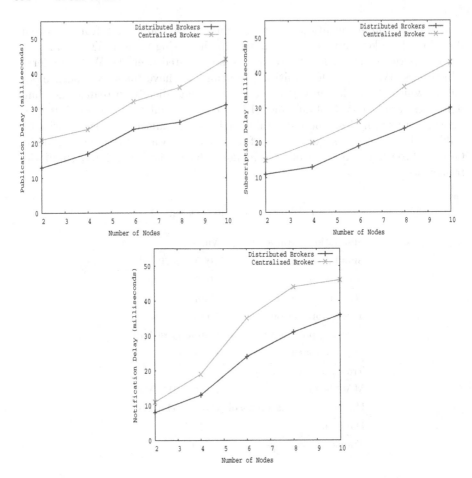

Fig. 4. Test-bed results of Publication Delay, Subscription Delay and Notification delay of fog nodes

The results presented in Fig. 4 depict the average time taken by publication/subscription messages to reach to the rendezvous broker. The publication and subscription delay of distributed fog nodes varies from 13–32 milliseconds, 11–28 milliseconds respectively. However, in case of centralized broker, the delay increases and varies from 20–45 milliseconds. The notification delay is also recorded which varies from 8–35 milliseconds in the case of distributed brokers. However, in the case of centralized broker, the notification delay varies from 12–46 milliseconds. This establishes that using fog nodes as distributed brokers is beneficial. It may be noted that publication/subscription delay is more than notification delay in our design because publication/subscription is routed in overlay towards rendezvous broker using Chord lookup procedure. On the other hand, notification can be directly sent to the subscriber.

5.2   Simulation Results and Discussion

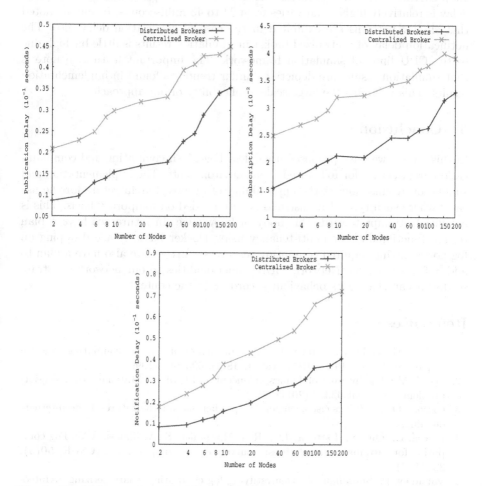

Fig. 5. Simulation results of Publication Delay, Subscription Delay and Notification Delay of fog nodes

The simulation results are compared to test-bed results by finding similar trends in simulation results of large scale network of our proposed approach. We have simulated similar infrastructure with 2, 4, 6, 8, 10, 20, 40, 60, 80, 100, 150 and 200 fog nodes in network. We have recorded simulation results with same parameters as in the case of test-bed results. Each instance of the fog network has been iterated 10 times to avoid any ambiguity in the results.

It is evident that delay in Fig. 5 is tolerable and provide enough encouragement to implement wireless Fog-Mesh near user devices. The delay for storing publication messages at fog nodes varies from 8 to 33 milliseconds. For storing subscription messages, the delay varies from 15 milliseconds to 32 milliseconds.

This delay is measured with respect to increasing number of fog nodes (from 2 to 200). On the other hand, in the case centralized brokers, publication/subscription delay is relatively higher and varies from 24 to 43 milliseconds. It may be noted that similar patterns are exhibited in the case of notification delay also. The notification delay of centralized broker in simulation results is little bit high due to the CPU limit of simulation framework. The important feature to note is that simulation results are depicting similar trends as found in implementation results. This validates the large scale applicability of our approach.

6   Conclusion

In this paper, we have proposed a wireless Fog-Mesh computing and communication architecture for IoT based smart environments. The implementation and simulation results suggest the applicability of proposed architecture for the use cases where such type of infrastructures are needed on temporary basis. This is an initial attempt towards this body of knowledge. In future, we have a plan to add functionality for multi-tenancy using Docker based image dropping on fog nodes having required computing resources. Further, we also have a plan to add Software Defined Network (SDN) functionalities to our network substrate so that it can change its behaviour according to the context.

References

1. Weiser, M., Gold, R., Brown, J.S.: The origins of ubiquitous computing research at parc in the late 1980s. IBM Syst. J. **38**(4), 693–696 (1999)
2. Lee, G.M.: The Internet of Things - Concept and Problem Statement draft-lee-iot-problem-statement-02.txt (2011)
3. Cisco. https://blogs.cisco.com/cle/10-predictions-for-the-future-of-the-internet-of-things
4. Perera, C., Qin, Y., Estrella, J.C., Reiff-Marganiec, S., Vasilakos, A.V.: Fog computing for sustainable smart cities: a survey. ACM Comput. Surv. (CSUR) **50(3)**, 32 (2017)
5. Varshney, P., Simmhan, Y.: Demystifying fog computing: characterizing architectures, applications and abstractions. In: 2017 IEEE 1st International Conference on Fog and Edge Computing (ICFEC), pp. 115–124. IEEE (2017)
6. Chiang, M., Zhang, T.: Fog and IoT: an overview of research opportunities. IEEE Internet Things J. **3**(6), 854–864 (2016)
7. Mouradian, C., Naboulsi, D., Yangui, S., Glitho, R.H., Morrow, M.J., Polakos, P.A.: A comprehensive survey on fog computing: state-of-the-art and research challenges. IEEE Commun. Surv. Tutorials **20**, 416–464 (2017)
8. Zhang, Q., Cheng, L., Boutaba, R.: Cloud computing: state-of-the-art and research challenges. J. Internet Serv. Appl. **1**(1), 7–18 (2010)
9. Díaz, M., Martín, C., Rubio, B.: State-of-the-art, challenges, and open issues in the integration of internet of things and cloud computing. J. Netw. Comput. Appl. **67**(Suppl. C), 99–117 (2016)
10. Buyya, R., Calheiros, R.N., Li, X.: Autonomic cloud computing: open challenges and architectural elements. In: 2012 Third International Conference on Emerging Applications of Information Technology (EAIT), pp. 3–10. IEEE (2012)

11. Managing crowd at events and venues of mass gathering
12. Akyildiz, I.F., Wang, X., Wang, W.: Wireless mesh networks: a survey. Comput. Netw. **47**(4), 445–487 (2005)
13. Liu, Y., Tong, K.F., Qiu, X., Liu, Y., Ding, X.: Wireless mesh networks in IoT networks. In: 2017 International Workshop on Electromagnetics: Applications and Student Innovation Competition (iWEM), pp. 183–185. IEEE (2017)
14. Muhendra, R., Rinaldi, A., Budiman, M., et al.: Development of wifi mesh infrastructure for internet of things applications. Procedia Eng. **170**, 332–337 (2017)
15. Garcia Lopez, P., et al.: Edge-centric computing: vision and challenges. ACM SIG-COMM Comput. Commun. Rev. **45**(5), 37–42 (2015)
16. Yang, X., Hu, Y.: A DHT-based infrastructure for content-based publish/subscribe services. In: Seventh IEEE International Conference on Peer-to-Peer Computing (P2P 2007), pp. 185–192. IEEE (2007)
17. Castro, M., Villanueva, E., Ruiz, I., Sargento, S., Kassler, A.: Performance evaluation of structured P2P over wireless multi-hop networks. In: Second International Conference on Sensor Technologies and Applications, SENSORCOMM 2008, pp. 796–801, August 2008
18. Banks, A., Gupta, R.: MQTT version 3.1. 1. OASIS standard (2014)
19. Al-Fuqaha, A., Guizani, M., Mohammadi, M., Aledhari, M., Ayyash, M.: Internet of things: a survey on enabling technologies, protocols, and applications. IEEE Commun. Surv. Tutorials **17**(4), 2347–2376 (2015)
20. Cirani, S., et al.: A scalable and self-configuring architecture for service discovery in the internet of things. IEEE Internet Things J. **1**(5), 508–521 (2014)
21. Tanganelli, G., Vallati, C., Mingozzi, E.: Edge-centric distributed discovery and access in the internet of things. IEEE Internet Things J. **5**(1), 425–438 (2018)
22. Tanganelli, G., Vallati, C., Mingozzi, E.: A fog-based distributed look-up service for intelligent transportation systems. In: 2017 IEEE 18th International Symposium on a World of Wireless, Mobile and Multimedia Networks (WoWMoM), pp. 1–6, June 2017
23. Chang, C., Liyanage, M., Soo, S., Srirama, S.N.: Fog computing as a resource-aware enhancement for vicinal mobile mesh social networking. In: 2017 IEEE 31st International Conference on Advanced Information Networking and Applications (AINA), pp. 894–901. IEEE (2017)
24. Ganti, R.K., Ye, F., Lei, H.: Mobile crowdsensing: current state and future challenges. IEEE Commun. Mag. **49**(11), 32–39 (2011)
25. Vaquero, L.M., Rodero-Merino, L.: Finding your way in the fog: towards a comprehensive definition of fog computing. ACM SIGCOMM Comput. Commun. Rev. **44**(5), 27–32 (2014)
26. Satyanarayanan, M., Bahl, P., Caceres, R., Davies, N.: The case for VM-based cloudlets in mobile computing. IEEE Perv. Comput. **8**(4), 14–23 (2009)
27. Cisco: Cisco fog computing solutions: Unleash the power of the internet of things (2015)
28. Tordera, E.M., et al.: What is a fog node a tutorial on current concepts towards a common definition. arXiv preprint arXiv:1611.09193 (2016)
29. Dastjerdi, A.V., Gupta, H., Calheiros, R.N., Ghosh, S.K., Buyya, R.: Fog computing: Principles, architectures, and applications. arXiv preprint arXiv:1601.02752 (2016)
30. Ismail, B.I., et al.: Evaluation of docker as edge computing platform. In: 2015 IEEE Conference on Open Systems (ICOS), pp. 130–135. IEEE (2015)

31. Patel, A.B., Birla, M., Nair, U.: Addressing big data problem using hadoop and map reduce. In: 2012 Nirma University International Conference on Engineering (NUiCONE), pp. 1–5. IEEE (2012)
32. Cisco Data in Motion API References
33. Hortonworks data flow
34. Apache Nifi (2017)
35. Apache Kafka (2017)
36. Apache Storm (2017)
37. Pardo-Castellote, G.: OMG data-distribution service: architectural overview. In: Proceedings of 23rd International Conference on Distributed Computing Systems Workshops, pp. 200–206. IEEE (2003)
38. Vinoski, S.: Advanced message queuing protocol. IEEE Internet Comput. **10**(6), 87–89 (2006)
39. Saint-Andre, P.: Extensible messaging and presence protocol (XMPP): Core (2011)
40. Eugster, P.T., Felber, P.A., Guerraoui, R., Kermarrec, A.M.: The many faces of publish/subscribe. ACM Comput. Surv. (CSUR) **35**(2), 114–131 (2003)
41. Hwmp protocol specification, working group ieee
42. Stoica, I., Morris, R., Karger, D., Kaashoek, M.F., Balakrishnan, H.: Chord: a scalable peer-to-peer lookup service for internet applications. In: Proceedings of the 2001 Conference on Applications, Technologies, Architectures, and Protocols for Computer Communications, SIGCOMM 2001, pp. 149–160. ACM, New York (2001)
43. Karsten, L., Sven, K.: Open-chord: Distributed and mobile systems group
44. Sigar api
45. Mosquitto: An Open Source MQTT
46. OverSim: The Overlay Simulation Framework
47. Quintana, A.A.: INET-MANET Framework
48. OMNeT++: Discrete Event Simulator
49. Ali, S., Sewak, A., Pandey, M., Tyagi, N.: Simulation of P2P overlays over MANETs: impediments and proposed solution. In: 2017 9th International Conference on Communication Systems and Networks (COMSNETS), pp. 338–345, January 2017
50. Varghese, B., Wang, N., Nikolopoulos, D.S., Buyya, R.: Feasibility of fog computing. arXiv preprint arXiv:1701.05451 (2017)

Author Index

Printed in the United States
By Bookmasters

Printed in the United States
By Bookmasters